KILL ME
Kiss Me

Volume 3
by Lee Young You

 TOKYOPOP®

Hamburg • London • Los Angeles • Tokyo

Kill Me Kiss Me Vol. 3
created by Lee Young You

Translation - Jihae Hong
English Adaptation - Paul Morrissey
Copy Editor - Alexis Kirsch
Retouch and Lettering - William Suh
Production Artist - James Dashiell
Cover Design - Anna Kernbaum

Editor - Bryce P. Coleman
Digital Imaging Manager - Chris Buford
Pre-Press Manager - Antonio DePietro
Production Managers - Jennifer Miller and Mutsumi Miyazaki
Art Director - Matt Alford
Managing Editor - Jill Freshney
VP of Production - Ron Klamert
President and C.O.O. - John Parker
Publisher and C.E.O. - Stuart Levy

A  Manga

TOKYOPOP Inc.
5900 Wilshire Blvd. Suite 2000
Los Angeles, CA 90036

E-mail: info@TOKYOPOP.com
Come visit us online at www.TOKYOPOP.com

ISBN: 1-59182-595-4

First TOKYOPOP printing: August 2004
10 9 8 7 6 5 4 3 2 1
Printed in the USA

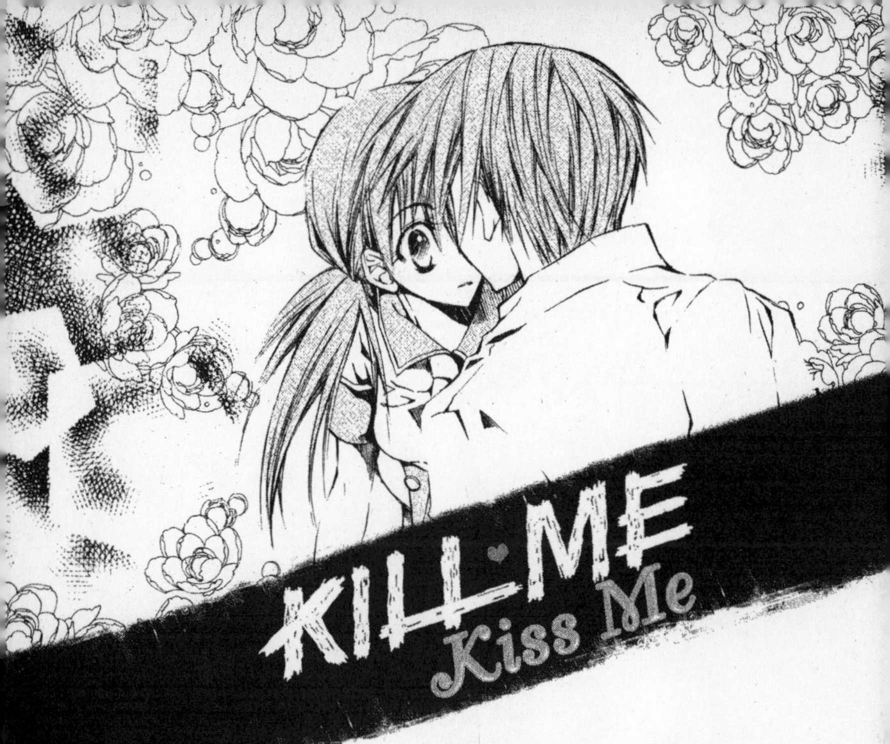
KILL ME
Kiss Me

Story So Far...

When Tae convinces her pretty-boy cousin, Jung-Woo, to switch places with her at their respective schools, it sets off a chain reaction of misunderstandings, mistaken identities and misdirected lust. But even after the duplicitous duo come clean, things still get down and dirty. It seems that local tough-chick Que-Min has taken a keen interest in the always-oblivious Jung-Woo, who doesn't even know her name. But one name he'll never forget is that of resident bad-ass Ghoon-Hahm, who inexplicably makes Jung-Woo the recipient of one serious beat-down.

Jung-Woo Im

Your typical lone wolf, his pretty-boy looks get him more attention than he'd like—especially from local gang leader Ghoon-Hahm.

A former tough-chick trying to leave her past
behind her. She's got a thing for poor Jung-Woo—
now if he could only remember her name.

He's made Jung-Woo the recipient of almost daily butt-kickings. Is it that he just doesn't like the pretty-boy's face...or that Que-Min does?

Tae Yeon Im

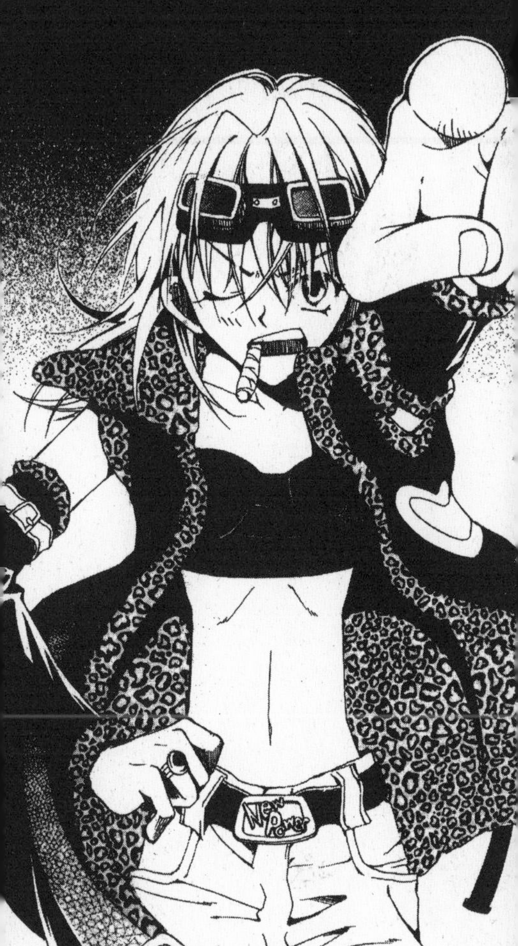
New Power

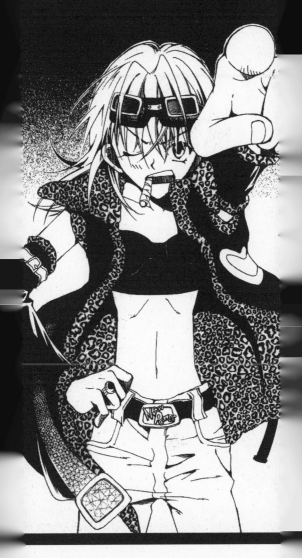

Jung-Woo's identical cousin—her good intentions frquently put him in chaotic situations.

Ga-Woon Kim

Pure Water High's resident bully, and one of the many who seem to enjoy handing out beatings to the oblivious Jung-Woo, until Tae sets him straight.

A male model who has reached idol status. Kun's glamorous newfound celebrity hides a rough and tumble past.

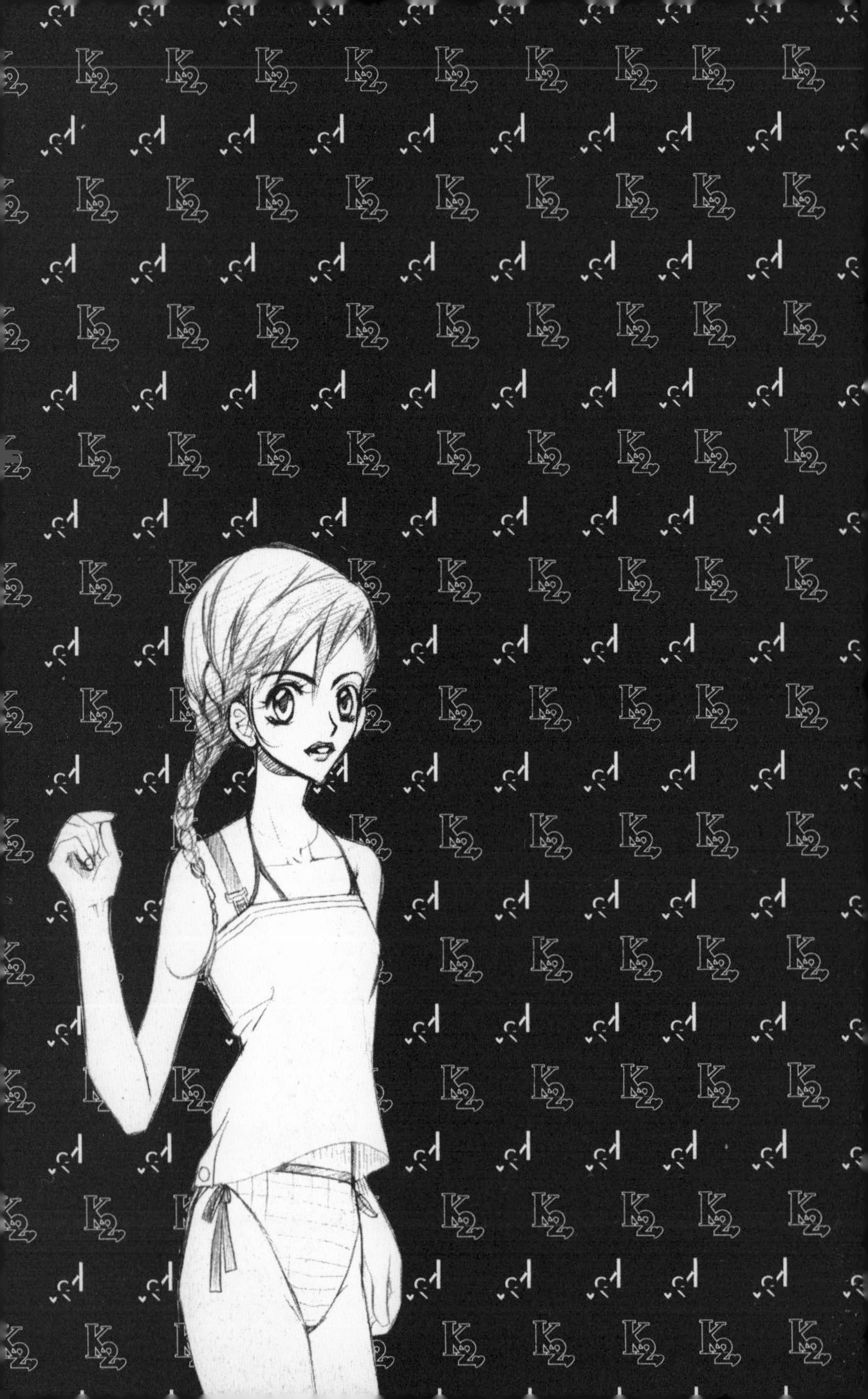

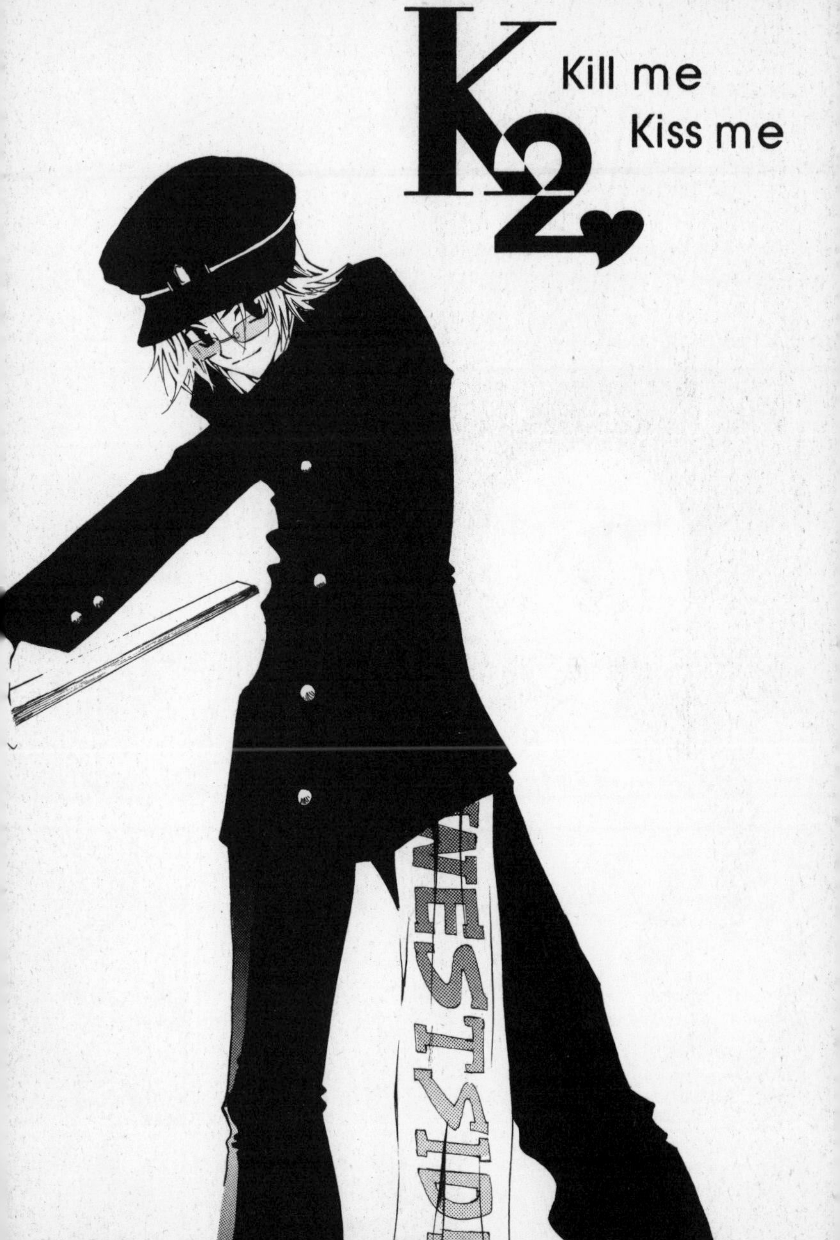
K2 Kill me Kiss me
WESTSIDE

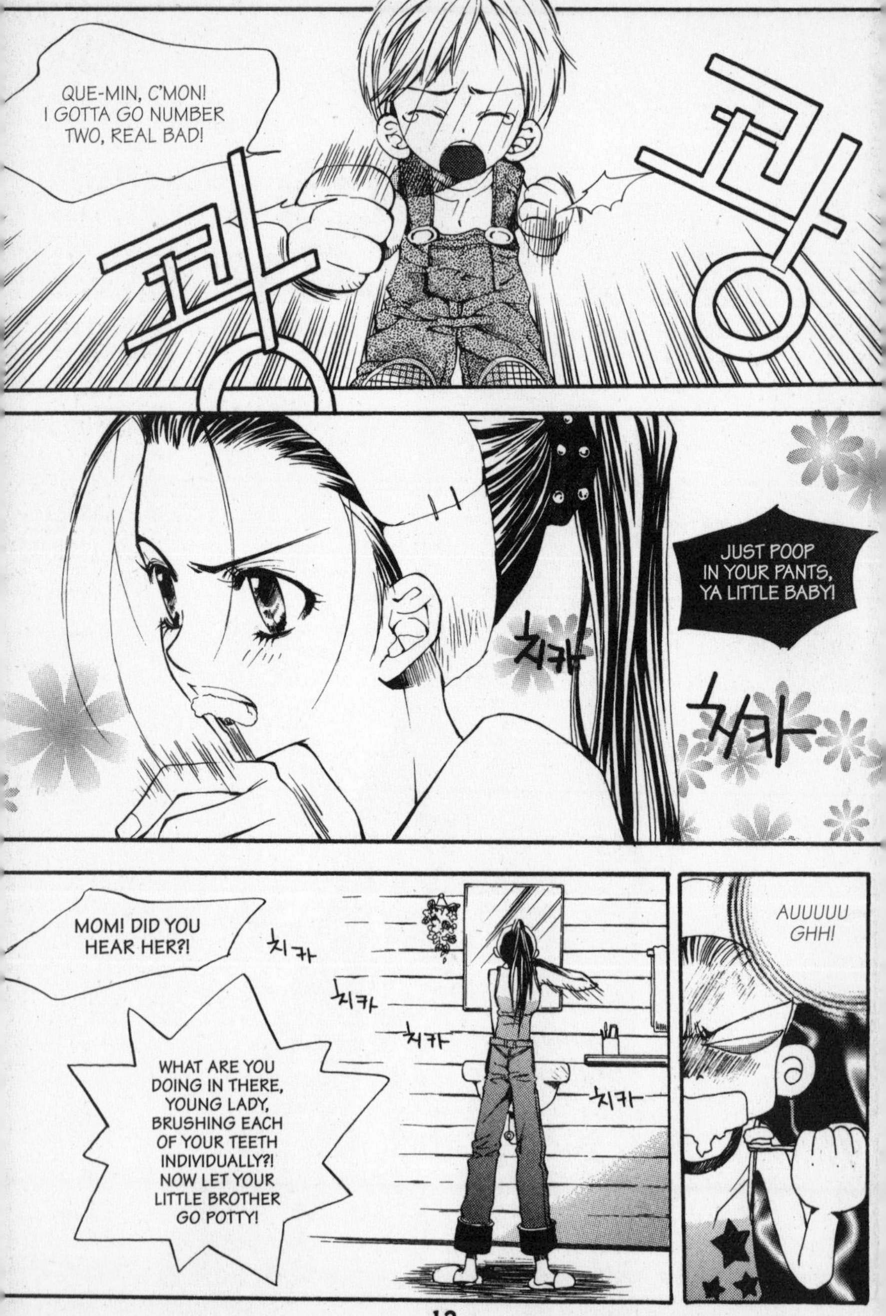
QUE-MIN, C'MON! I GOTTA GO NUMBER TWO, REAL BAD!
쾅
쾅
JUST POOP IN YOUR PANTS, YA LITTLE BABY!
치카
치카
MOM! DID YOU HEAR HER?!
치카
치카
치카
치카
WHAT ARE YOU DOING IN THERE, YOUNG LADY, BRUSHING EACH OF YOUR TEETH INDIVIDUALLY?! NOW LET YOUR LITTLE BROTHER GO POTTY!
AUUUUU GHH!

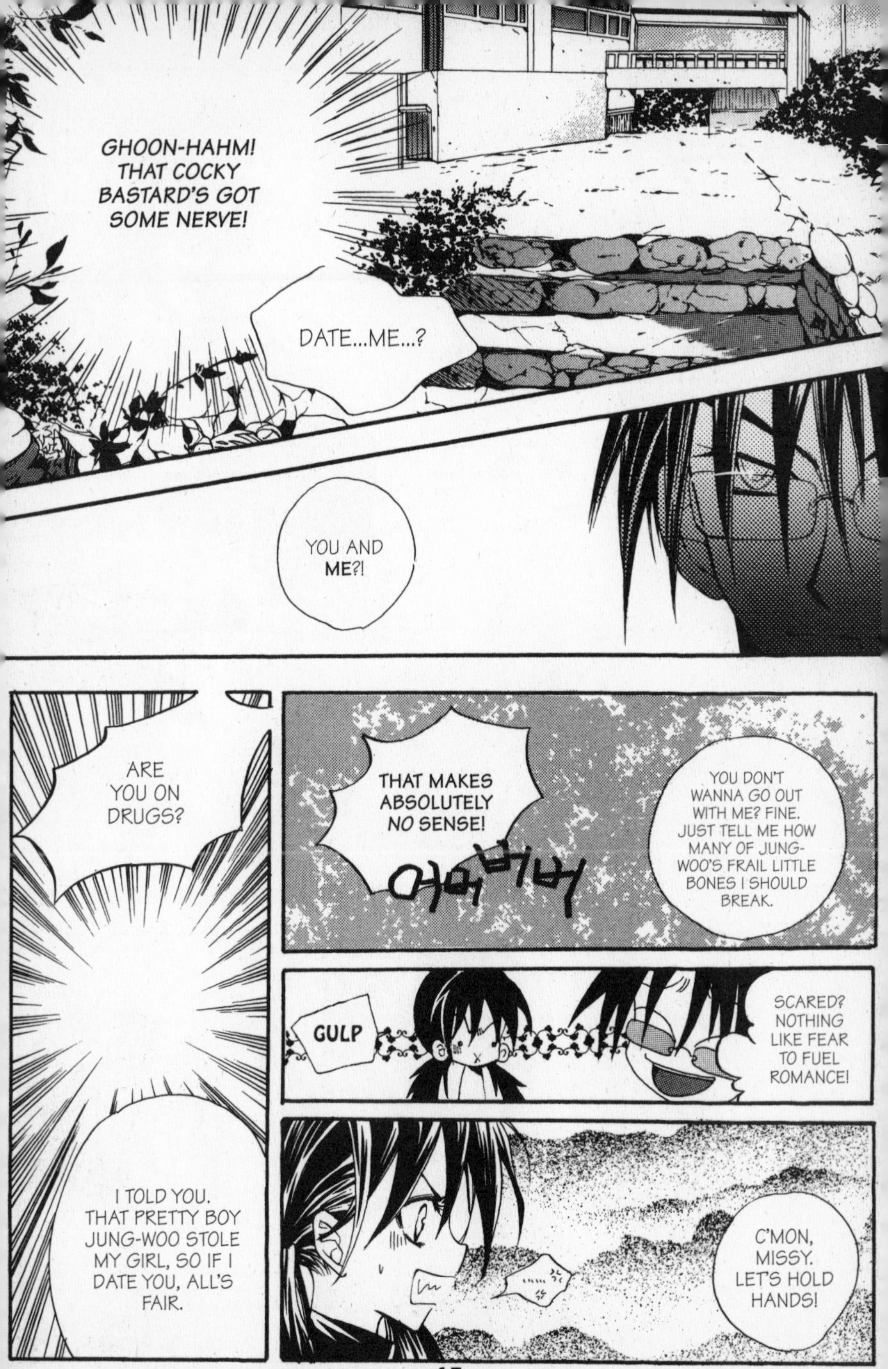
GHOON-HAHM! THAT COCKY BASTARD'S GOT SOME NERVE!
DATE...ME...?
YOU AND **ME**?!
ARE YOU ON DRUGS?
I TOLD YOU. THAT PRETTY BOY JUNG-WOO STOLE MY GIRL, SO IF I DATE YOU, ALL'S FAIR.
THAT MAKES ABSOLUTELY NO SENSE!
YOU DON'T WANNA GO OUT WITH ME? FINE. JUST TELL ME HOW MANY OF JUNG-WOO'S FRAIL LITTLE BONES I SHOULD BREAK.
GULP
SCARED? NOTHING LIKE FEAR TO FUEL ROMANCE!
C'MON, MISSY. LET'S HOLD HANDS!

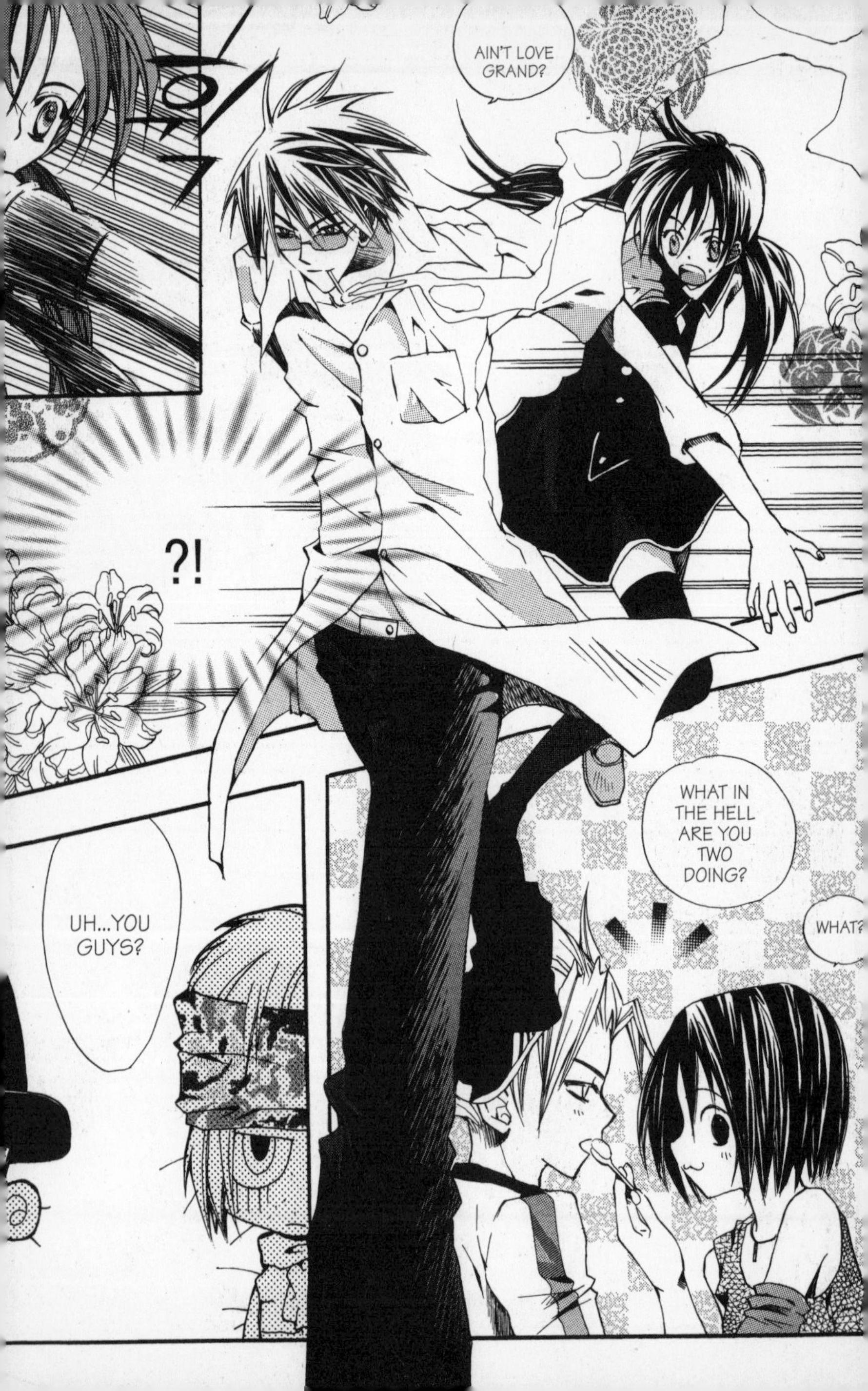
AIN'T LOVE GRAND?
?!
UH...YOU GUYS?
WHAT IN THE HELL ARE YOU TWO DOING?
WHAT?

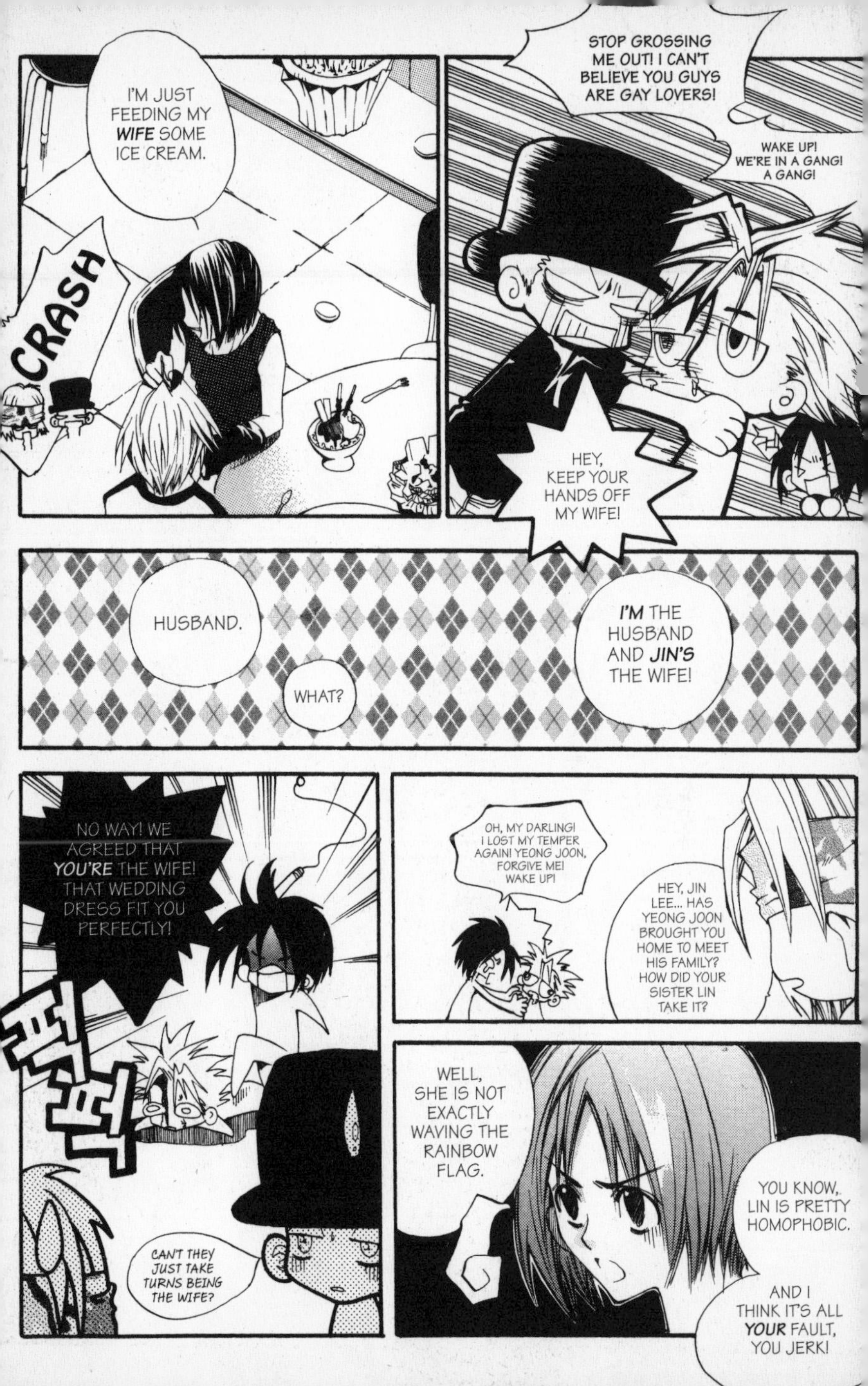
I'M JUST FEEDING MY WIFE SOME ICE CREAM.
CRASH
STOP GROSSING ME OUT! I CAN'T BELIEVE YOU GUYS ARE GAY LOVERS!
WAKE UP! WE'RE IN A GANG! A GANG!
HEY, KEEP YOUR HANDS OFF MY WIFE!
HUSBAND.
WHAT?
I'M THE HUSBAND AND JIN'S THE WIFE!
NO WAY! WE AGREED THAT YOU'RE THE WIFE! THAT WEDDING DRESS FIT YOU PERFECTLY!
CAN'T THEY JUST TAKE TURNS BEING THE WIFE?
OH, MY DARLING! I LOST MY TEMPER AGAIN! YEONG JOON, FORGIVE ME! WAKE UP!
HEY, JIN LEE... HAS YEONG JOON BROUGHT YOU HOME TO MEET HIS FAMILY? HOW DID YOUR SISTER LIN TAKE IT?
WELL, SHE IS NOT EXACTLY WAVING THE RAINBOW FLAG.
YOU KNOW, LIN IS PRETTY HOMOPHOBIC.
AND I THINK IT'S ALL YOUR FAULT, YOU JERK!

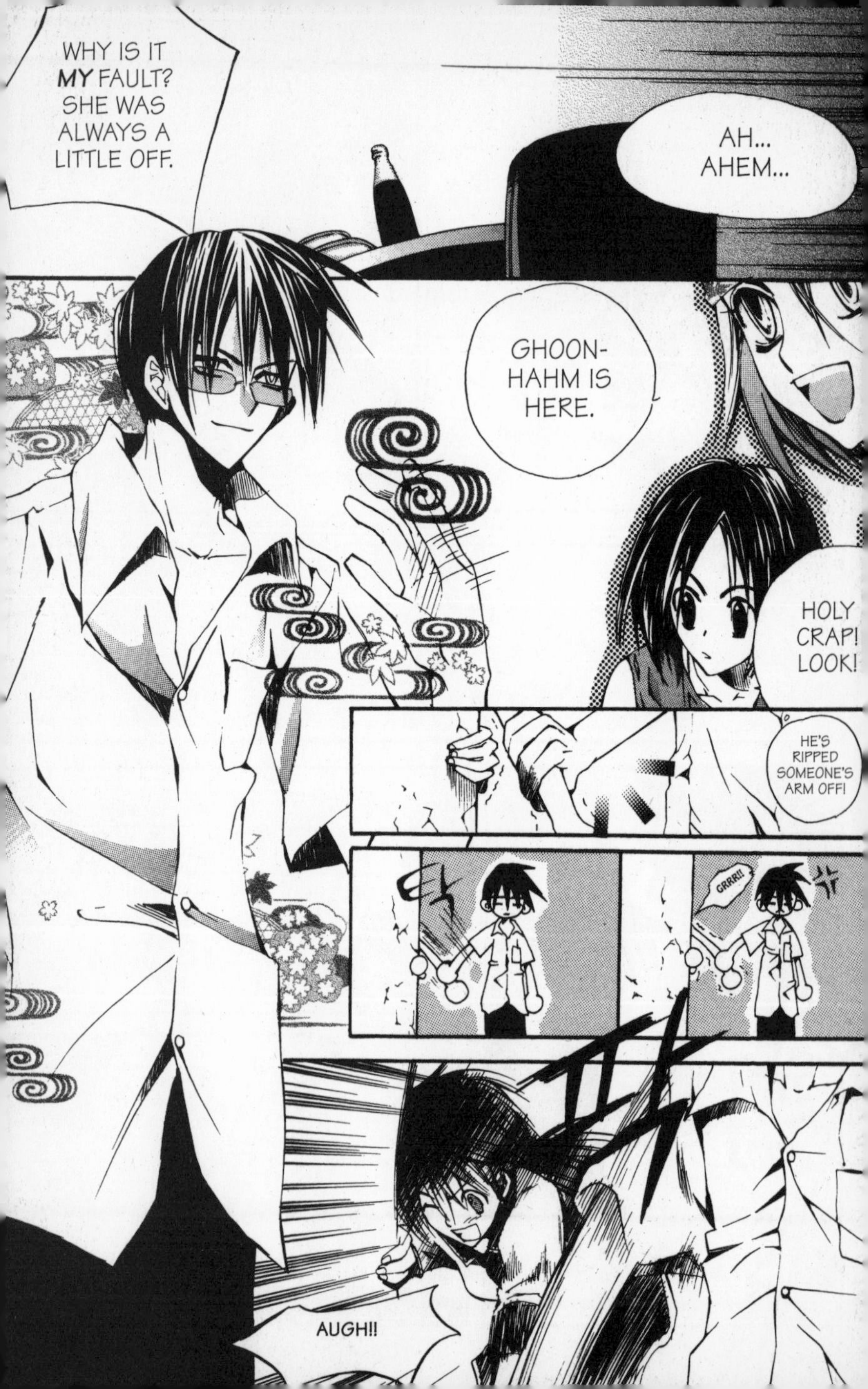
WHY IS IT **MY** FAULT? SHE WAS ALWAYS A LITTLE OFF.
AH... AHEM...
GHOON-HAHM IS HERE.
HOLY CRAP! LOOK!
HE'S RIPPED SOMEONE'S ARM OFF!
GRRR!!
AUGH!!

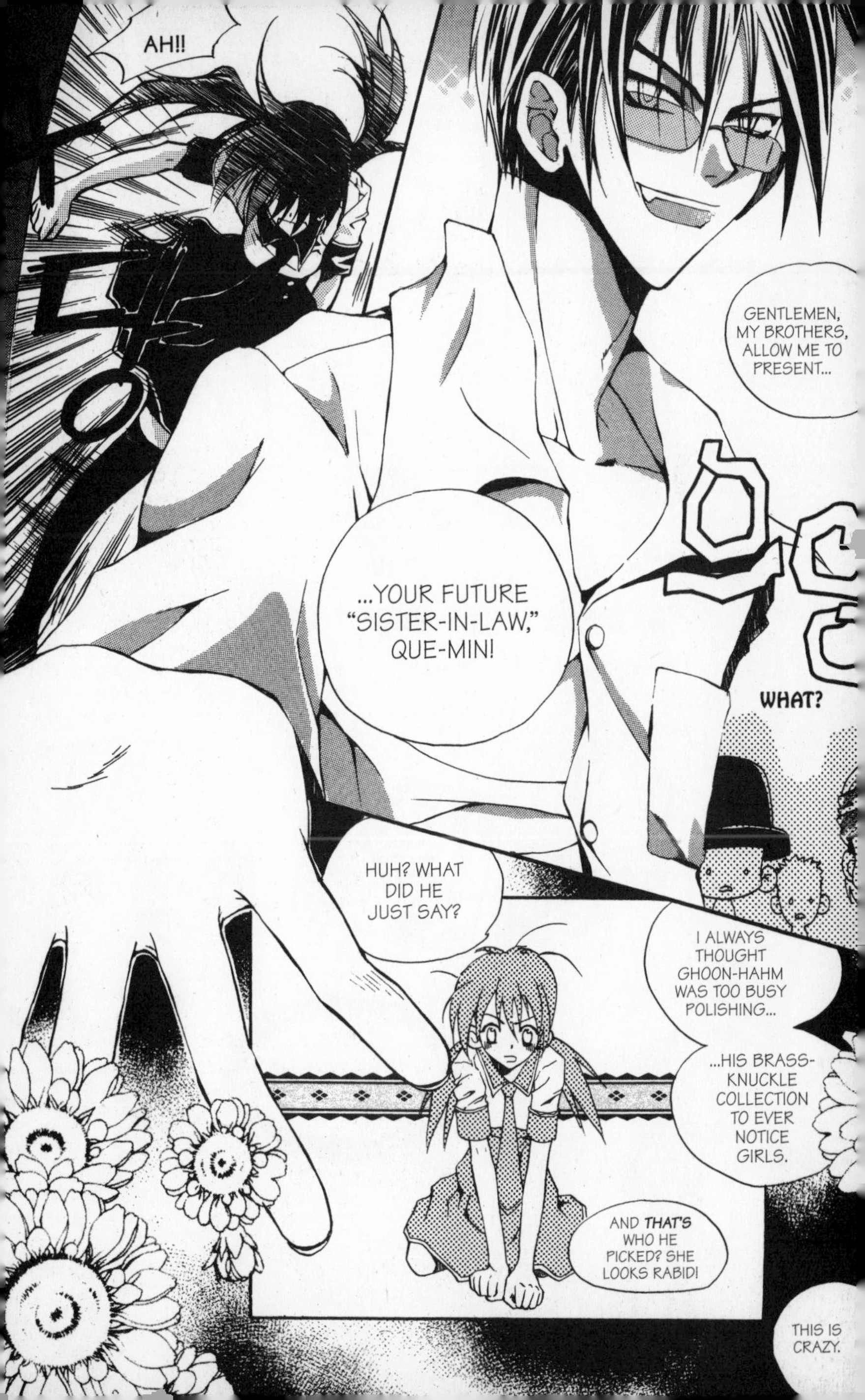
AH!!
GENTLEMEN, MY BROTHERS, ALLOW ME TO PRESENT...
...YOUR FUTURE "SISTER-IN-LAW," QUE-MIN!
WHAT?
HUH? WHAT DID HE JUST SAY?
I ALWAYS THOUGHT GHOON-HAHM WAS TOO BUSY POLISHING...
...HIS BRASS-KNUCKLE COLLECTION TO EVER NOTICE GIRLS.
AND **THAT'S** WHO HE PICKED? SHE LOOKS RABID!
THIS IS CRAZY.

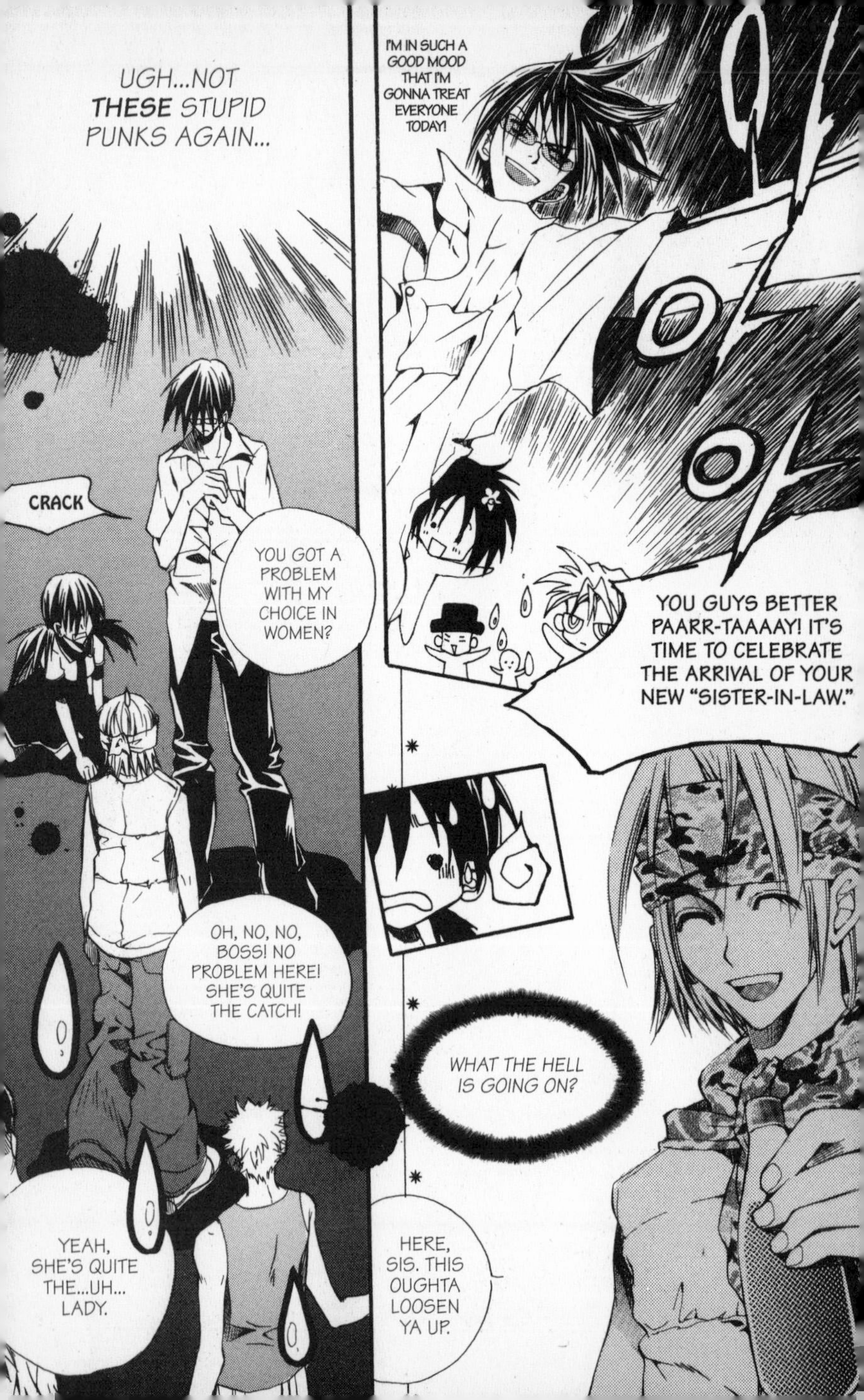
UGH...NOT THESE STUPID PUNKS AGAIN...
CRACK
YOU GOT A PROBLEM WITH MY CHOICE IN WOMEN?
OH, NO, NO, BOSS! NO PROBLEM HERE! SHE'S QUITE THE CATCH!
YEAH, SHE'S QUITE THE...UH... LADY.
I'M IN SUCH A GOOD MOOD THAT I'M GONNA TREAT EVERYONE TODAY!
YOU GUYS BETTER PAARR-TAAAAY! IT'S TIME TO CELEBRATE THE ARRIVAL OF YOUR NEW "SISTER-IN-LAW."
WHAT THE HELL IS GOING ON?
HERE, SIS. THIS OUGHTA LOOSEN YA UP.

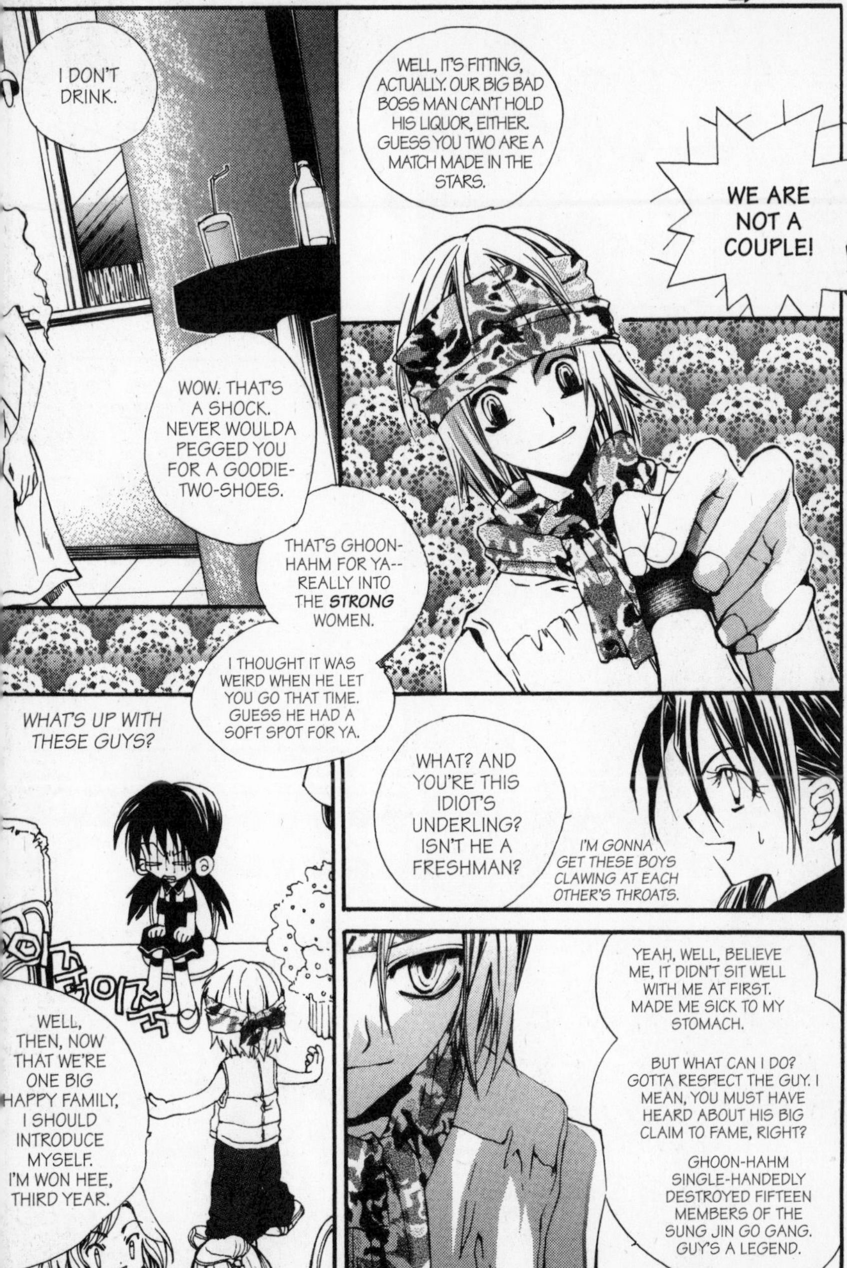
I DON'T DRINK.
WELL, IT'S FITTING, ACTUALLY. OUR BIG BAD BOSS MAN CAN'T HOLD HIS LIQUOR, EITHER. GUESS YOU TWO ARE A MATCH MADE IN THE STARS.
WE ARE NOT A COUPLE!
WOW. THAT'S A SHOCK. NEVER WOULDA PEGGED YOU FOR A GOODIE-TWO-SHOES.
THAT'S GHOON-HAHM FOR YA-- REALLY INTO THE **STRONG** WOMEN.
I THOUGHT IT WAS WEIRD WHEN HE LET YOU GO THAT TIME. GUESS HE HAD A SOFT SPOT FOR YA.
WHAT'S UP WITH THESE GUYS?
WELL, THEN, NOW THAT WE'RE ONE BIG HAPPY FAMILY, I SHOULD INTRODUCE MYSELF. I'M WON HEE, THIRD YEAR.
WHAT? AND YOU'RE THIS IDIOT'S UNDERLING? ISN'T HE A FRESHMAN?
I'M GONNA GET THESE BOYS CLAWING AT EACH OTHER'S THROATS.
YEAH, WELL, BELIEVE ME, IT DIDN'T SIT WELL WITH ME AT FIRST. MADE ME SICK TO MY STOMACH.
BUT WHAT CAN I DO? GOTTA RESPECT THE GUY. I MEAN, YOU MUST HAVE HEARD ABOUT HIS BIG CLAIM TO FAME, RIGHT?
GHOON-HAHM SINGLE-HANDEDLY DESTROYED FIFTEEN MEMBERS OF THE SUNG JIN GO GANG. GUY'S A LEGEND.

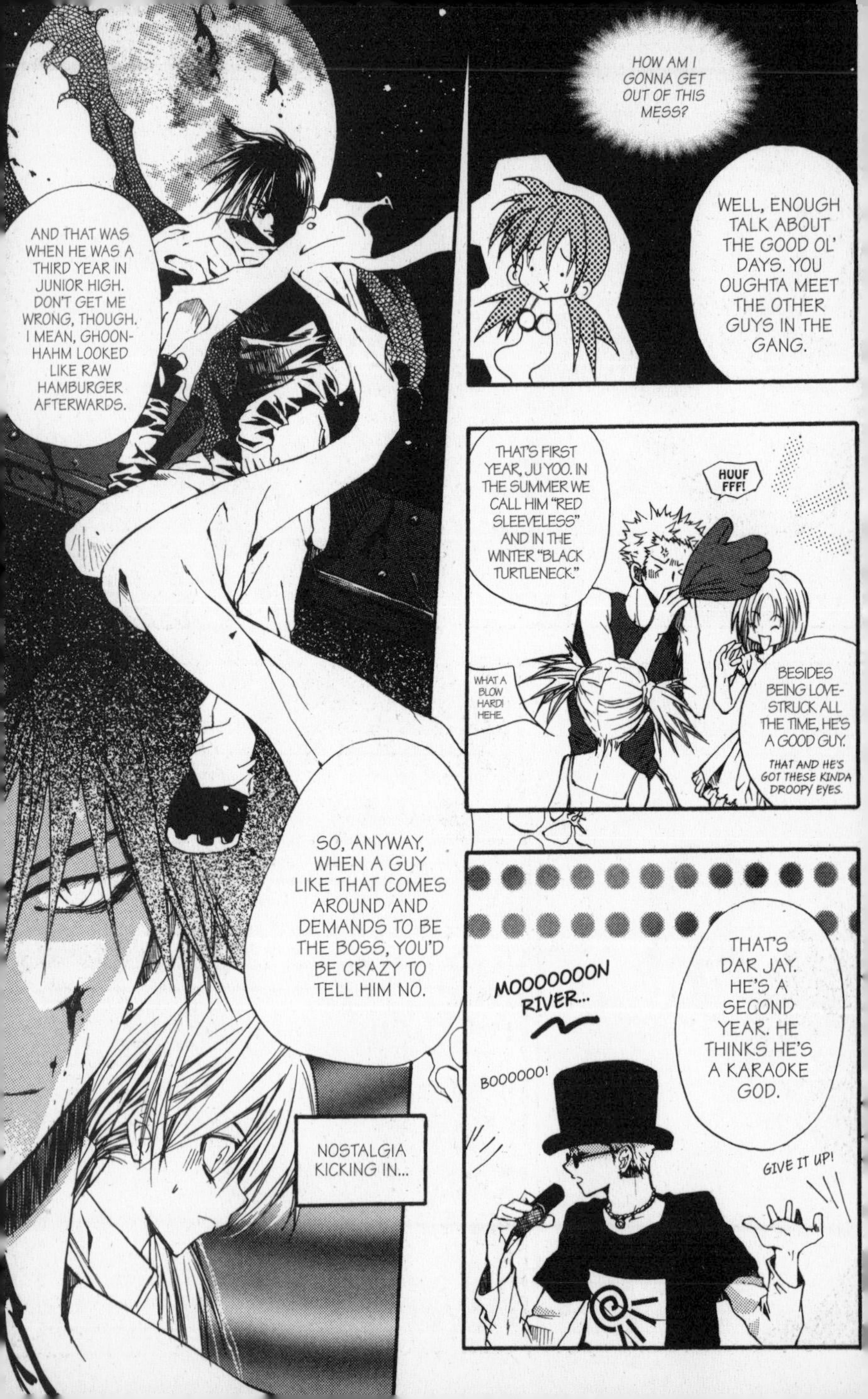
AND THAT WAS WHEN HE WAS A THIRD YEAR IN JUNIOR HIGH. DON'T GET ME WRONG, THOUGH. I MEAN, GHOON-HAHM LOOKED LIKE RAW HAMBURGER AFTERWARDS.
SO, ANYWAY, WHEN A GUY LIKE THAT COMES AROUND AND DEMANDS TO BE THE BOSS, YOU'D BE CRAZY TO TELL HIM NO.
NOSTALGIA KICKING IN...
HOW AM I GONNA GET OUT OF THIS MESS?
WELL, ENOUGH TALK ABOUT THE GOOD OL' DAYS. YOU OUGHTA MEET THE OTHER GUYS IN THE GANG.
THAT'S FIRST YEAR, JU YOO. IN THE SUMMER WE CALL HIM "RED SLEEVELESS" AND IN THE WINTER "BLACK TURTLENECK."
HUUF FFF!
WHAT A BLOW HARD! HEHE.
BESIDES BEING LOVE-STRUCK ALL THE TIME, HE'S A GOOD GUY.
THAT AND HE'S GOT THESE KINDA DROOPY EYES.
MOOOOOOON RIVER...
BOOOOOO!
THAT'S DAR JAY. HE'S A SECOND YEAR. HE THINKS HE'S A KARAOKE GOD.
GIVE IT UP!

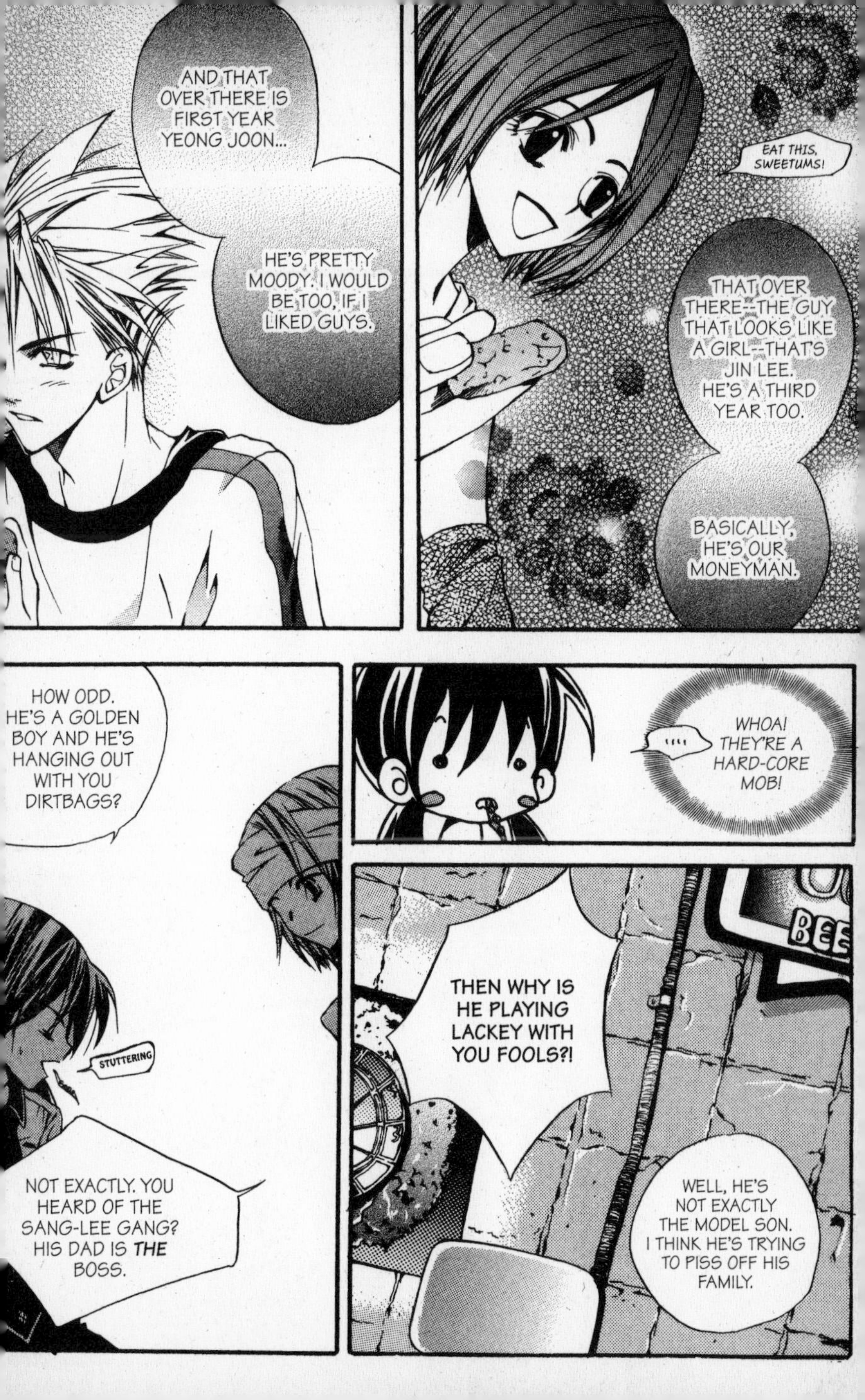
AND THAT OVER THERE IS FIRST YEAR YEONG JOON...
HE'S PRETTY MOODY. I WOULD BE TOO, IF I LIKED GUYS.
EAT THIS, SWEETUMS!
THAT OVER THERE--THE GUY THAT LOOKS LIKE A GIRL--THAT'S JIN LEE. HE'S A THIRD YEAR TOO.
BASICALLY, HE'S OUR MONEYMAN.
HOW ODD. HE'S A GOLDEN BOY AND HE'S HANGING OUT WITH YOU DIRTBAGS?
....
WHOA! THEY'RE A HARD-CORE MOB!
STUTTERING
NOT EXACTLY. YOU HEARD OF THE SANG-LEE GANG? HIS DAD IS **THE** BOSS.
THEN WHY IS HE PLAYING LACKEY WITH YOU FOOLS?!
WELL, HE'S NOT EXACTLY THE MODEL SON. I THINK HE'S TRYING TO PISS OFF HIS FAMILY.

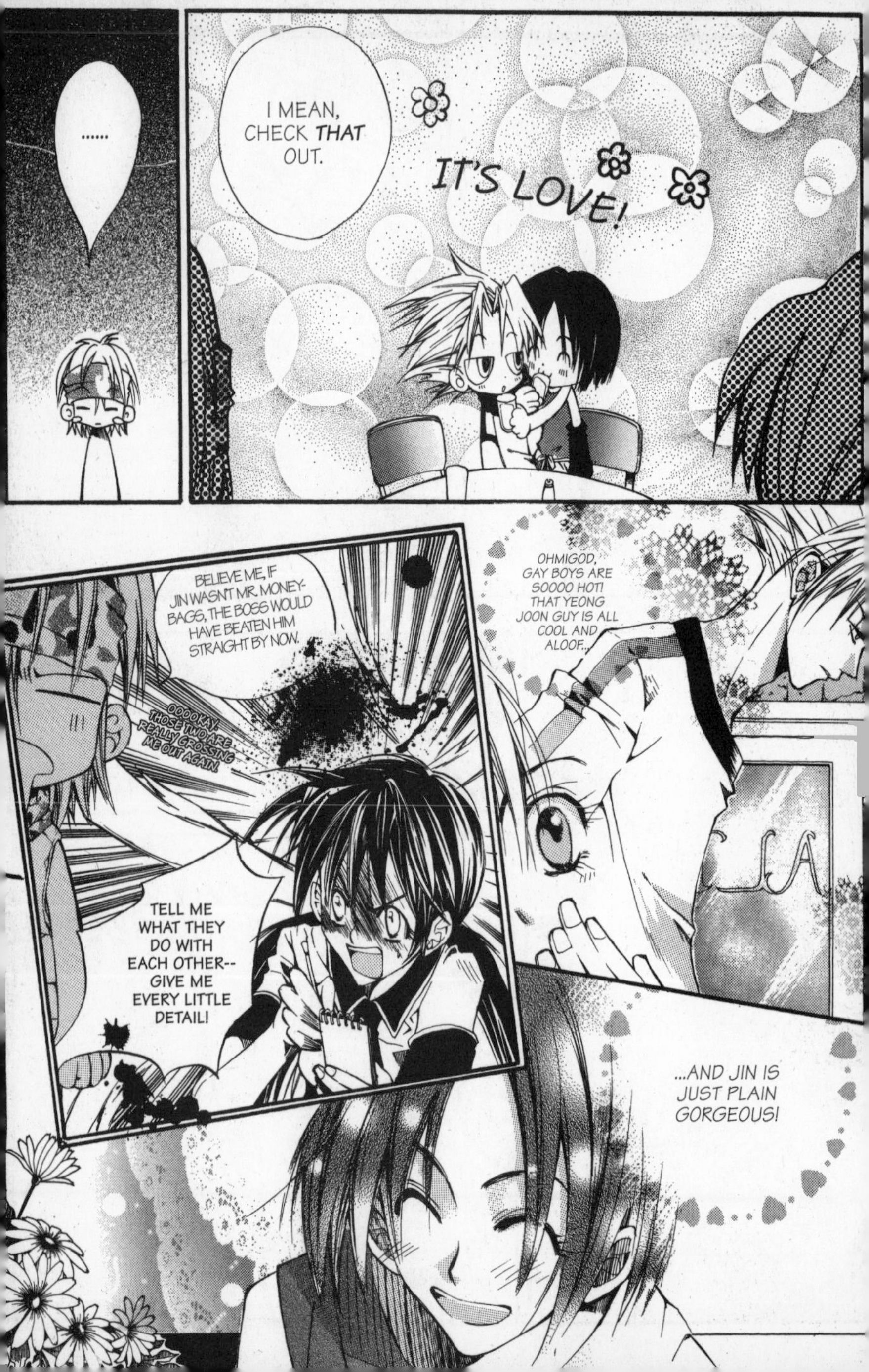
......
I MEAN, CHECK THAT OUT.
IT'S LOVE!
BELIEVE ME, IF JIN WASN'T MR. MONEY-BAGS, THE BOSS WOULD HAVE BEATEN HIM STRAIGHT BY NOW.
OOOOKAY. THOSE TWO ARE REALLY GROSSING ME OUT AGAIN.
TELL ME WHAT THEY DO WITH EACH OTHER-- GIVE ME EVERY LITTLE DETAIL!
OHMIGOD, GAY BOYS ARE SOOOO HOT! THAT YEONG JOON GUY IS ALL COOL AND ALOOF...
...AND JIN IS JUST PLAIN GORGEOUS!

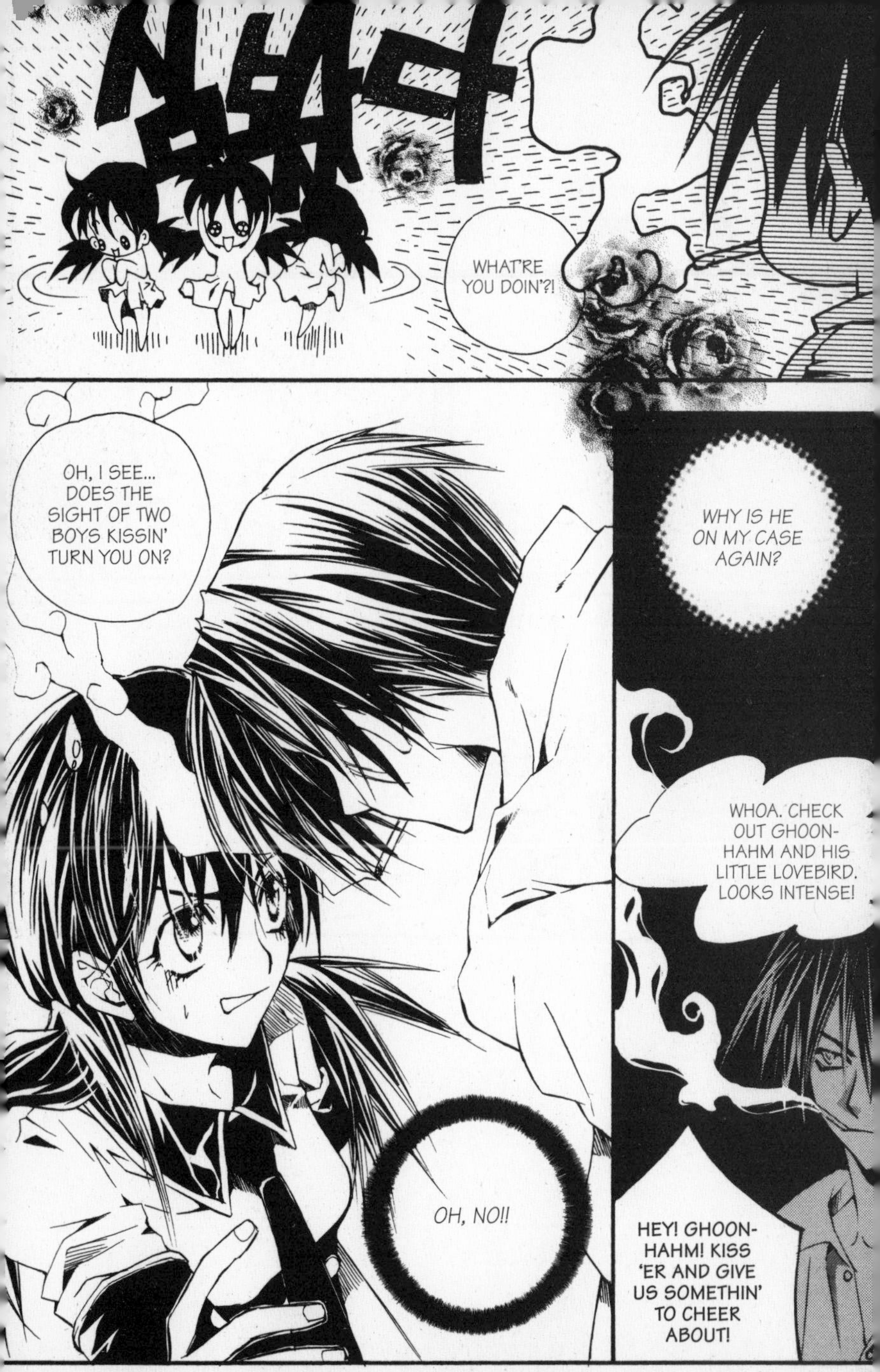
WHAT'RE YOU DOIN'?!
OH, I SEE... DOES THE SIGHT OF TWO BOYS KISSIN' TURN YOU ON?
OH, NO!!
WHY IS HE ON MY CASE AGAIN?
WHOA. CHECK OUT GHOON-HAHM AND HIS LITTLE LOVEBIRD. LOOKS INTENSE!
HEY! GHOON-HAHM! KISS 'ER AND GIVE US SOMETHIN' TO CHEER ABOUT!

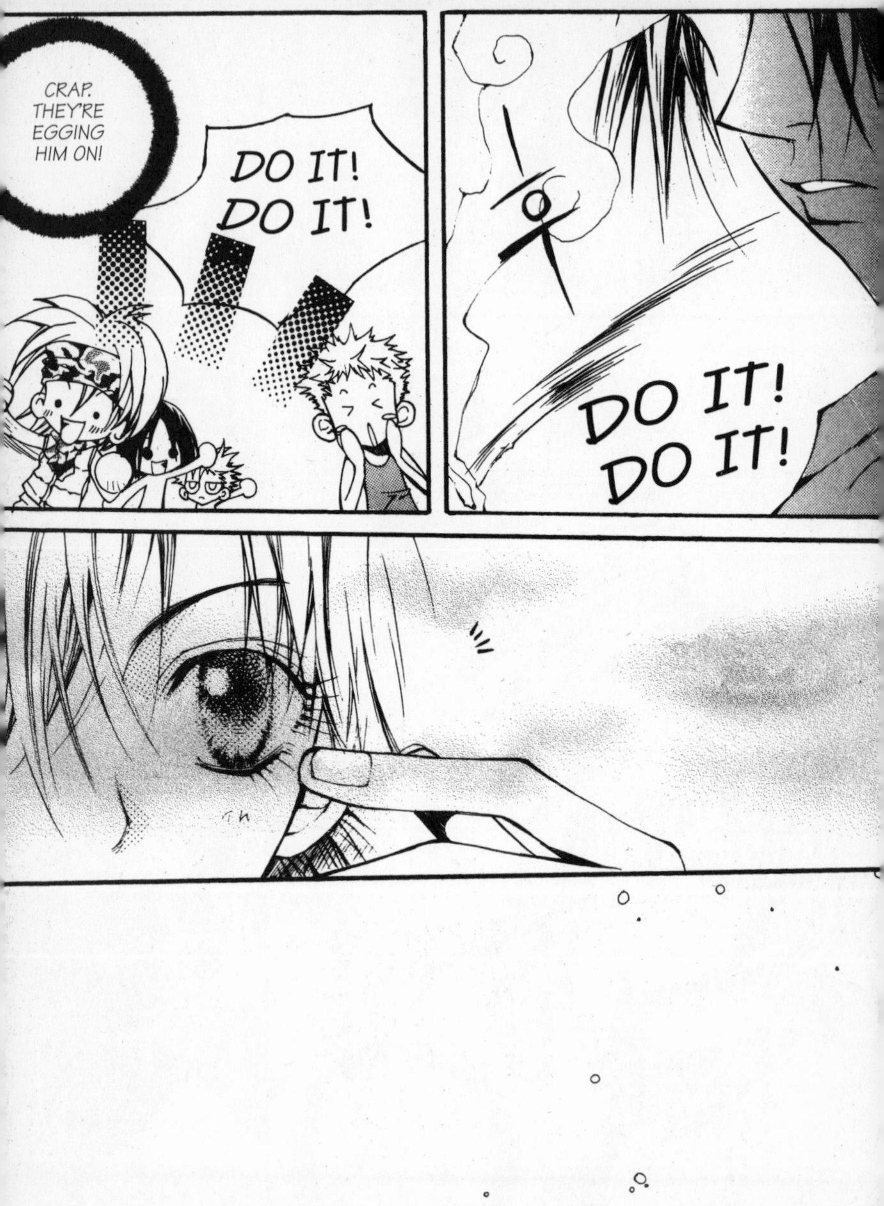
CRAP. THEY'RE EGGING HIM ON!
DO IT! DO IT!
DO IT! DO IT!

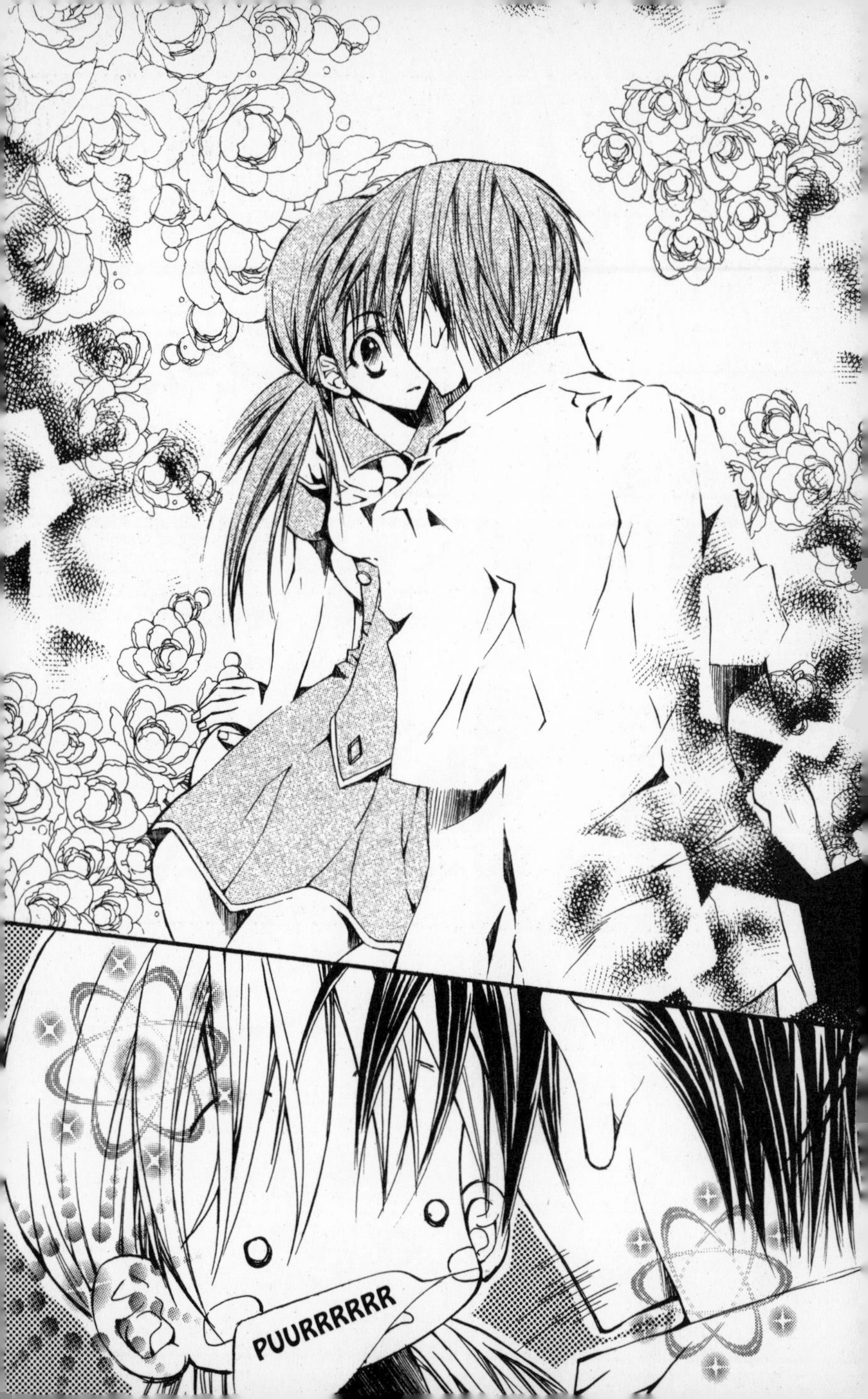
PUURRRRRR

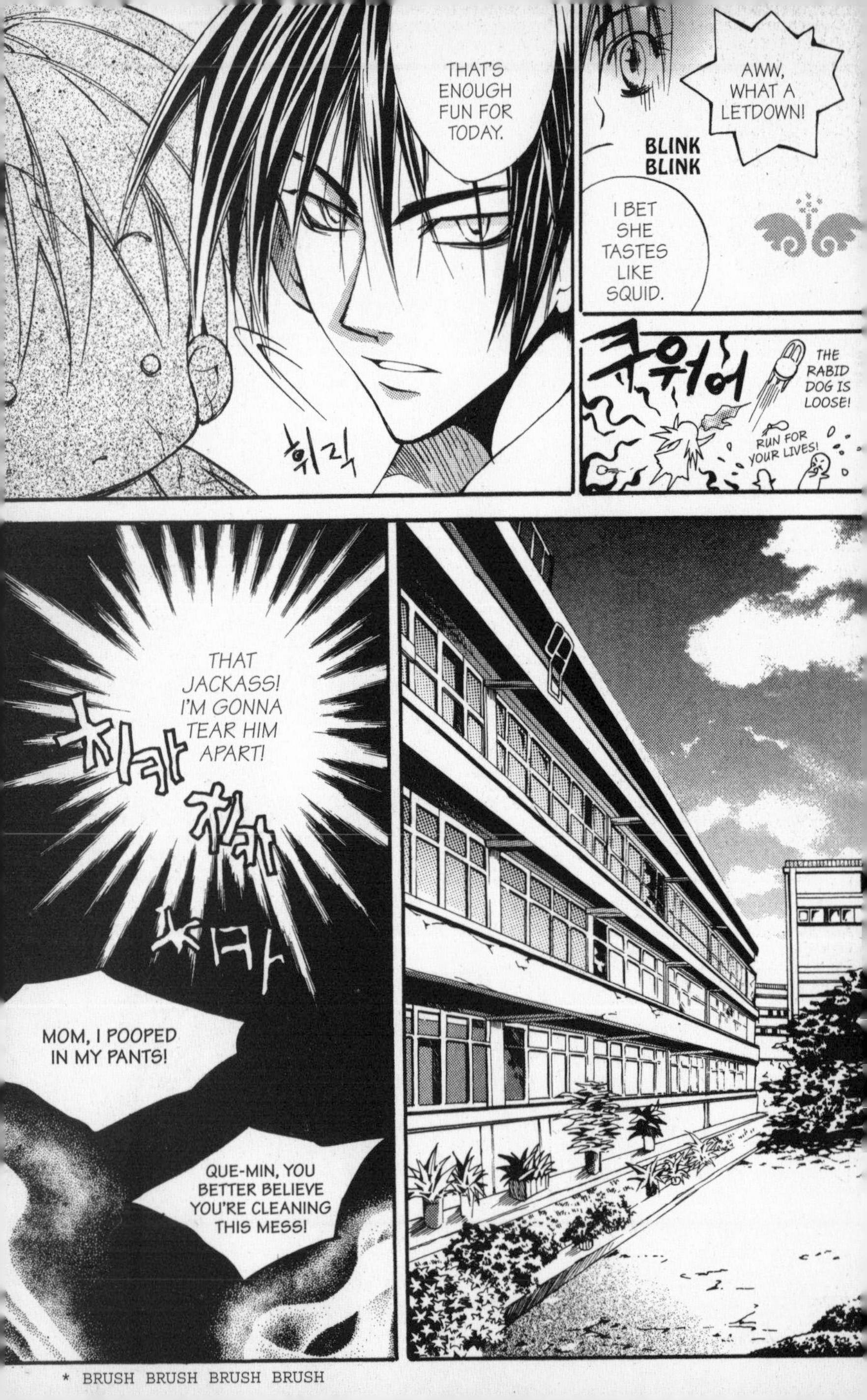
THAT'S ENOUGH FUN FOR TODAY.
휘릭
AWW, WHAT A LETDOWN!
BLINK BLINK
I BET SHE TASTES LIKE SQUID.
쿠워어
THE RABID DOG IS LOOSE!
RUN FOR YOUR LIVES!
THAT JACKASS! I'M GONNA TEAR HIM APART!
치카
치카
치카
MOM, I POOPED IN MY PANTS!
QUE-MIN, YOU BETTER BELIEVE YOU'RE CLEANING THIS MESS!

* BRUSH BRUSH BRUSH BRUSH

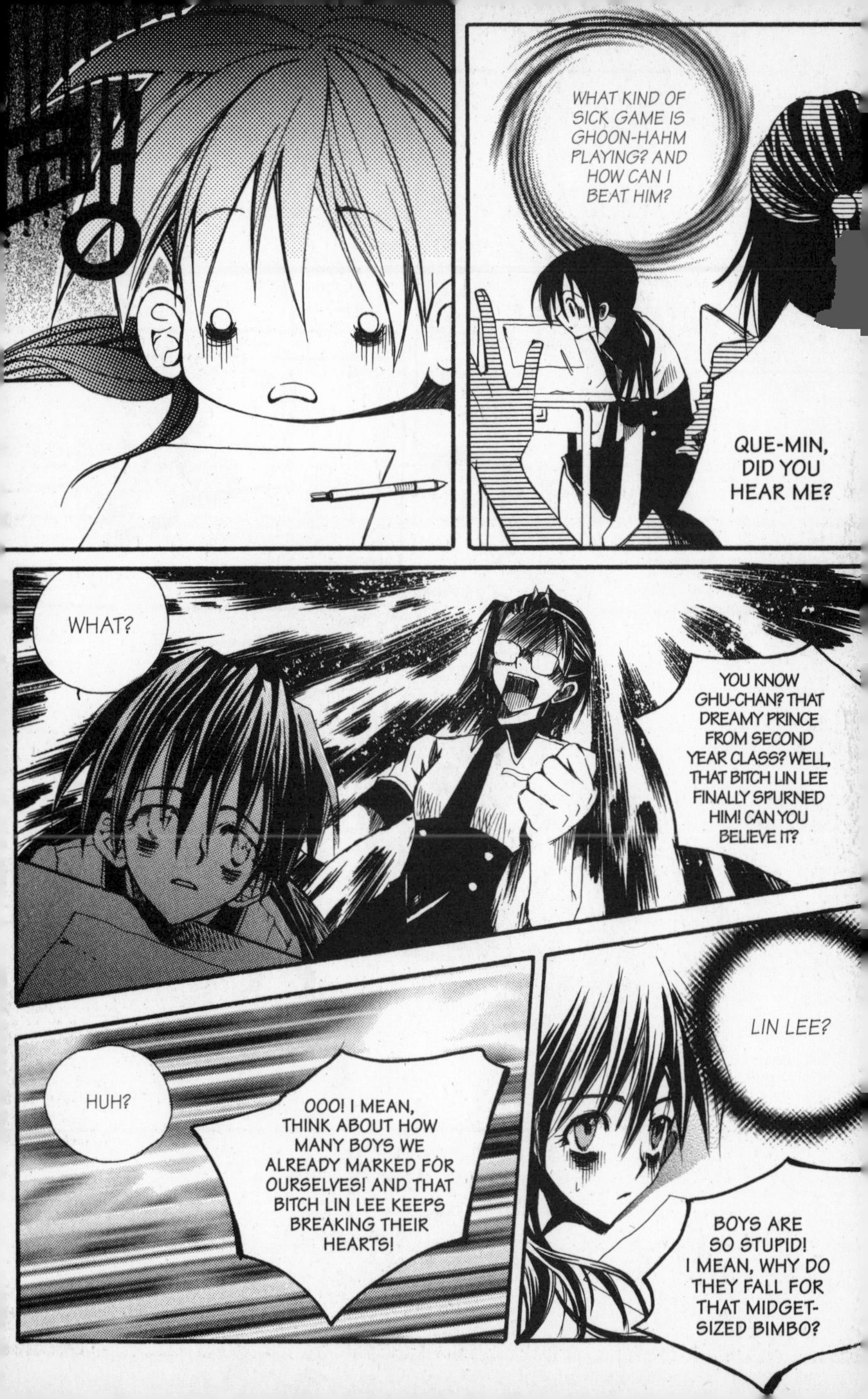
WHAT KIND OF SICK GAME IS GHOON-HAHM PLAYING? AND HOW CAN I BEAT HIM?
QUE-MIN, DID YOU HEAR ME?
WHAT?
YOU KNOW GHU-CHAN? THAT DREAMY PRINCE FROM SECOND YEAR CLASS? WELL, THAT BITCH LIN LEE FINALLY SPURNED HIM! CAN YOU BELIEVE IT?
HUH?
OOO! I MEAN, THINK ABOUT HOW MANY BOYS WE ALREADY MARKED FOR OURSELVES! AND THAT BITCH LIN LEE KEEPS BREAKING THEIR HEARTS!
LIN LEE?
BOYS ARE SO STUPID! I MEAN, WHY DO THEY FALL FOR THAT MIDGET-SIZED BIMBO?

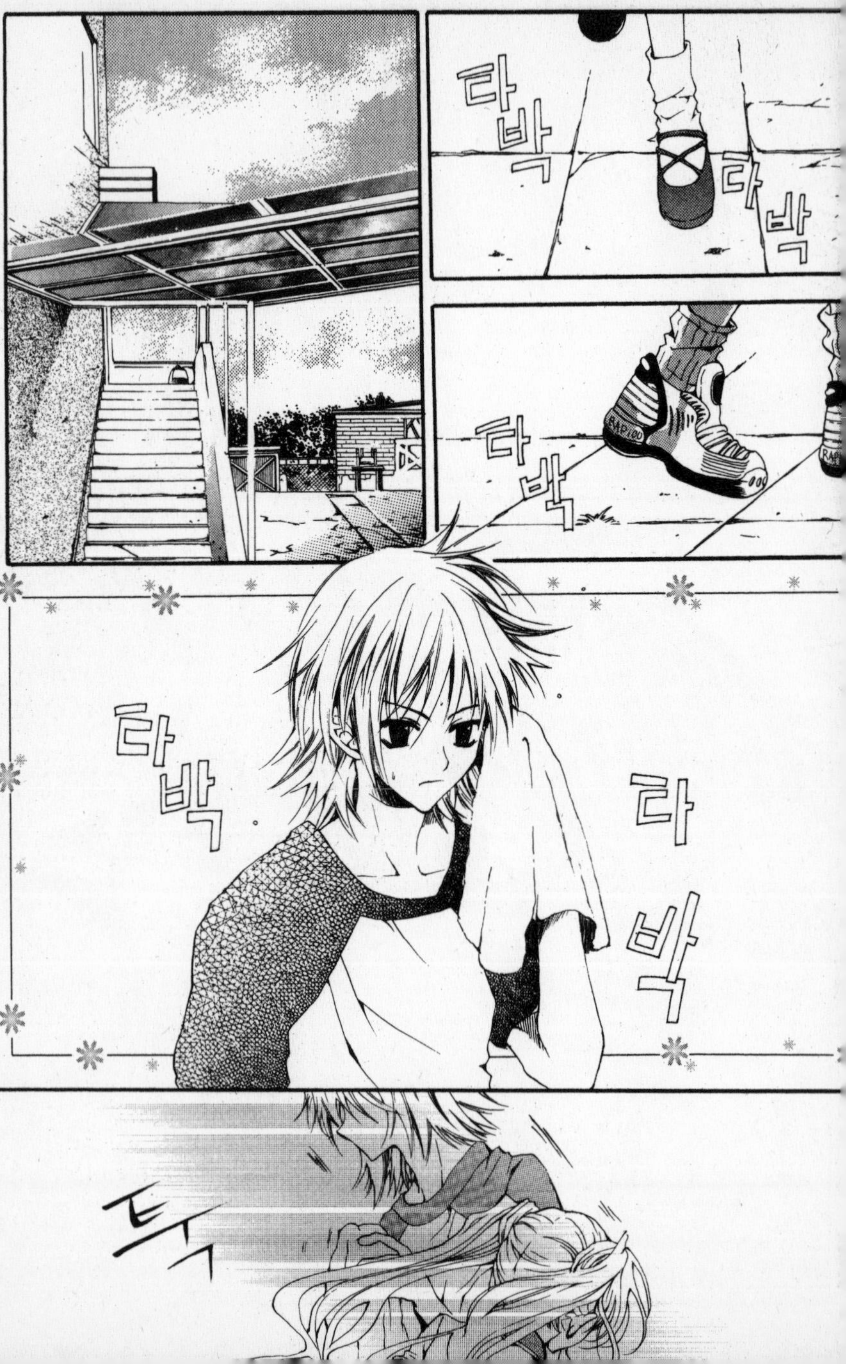
타박
타박
타박
타박
타박
타박
툭

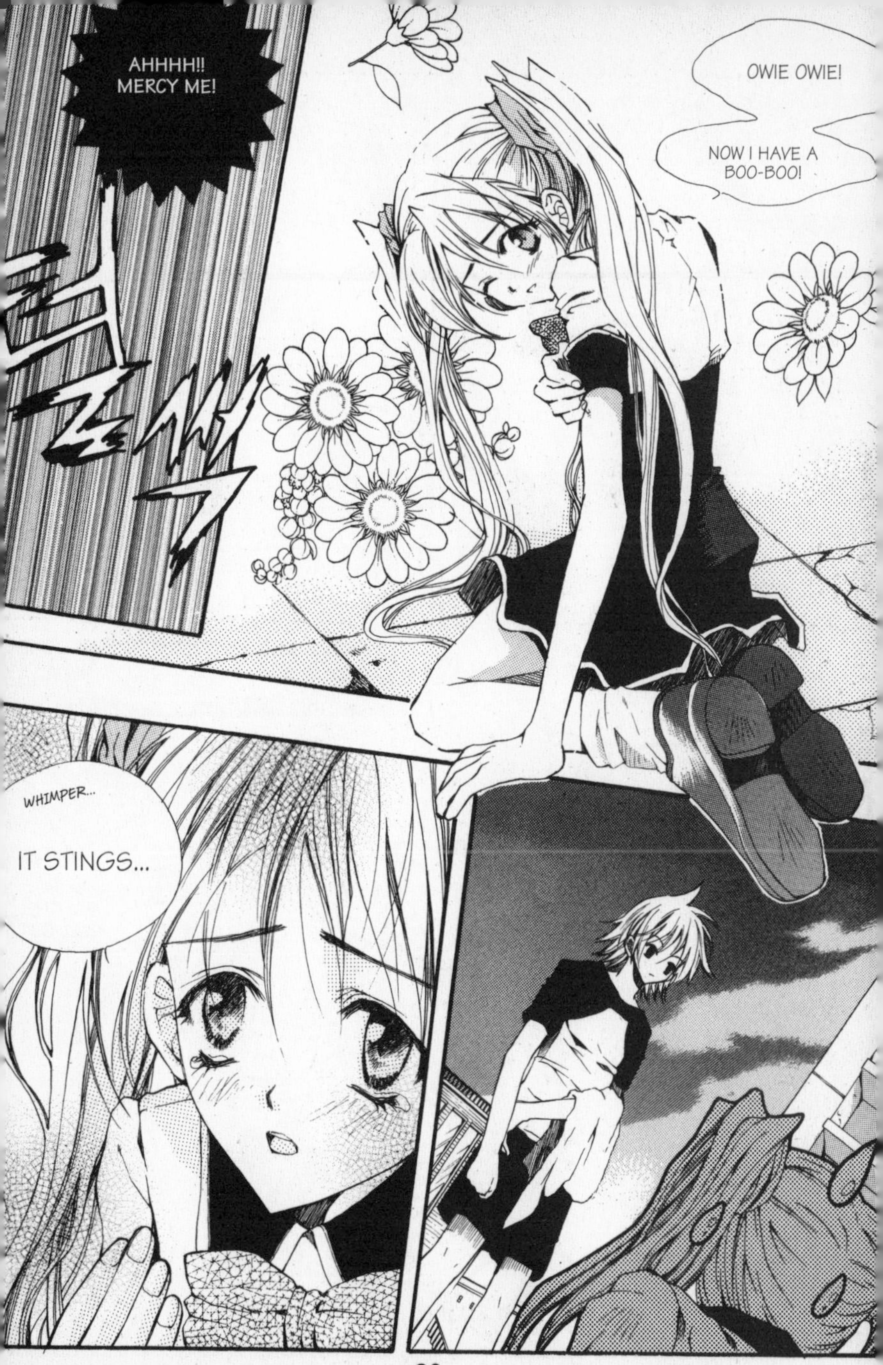
AHHHH!! MERCY ME!
OWIE OWIE!
NOW I HAVE A BOO-BOO!
WHIMPER...
IT STINGS...

* CLUELESS

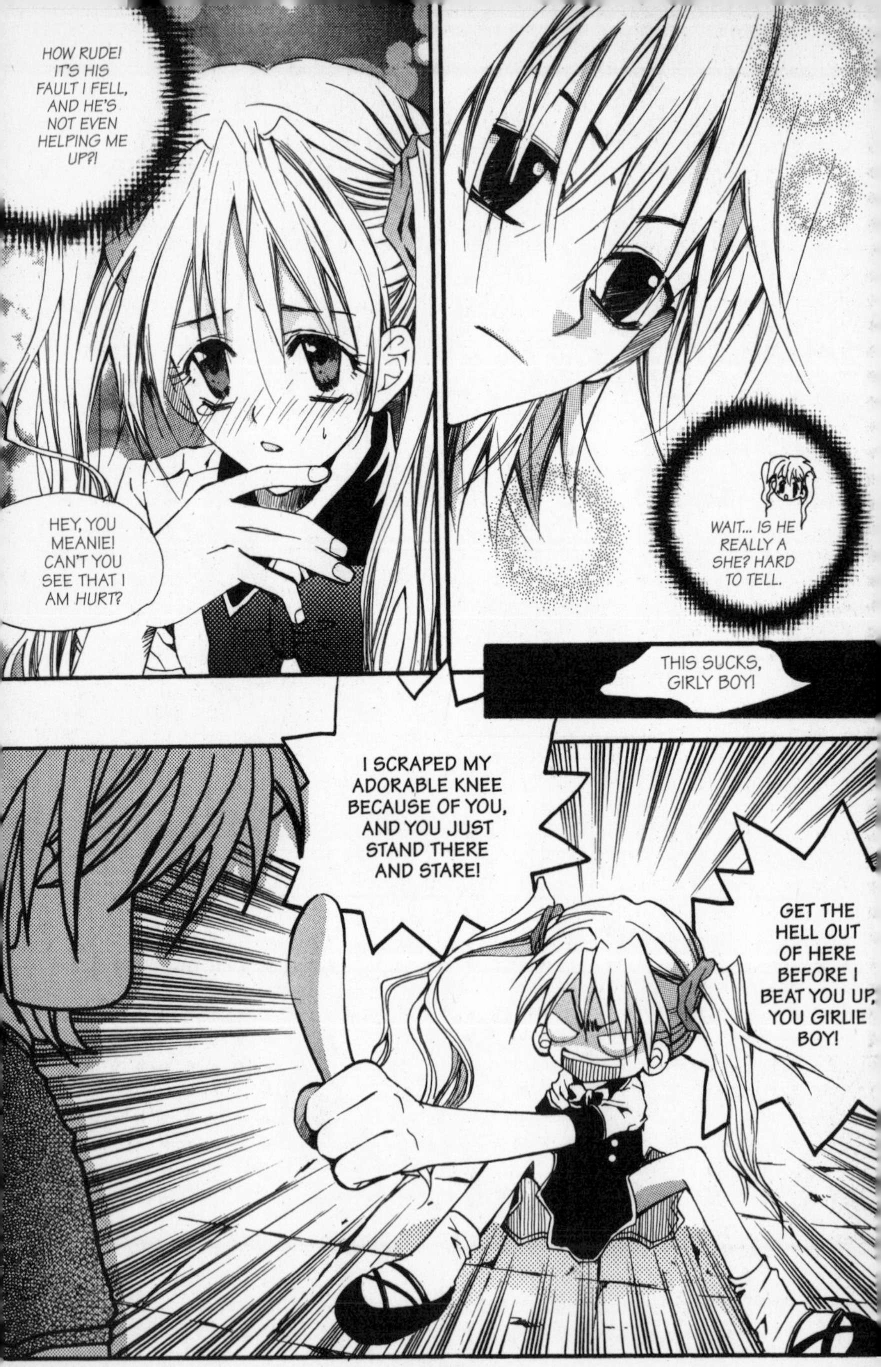
HOW RUDE! IT'S HIS FAULT I FELL, AND HE'S NOT EVEN HELPING ME UP?!
HEY, YOU MEANIE! CAN'T YOU SEE THAT I AM HURT?
WAIT... IS HE REALLY A SHE? HARD TO TELL.
THIS SUCKS, GIRLY BOY!
I SCRAPED MY ADORABLE KNEE BECAUSE OF YOU, AND YOU JUST STAND THERE AND STARE!
GET THE HELL OUT OF HERE BEFORE I BEAT YOU UP, YOU GIRLIE BOY!

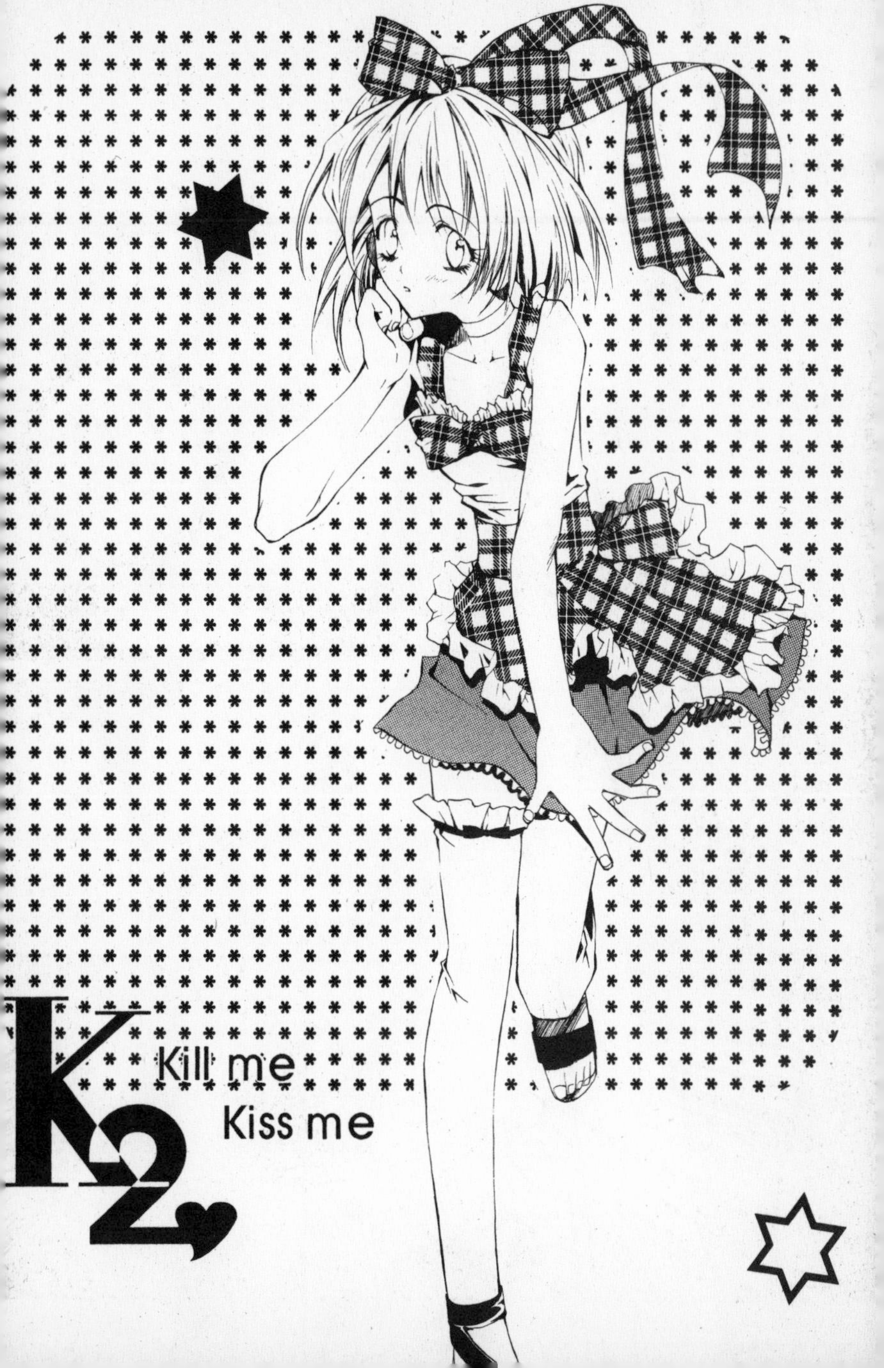

K2
Kill me
Kiss me

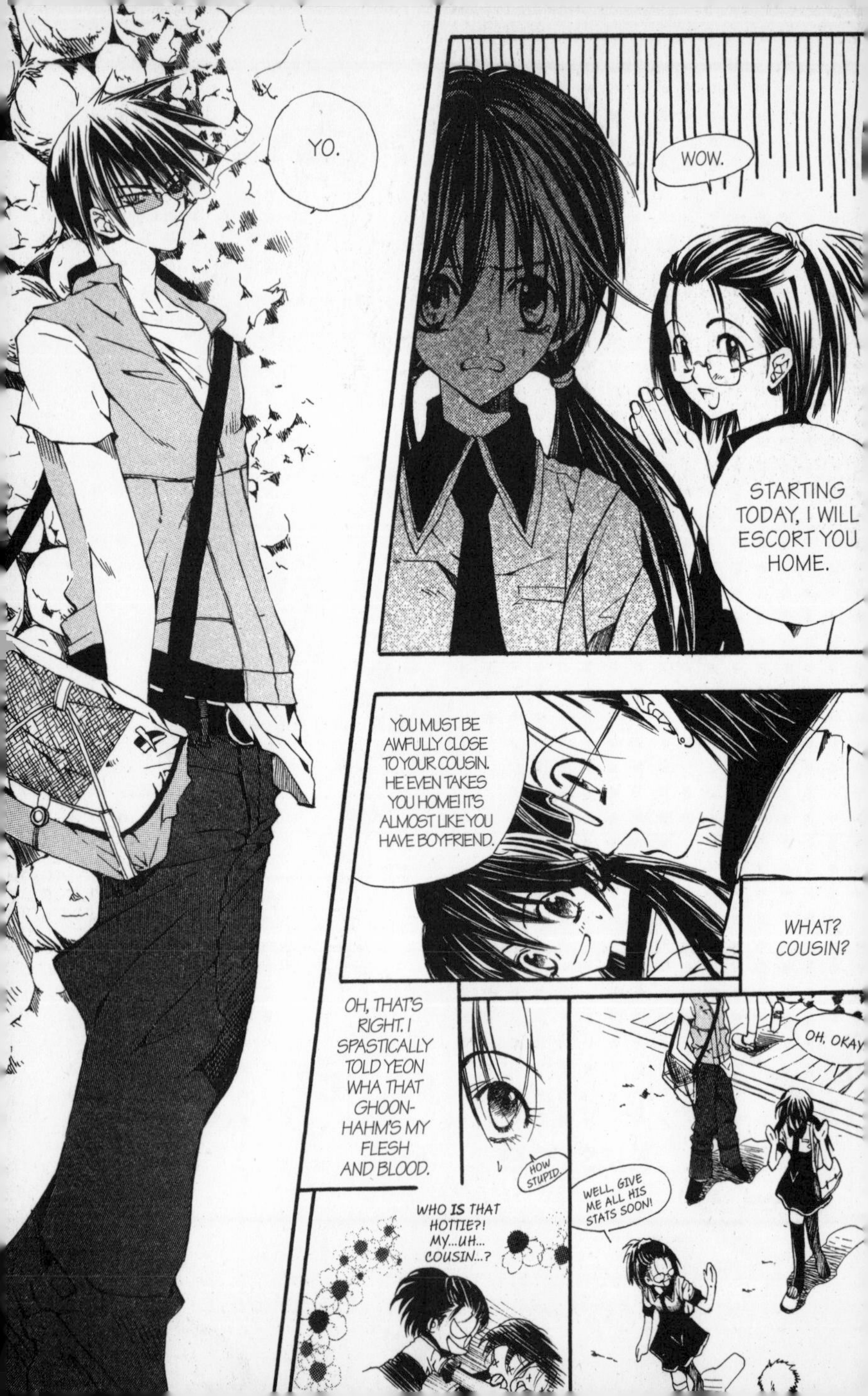

YO.
WOW.
STARTING TODAY, I WILL ESCORT YOU HOME.
YOU MUST BE AWFULLY CLOSE TO YOUR COUSIN. HE EVEN TAKES YOU HOME! IT'S ALMOST LIKE YOU HAVE BOYFRIEND.
WHAT? COUSIN?
OH, THAT'S RIGHT. I SPASTICALLY TOLD YEON WHA THAT GHOON-HAHM'S MY FLESH AND BLOOD.
HOW STUPID.
WHO IS THAT HOTTIE?! MY...UH... COUSIN...?
OH, OKAY
WELL, GIVE ME ALL HIS STATS SOON!

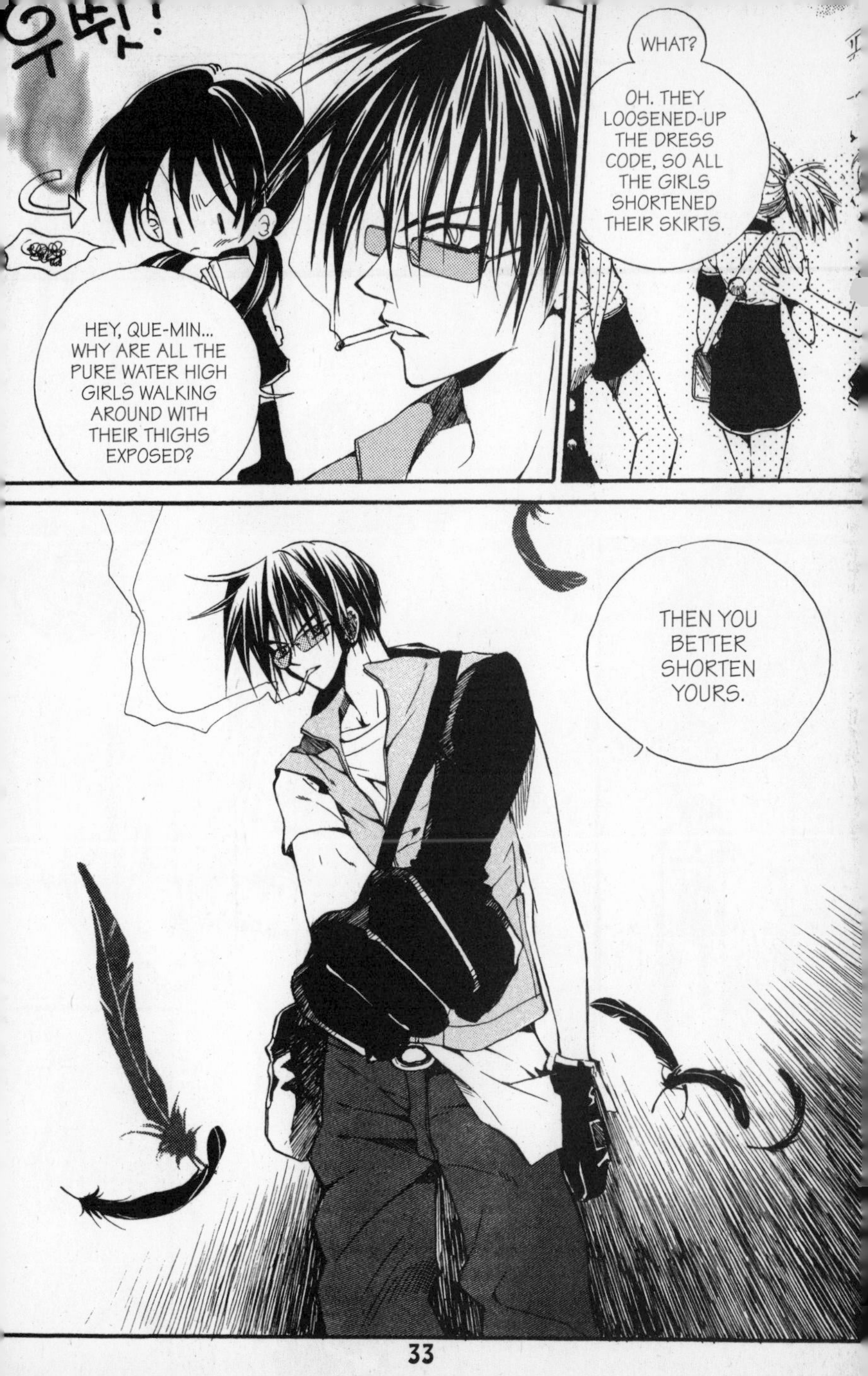
HEY, QUE-MIN... WHY ARE ALL THE PURE WATER HIGH GIRLS WALKING AROUND WITH THEIR THIGHS EXPOSED?
WHAT?
OH. THEY LOOSENED-UP THE DRESS CODE, SO ALL THE GIRLS SHORTENED THEIR SKIRTS.
THEN YOU BETTER SHORTEN YOURS.

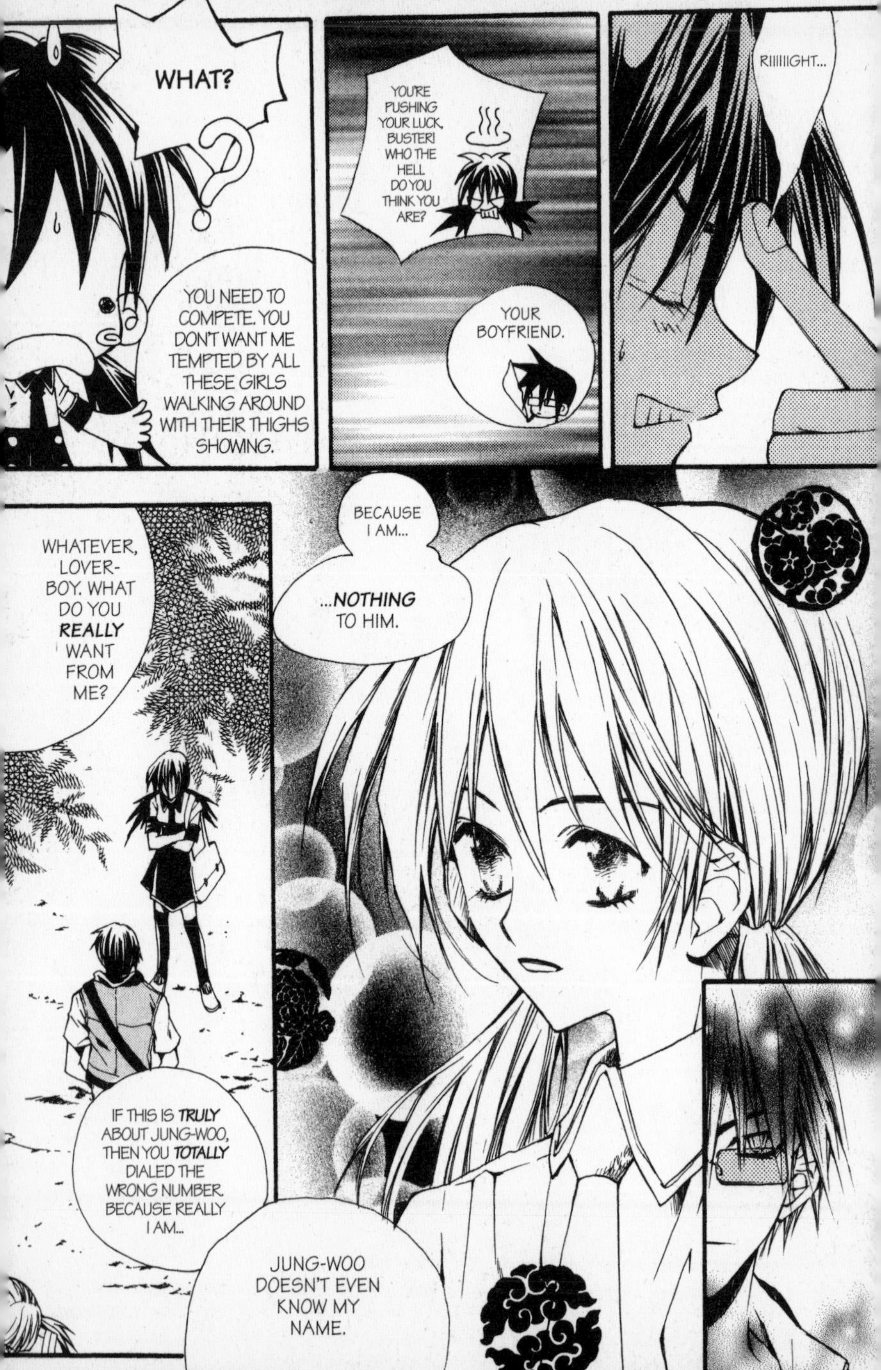
WHAT?
YOU NEED TO COMPETE. YOU DON'T WANT ME TEMPTED BY ALL THESE GIRLS WALKING AROUND WITH THEIR THIGHS SHOWING.
YOU'RE PUSHING YOUR LUCK, BUSTER! WHO THE HELL DO YOU THINK YOU ARE?
YOUR BOYFRIEND.
RIIIIIIGHT...
WHATEVER, LOVER-BOY. WHAT DO YOU REALLY WANT FROM ME?
IF THIS IS TRULY ABOUT JUNG-WOO, THEN YOU TOTALLY DIALED THE WRONG NUMBER. BECAUSE REALLY I AM...
BECAUSE I AM...
...NOTHING TO HIM.
JUNG-WOO DOESN'T EVEN KNOW MY NAME.

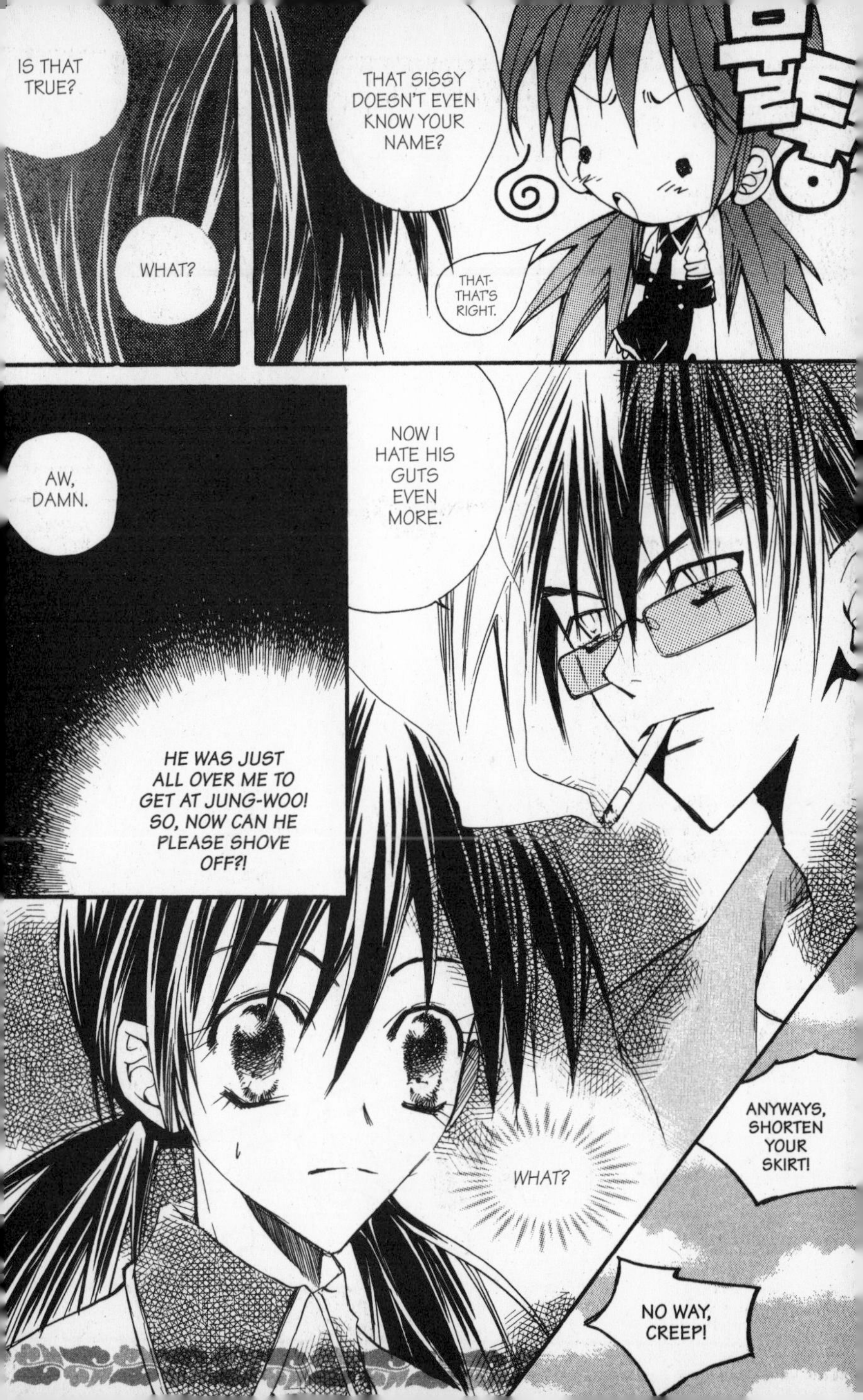
IS THAT TRUE?
WHAT?
THAT SISSY DOESN'T EVEN KNOW YOUR NAME?
THAT-THAT'S RIGHT.
AW, DAMN.
NOW I HATE HIS GUTS EVEN MORE.
HE WAS JUST ALL OVER ME TO GET AT JUNG-WOO! SO, NOW CAN HE PLEASE SHOVE OFF?!
WHAT?
ANYWAYS, SHORTEN YOUR SKIRT!
NO WAY, CREEP!

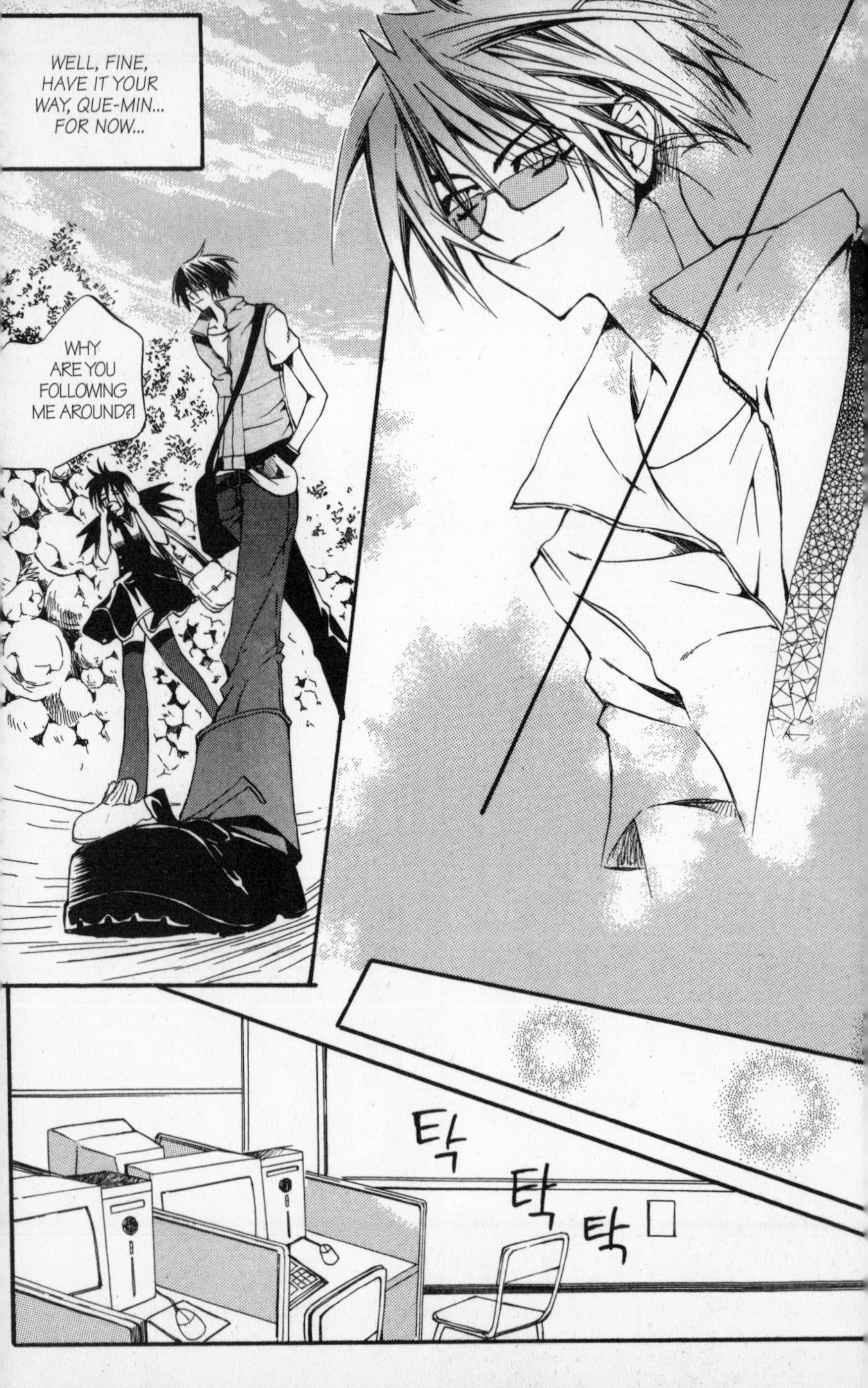
WELL, FINE, HAVE IT YOUR WAY, QUE-MIN... FOR NOW...
WHY ARE YOU FOLLOWING ME AROUND?!
탁
탁
탁

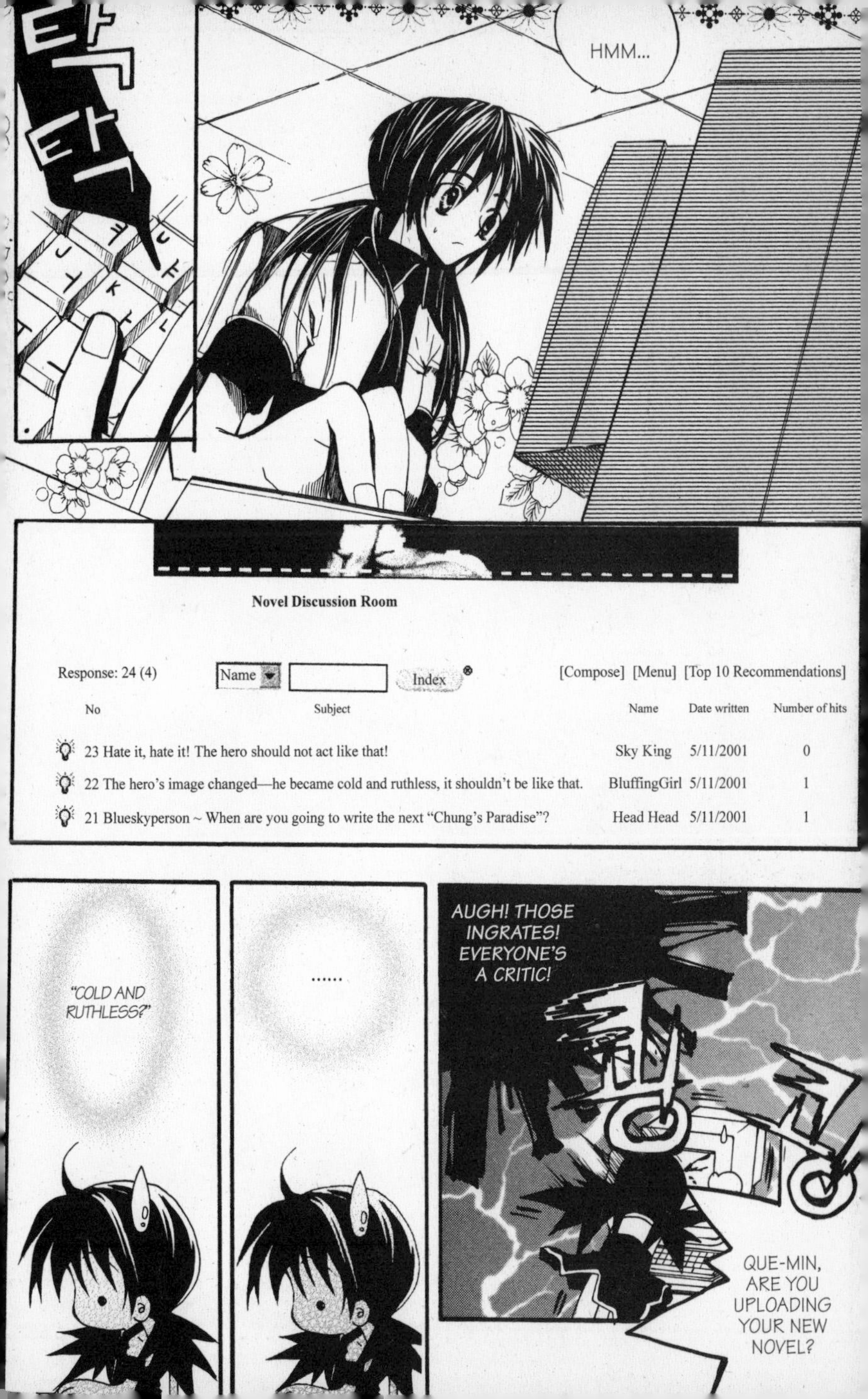
HMM...
Novel Discussion Room
Response: 24 (4)
Name
Index
[Compose] [Menu] [Top 10 Recommendations]
No
Subject
Name
Date written
Number of hits
23 Hate it, hate it! The hero should not act like that! Sky King 5/11/2001 0
22 The hero's image changed—he became cold and ruthless, it shouldn't be like that. BluffingGirl 5/11/2001 1
21 Blueskyperson ~ When are you going to write the next "Chung's Paradise"? Head Head 5/11/2001 1
"COLD AND RUTHLESS?"
......
AUGH! THOSE INGRATES! EVERYONE'S A CRITIC!
QUE-MIN, ARE YOU UPLOADING YOUR NEW NOVEL?

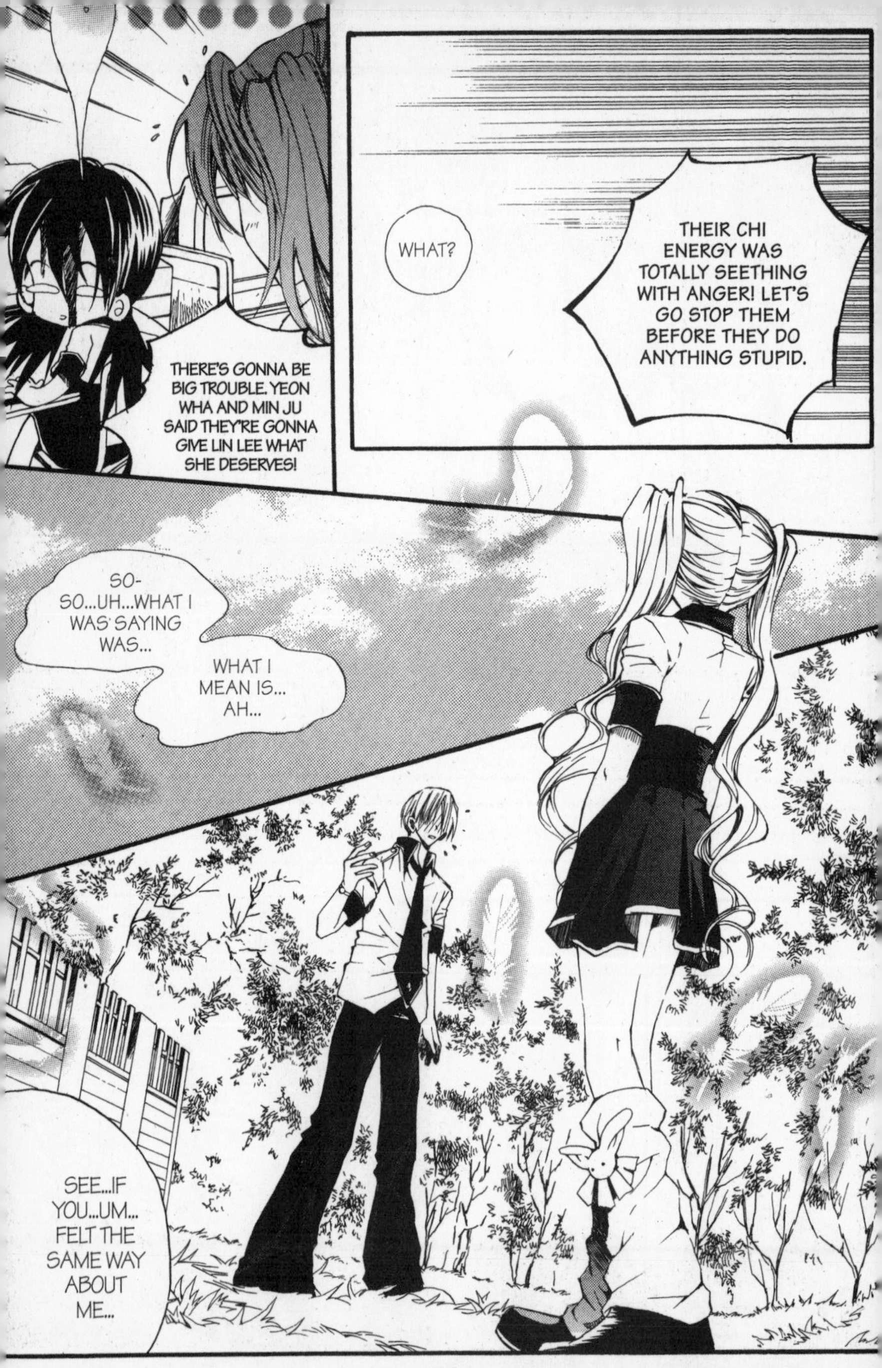
THERE'S GONNA BE BIG TROUBLE. YEON WHA AND MIN JU SAID THEY'RE GONNA GIVE LIN LEE WHAT SHE DESERVES!
WHAT?
THEIR CHI ENERGY WAS TOTALLY SEETHING WITH ANGER! LET'S GO STOP THEM BEFORE THEY DO ANYTHING STUPID.
SO-SO...UH...WHAT I WAS SAYING WAS...
WHAT I MEAN IS... AH...
SEE...IF YOU...UM... FELT THE SAME WAY ABOUT ME...

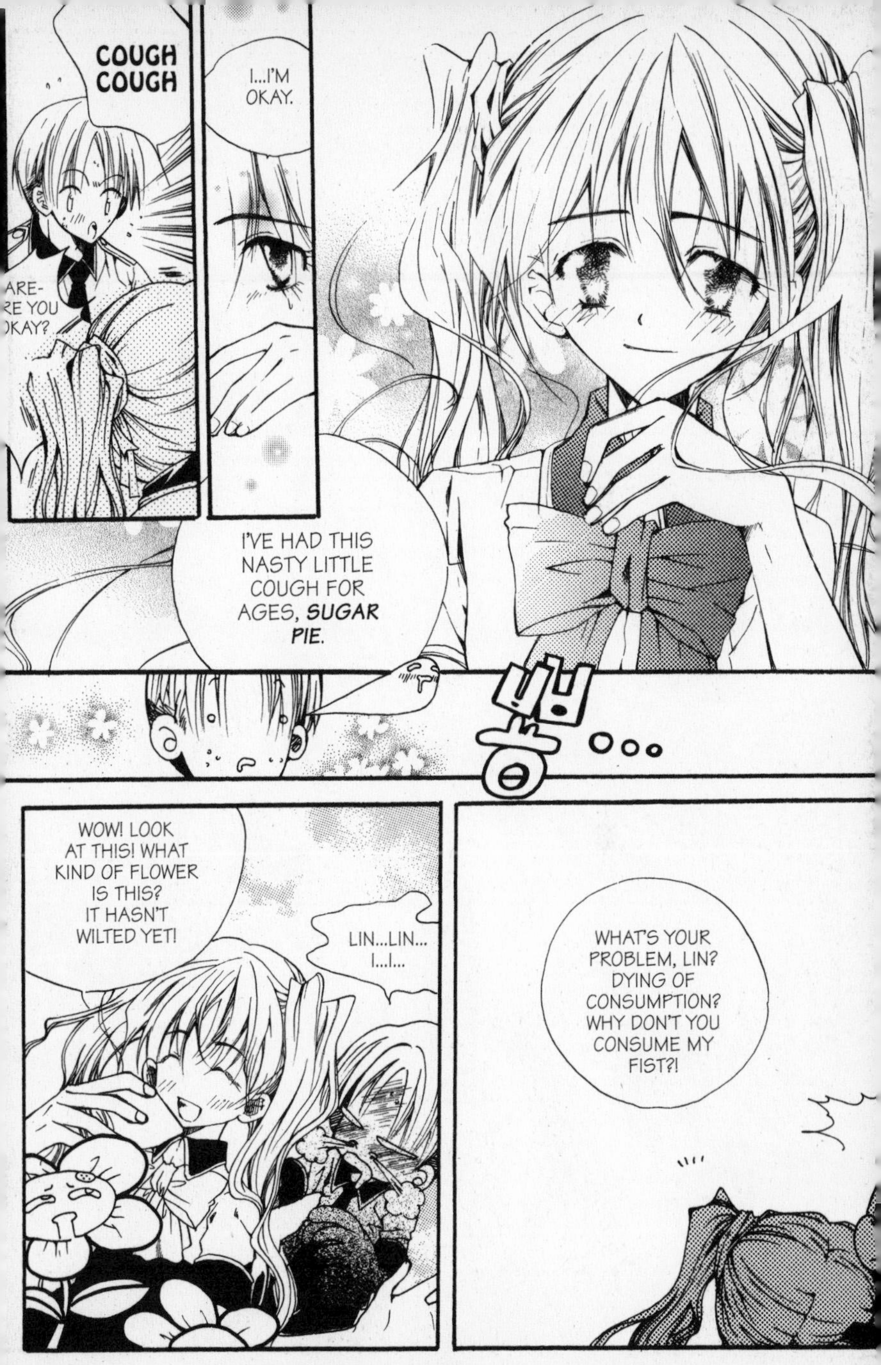
COUGH COUGH
ARE- RE YOU KAY?
I...I'M OKAY.
I'VE HAD THIS NASTY LITTLE COUGH FOR AGES, **SUGAR PIE**.
WOW! LOOK AT THIS! WHAT KIND OF FLOWER IS THIS? IT HASN'T WILTED YET!
LIN...LIN... I...I...
WHAT'S YOUR PROBLEM, LIN? DYING OF CONSUMPTION? WHY DON'T YOU CONSUME MY FIST?!

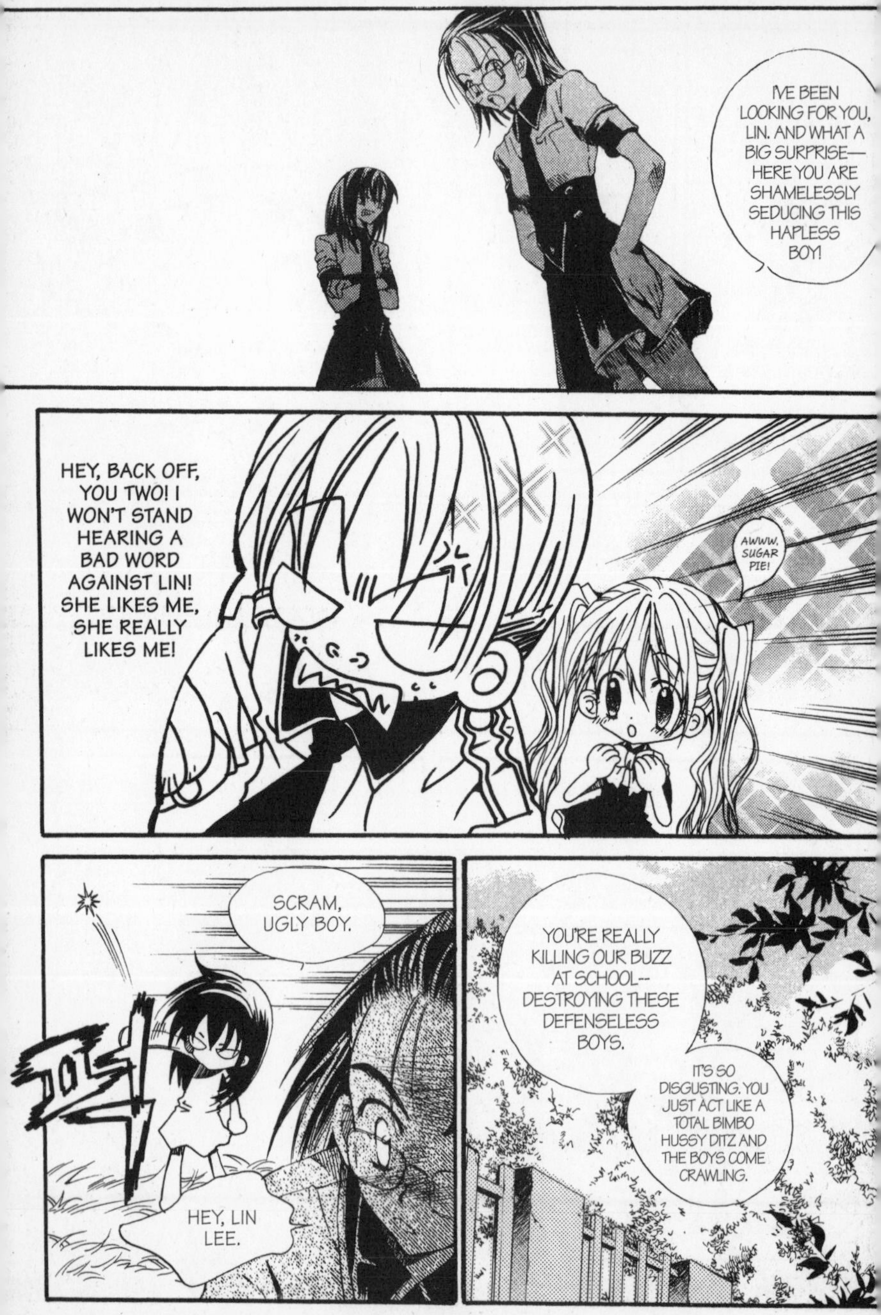
I'VE BEEN LOOKING FOR YOU, LIN. AND WHAT A BIG SURPRISE— HERE YOU ARE SHAMELESSLY SEDUCING THIS HAPLESS BOY!
HEY, BACK OFF, YOU TWO! I WON'T STAND HEARING A BAD WORD AGAINST LIN! SHE LIKES ME, SHE REALLY LIKES ME!
AWWW, SUGAR PIE!
SCRAM, UGLY BOY.
HEY, LIN LEE.
YOU'RE REALLY KILLING OUR BUZZ AT SCHOOL-- DESTROYING THESE DEFENSELESS BOYS.
IT'S SO DISGUSTING. YOU JUST ACT LIKE A TOTAL BIMBO HUSSY DITZ AND THE BOYS COME CRAWLING.

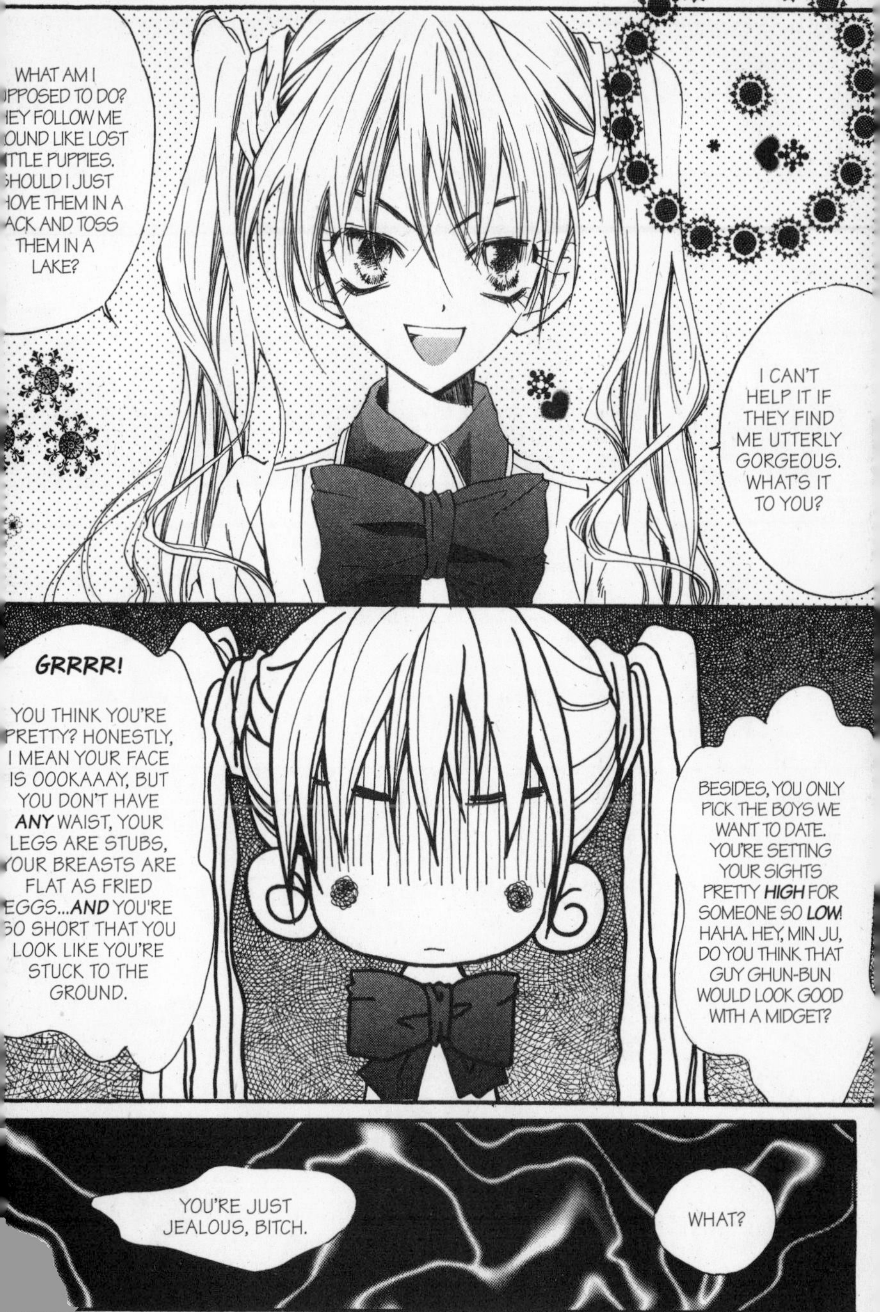
WHAT AM I PPOSED TO DO? IEY FOLLOW ME OUND LIKE LOST TTLE PUPPIES. SHOULD I JUST HOVE THEM IN A ACK AND TOSS THEM IN A LAKE?
I CAN'T HELP IT IF THEY FIND ME UTTERLY GORGEOUS. WHAT'S IT TO YOU?
GRRRR!
YOU THINK YOU'RE PRETTY? HONESTLY, I MEAN YOUR FACE IS OOOKAAAY, BUT YOU DON'T HAVE ANY WAIST, YOUR LEGS ARE STUBS, OUR BREASTS ARE FLAT AS FRIED EGGS...AND YOU'RE SO SHORT THAT YOU LOOK LIKE YOU'RE STUCK TO THE GROUND.
BESIDES, YOU ONLY PICK THE BOYS WE WANT TO DATE. YOU'RE SETTING YOUR SIGHTS PRETTY HIGH FOR SOMEONE SO LOW! HAHA. HEY, MIN JU, DO YOU THINK THAT GUY GHUN-BUN WOULD LOOK GOOD WITH A MIDGET?
YOU'RE JUST JEALOUS, BITCH.
WHAT?

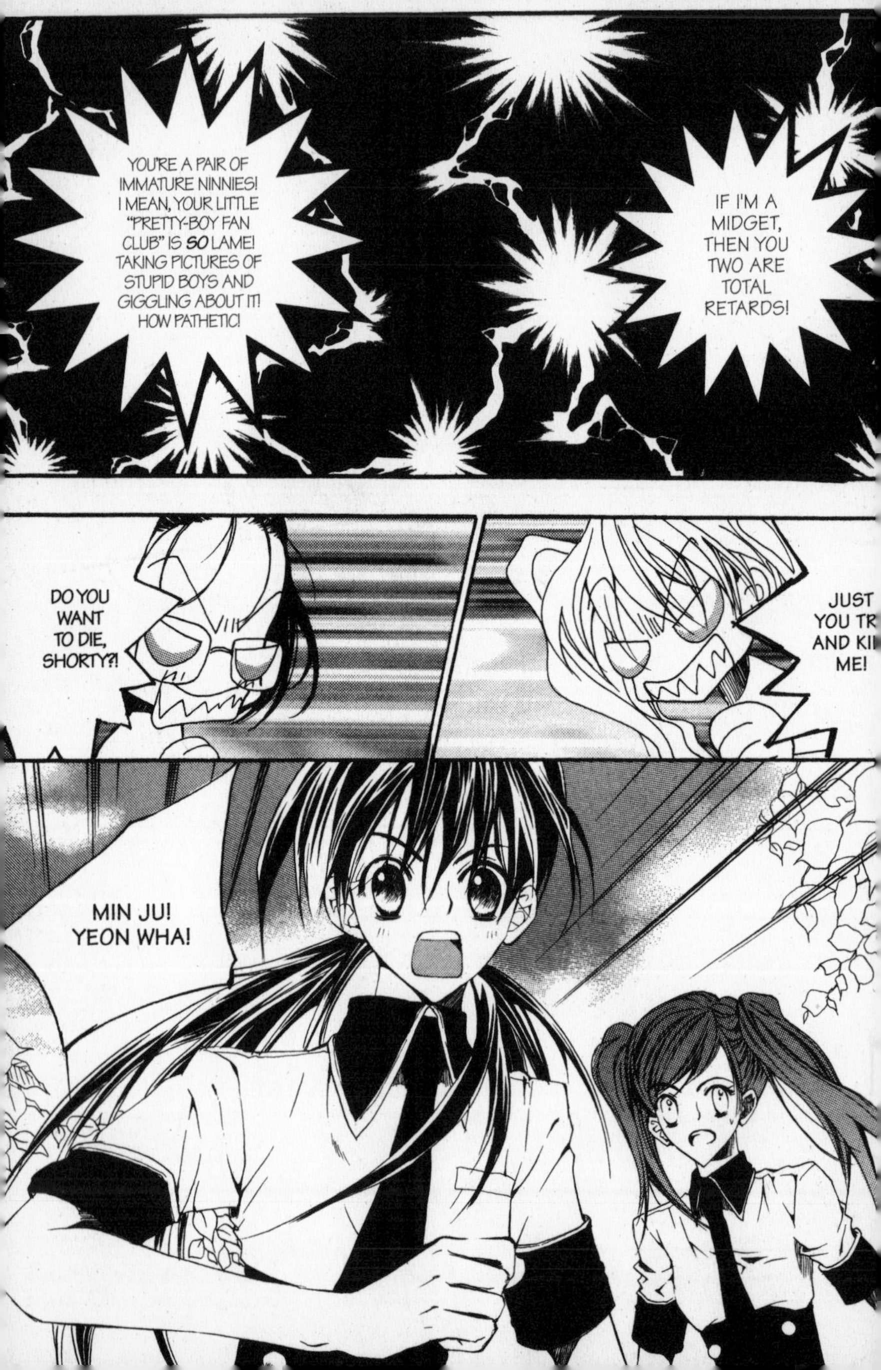

YOU'RE A PAIR OF IMMATURE NINNIES! I MEAN, YOUR LITTLE "PRETTY-BOY FAN CLUB" IS *SO* LAME! TAKING PICTURES OF STUPID BOYS AND GIGGLING ABOUT IT! HOW PATHETIC!
IF I'M A MIDGET, THEN YOU TWO ARE TOTAL RETARDS!
DO YOU WANT TO DIE, SHORTY?!
JUST YOU TR AND KI ME!
MIN JU! YEON WHA!

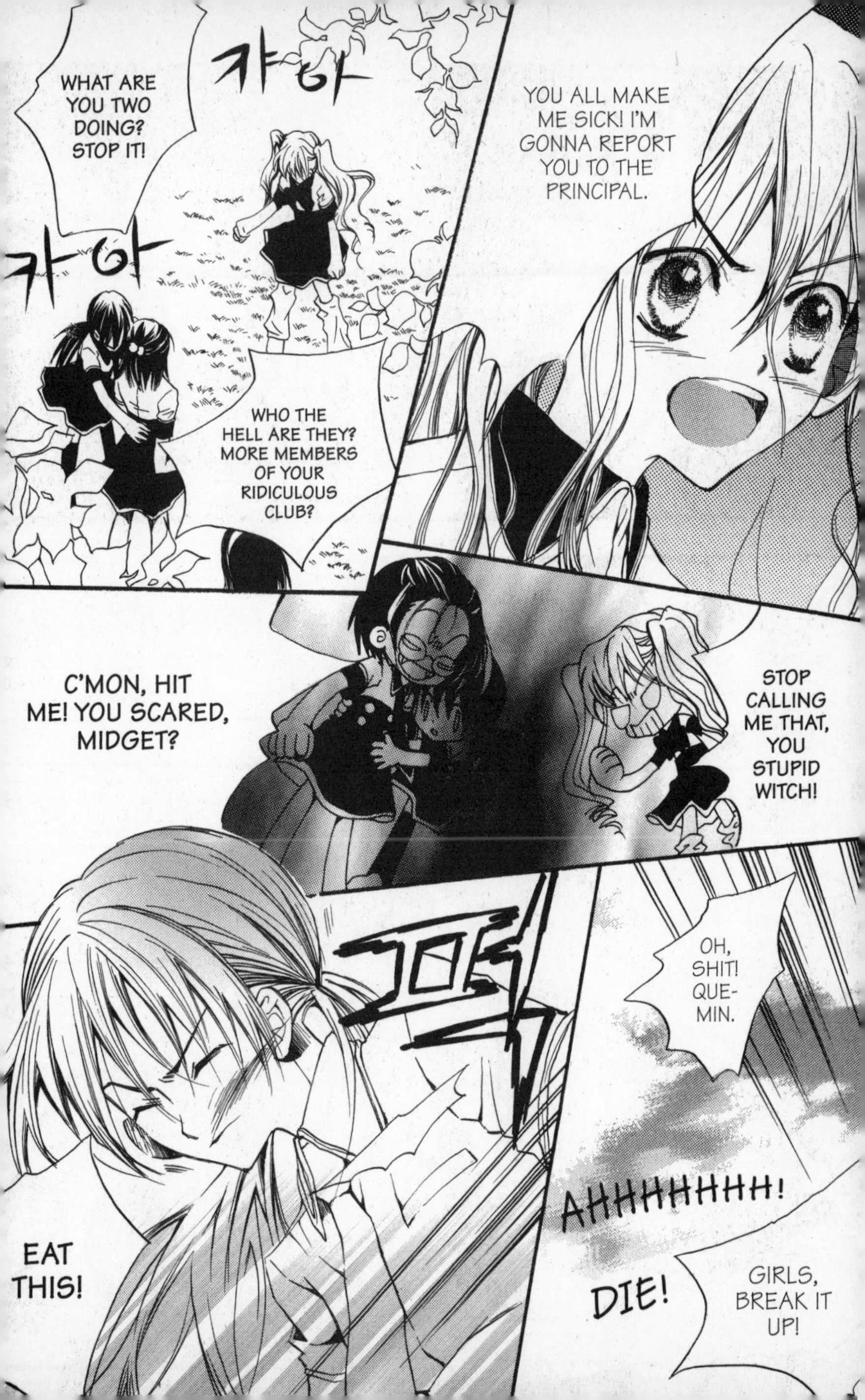
WHAT ARE YOU TWO DOING? STOP IT!
카아
카아
WHO THE HELL ARE THEY? MORE MEMBERS OF YOUR RIDICULOUS CLUB?
YOU ALL MAKE ME SICK! I'M GONNA REPORT YOU TO THE PRINCIPAL.
C'MON, HIT ME! YOU SCARED, MIDGET?
STOP CALLING ME THAT, YOU STUPID WITCH!
EAT THIS!
OH, SHIT! QUE-MIN.
AHHHHHHHH!
DIE!
GIRLS, BREAK IT UP!

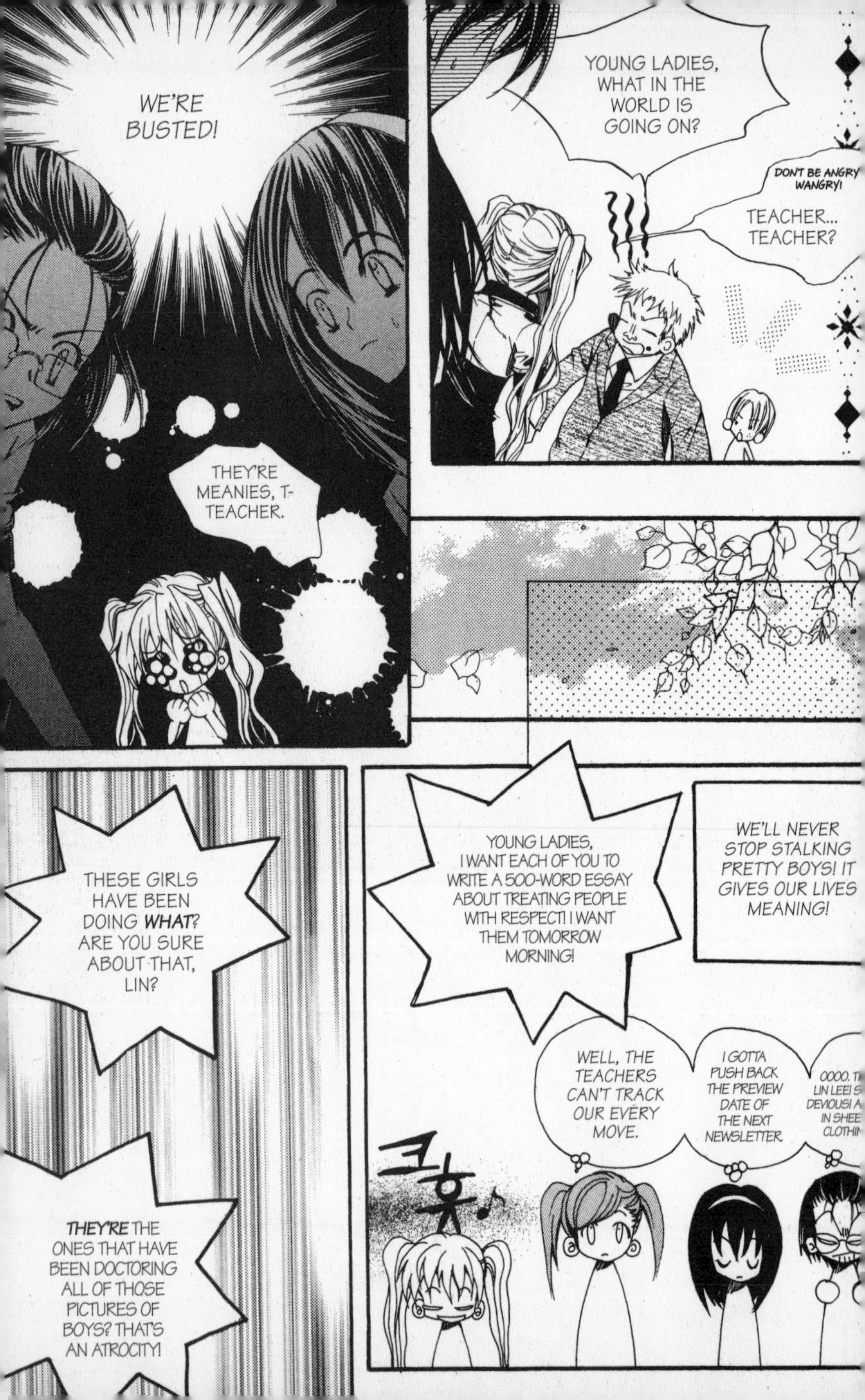
WE'RE BUSTED!
THEY'RE MEANIES, T-TEACHER.
YOUNG LADIES, WHAT IN THE WORLD IS GOING ON?
DON'T BE ANGRY WANGRY!
TEACHER... TEACHER?
THESE GIRLS HAVE BEEN DOING **WHAT**? ARE YOU SURE ABOUT THAT, LIN?
THEY'RE THE ONES THAT HAVE BEEN DOCTORING ALL OF THOSE PICTURES OF BOYS? THAT'S AN ATROCITY!
YOUNG LADIES, I WANT EACH OF YOU TO WRITE A 500-WORD ESSAY ABOUT TREATING PEOPLE WITH RESPECT! I WANT THEM TOMORROW MORNING!
WE'LL NEVER STOP STALKING PRETTY BOYS! IT GIVES OUR LIVES MEANING!
WELL, THE TEACHERS CAN'T TRACK OUR EVERY MOVE.
I GOTTA PUSH BACK THE PREVIEW DATE OF THE NEXT NEWSLETTER.

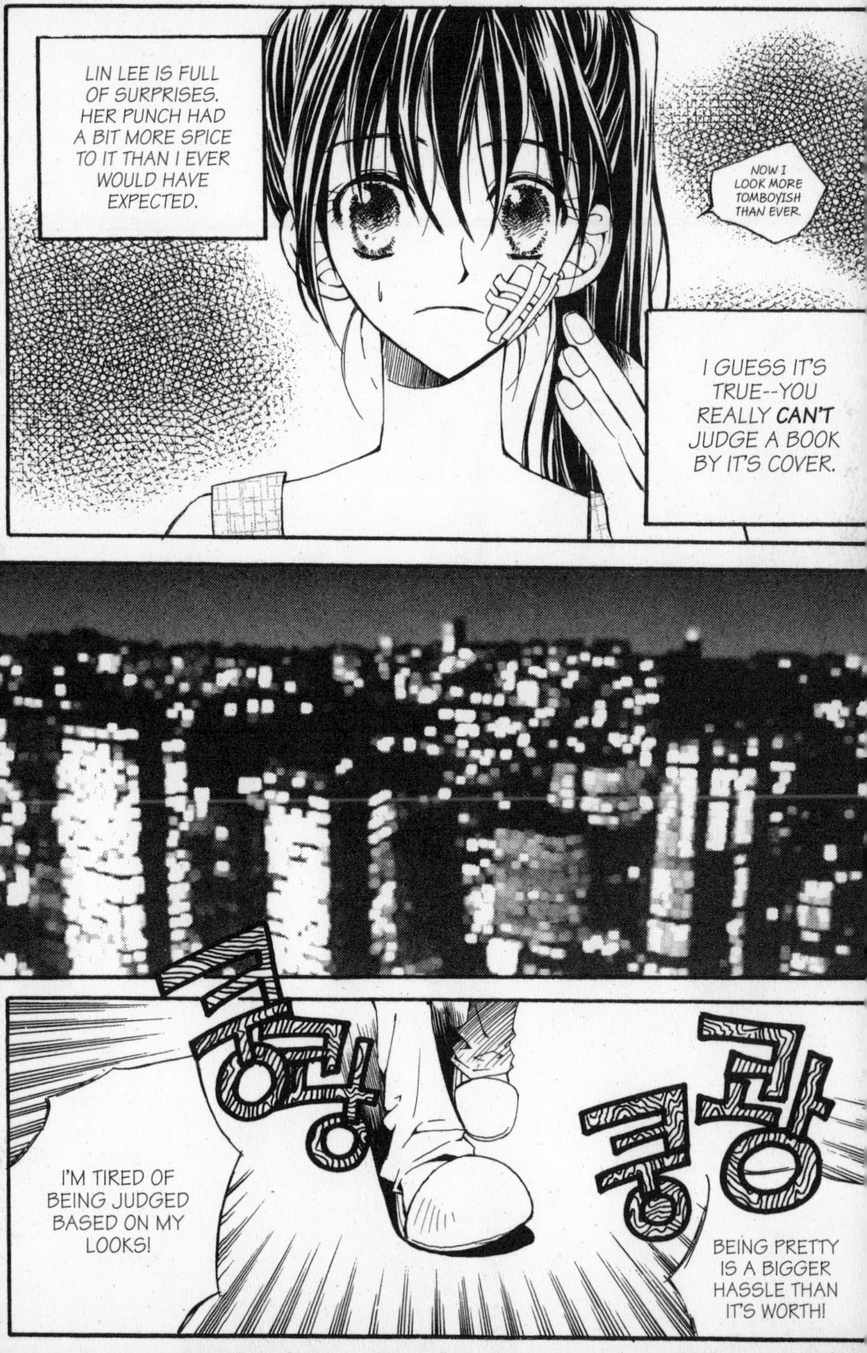
LIN LEE IS FULL OF SURPRISES. HER PUNCH HAD A BIT MORE SPICE TO IT THAN I EVER WOULD HAVE EXPECTED.
NOW I LOOK MORE TOMBOYISH THAN EVER.
I GUESS IT'S TRUE--YOU REALLY **CAN'T** JUDGE A BOOK BY IT'S COVER.
I'M TIRED OF BEING JUDGED BASED ON MY LOOKS!
BEING PRETTY IS A BIGGER HASSLE THAN IT'S WORTH!

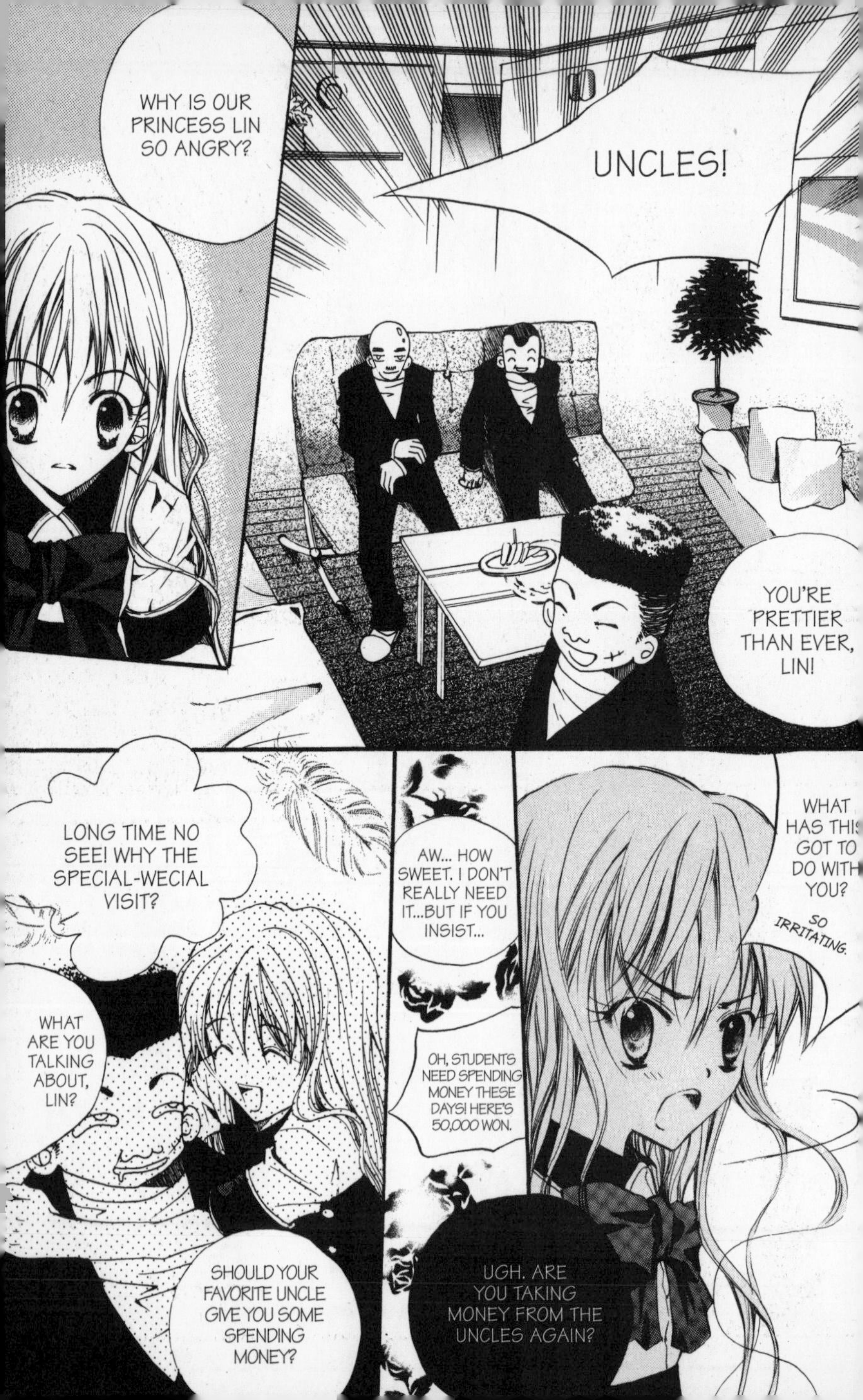
WHY IS OUR PRINCESS LIN SO ANGRY?
UNCLES!
YOU'RE PRETTIER THAN EVER, LIN!
LONG TIME NO SEE! WHY THE SPECIAL-WECIAL VISIT?
WHAT ARE YOU TALKING ABOUT, LIN?
SHOULD YOUR FAVORITE UNCLE GIVE YOU SOME SPENDING MONEY?
AW... HOW SWEET. I DON'T REALLY NEED IT...BUT IF YOU INSIST...
OH, STUDENTS NEED SPENDING MONEY THESE DAYS! HERE'S 50,000 WON.
WHAT HAS THIS GOT TO DO WITH YOU?
SO IRRITATING.
UGH. ARE YOU TAKING MONEY FROM THE UNCLES AGAIN?

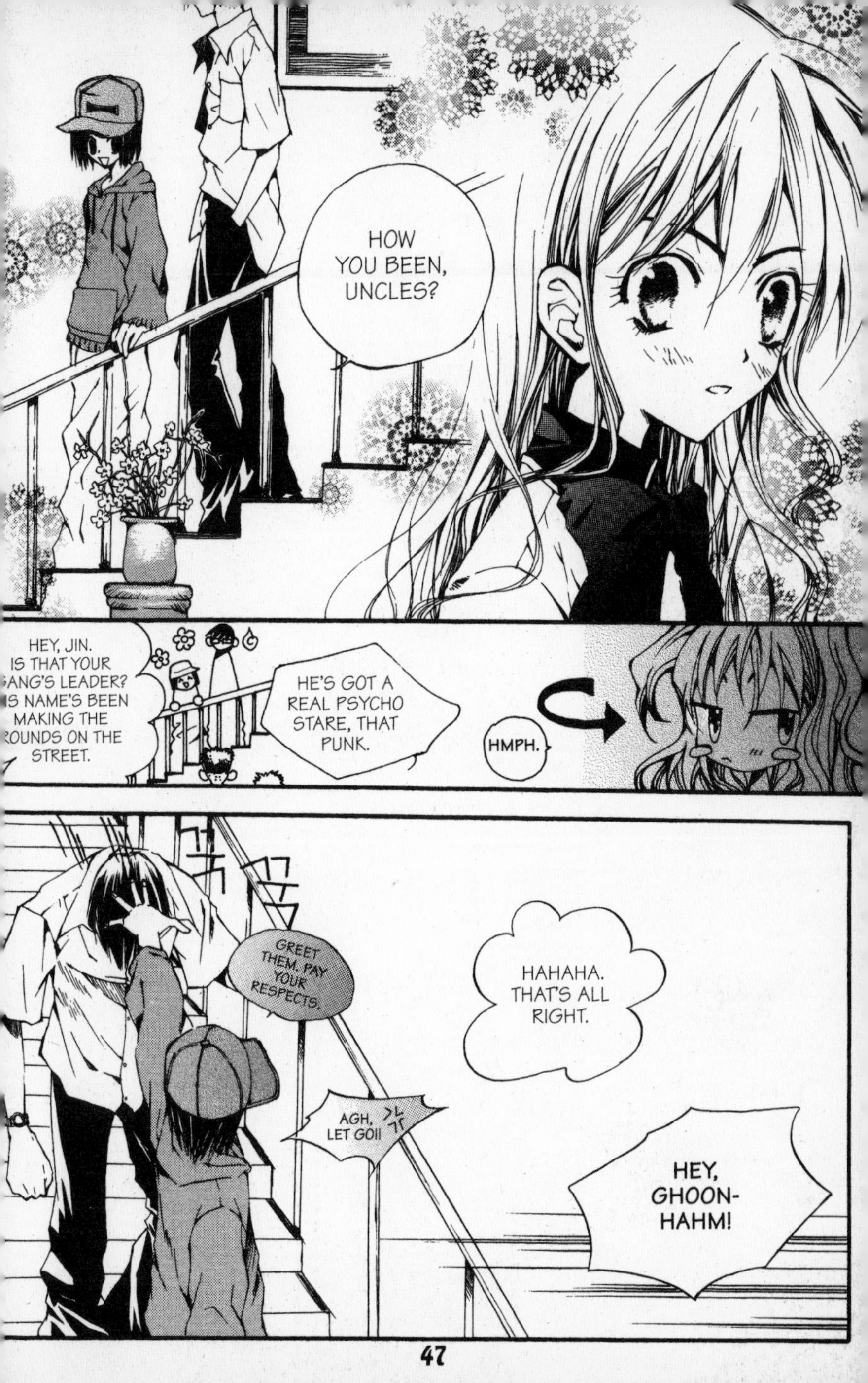
HOW YOU BEEN, UNCLES?
HEY, JIN. IS THAT YOUR ANG'S LEADER? S NAME'S BEEN MAKING THE ROUNDS ON THE STREET.
HE'S GOT A REAL PSYCHO STARE, THAT PUNK.
HMPH.
GREET THEM. PAY YOUR RESPECTS.
AGH, LET GO!!
HAHAHA. THAT'S ALL RIGHT.
HEY, GHOON-HAHM!

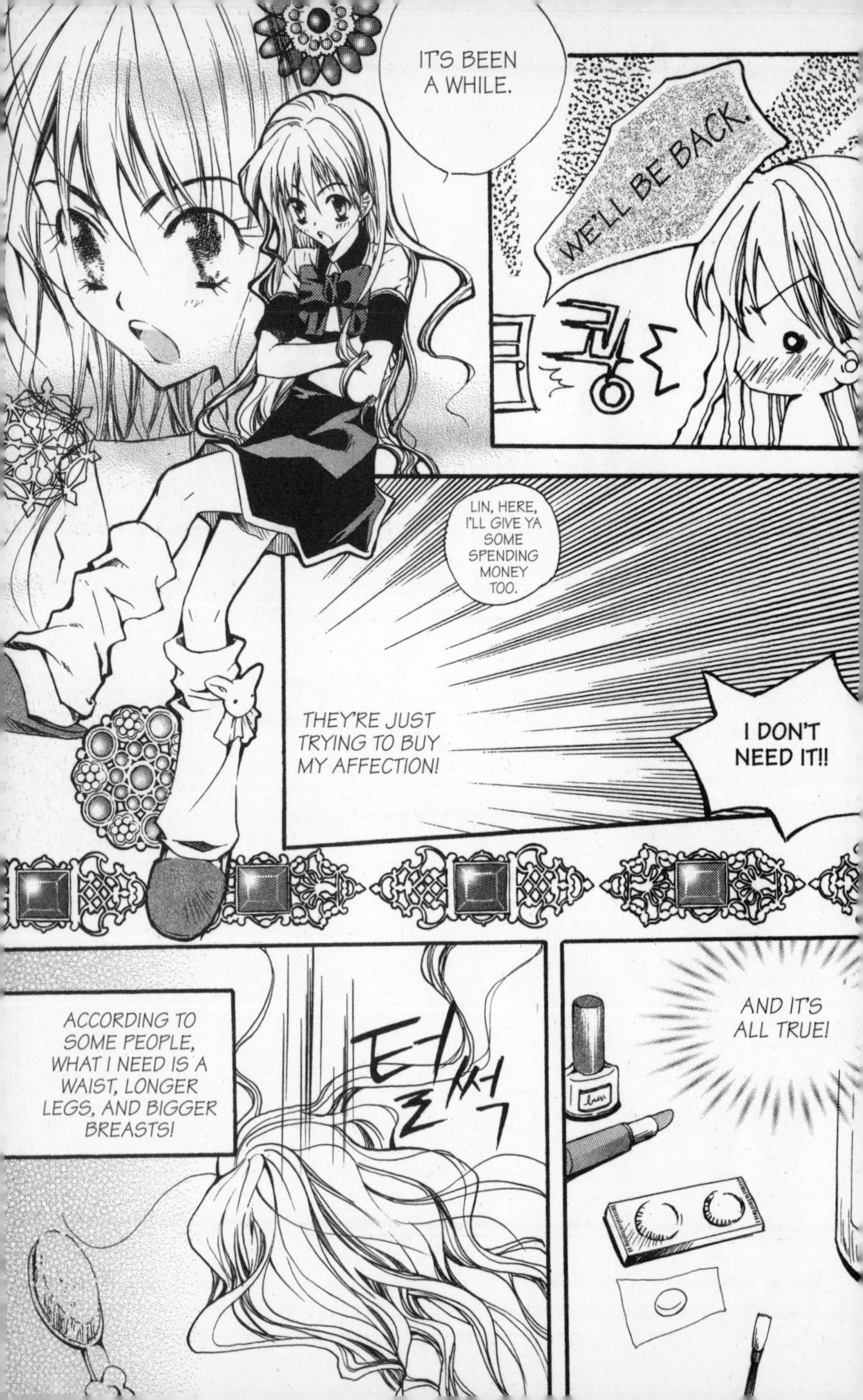
IT'S BEEN A WHILE.
WE'LL BE BACK.
쾅
LIN, HERE, I'LL GIVE YA SOME SPENDING MONEY TOO.
THEY'RE JUST TRYING TO BUY MY AFFECTION!
I DON'T NEED IT!!
ACCORDING TO SOME PEOPLE, WHAT I NEED IS A WAIST, LONGER LEGS, AND BIGGER BREASTS!
털썩
AND IT'S ALL TRUE!

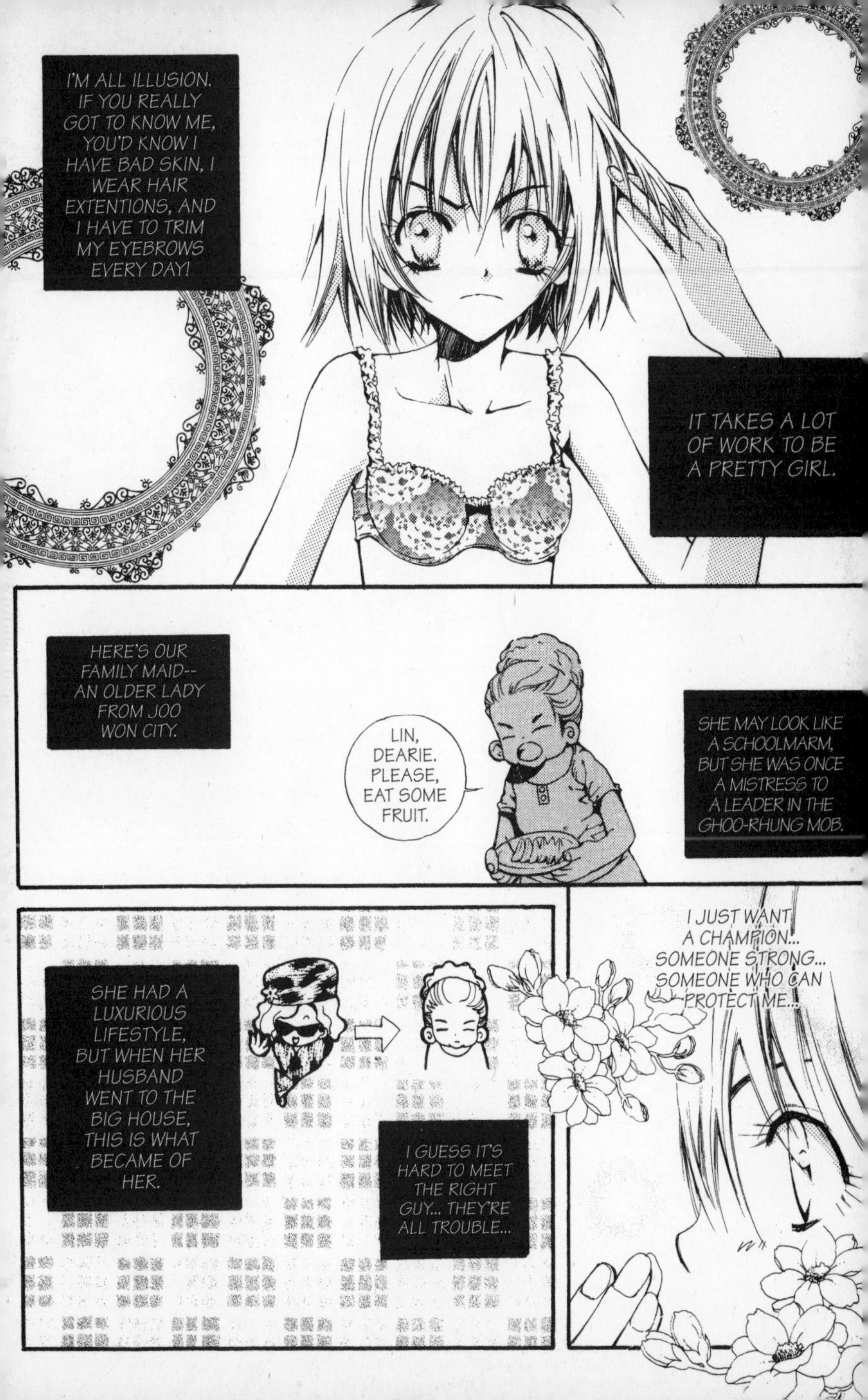

I'M ALL ILLUSION. IF YOU REALLY GOT TO KNOW ME, YOU'D KNOW I HAVE BAD SKIN, I WEAR HAIR EXTENTIONS, AND I HAVE TO TRIM MY EYEBROWS EVERY DAY!
IT TAKES A LOT OF WORK TO BE A PRETTY GIRL.
HERE'S OUR FAMILY MAID-- AN OLDER LADY FROM JOO WON CITY.
LIN, DEARIE. PLEASE, EAT SOME FRUIT.
SHE MAY LOOK LIKE A SCHOOLMARM, BUT SHE WAS ONCE A MISTRESS TO A LEADER IN THE GHOO-RHUNG MOB.
SHE HAD A LUXURIOUS LIFESTYLE, BUT WHEN HER HUSBAND WENT TO THE BIG HOUSE, THIS IS WHAT BECAME OF HER.
I GUESS IT'S HARD TO MEET THE RIGHT GUY... THEY'RE ALL TROUBLE...
I JUST WANT A CHAMPION... SOMEONE STRONG... SOMEONE WHO CAN PROTECT ME...

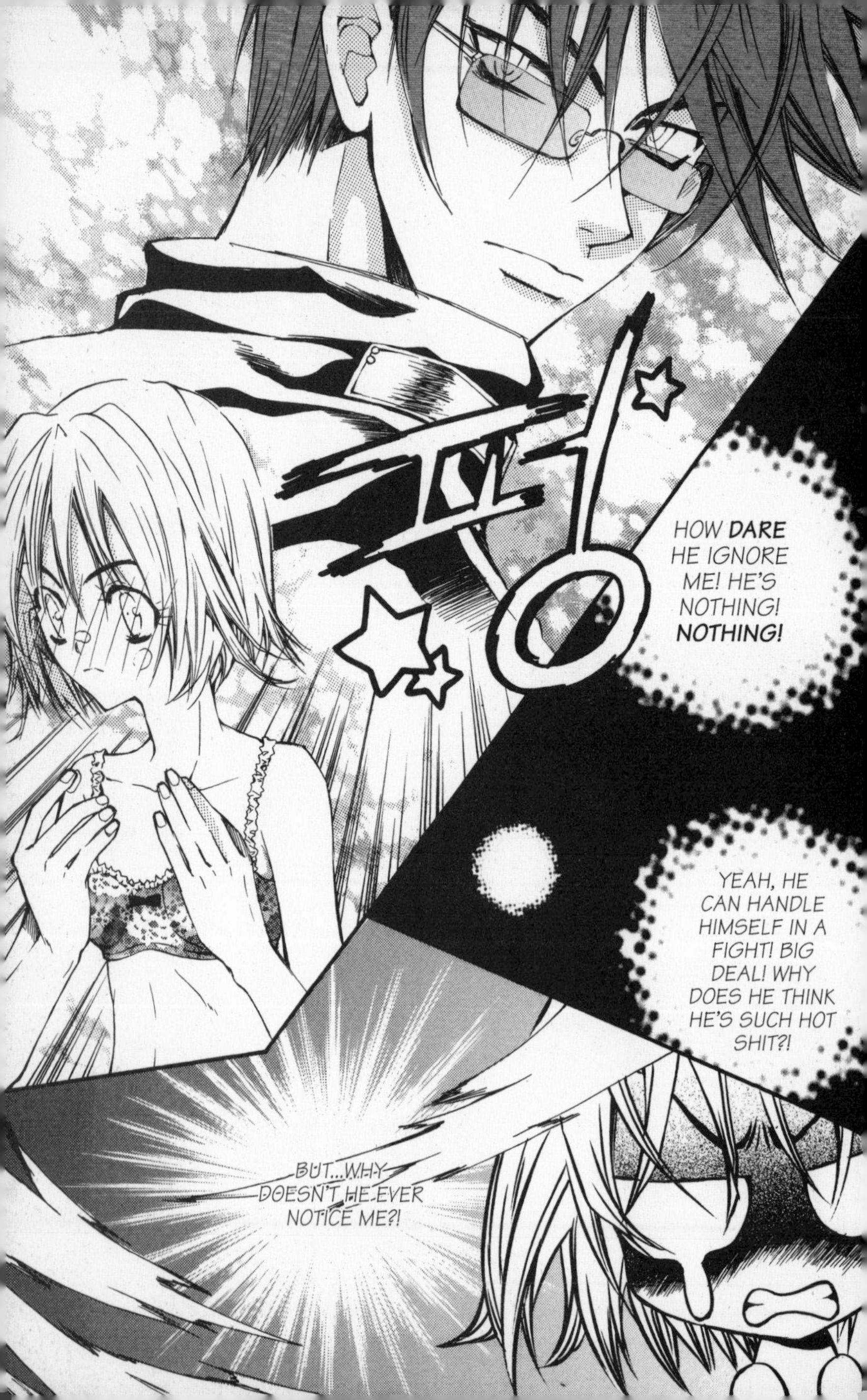
HOW DARE HE IGNORE ME! HE'S NOTHING! NOTHING!
YEAH, HE CAN HANDLE HIMSELF IN A FIGHT! BIG DEAL! WHY DOES HE THINK HE'S SUCH HOT SHIT?!
BUT...WHY DOESN'T HE EVER NOTICE ME?!

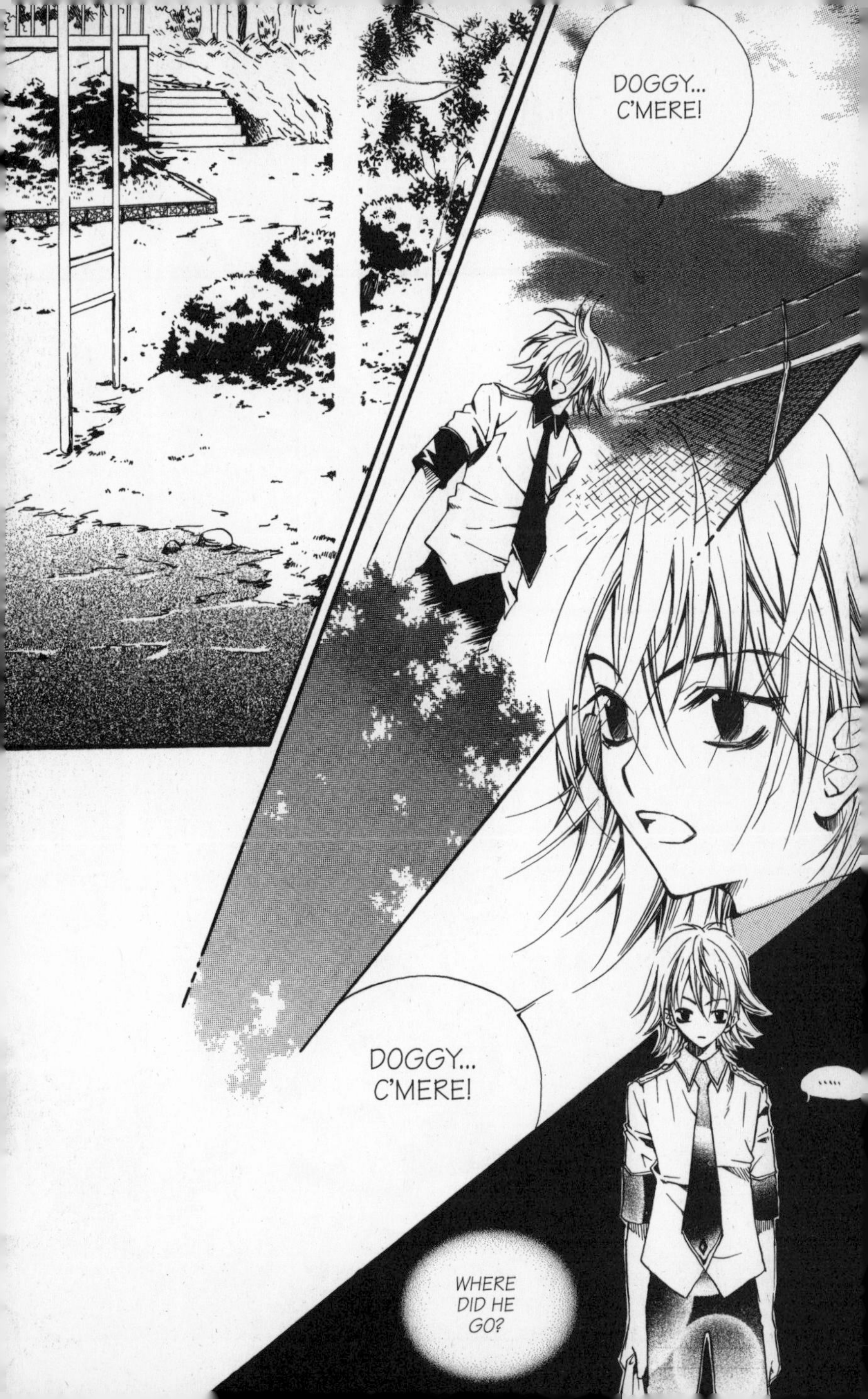
DOGGY...
C'MERE!
DOGGY...
C'MERE!
......
WHERE DID HE GO?

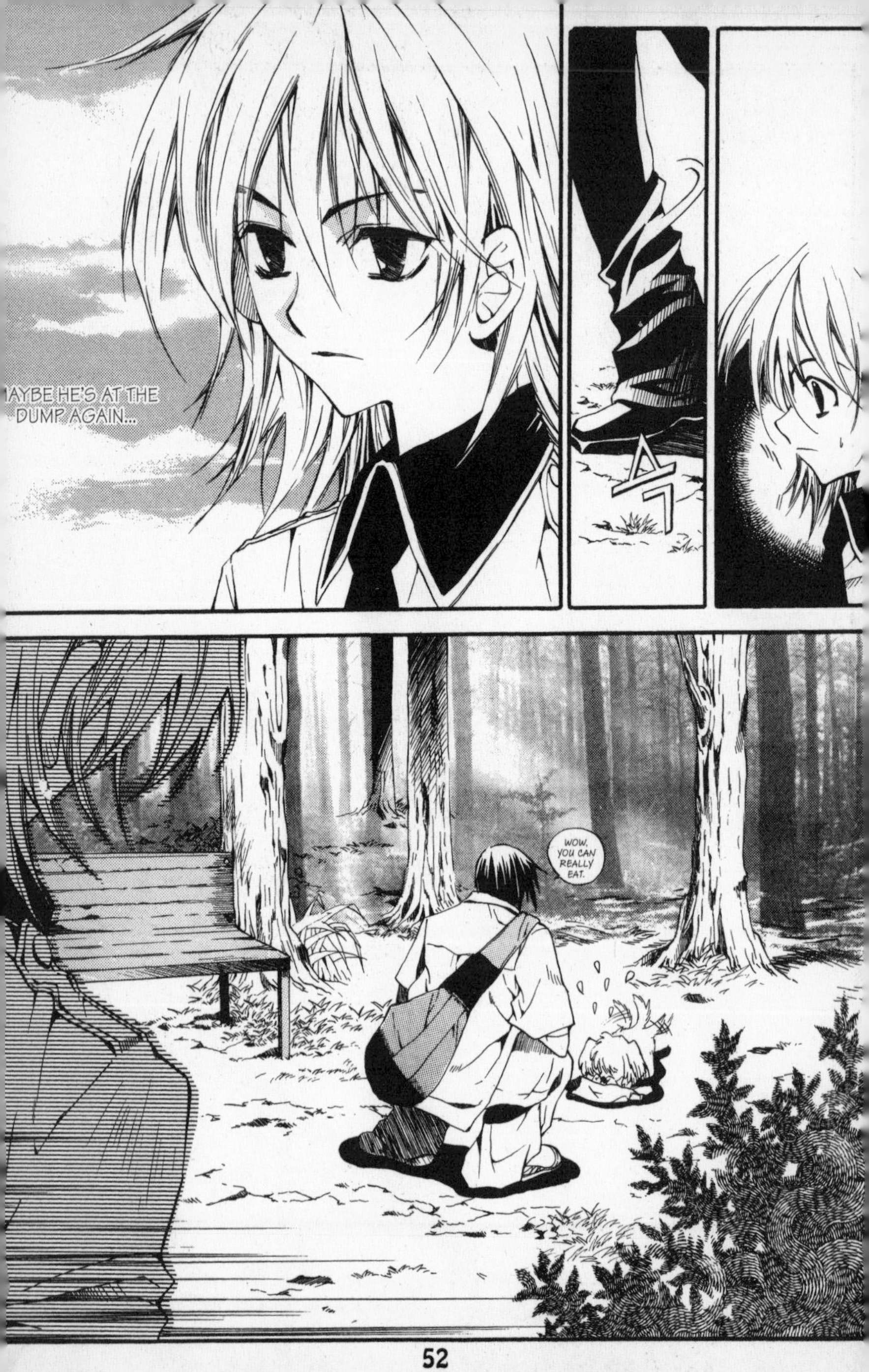
AYBE HE'S AT THE DUMP AGAIN...
WOW, YOU CAN REALLY EAT.

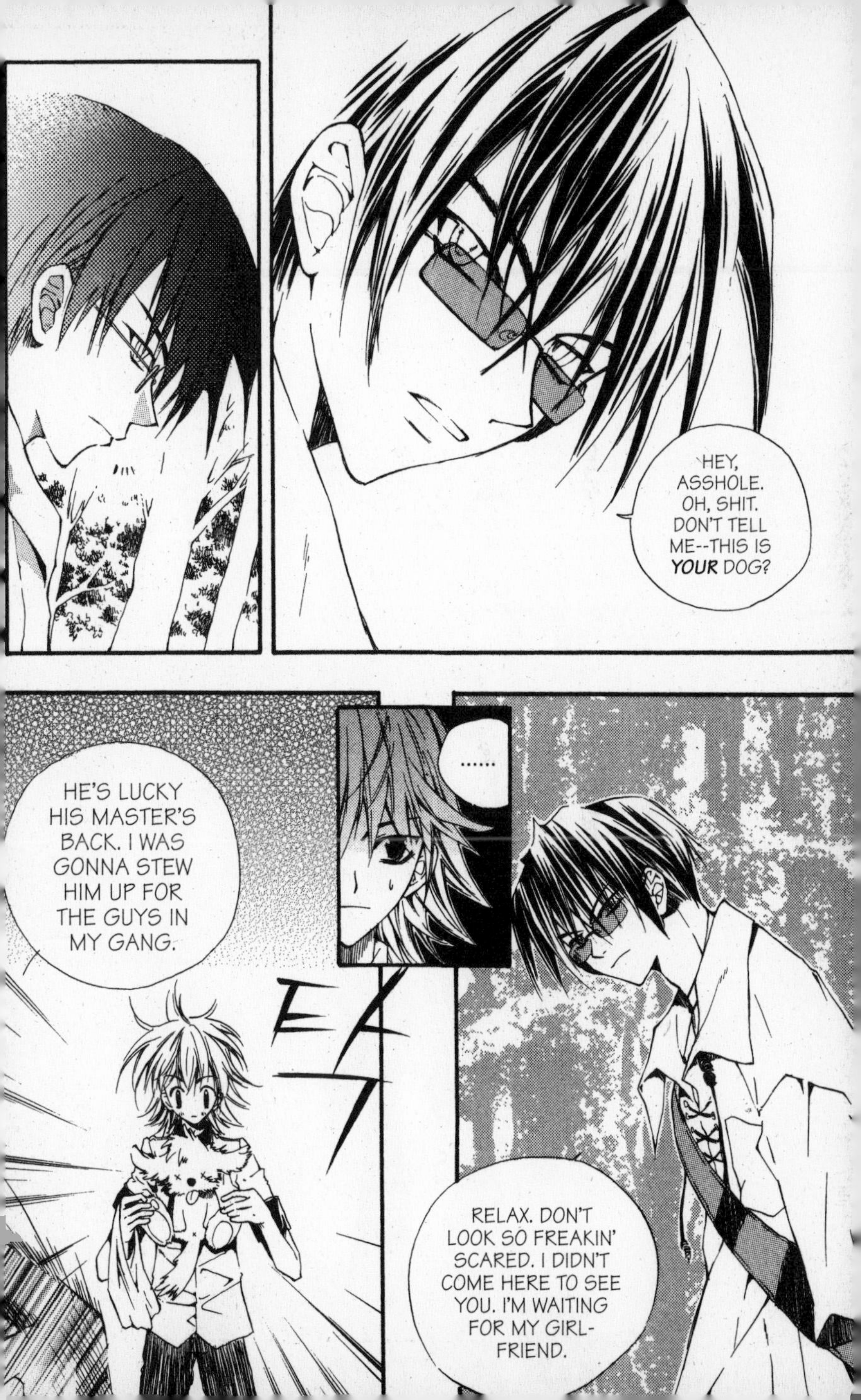
HEY, ASSHOLE. OH, SHIT. DON'T TELL ME--THIS IS ***YOUR*** DOG?
HE'S LUCKY HIS MASTER'S BACK. I WAS GONNA STEW HIM UP FOR THE GUYS IN MY GANG.
......
RELAX. DON'T LOOK SO FREAKIN' SCARED. I DIDN'T COME HERE TO SEE YOU. I'M WAITING FOR MY GIRL-FRIEND.

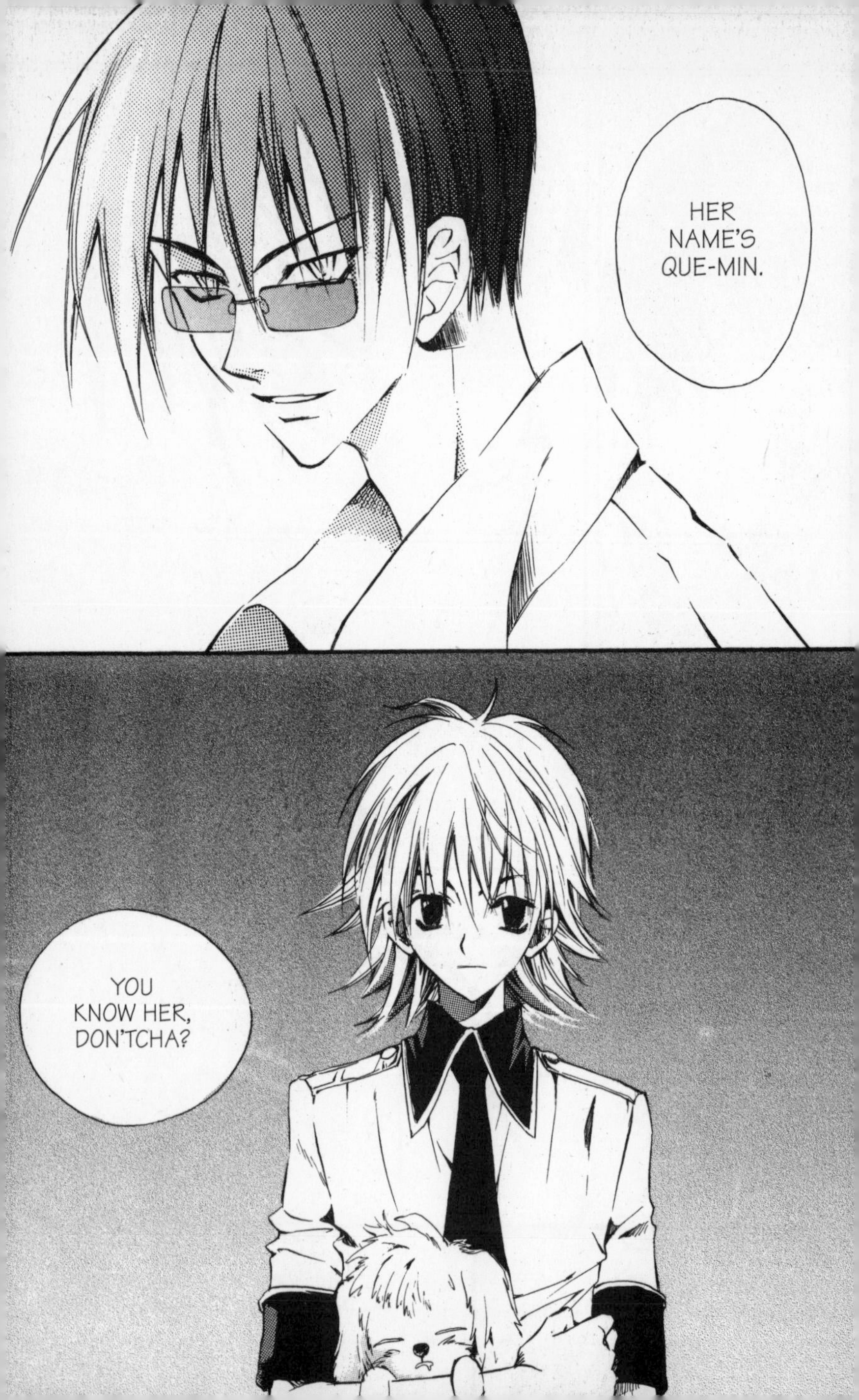
HER NAME'S QUE-MIN.
YOU KNOW HER, DON'TCHA?

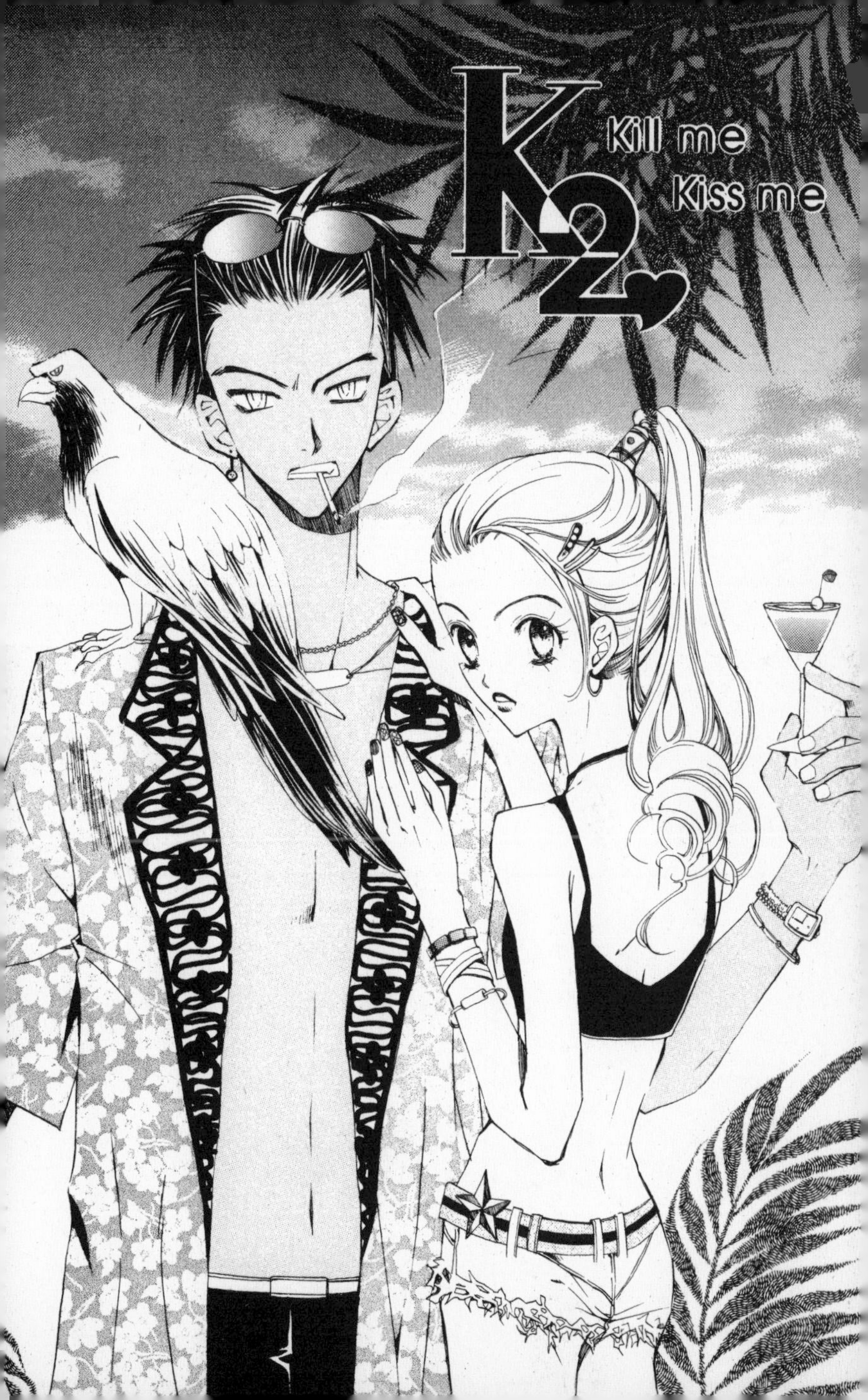
K2
Kill me
Kiss me

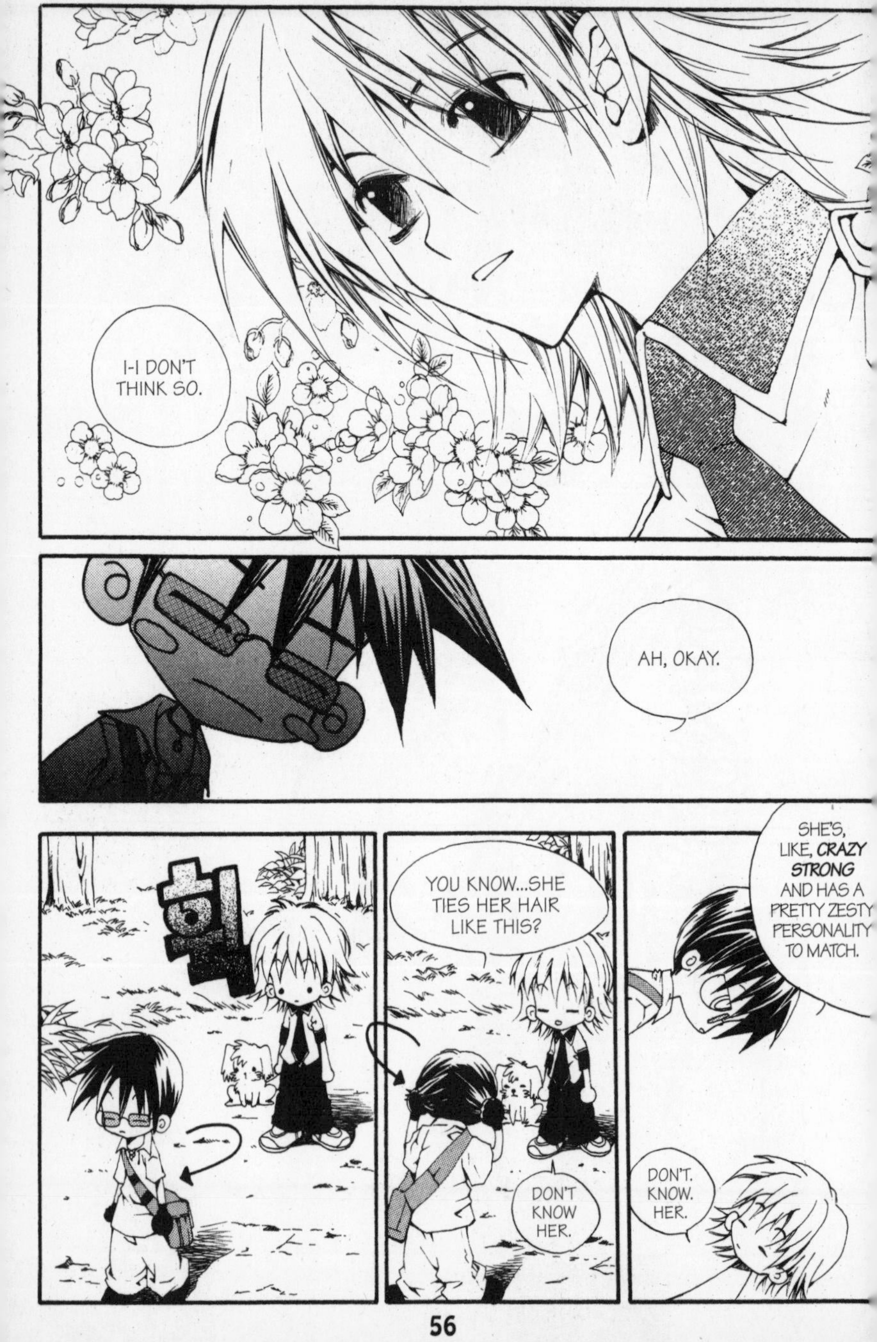
I-I DON'T THINK SO.
AH, OKAY.
YOU KNOW...SHE TIES HER HAIR LIKE THIS?
DON'T KNOW HER.
SHE'S, LIKE, **CRAZY STRONG** AND HAS A PRETTY ZESTY PERSONALITY TO MATCH.
DON'T. KNOW. HER.

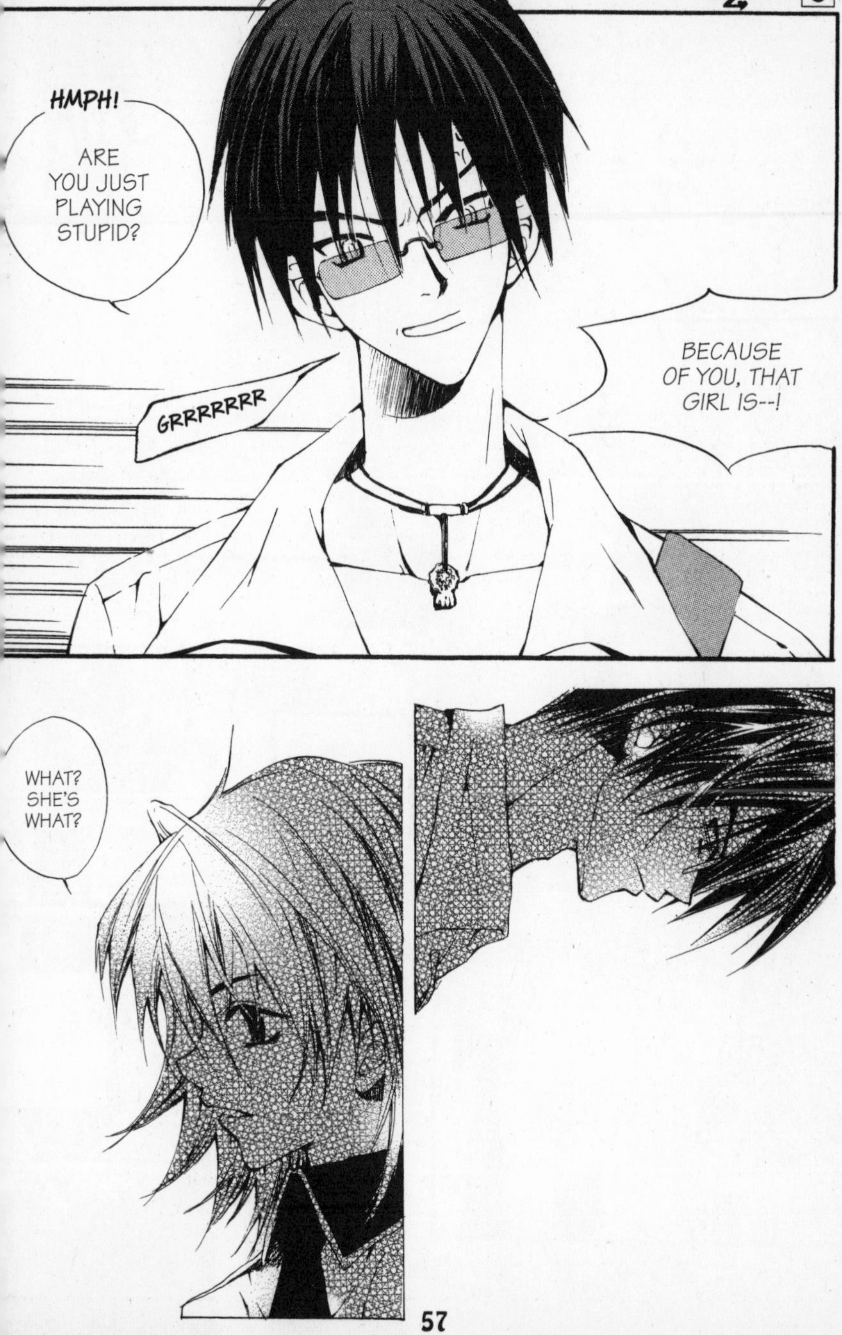
HMPH!
ARE YOU JUST PLAYING STUPID?
GRRRRRRR
BECAUSE OF YOU, THAT GIRL IS--!
WHAT? SHE'S WHAT?

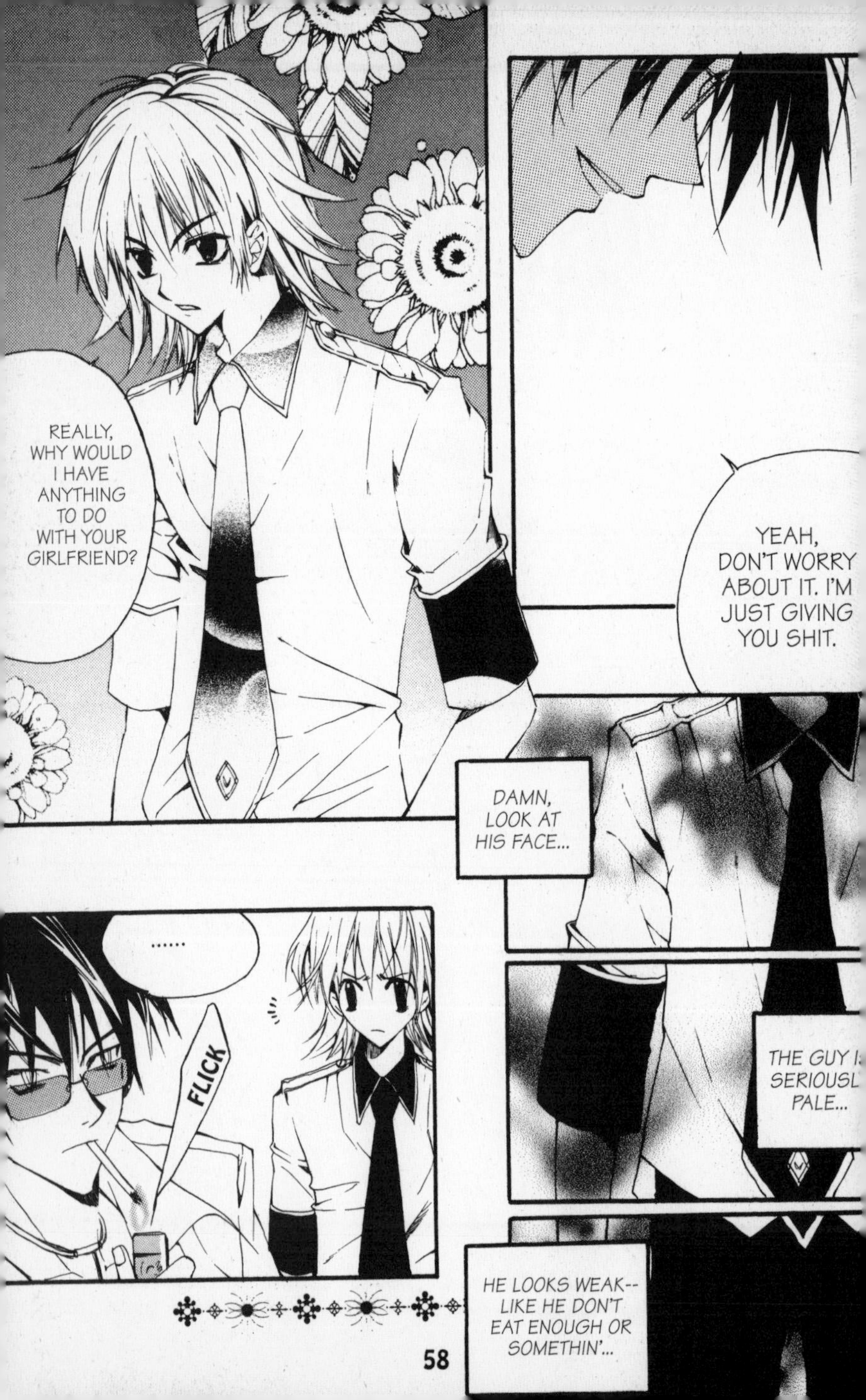
REALLY, WHY WOULD I HAVE ANYTHING TO DO WITH YOUR GIRLFRIEND?
YEAH, DON'T WORRY ABOUT IT. I'M JUST GIVING YOU SHIT.
DAMN, LOOK AT HIS FACE...
......
FLICK
THE GUY I SERIOUSL PALE...
HE LOOKS WEAK--LIKE HE DON'T EAT ENOUGH OR SOMETHIN'...

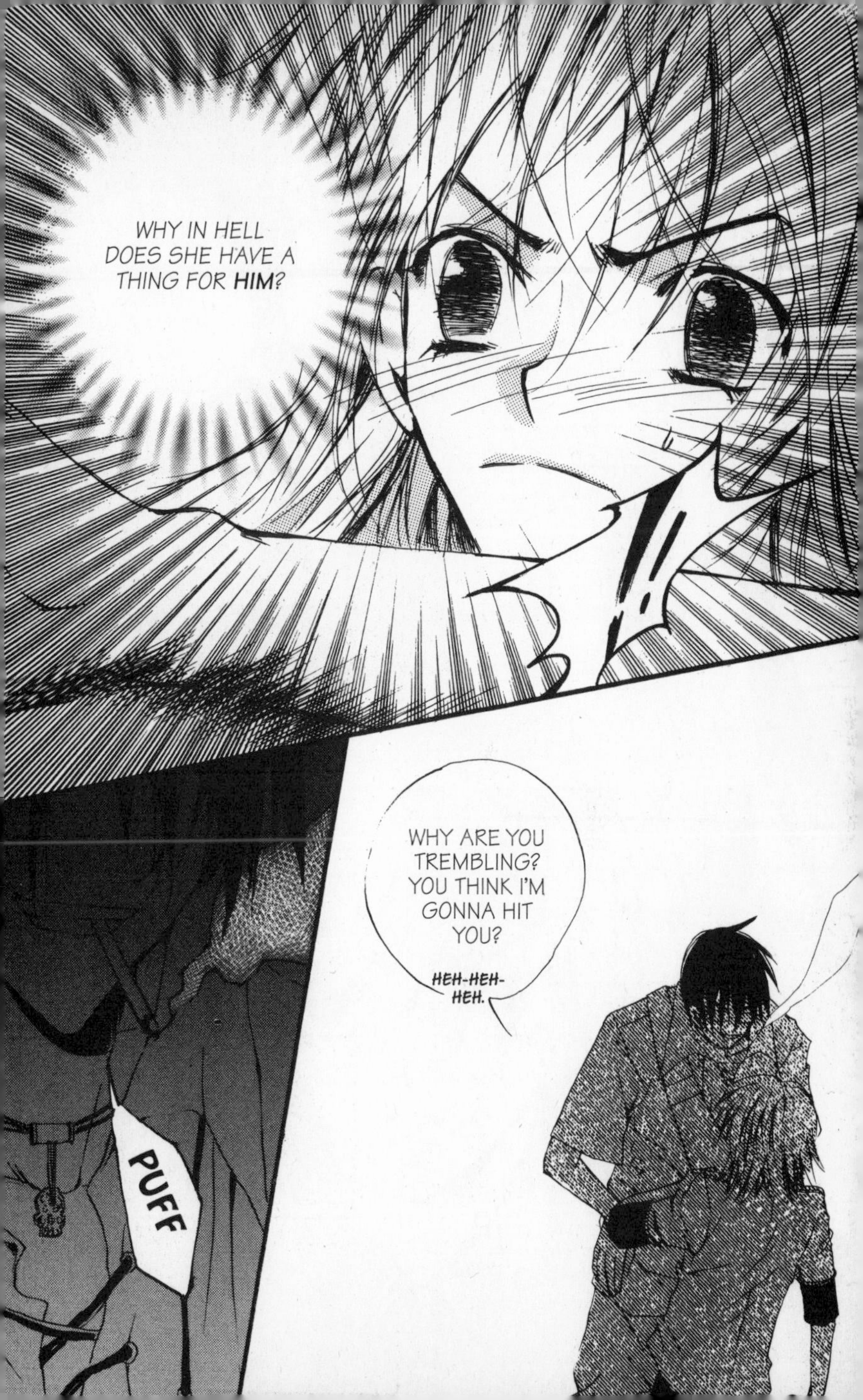
WHY IN HELL DOES SHE HAVE A THING FOR **HIM**?
PUFF
WHY ARE YOU TREMBLING? YOU THINK I'M GONNA HIT YOU?
HEH-HEH-HEH.

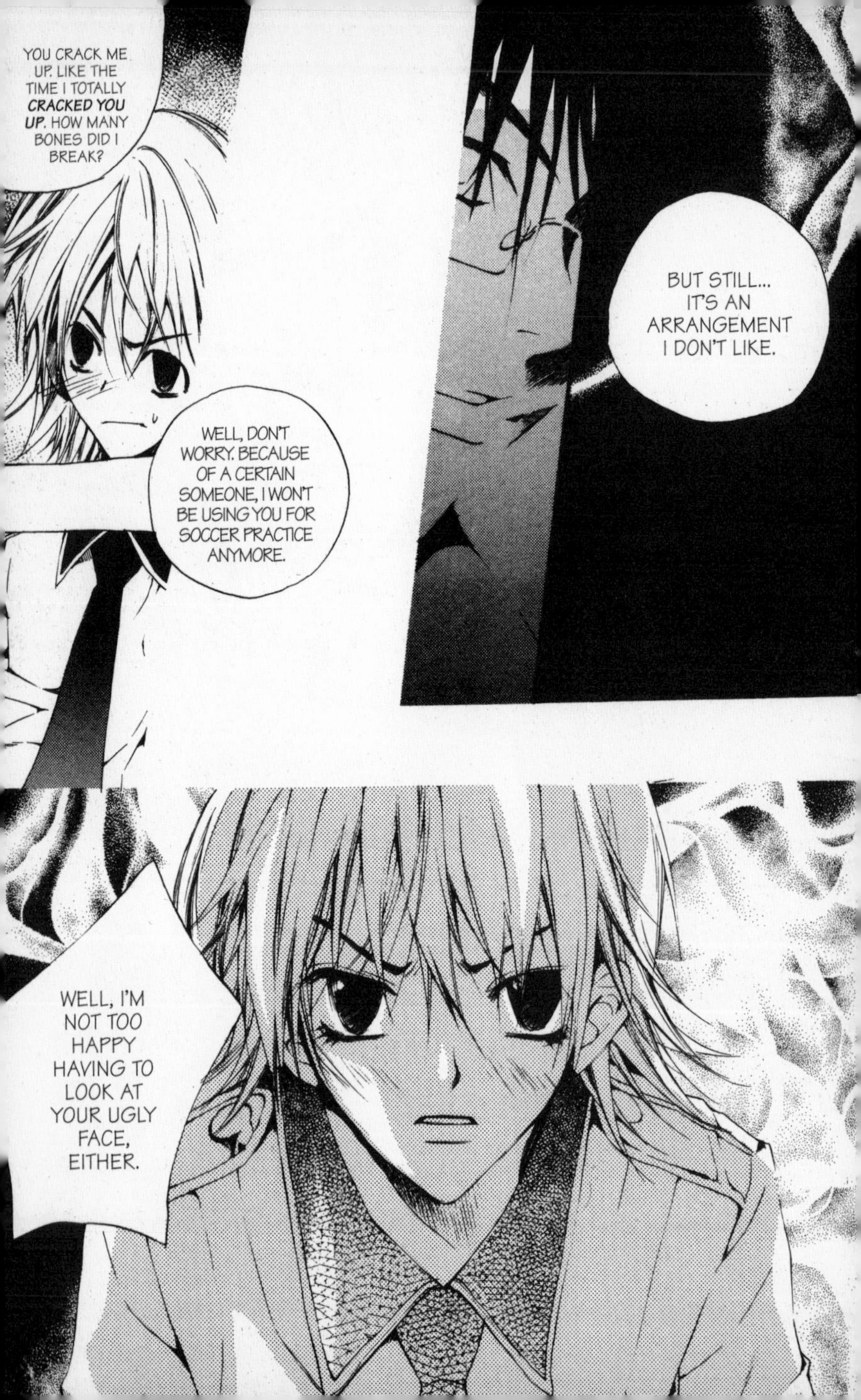
YOU CRACK ME UP. LIKE THE TIME I TOTALLY **CRACKED YOU UP**. HOW MANY BONES DID I BREAK?
WELL, DON'T WORRY. BECAUSE OF A CERTAIN SOMEONE, I WON'T BE USING YOU FOR SOCCER PRACTICE ANYMORE.
BUT STILL... IT'S AN ARRANGEMENT I DON'T LIKE.
WELL, I'M NOT TOO HAPPY HAVING TO LOOK AT YOUR UGLY FACE, EITHER.

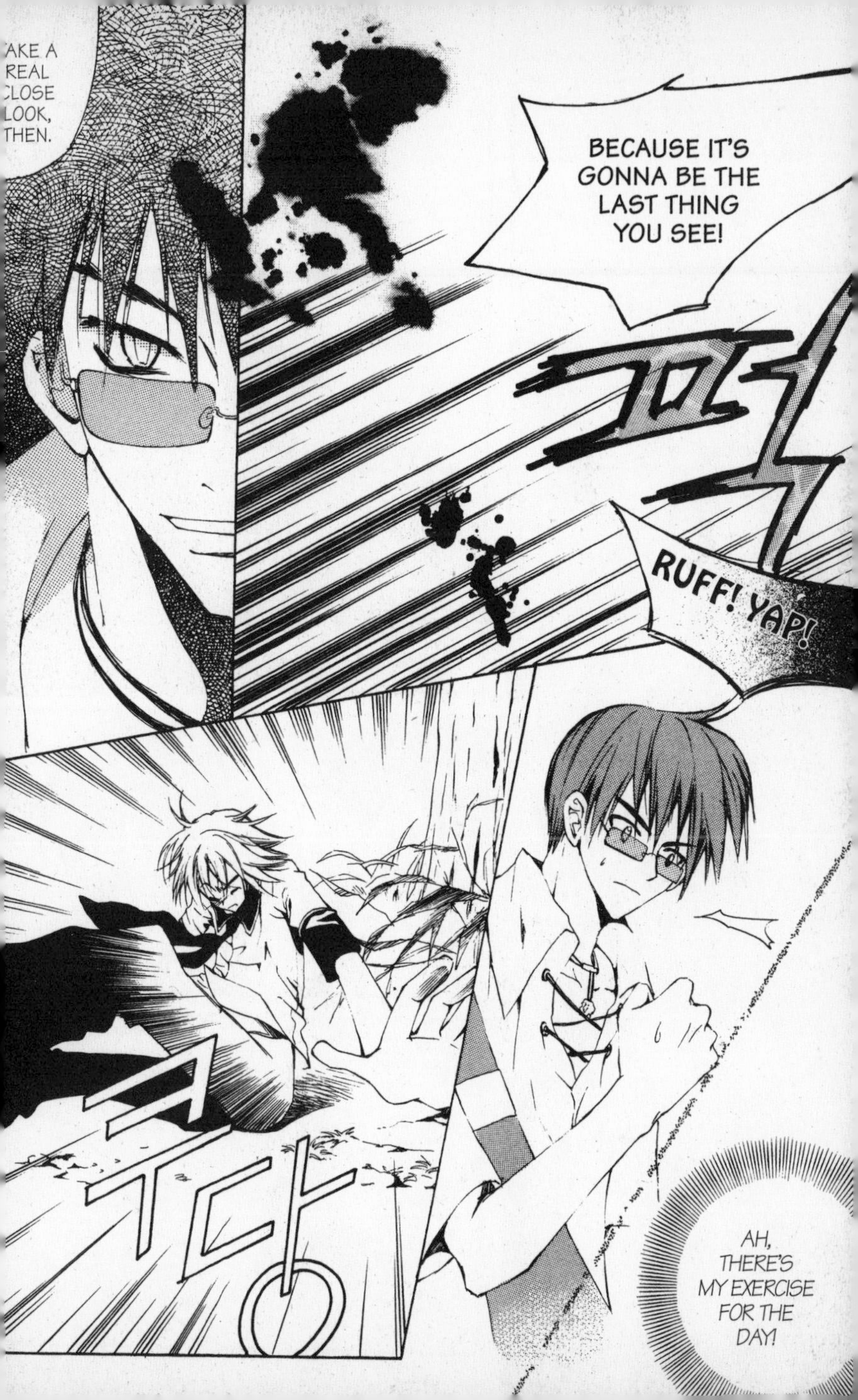

AKE A REAL CLOSE LOOK, THEN.
BECAUSE IT'S GONNA BE THE LAST THING YOU SEE!
RUFF! YAP!
AH, THERE'S MY EXERCISE FOR THE DAY!

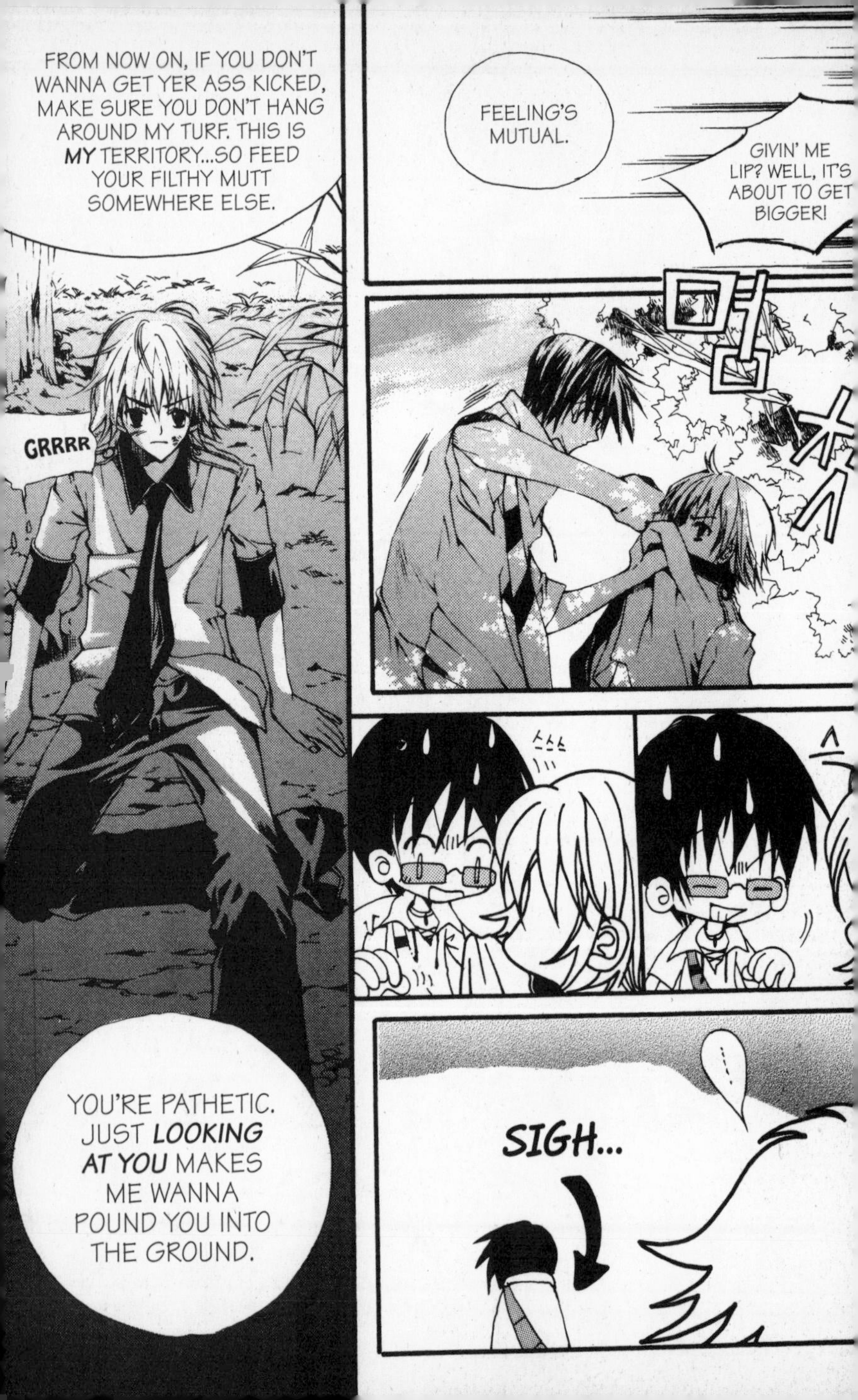
FROM NOW ON, IF YOU DON'T WANNA GET YER ASS KICKED, MAKE SURE YOU DON'T HANG AROUND MY TURF. THIS IS **MY** TERRITORY...SO FEED YOUR FILTHY MUTT SOMEWHERE ELSE.
GRRRR
YOU'RE PATHETIC. JUST **LOOKING AT YOU** MAKES ME WANNA POUND YOU INTO THE GROUND.
FEELING'S MUTUAL.
GIVIN' ME LIP? WELL, IT'S ABOUT TO GET BIGGER!
멈칫
....
SIGH...

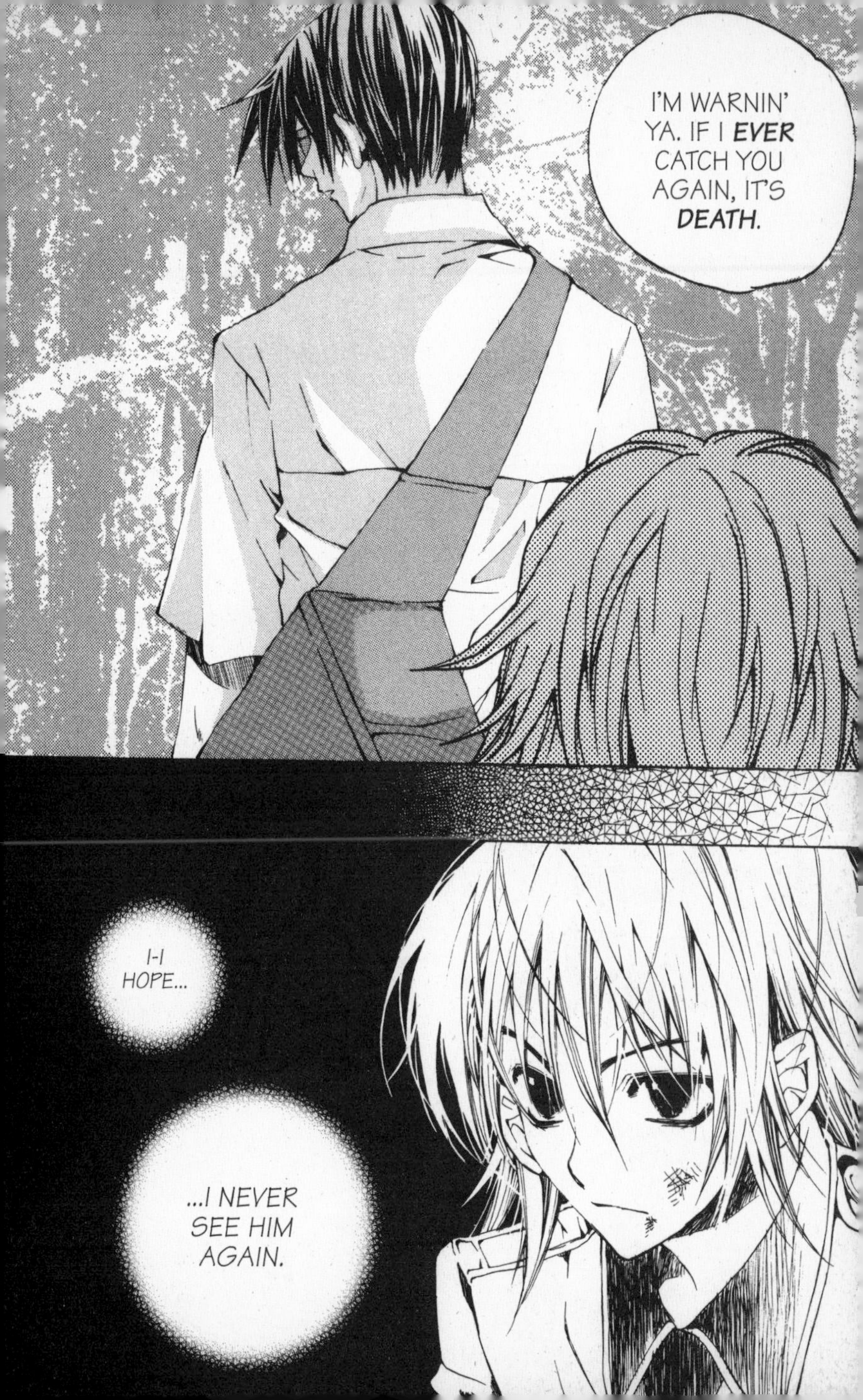
I'M WARNIN' YA. IF I **EVER** CATCH YOU AGAIN, IT'S **DEATH**.
I-I HOPE...
...I NEVER SEE HIM AGAIN.

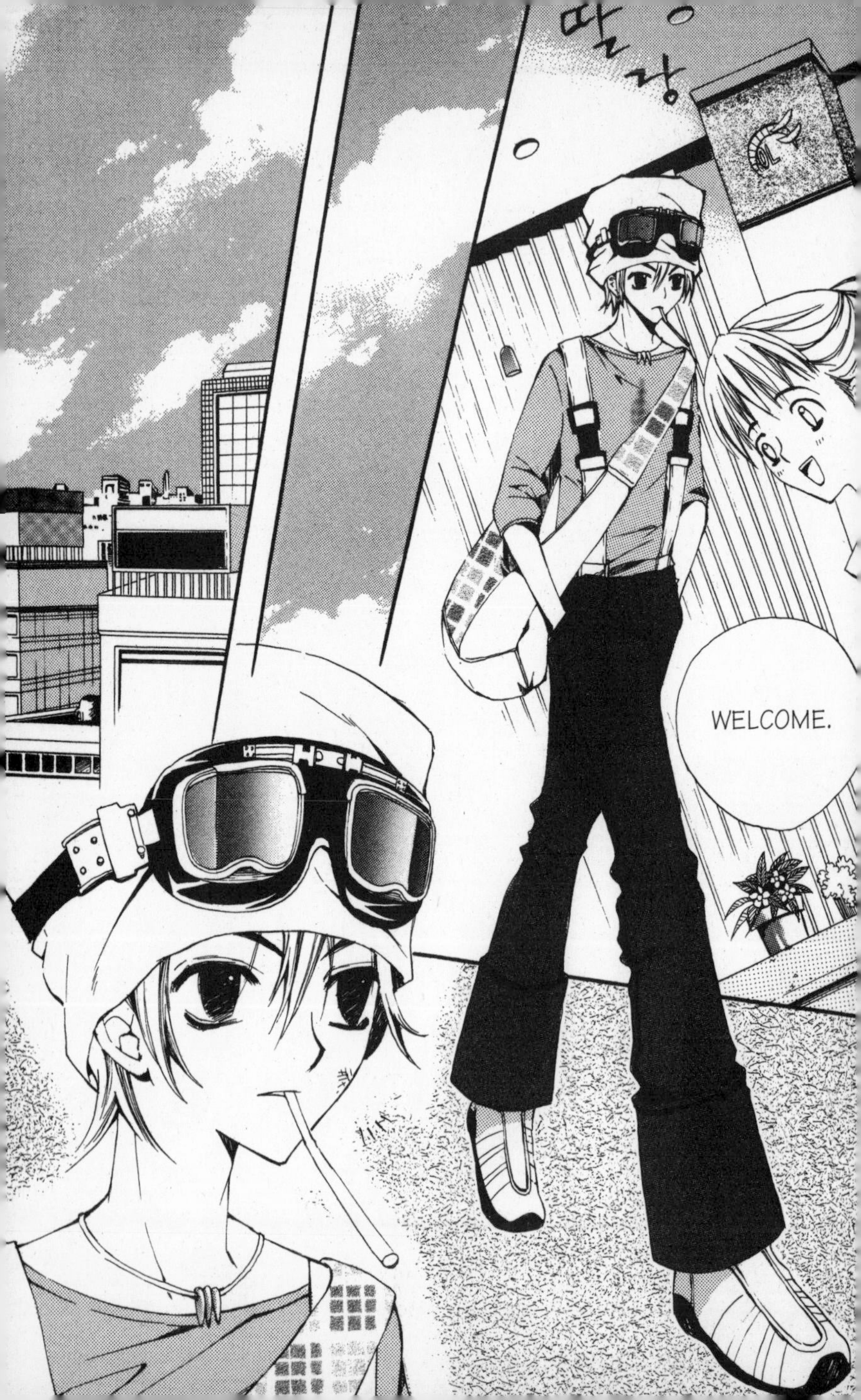
딸랑
WELCOME.

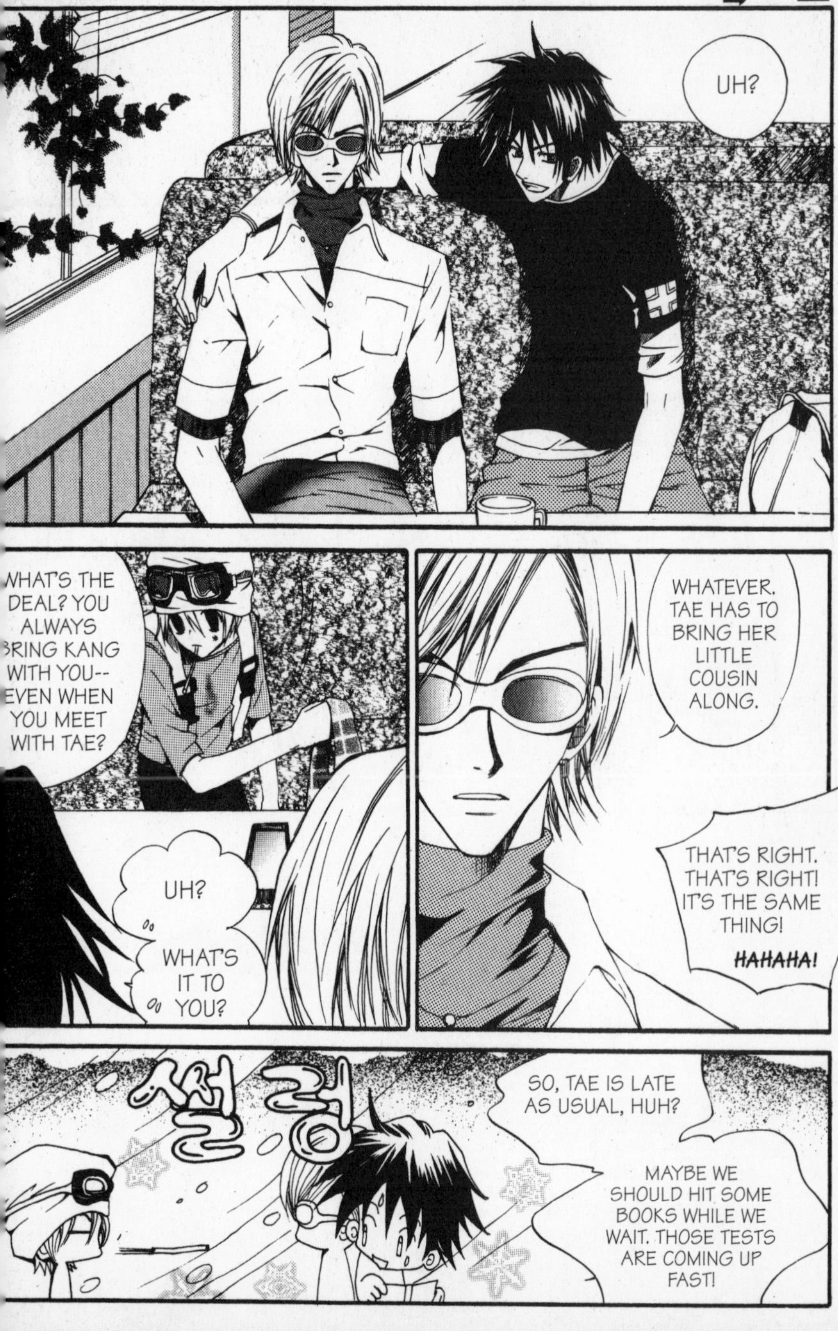
UH?
WHAT'S THE DEAL? YOU ALWAYS BRING KANG WITH YOU--EVEN WHEN YOU MEET WITH TAE?
UH? WHAT'S IT TO YOU?
WHATEVER. TAE HAS TO BRING HER LITTLE COUSIN ALONG.
THAT'S RIGHT. THAT'S RIGHT! IT'S THE SAME THING!
HAHAHA!
썰렁
SO, TAE IS LATE AS USUAL, HUH?
MAYBE WE SHOULD HIT SOME BOOKS WHILE WE WAIT. THOSE TESTS ARE COMING UP FAST!

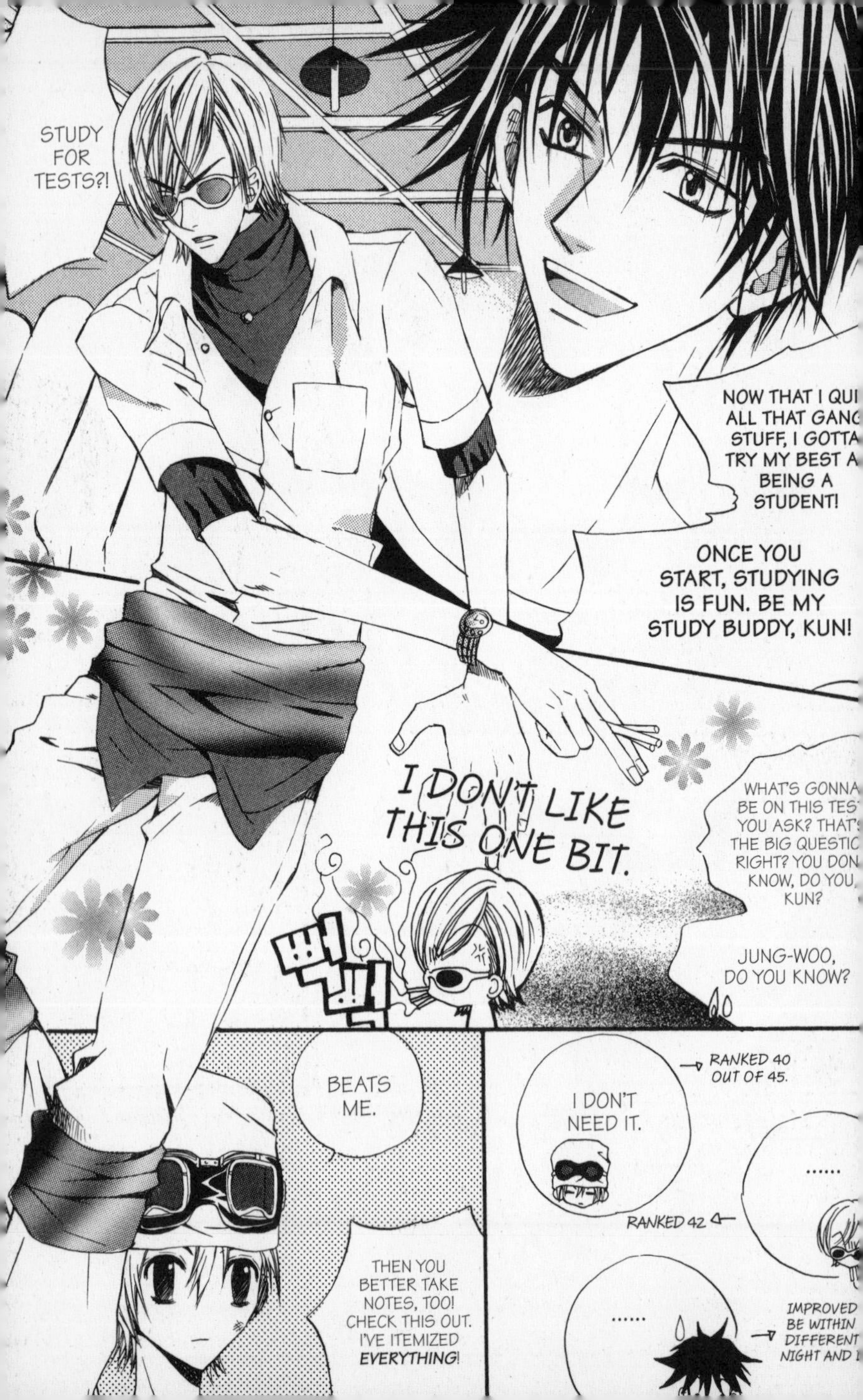

STUDY FOR TESTS?!
NOW THAT I QUI ALL THAT GANG STUFF, I GOTTA TRY MY BEST A BEING A STUDENT!
ONCE YOU START, STUDYING IS FUN. BE MY STUDY BUDDY, KUN!
I DON'T LIKE THIS ONE BIT.
WHAT'S GONNA BE ON THIS TES YOU ASK? THAT' THE BIG QUESTIC RIGHT? YOU DON KNOW, DO YOU, KUN?
JUNG-WOO, DO YOU KNOW?
BEATS ME.
THEN YOU BETTER TAKE NOTES, TOO! CHECK THIS OUT. I'VE ITEMIZED EVERYTHING!
RANKED 40 OUT OF 45.
I DON'T NEED IT.
......
RANKED 42
......
IMPROVED BE WITHIN DIFFERENT NIGHT AND

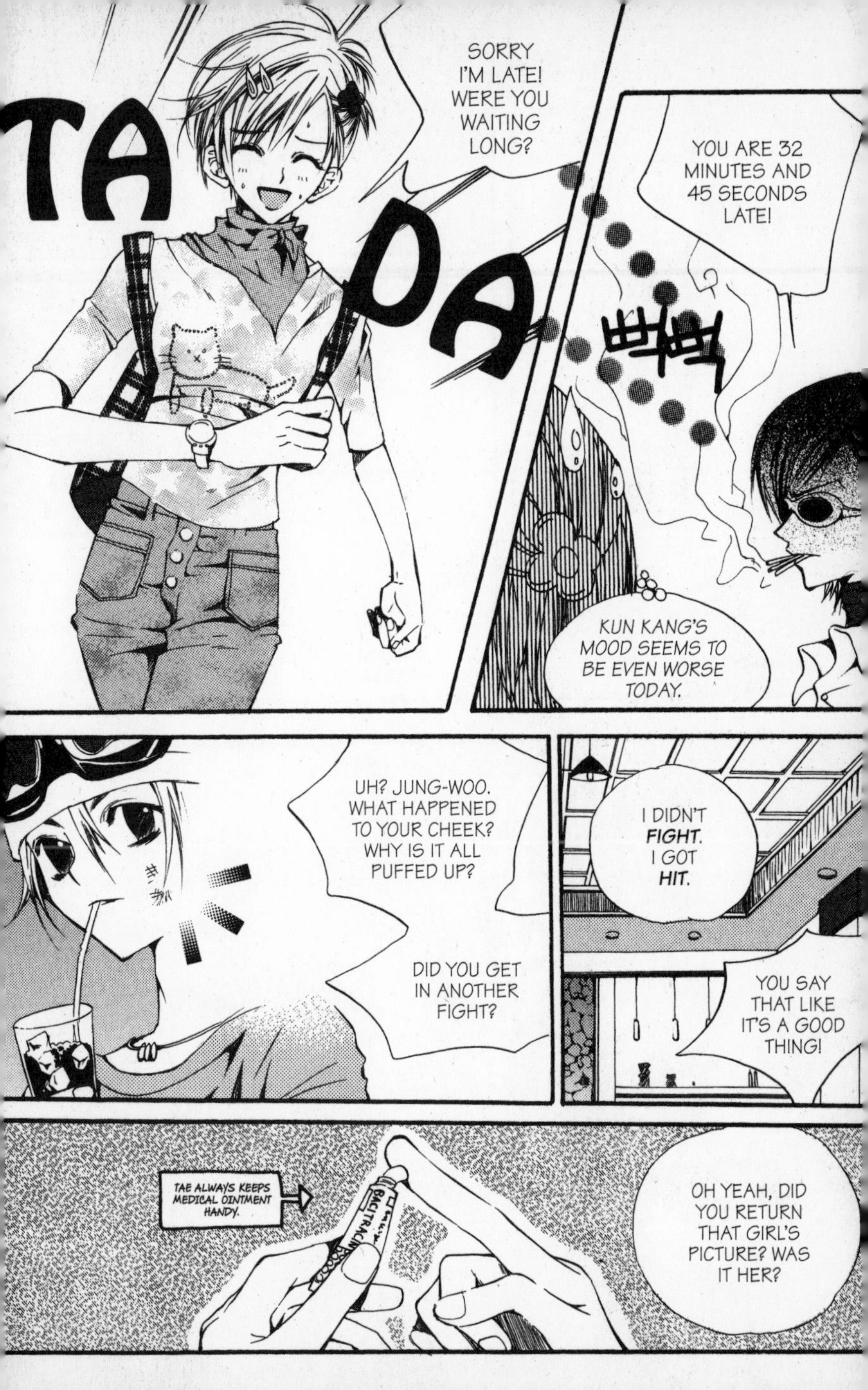
TA
SORRY I'M LATE! WERE YOU WAITING LONG?
DA
YOU ARE 32 MINUTES AND 45 SECONDS LATE!
KUN KANG'S MOOD SEEMS TO BE EVEN WORSE TODAY.
UH? JUNG-WOO. WHAT HAPPENED TO YOUR CHEEK? WHY IS IT ALL PUFFED UP?
DID YOU GET IN ANOTHER FIGHT?
I DIDN'T FIGHT. I GOT HIT.
YOU SAY THAT LIKE IT'S A GOOD THING!
TAE ALWAYS KEEPS MEDICAL OINTMENT HANDY.
BACITRACIN
OH YEAH, DID YOU RETURN THAT GIRL'S PICTURE? WAS IT HER?

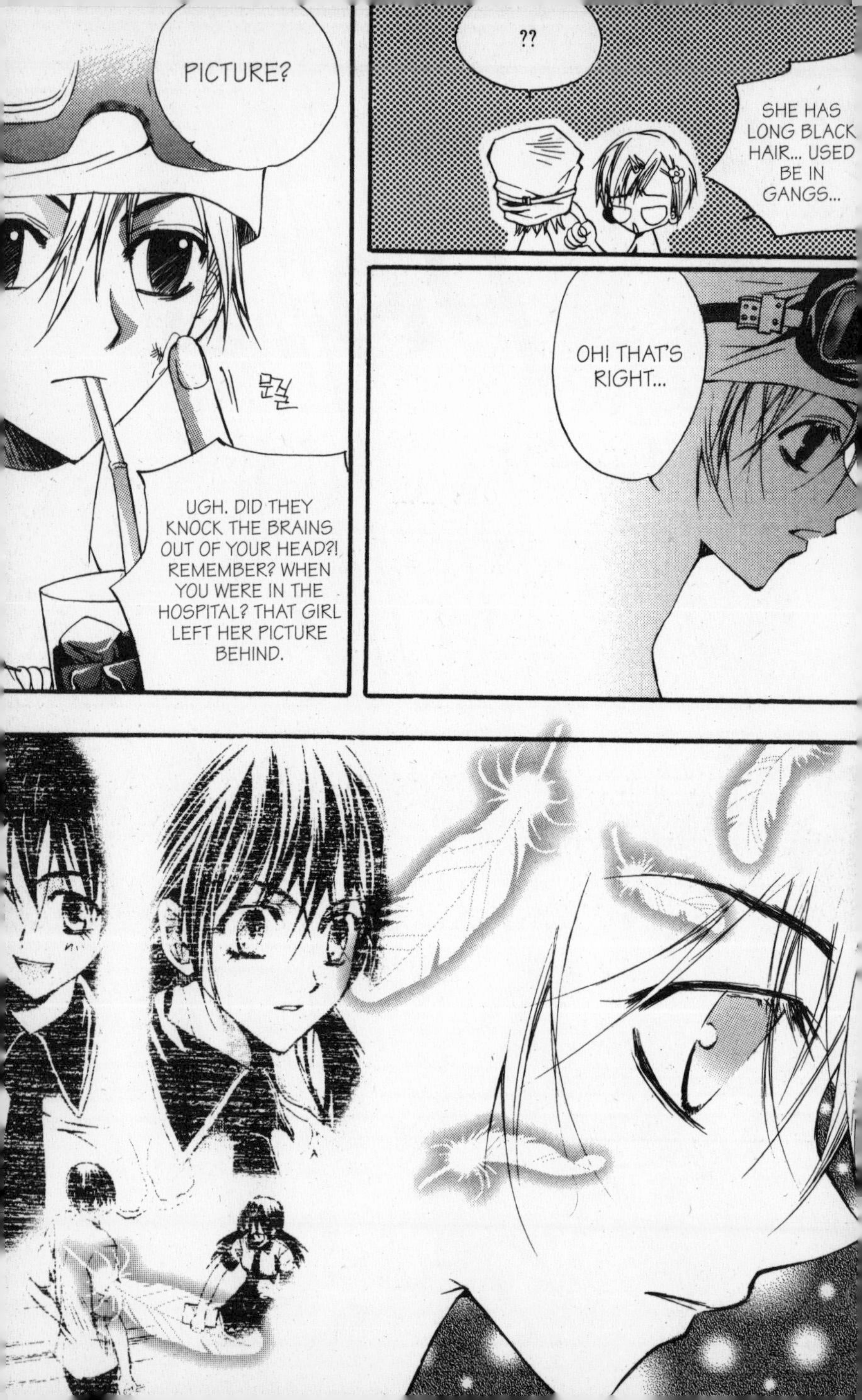
PICTURE?
문질
UGH. DID THEY KNOCK THE BRAINS OUT OF YOUR HEAD?! REMEMBER? WHEN YOU WERE IN THE HOSPITAL? THAT GIRL LEFT HER PICTURE BEHIND.
??
SHE HAS LONG BLACK HAIR... USED BE IN GANGS...
OH! THAT'S RIGHT...

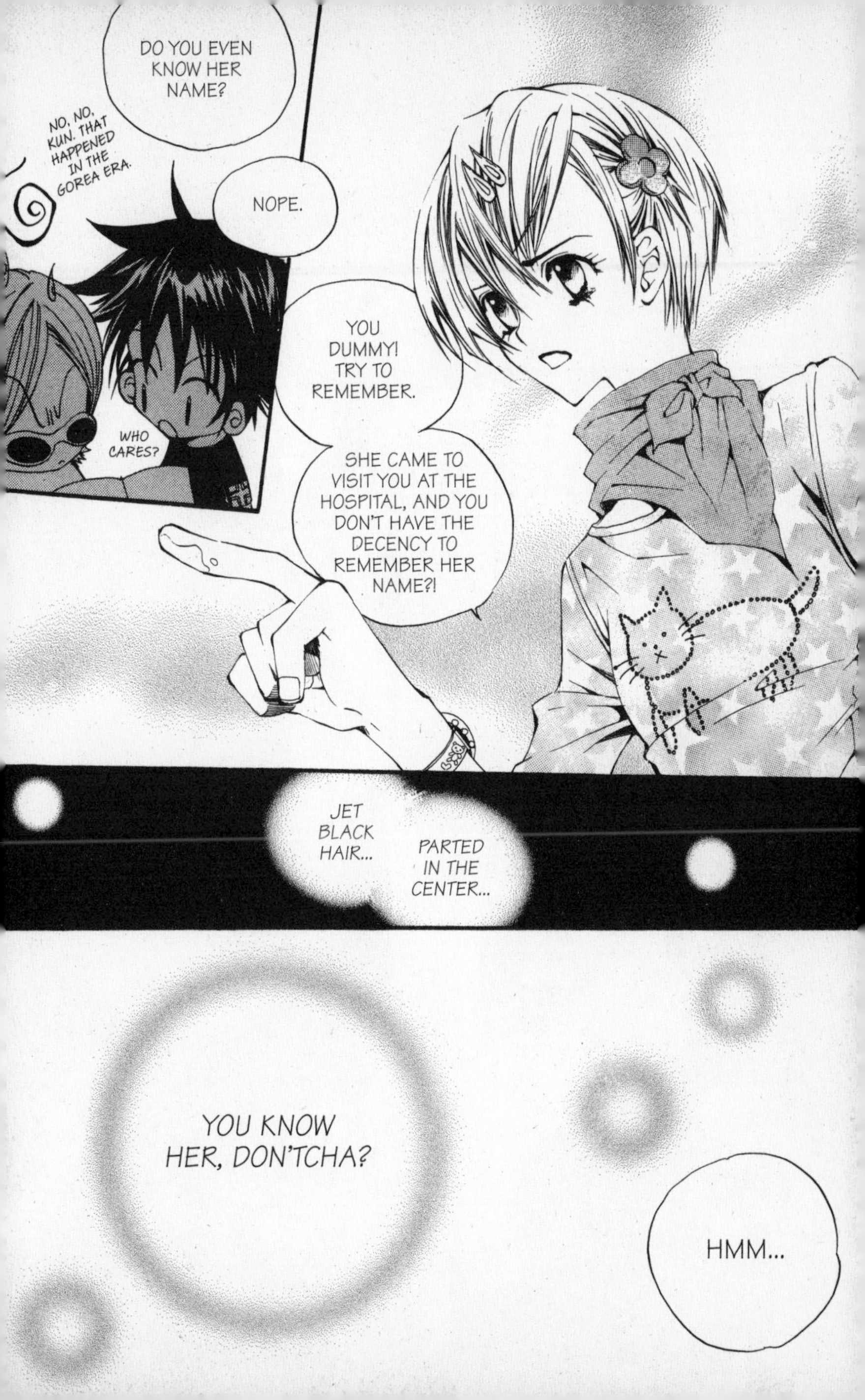
DO YOU EVEN KNOW HER NAME?
NOPE.
NO, NO, KUN. THAT HAPPENED IN THE GOREA ERA.
WHO CARES?
YOU DUMMY! TRY TO REMEMBER.
SHE CAME TO VISIT YOU AT THE HOSPITAL, AND YOU DON'T HAVE THE DECENCY TO REMEMBER HER NAME?!
JET BLACK HAIR...
PARTED IN THE CENTER...
YOU KNOW HER, DON'TCHA?
HMM...

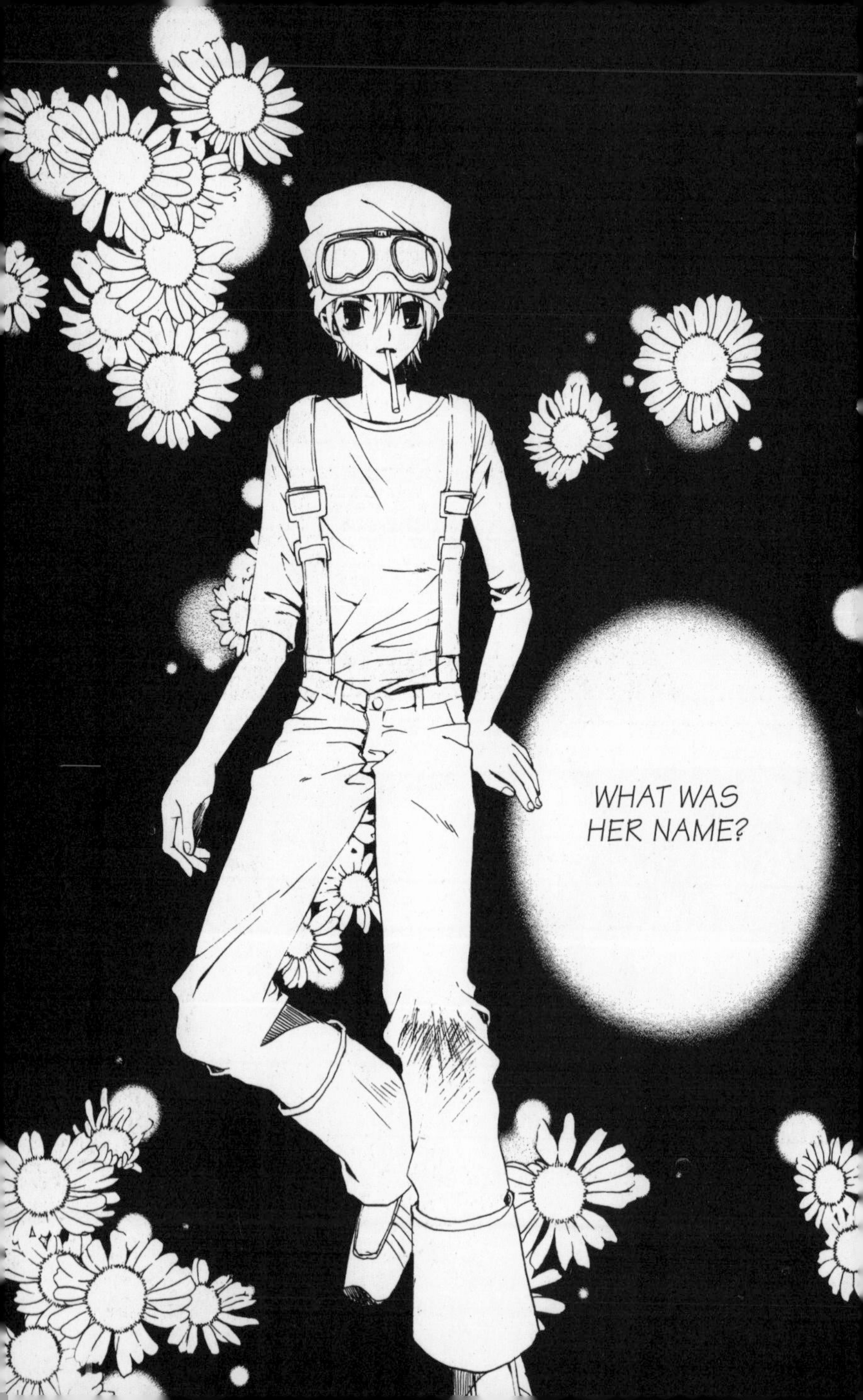
WHAT WAS HER NAME?

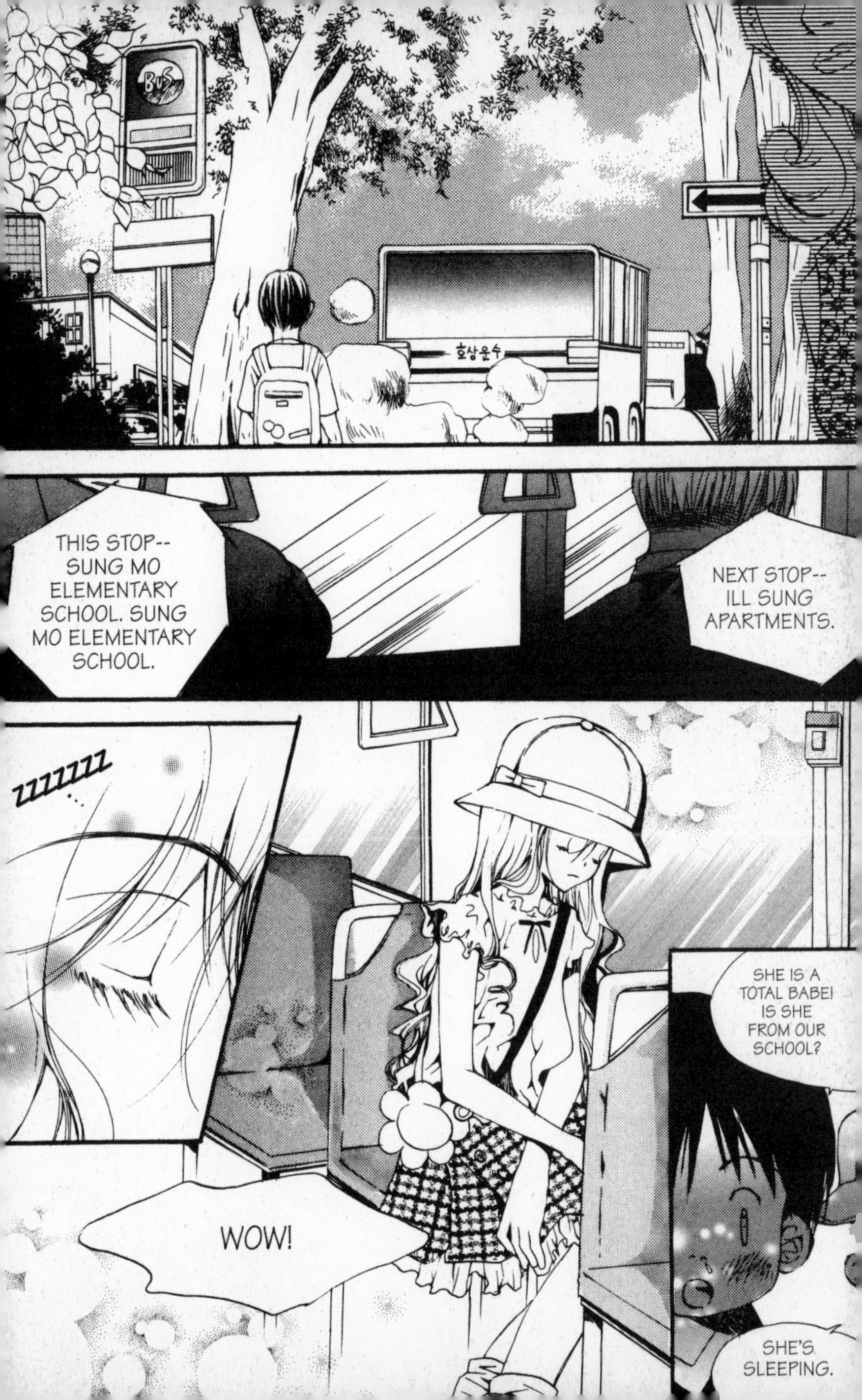
BUS
호상운수
THIS STOP-- SUNG MO ELEMENTARY SCHOOL. SUNG MO ELEMENTARY SCHOOL.
NEXT STOP-- ILL SUNG APARTMENTS.
ZZZZZZZ...
WOW!
SHE IS A TOTAL BABE! IS SHE FROM OUR SCHOOL?
SHE'S SLEEPING.

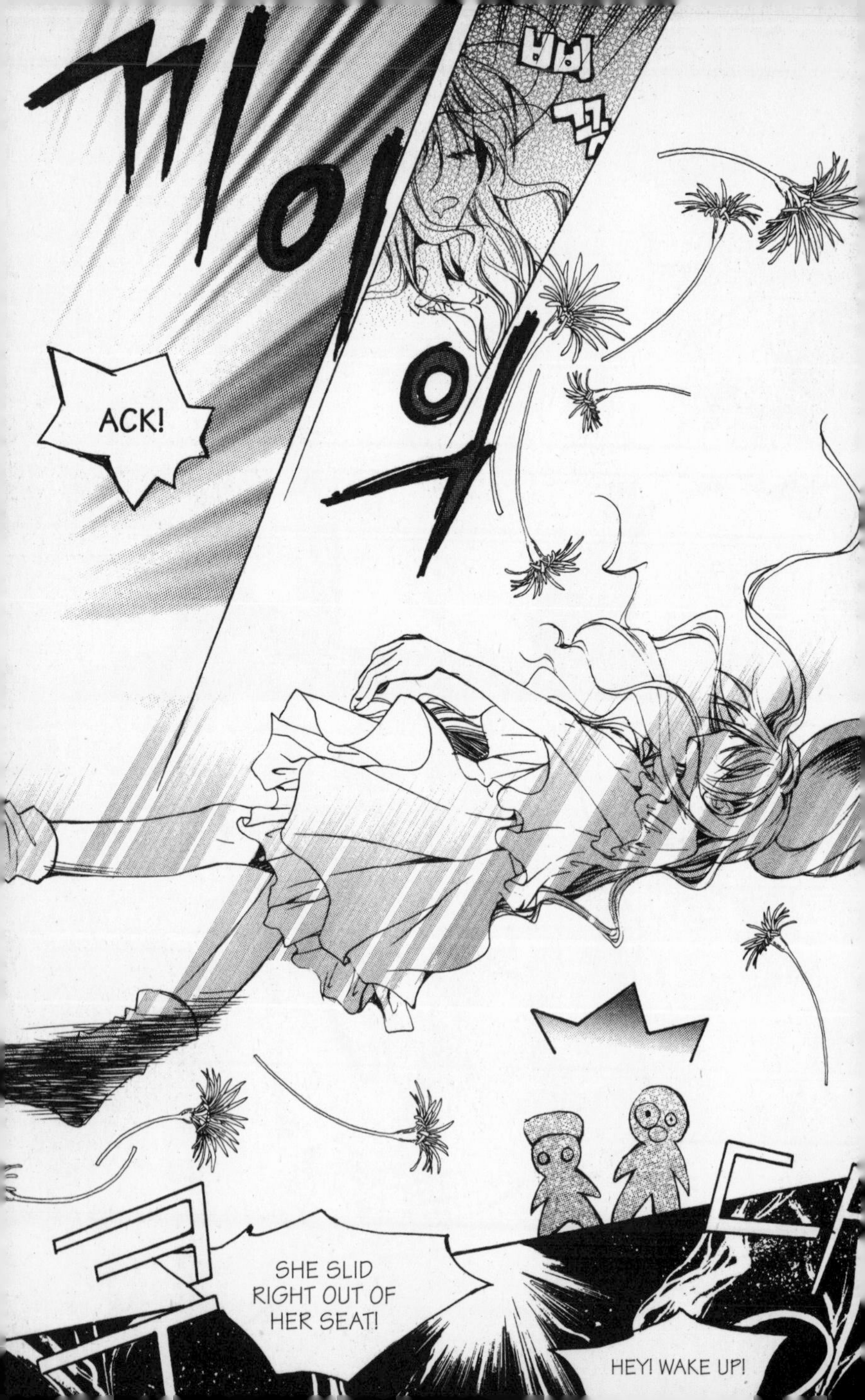
끼이익
삐끗
ACK!
SHE SLID RIGHT OUT OF HER SEAT!
HEY! WAKE UP!

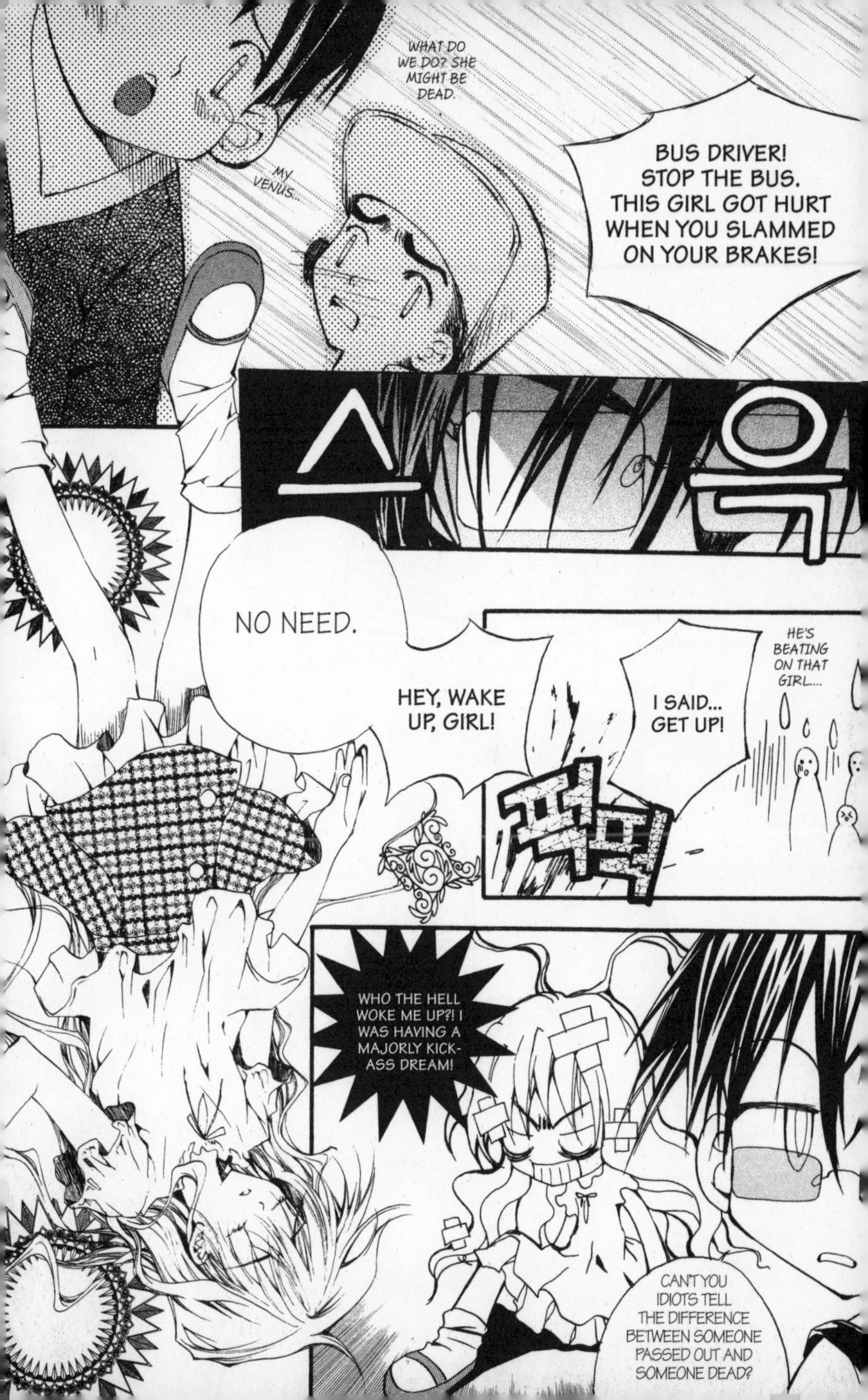
WHAT DO WE DO? SHE MIGHT BE DEAD.
MY VENUS...
BUS DRIVER! STOP THE BUS. THIS GIRL GOT HURT WHEN YOU SLAMMED ON YOUR BRAKES!
스윽
NO NEED.
HEY, WAKE UP, GIRL!
I SAID... GET UP!
HE'S BEATING ON THAT GIRL....
퍽
WHO THE HELL WOKE ME UP?! I WAS HAVING A MAJORLY KICK-ASS DREAM!
CAN'T YOU IDIOTS TELL THE DIFFERENCE BETWEEN SOMEONE PASSED OUT AND SOMEONE DEAD?

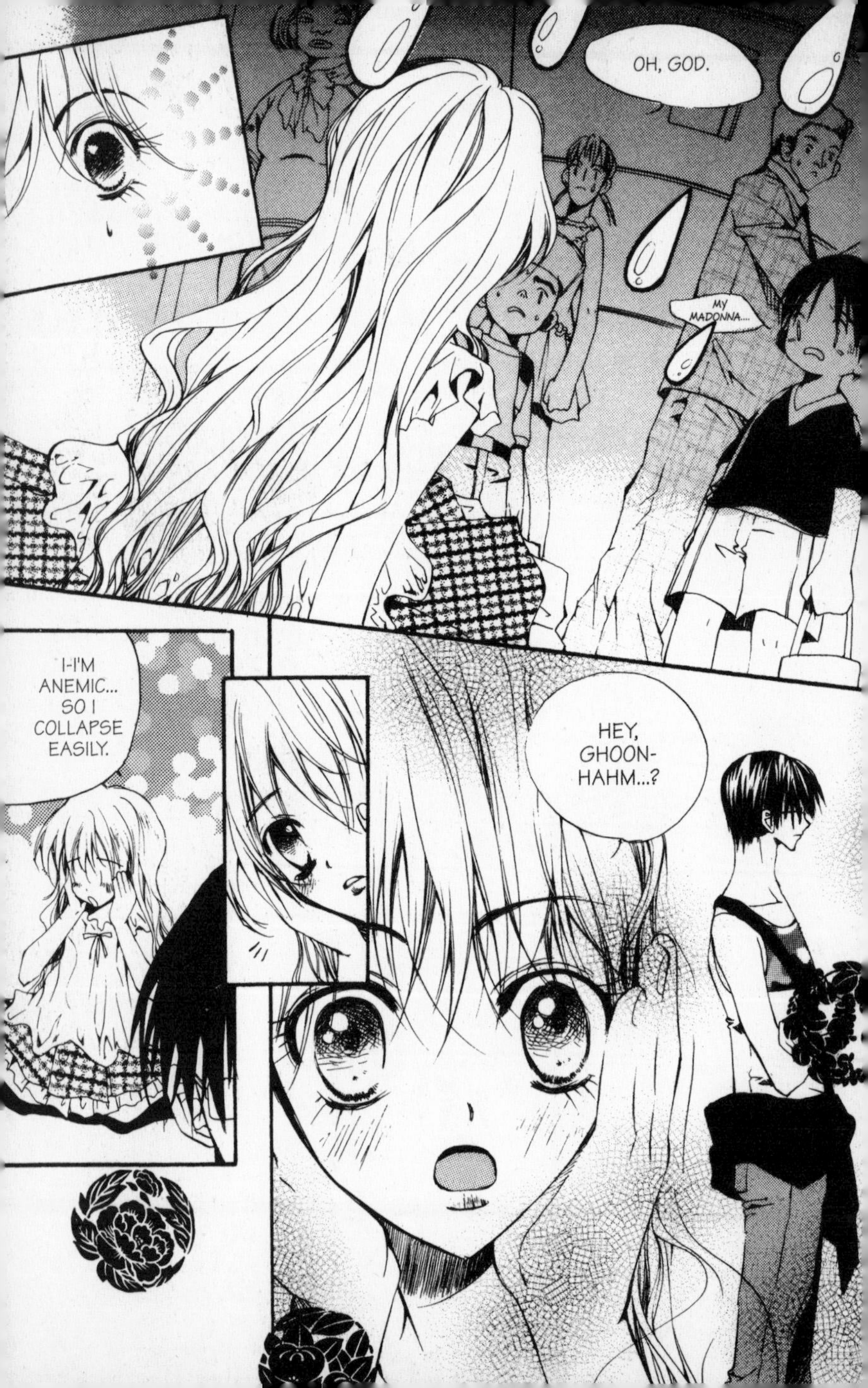
OH, GOD.
MY MADONNA....
I-I'M ANEMIC... SO I COLLAPSE EASILY.
HEY, GHOON-HAHM...?

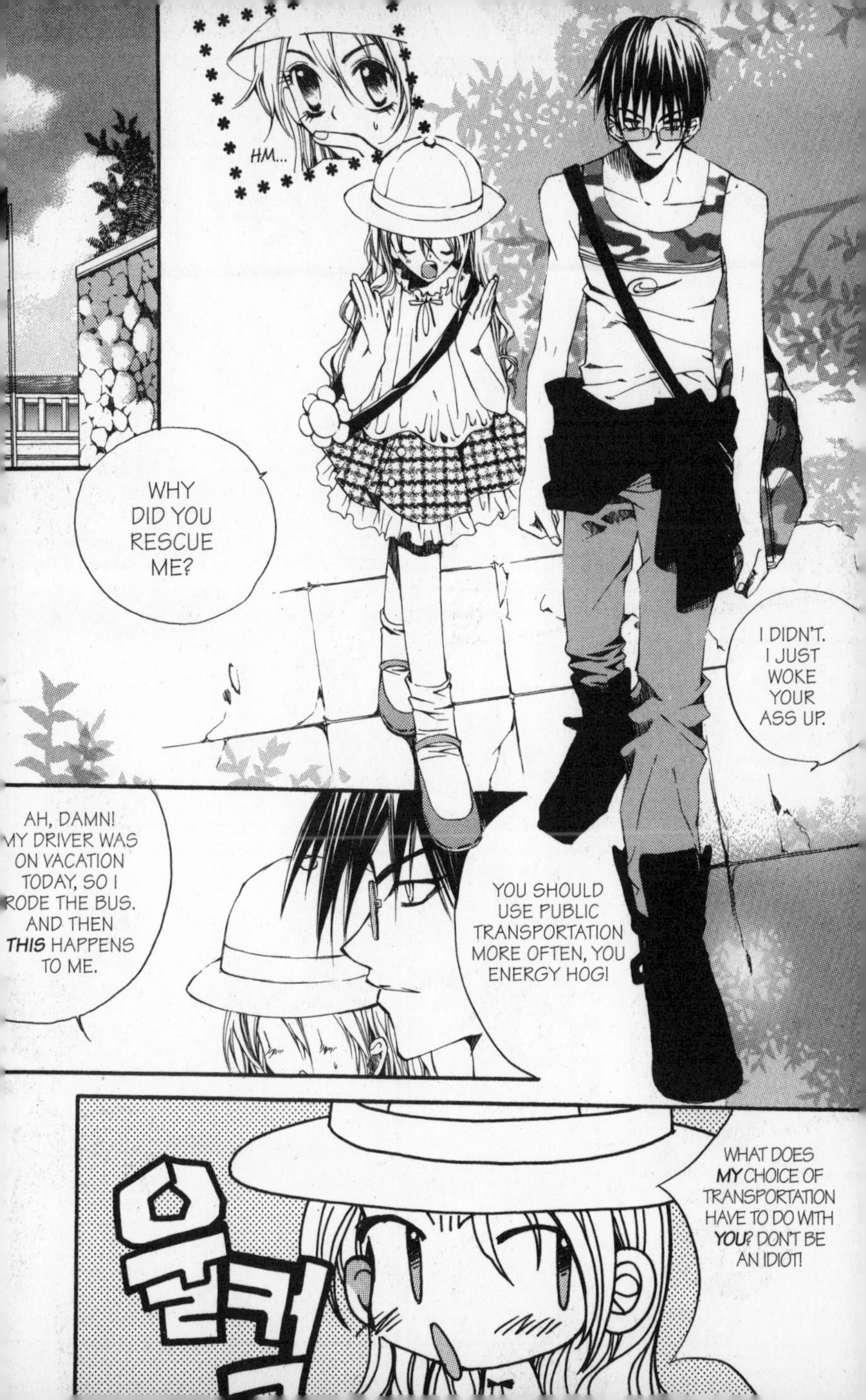
HM...
WHY DID YOU RESCUE ME?
I DIDN'T. I JUST WOKE YOUR ASS UP.
AH, DAMN! MY DRIVER WAS ON VACATION TODAY, SO I RODE THE BUS. AND THEN **THIS** HAPPENS TO ME.
YOU SHOULD USE PUBLIC TRANSPORTATION MORE OFTEN, YOU ENERGY HOG!
WHAT DOES **MY** CHOICE OF TRANSPORTATION HAVE TO DO WITH **YOU**? DON'T BE AN IDIOT!

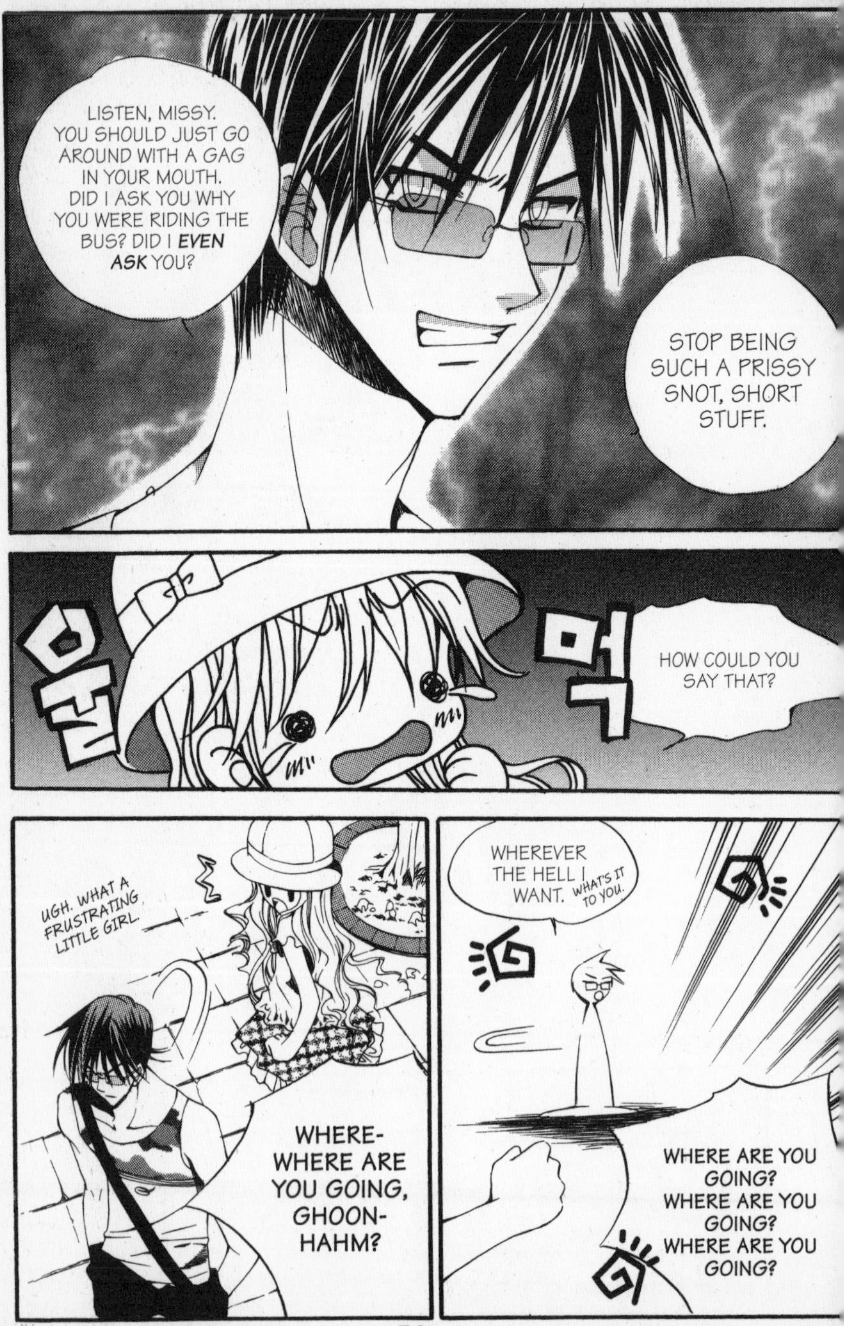

LISTEN, MISSY. YOU SHOULD JUST GO AROUND WITH A GAG IN YOUR MOUTH. DID I ASK YOU WHY YOU WERE RIDING THE BUS? DID I **EVEN ASK** YOU?
STOP BEING SUCH A PRISSY SNOT, SHORT STUFF.
얼
먹
HOW COULD YOU SAY THAT?
UGH. WHAT A FRUSTRATING LITTLE GIRL.
WHERE- WHERE ARE YOU GOING, GHOON-HAHM?
WHEREVER THE HELL I WANT.
WHAT'S IT TO YOU.
WHERE ARE YOU GOING? WHERE ARE YOU GOING? WHERE ARE YOU GOING?

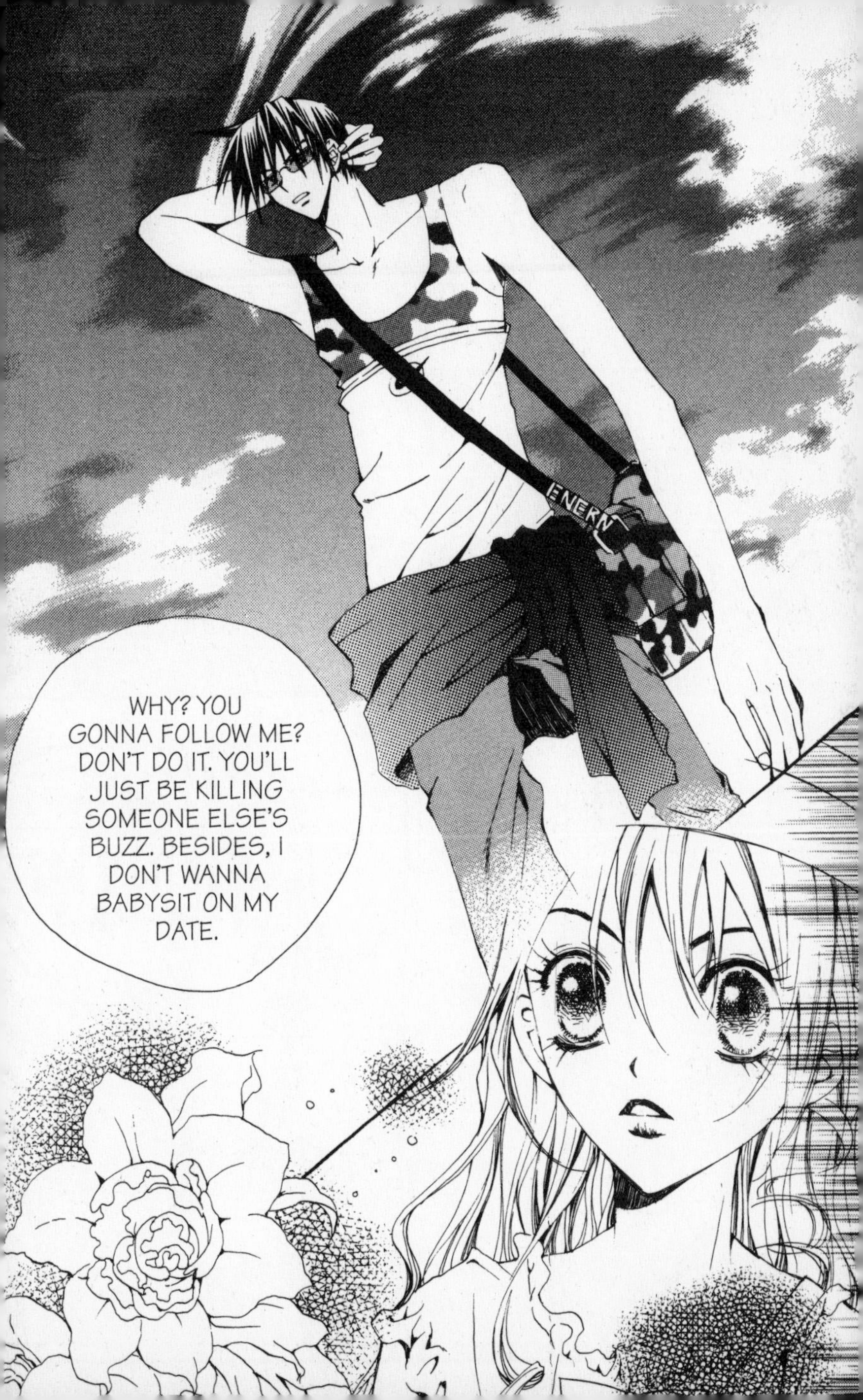
WHY? YOU GONNA FOLLOW ME? DON'T DO IT. YOU'LL JUST BE KILLING SOMEONE ELSE'S BUZZ. BESIDES, I DON'T WANNA BABYSIT ON MY DATE.
ENERN

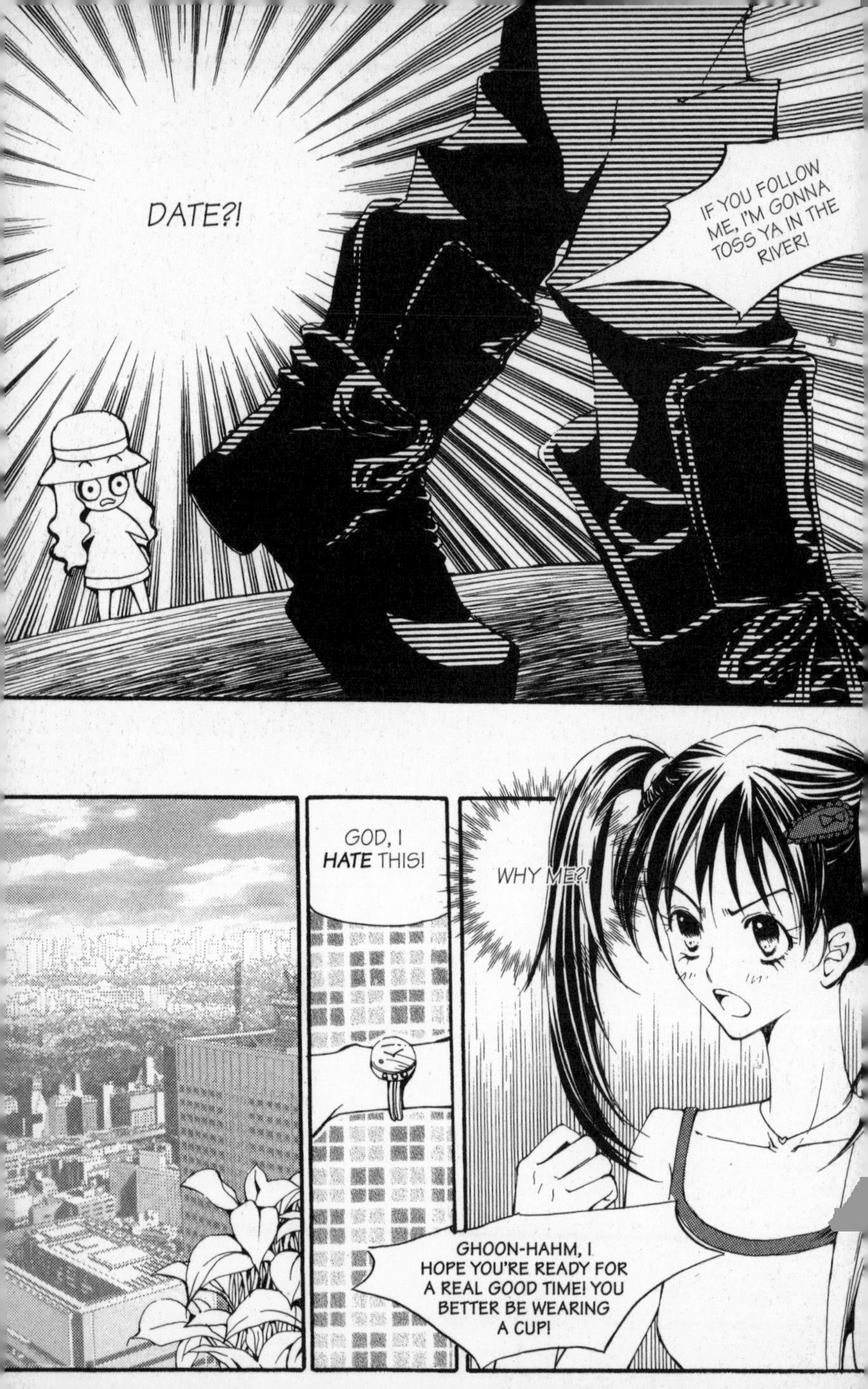
DATE?!
IF YOU FOLLOW ME, I'M GONNA TOSS YA IN THE RIVER!
GOD, I HATE THIS!
WHY ME?!
GHOON-HAHM, I HOPE YOU'RE READY FOR A REAL GOOD TIME! YOU BETTER BE WEARING A CUP!

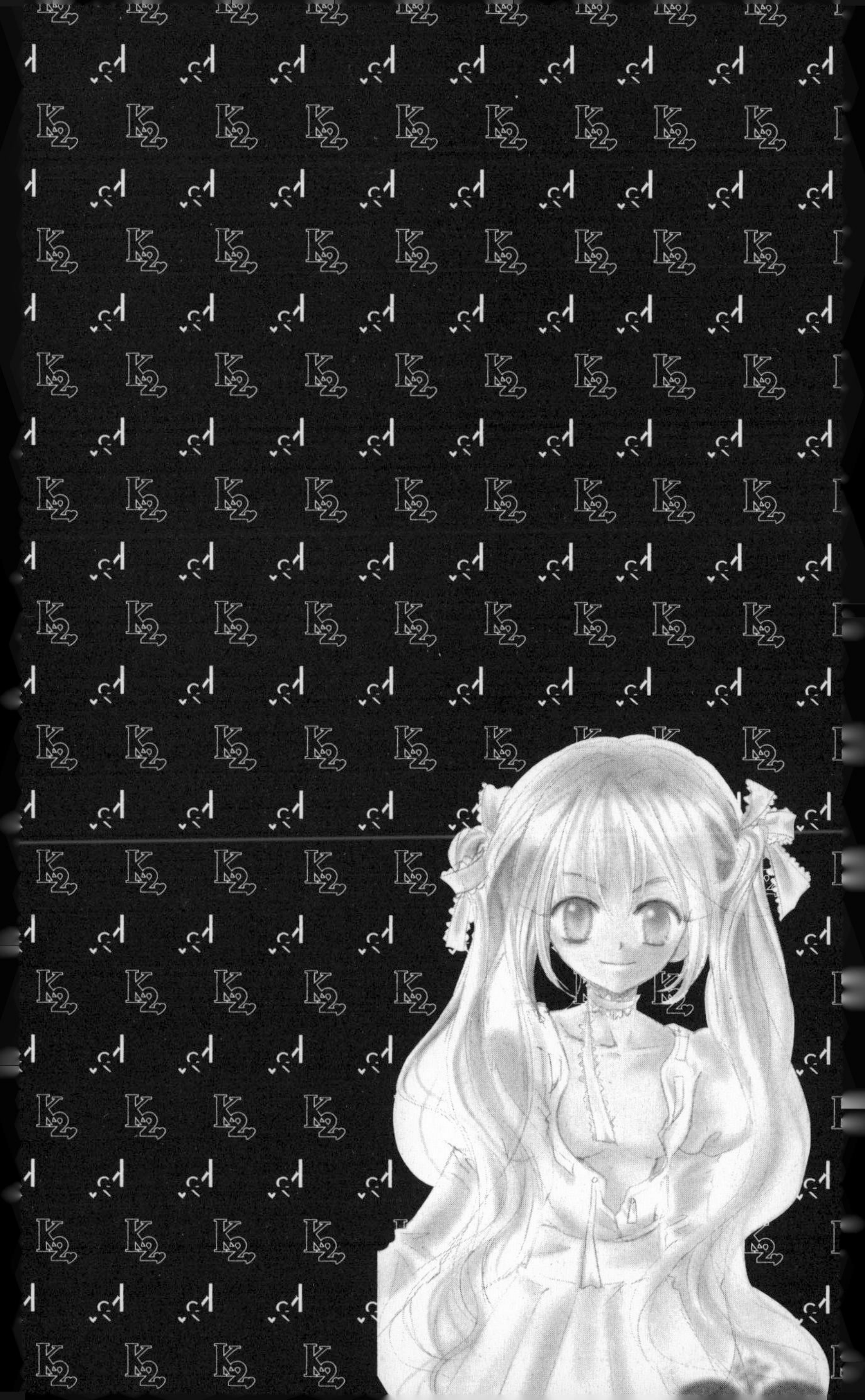

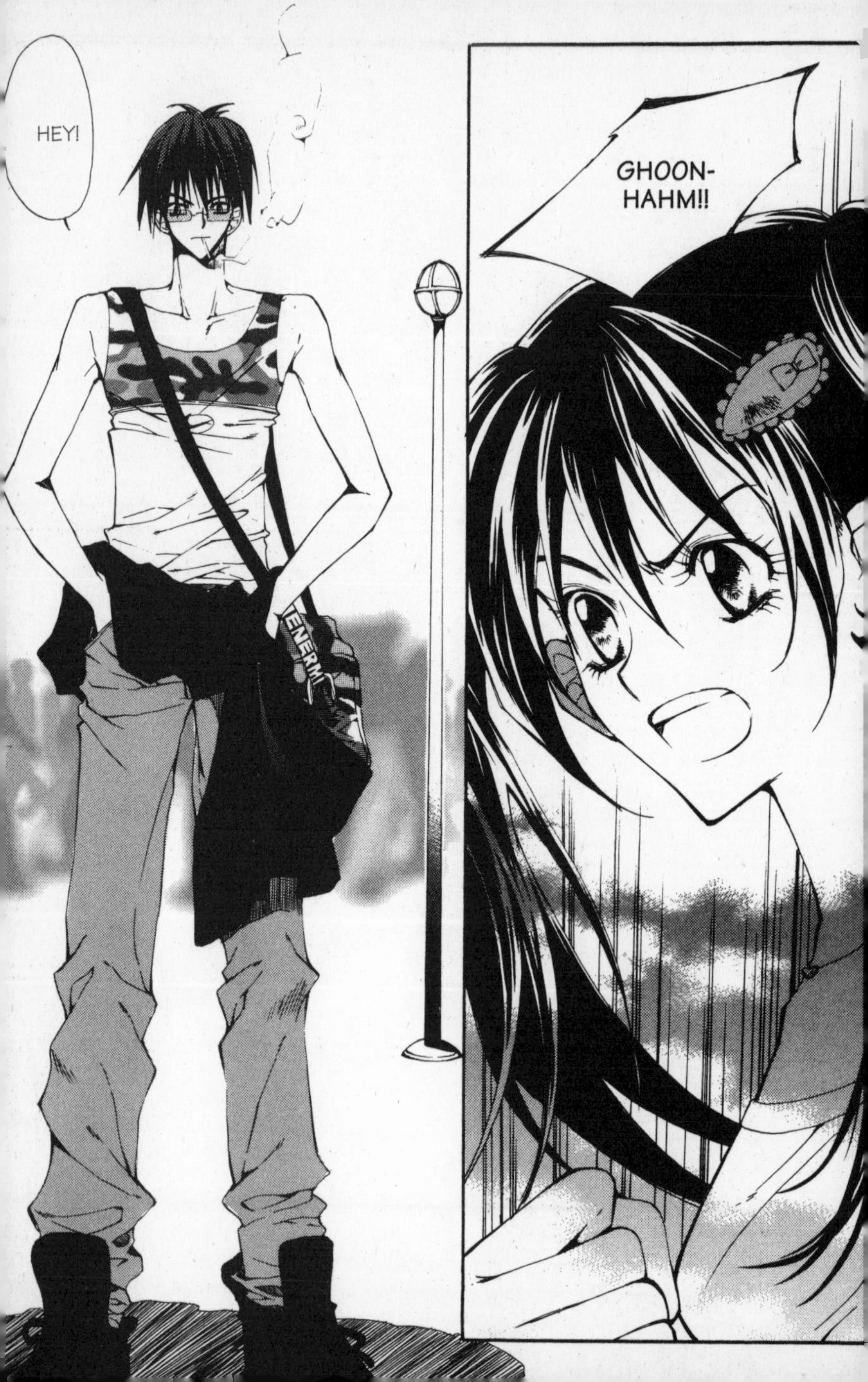
HEY!
GHOON-HAHM!!

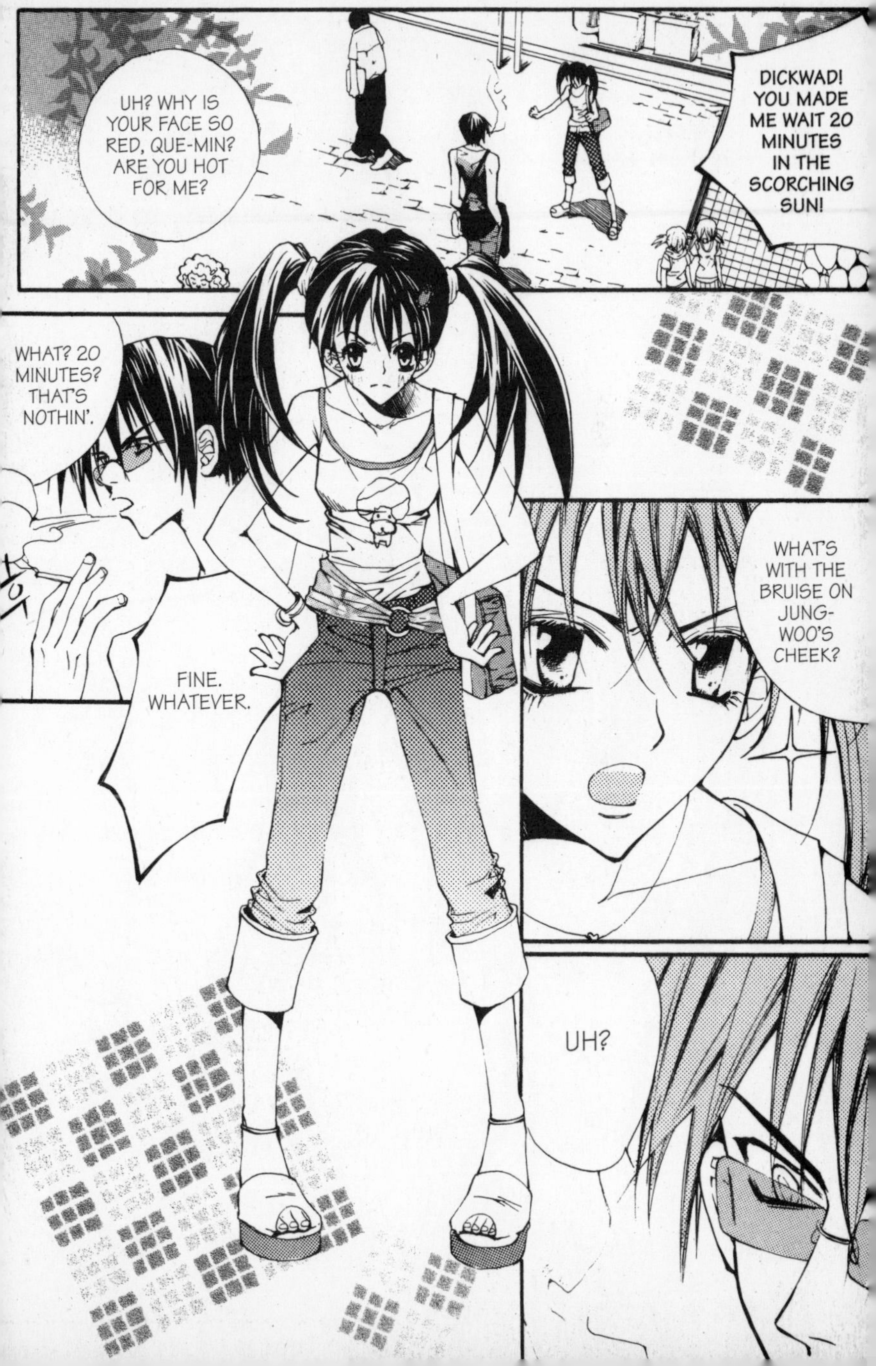
UH? WHY IS YOUR FACE SO RED, QUE-MIN? ARE YOU HOT FOR ME?
DICKWAD! YOU MADE ME WAIT 20 MINUTES IN THE SCORCHING SUN!
WHAT? 20 MINUTES? THAT'S NOTHIN'.
FINE. WHATEVER.
WHAT'S WITH THE BRUISE ON JUNG-WOO'S CHEEK?
UH?

* LOOK OF SUSPICION

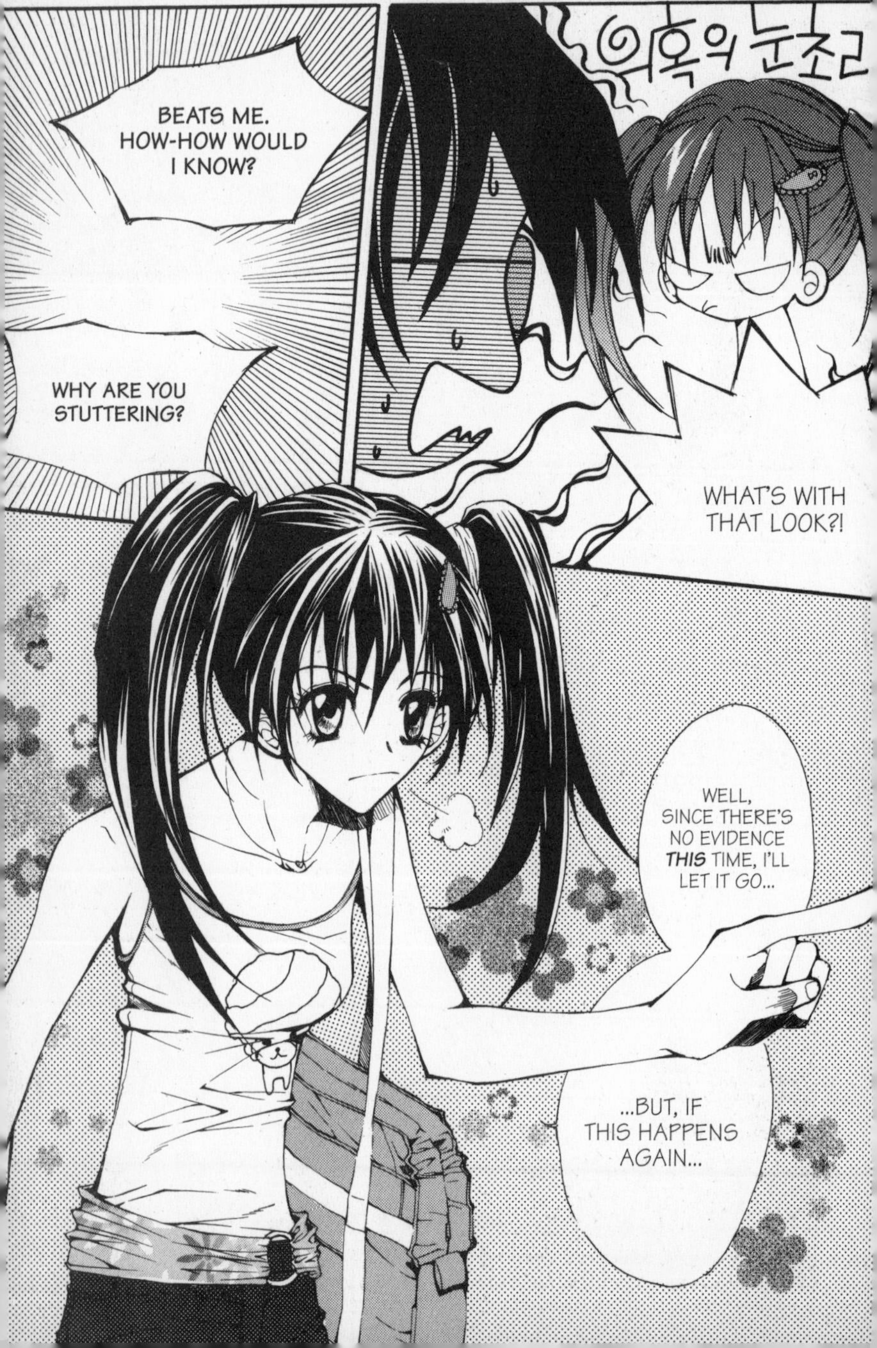

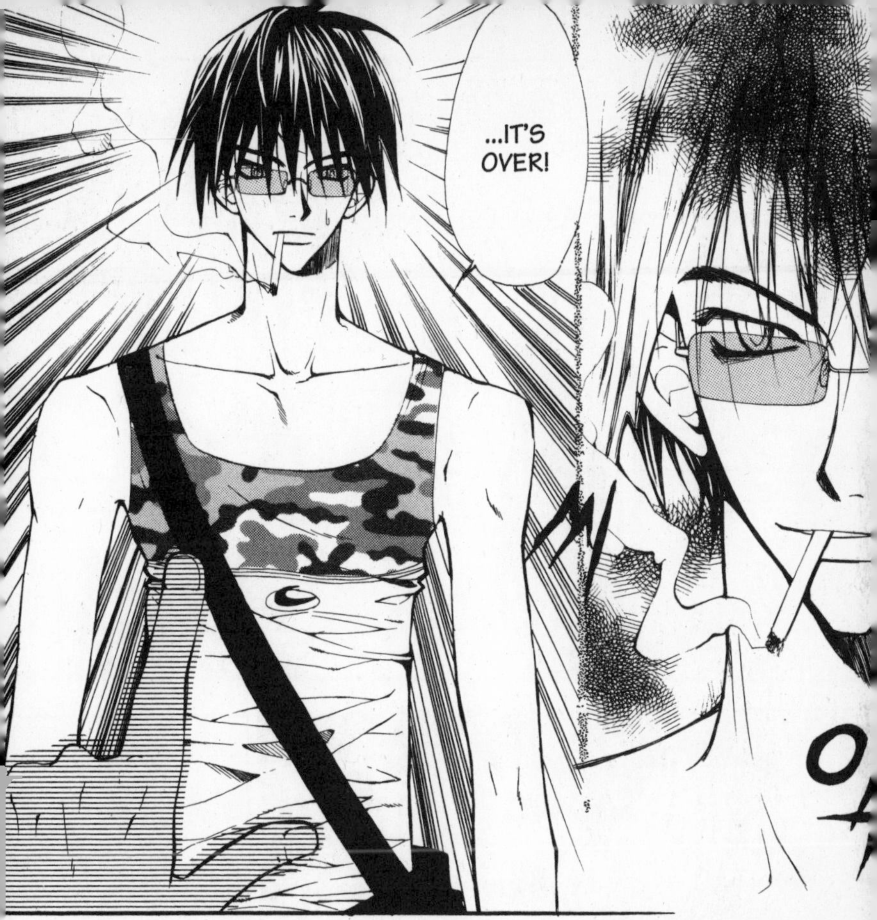
...IT'S OVER!

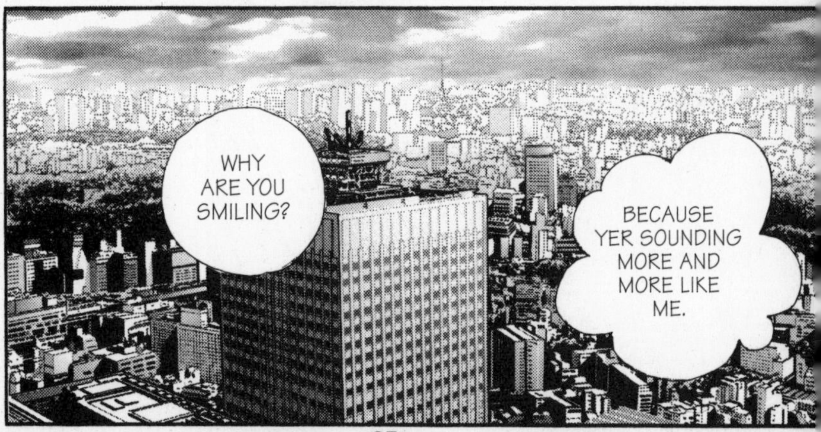
WHY ARE YOU SMILING?
BECAUSE YER SOUNDING MORE AND MORE LIKE ME.

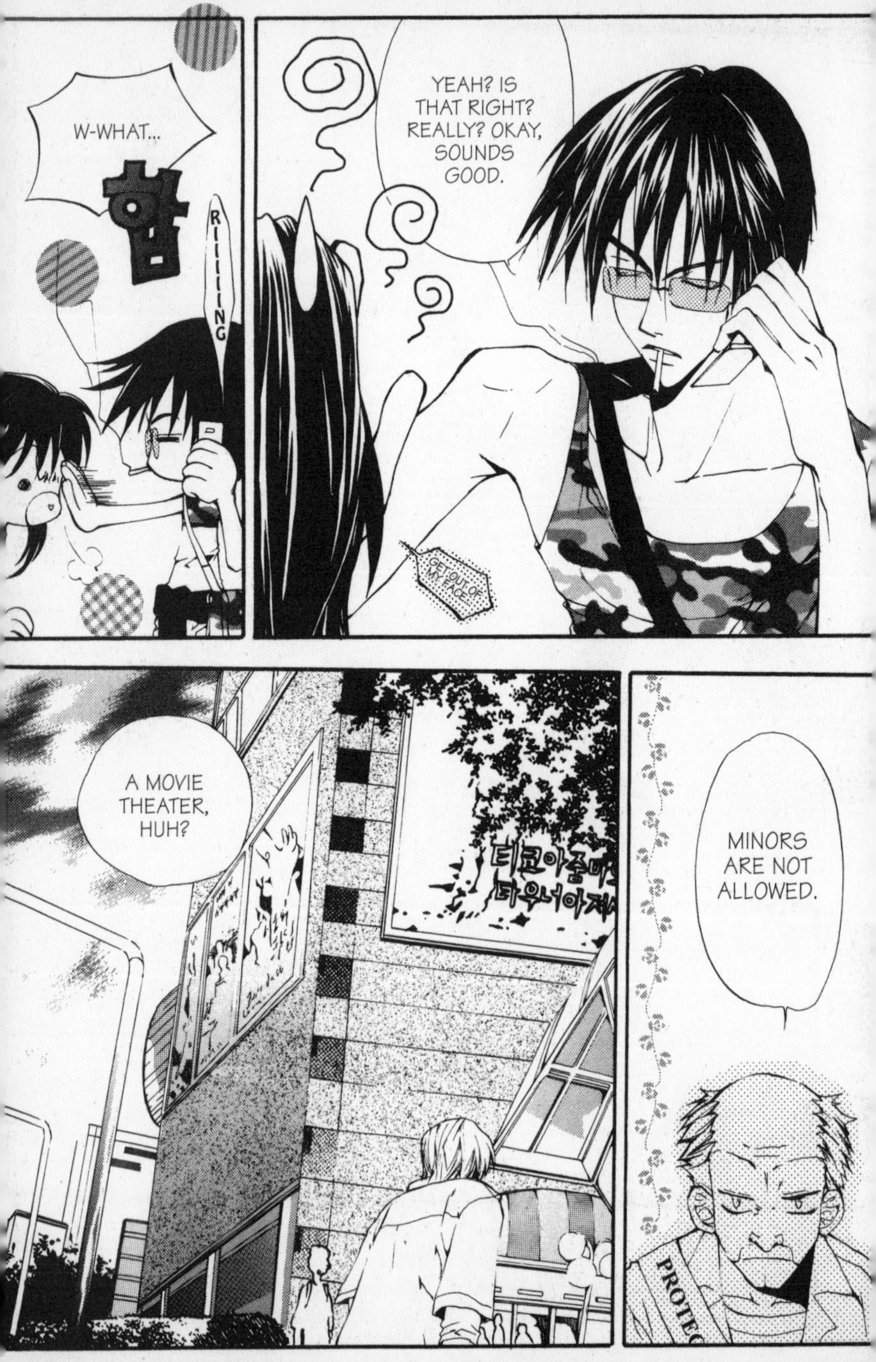
W-WHAT...
RIIIIING
YEAH? IS THAT RIGHT? REALLY? OKAY, SOUNDS GOOD.
GET OUT OF MY FACE.
A MOVIE THEATER, HUH?
MINORS ARE NOT ALLOWED.
PROTEC

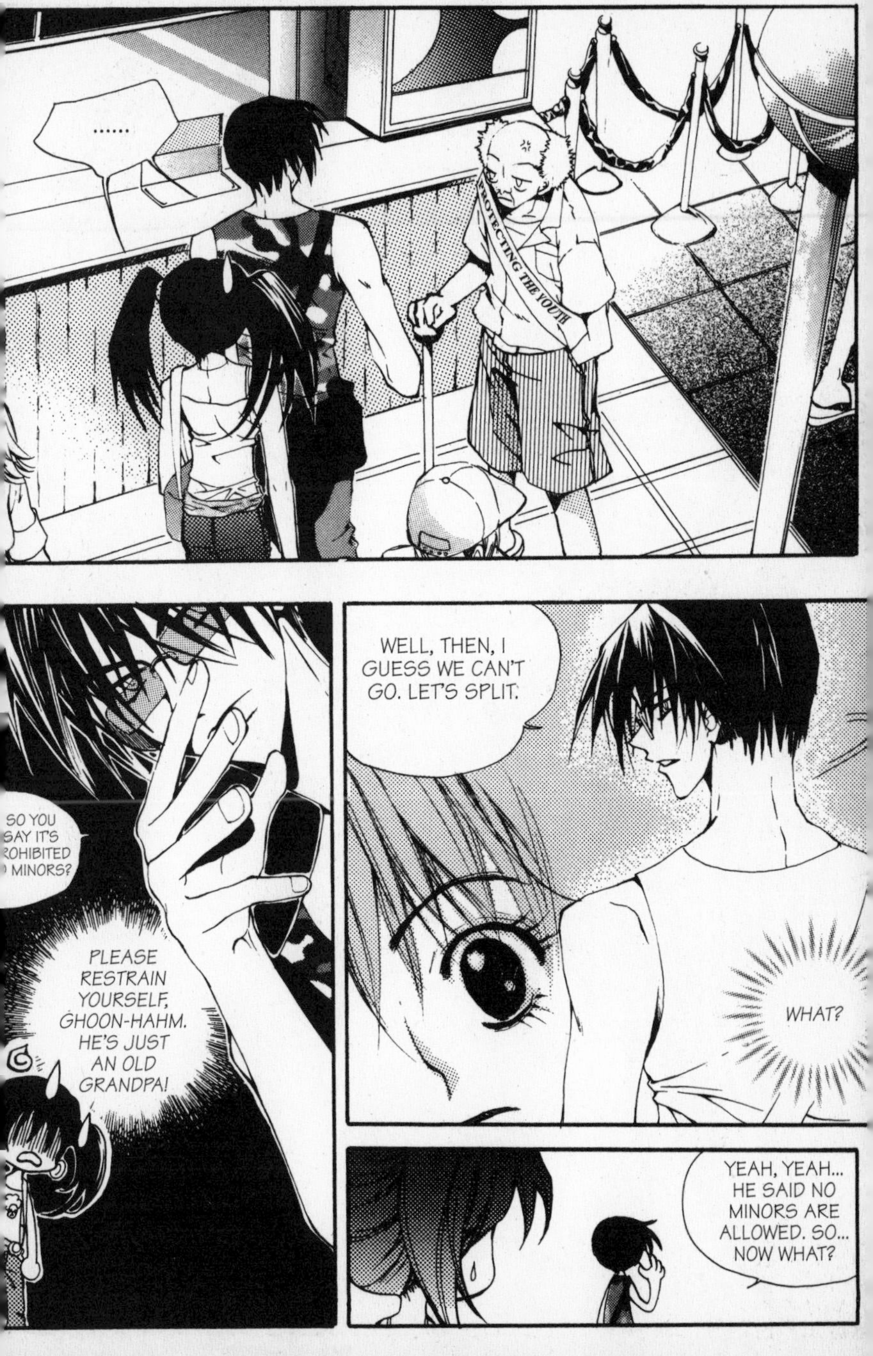
......
PROTECTING THE YOUTH
SO YOU SAY IT'S ROHIBITED MINORS?
PLEASE RESTRAIN YOURSELF, GHOON-HAHM. HE'S JUST AN OLD GRANDPA!
WELL, THEN, I GUESS WE CAN'T GO. LET'S SPLIT.
WHAT?
YEAH, YEAH... HE SAID NO MINORS ARE ALLOWED. SO... NOW WHAT?

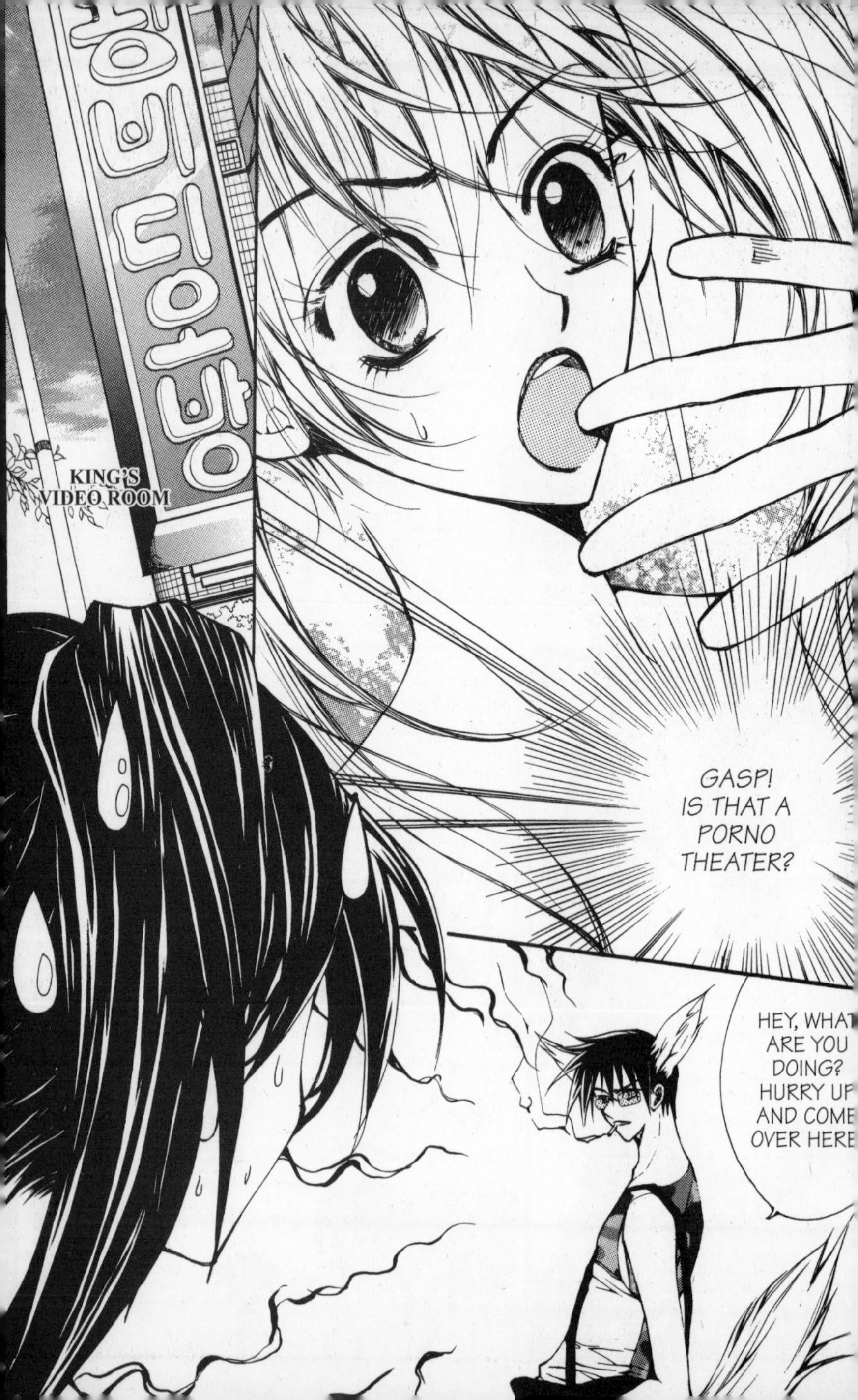
비디오방
KING'S VIDEO ROOM
GASP! IS THAT A PORNO THEATER?
HEY, WHAT ARE YOU DOING? HURRY UP AND COME OVER HERE

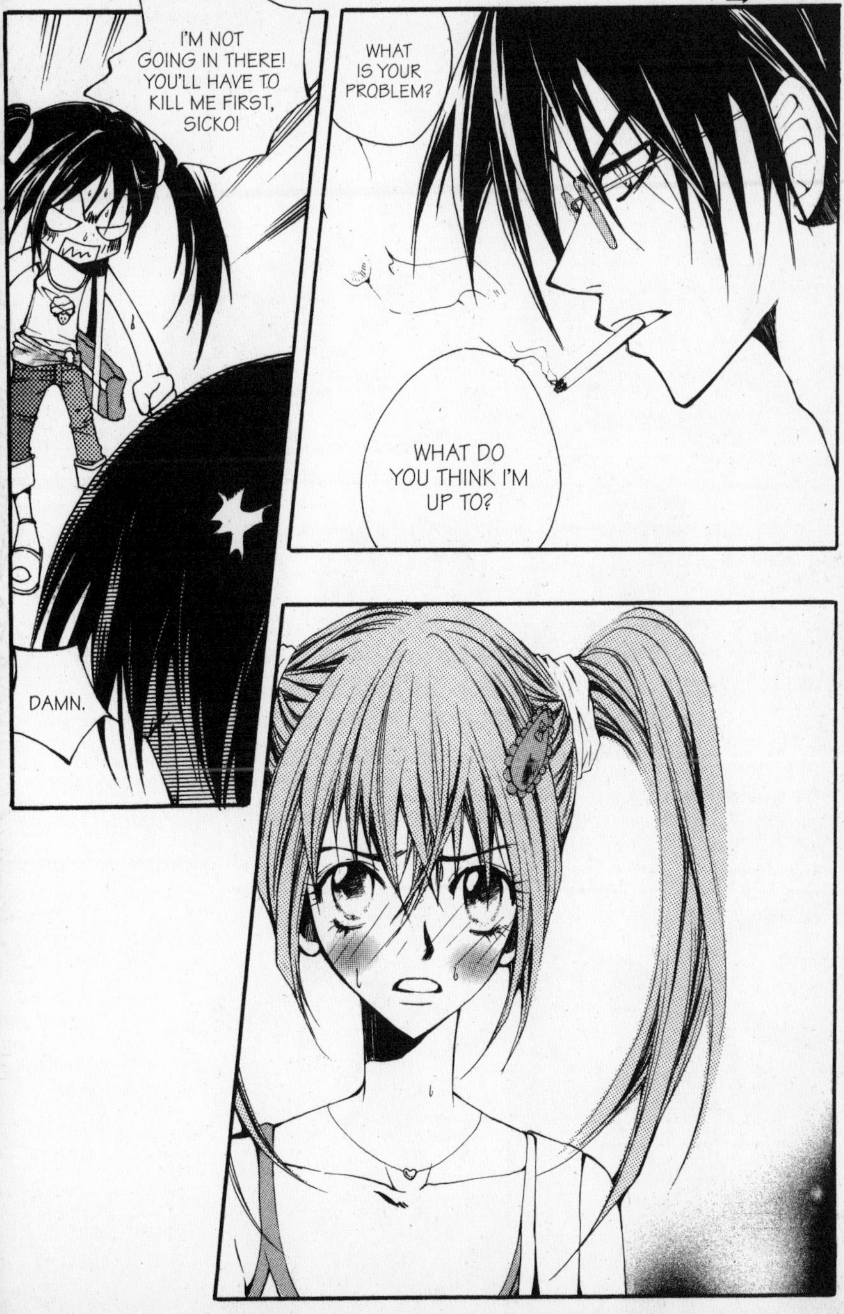
I'M NOT GOING IN THERE! YOU'LL HAVE TO KILL ME FIRST, SICKO!
DAMN.
WHAT IS YOUR PROBLEM?
WHAT DO YOU THINK I'M UP TO?

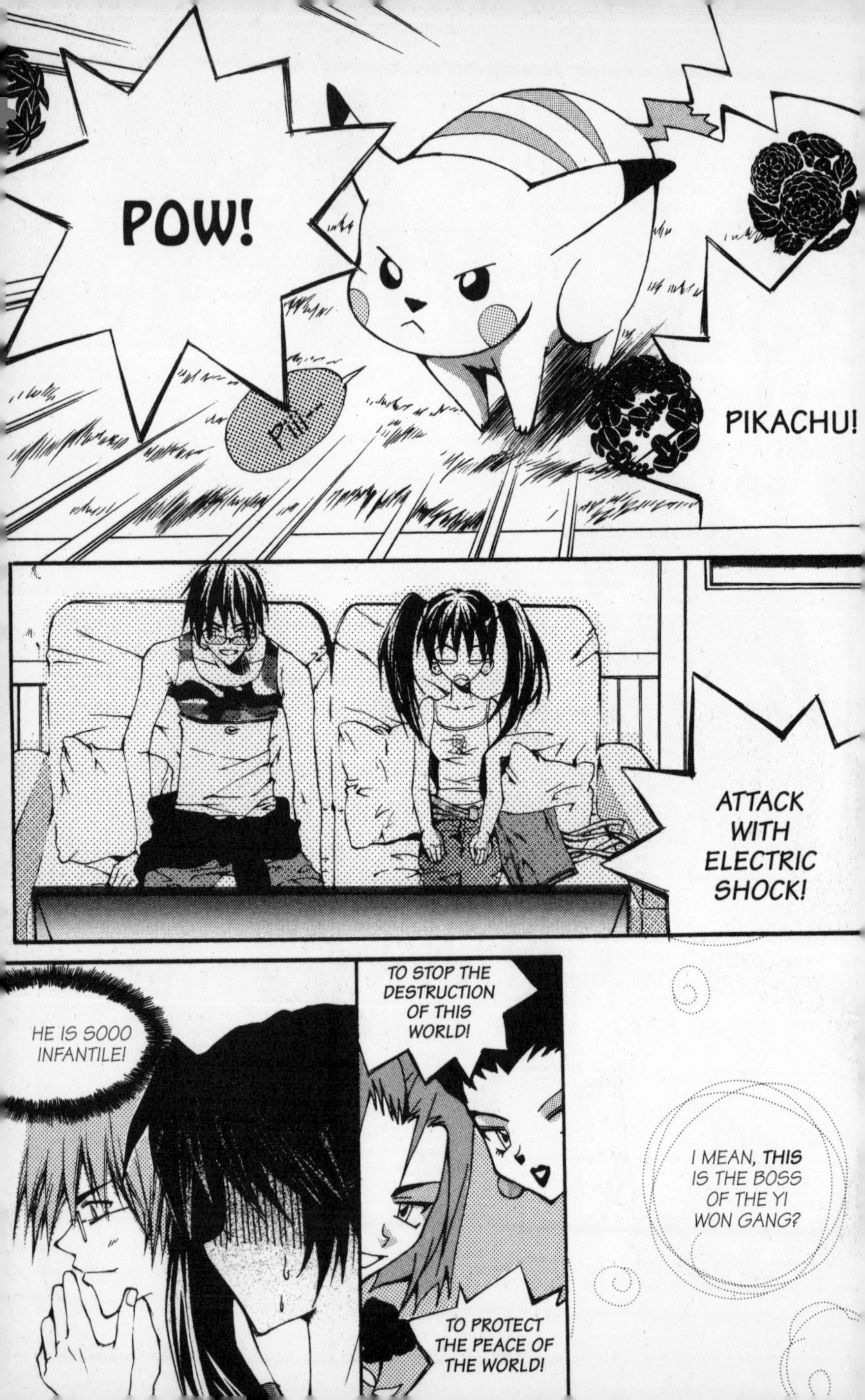
POW!
Piii—
PIKACHU!
ATTACK WITH ELECTRIC SHOCK!
HE IS SOOO INFANTILE!
TO STOP THE DESTRUCTION OF THIS WORLD!
TO PROTECT THE PEACE OF THE WORLD!
I MEAN, THIS IS THE BOSS OF THE YI WON GANG?

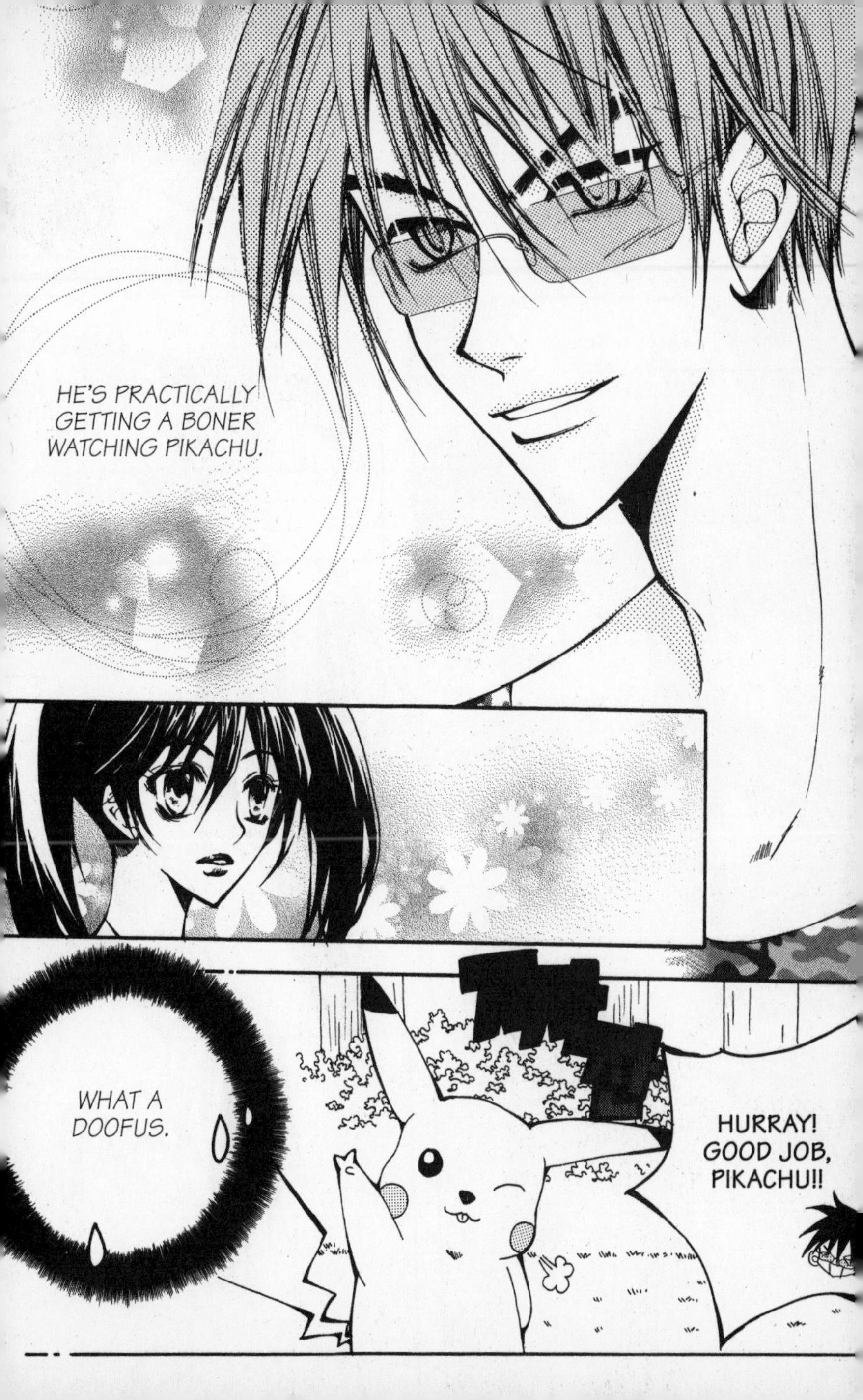
HE'S PRACTICALLY GETTING A BONER WATCHING PIKACHU.
WHAT A DOOFUS.
HURRAY! GOOD JOB, PIKACHU!!

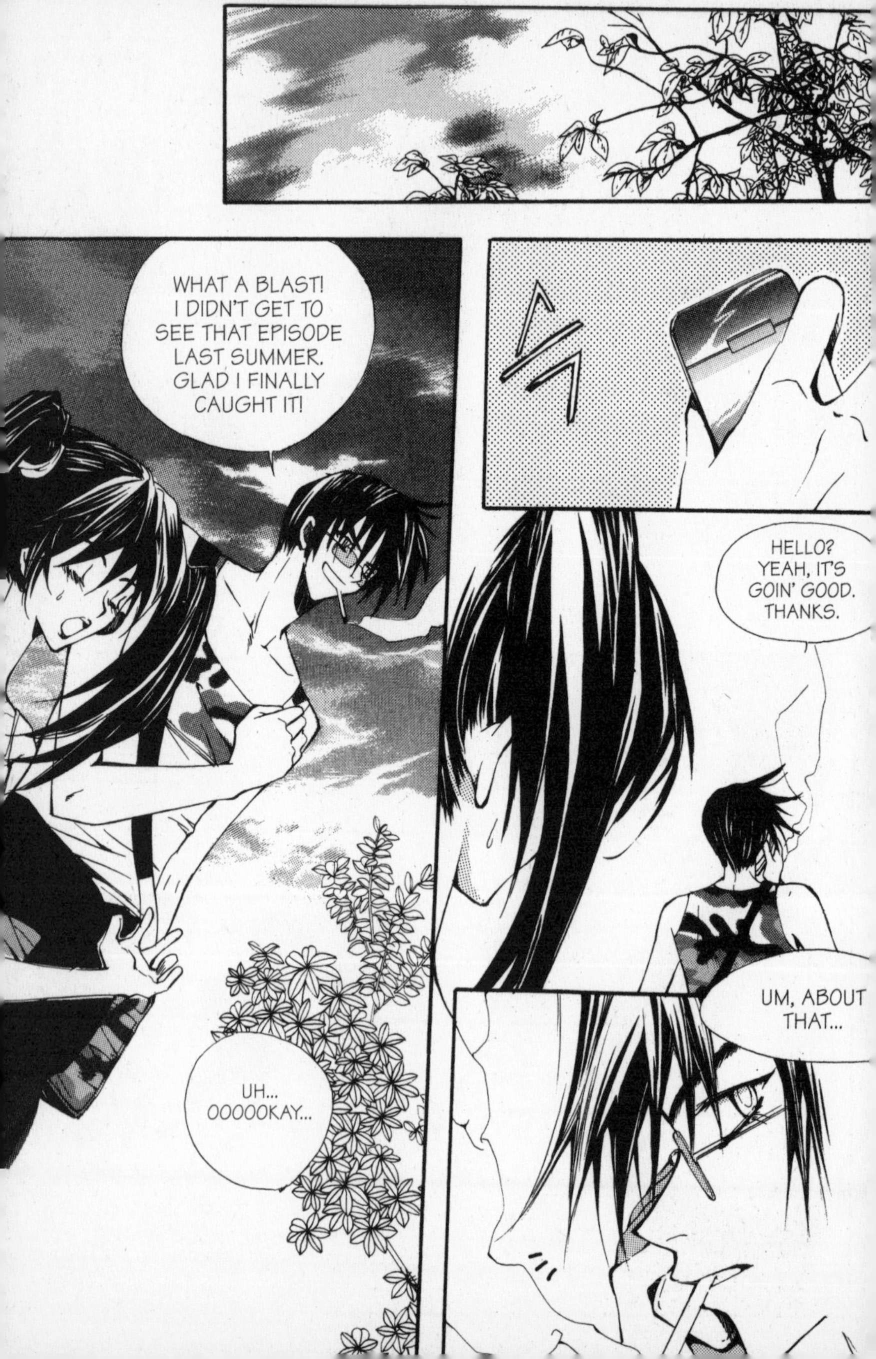
WHAT A BLAST! I DIDN'T GET TO SEE THAT EPISODE LAST SUMMER. GLAD I FINALLY CAUGHT IT!
UH... OOOOOKAY...
HELLO? YEAH, IT'S GOIN' GOOD. THANKS.
UM, ABOUT THAT...

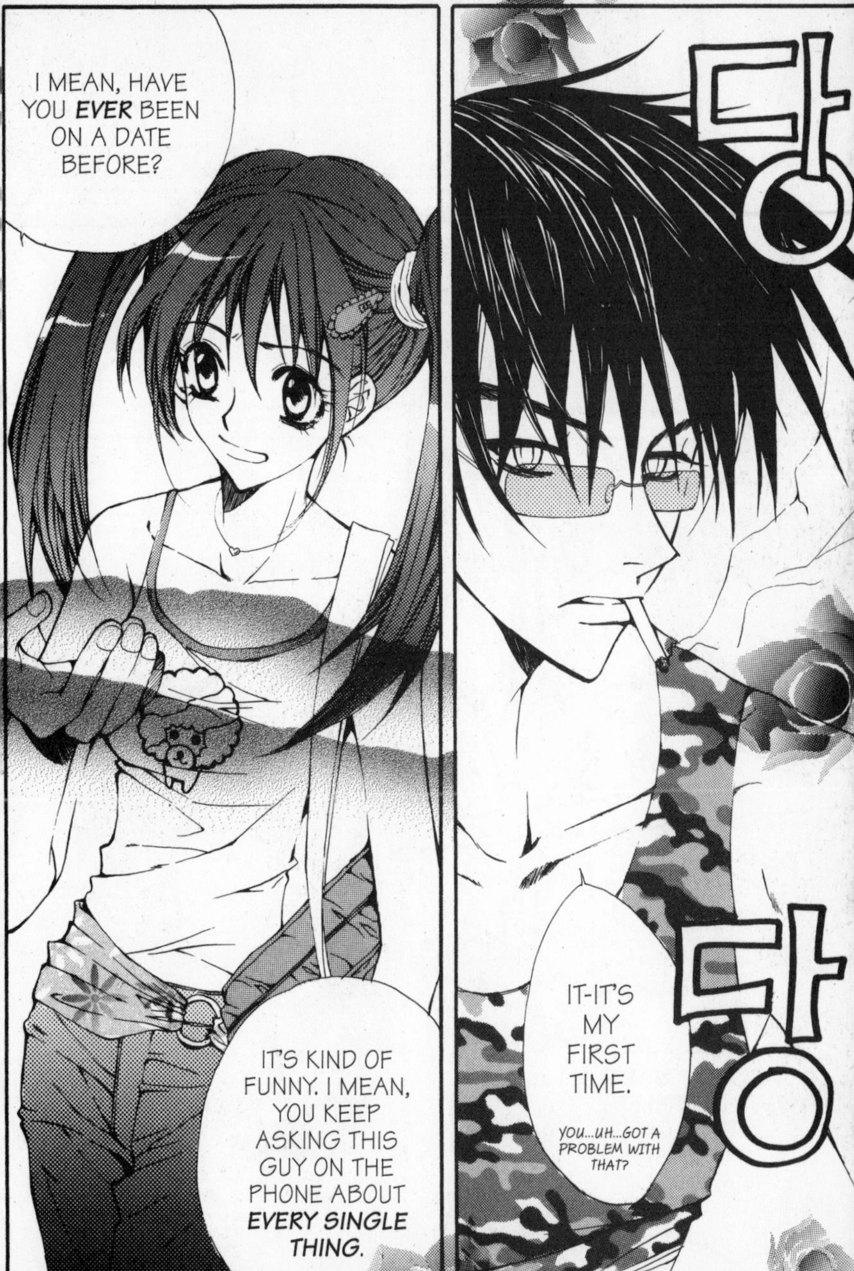
I MEAN, HAVE YOU **EVER** BEEN ON A DATE BEFORE?
IT'S KIND OF FUNNY. I MEAN, YOU KEEP ASKING THIS GUY ON THE PHONE ABOUT **EVERY SINGLE THING.**
당
IT-IT'S MY FIRST TIME.
YOU...UH...GOT A PROBLEM WITH THAT?
당

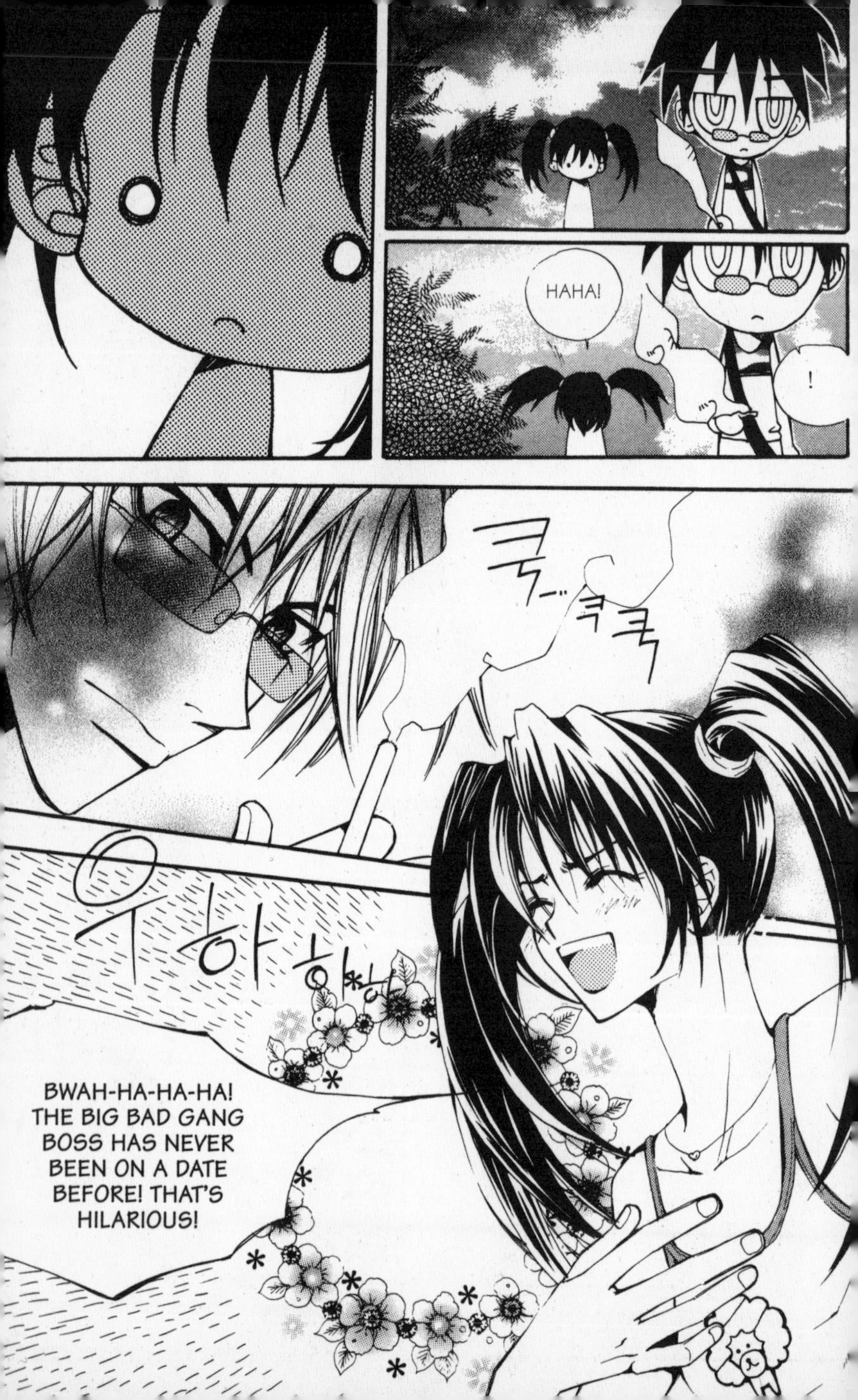
HAHA!
!
BWAH-HA-HA-HA! THE BIG BAD GANG BOSS HAS NEVER BEEN ON A DATE BEFORE! THAT'S HILARIOUS!

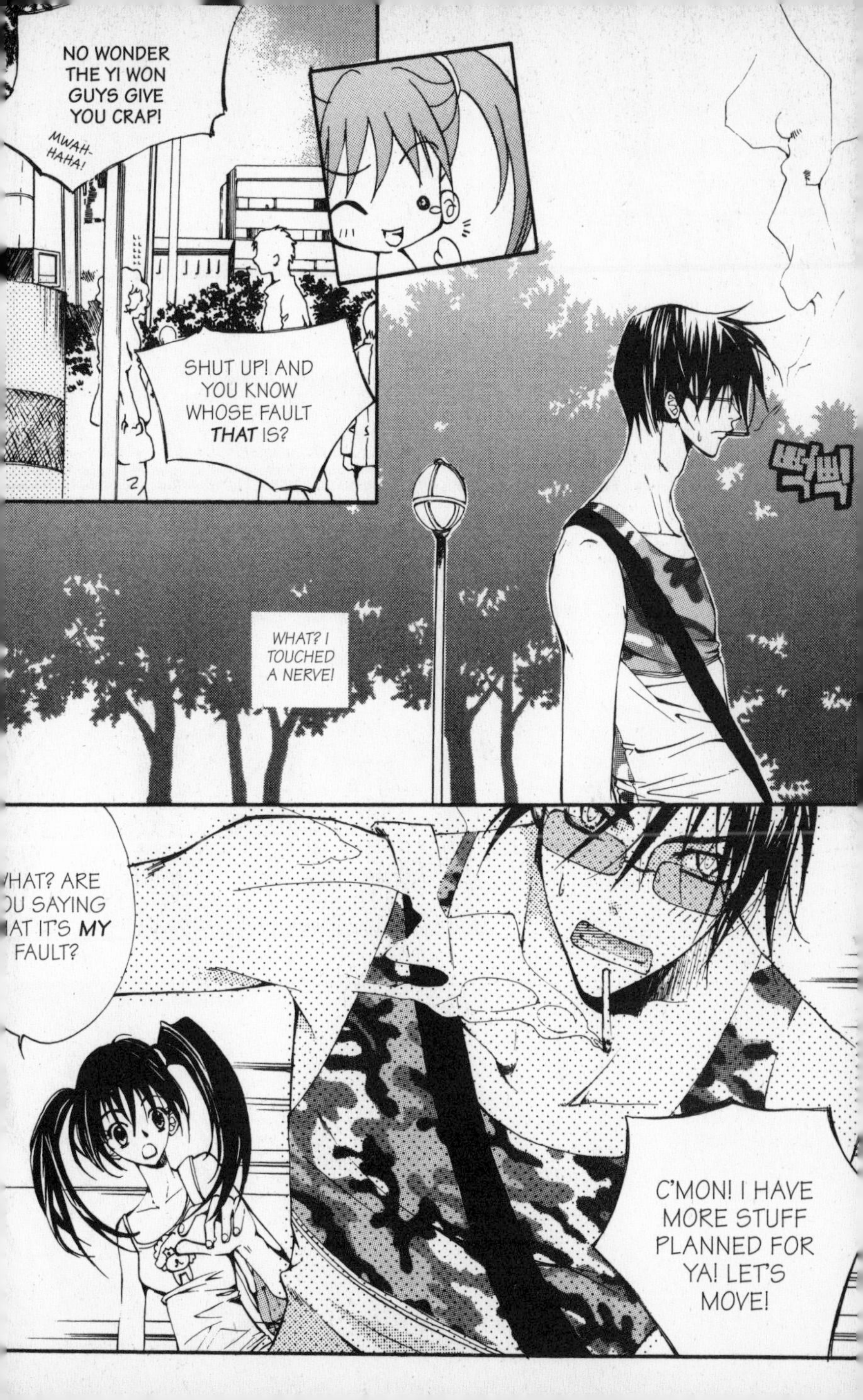
NO WONDER THE YI WON GUYS GIVE YOU CRAP!
MWAH-HAHA!
SHUT UP! AND YOU KNOW WHOSE FAULT THAT IS?
WHAT? I TOUCHED A NERVE!
HAT? ARE U SAYING AT IT'S MY FAULT?
C'MON! I HAVE MORE STUFF PLANNED FOR YA! LET'S MOVE!

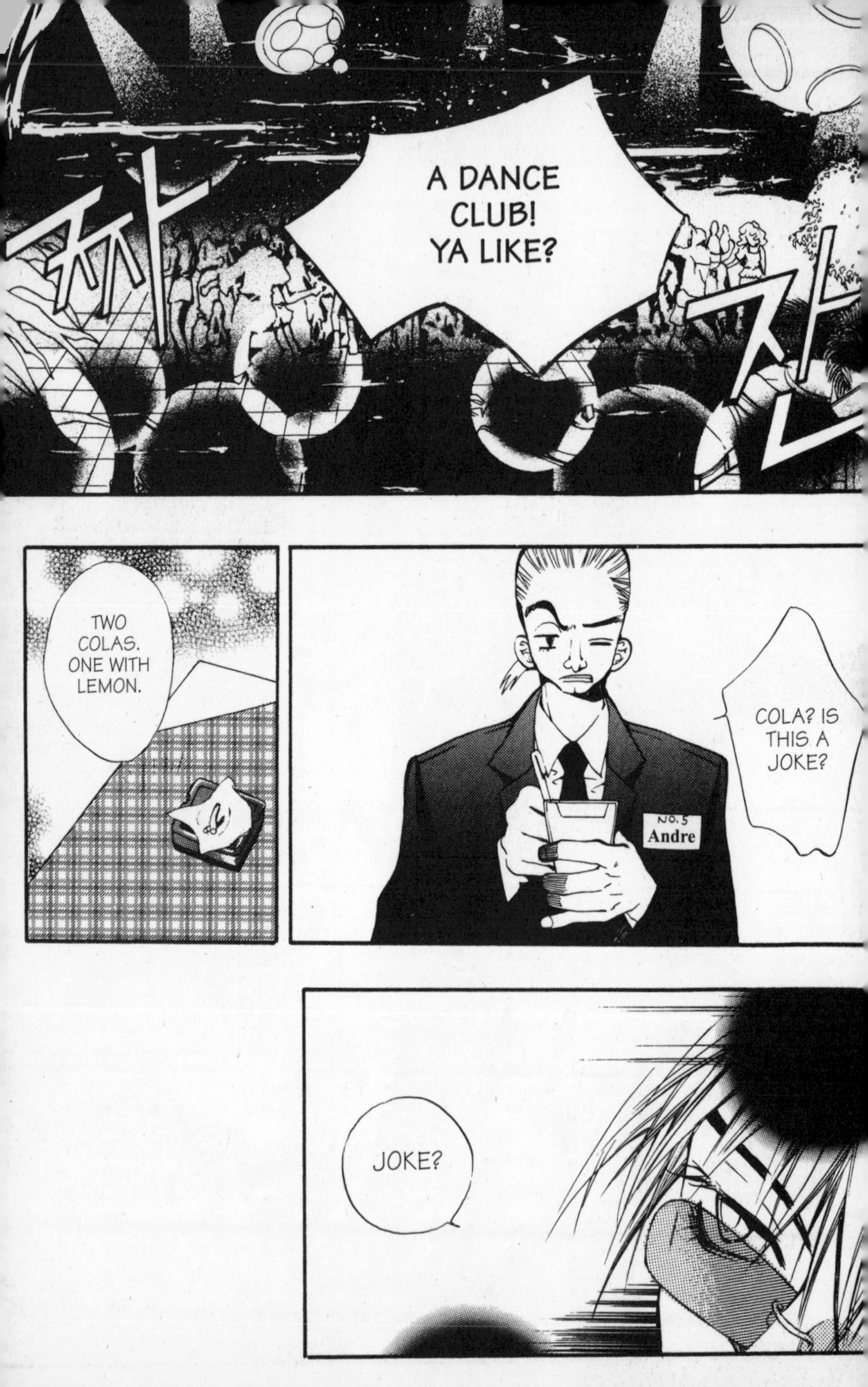
A DANCE CLUB! YA LIKE?
TWO COLAS. ONE WITH LEMON.
NO. 5 Andre
COLA? IS THIS A JOKE?
JOKE?

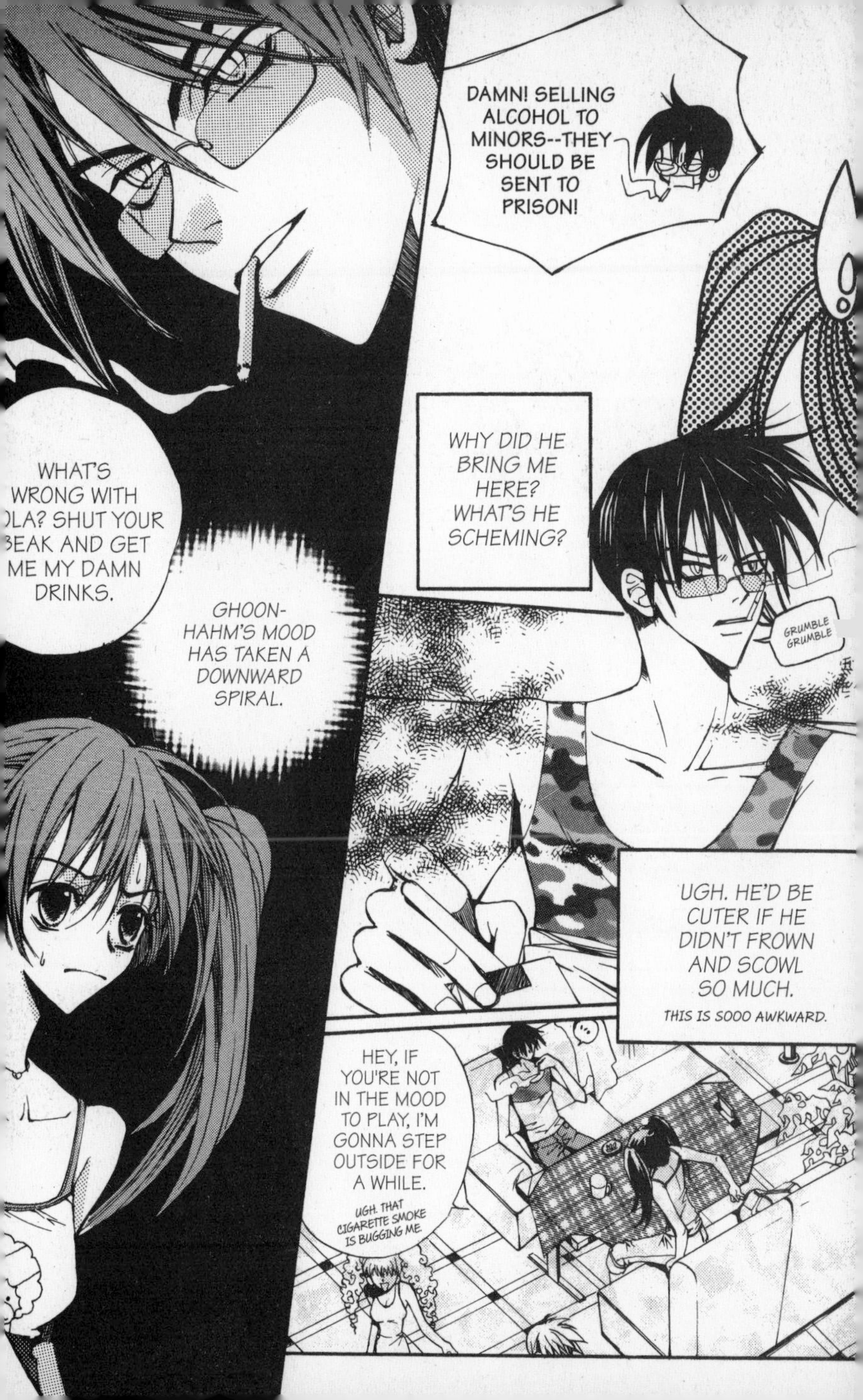
WHAT'S WRONG WITH OLA? SHUT YOUR BEAK AND GET ME MY DAMN DRINKS.
GHOON-HAHM'S MOOD HAS TAKEN A DOWNWARD SPIRAL.
DAMN! SELLING ALCOHOL TO MINORS--THEY SHOULD BE SENT TO PRISON!
WHY DID HE BRING ME HERE? WHAT'S HE SCHEMING?
GRUMBLE GRUMBLE
UGH. HE'D BE CUTER IF HE DIDN'T FROWN AND SCOWL SO MUCH.
THIS IS SOOO AWKWARD.
HEY, IF YOU'RE NOT IN THE MOOD TO PLAY, I'M GONNA STEP OUTSIDE FOR A WHILE.
UGH. THAT CIGARETTE SMOKE IS BUGGING ME.

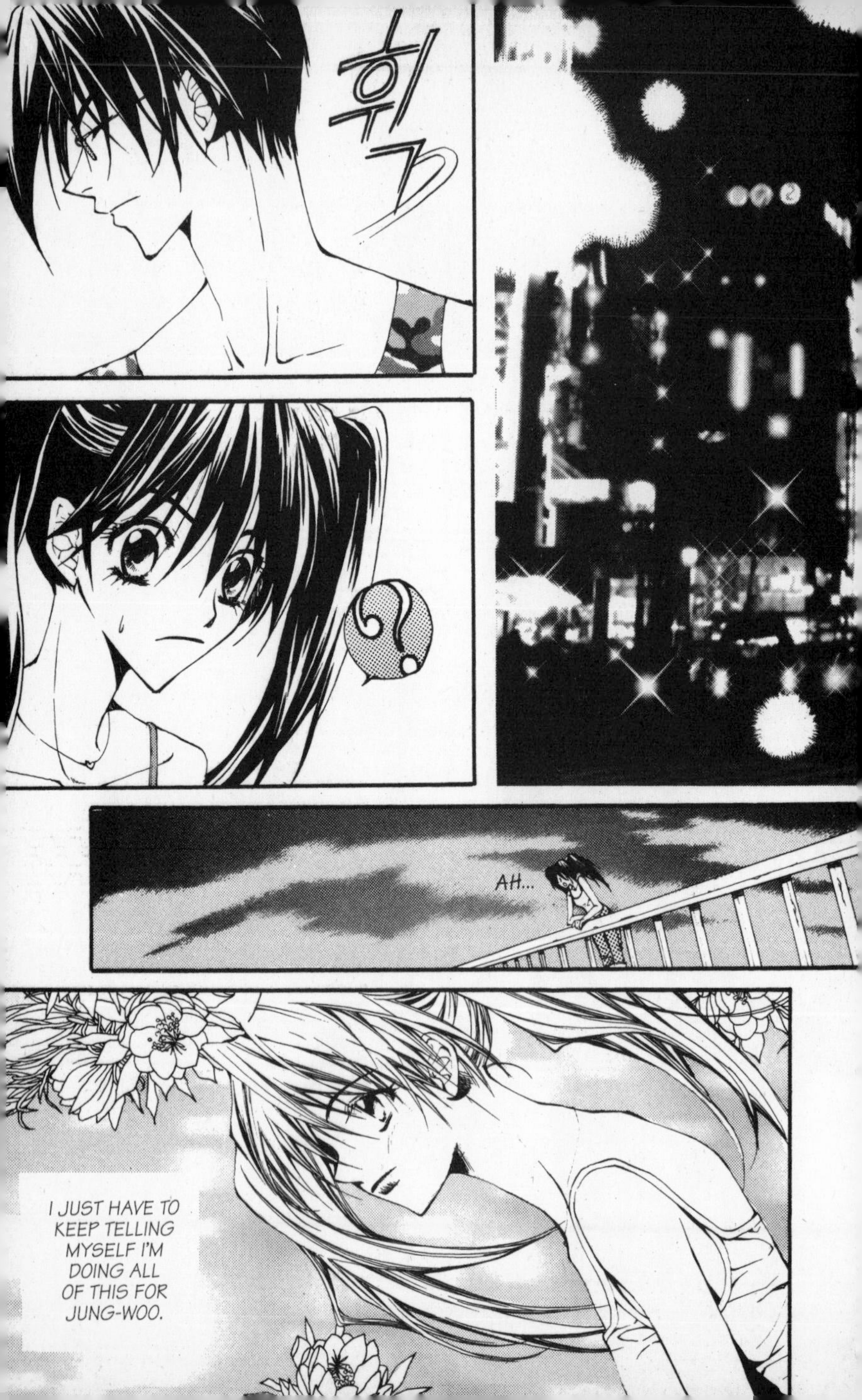
휙
?
AH...
I JUST HAVE TO KEEP TELLING MYSELF I'M DOING ALL OF THIS FOR JUNG-WOO.

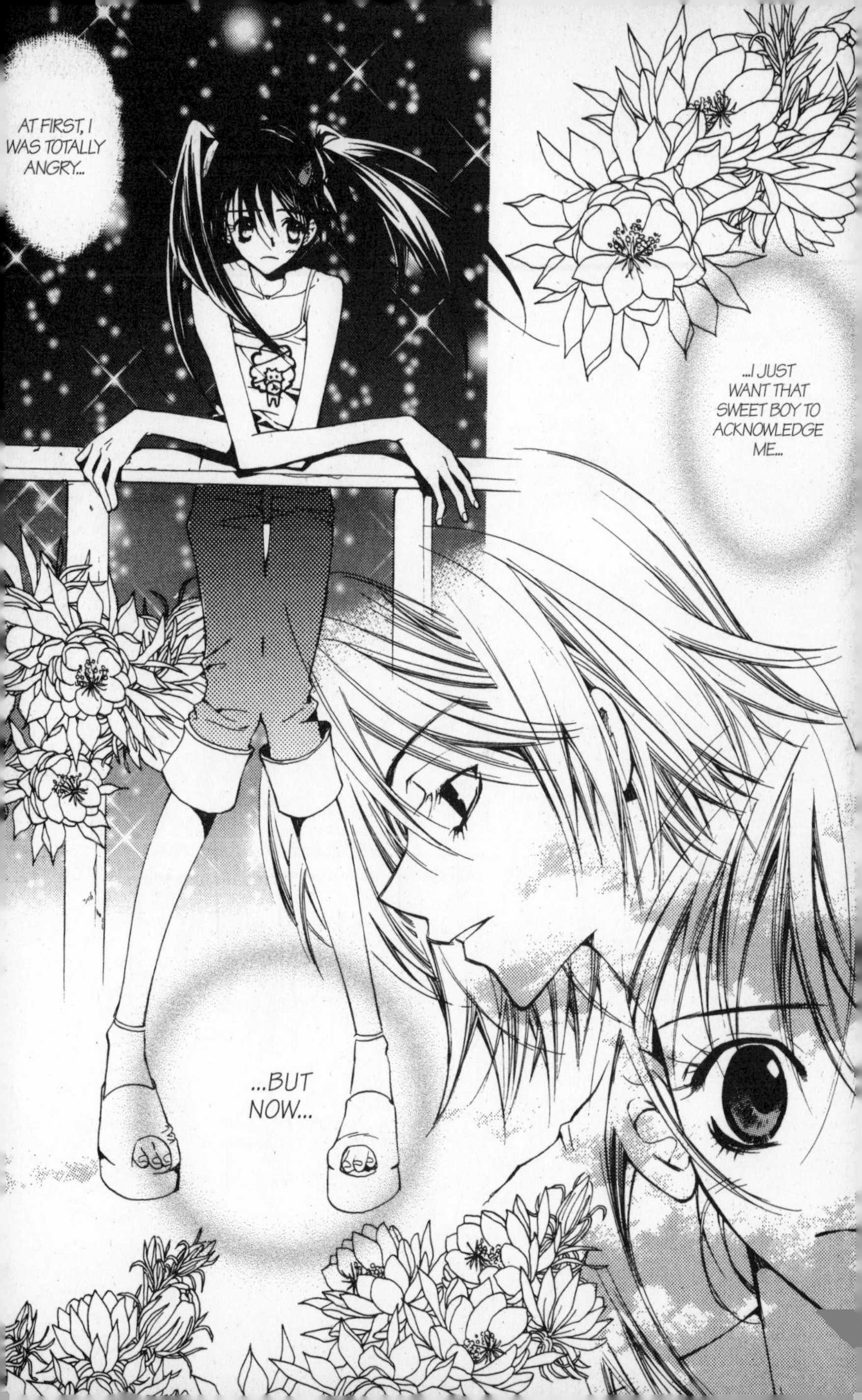
AT FIRST, I WAS TOTALLY ANGRY...
...BUT NOW...
...I JUST WANT THAT SWEET BOY TO ACKNOWLEDGE ME...

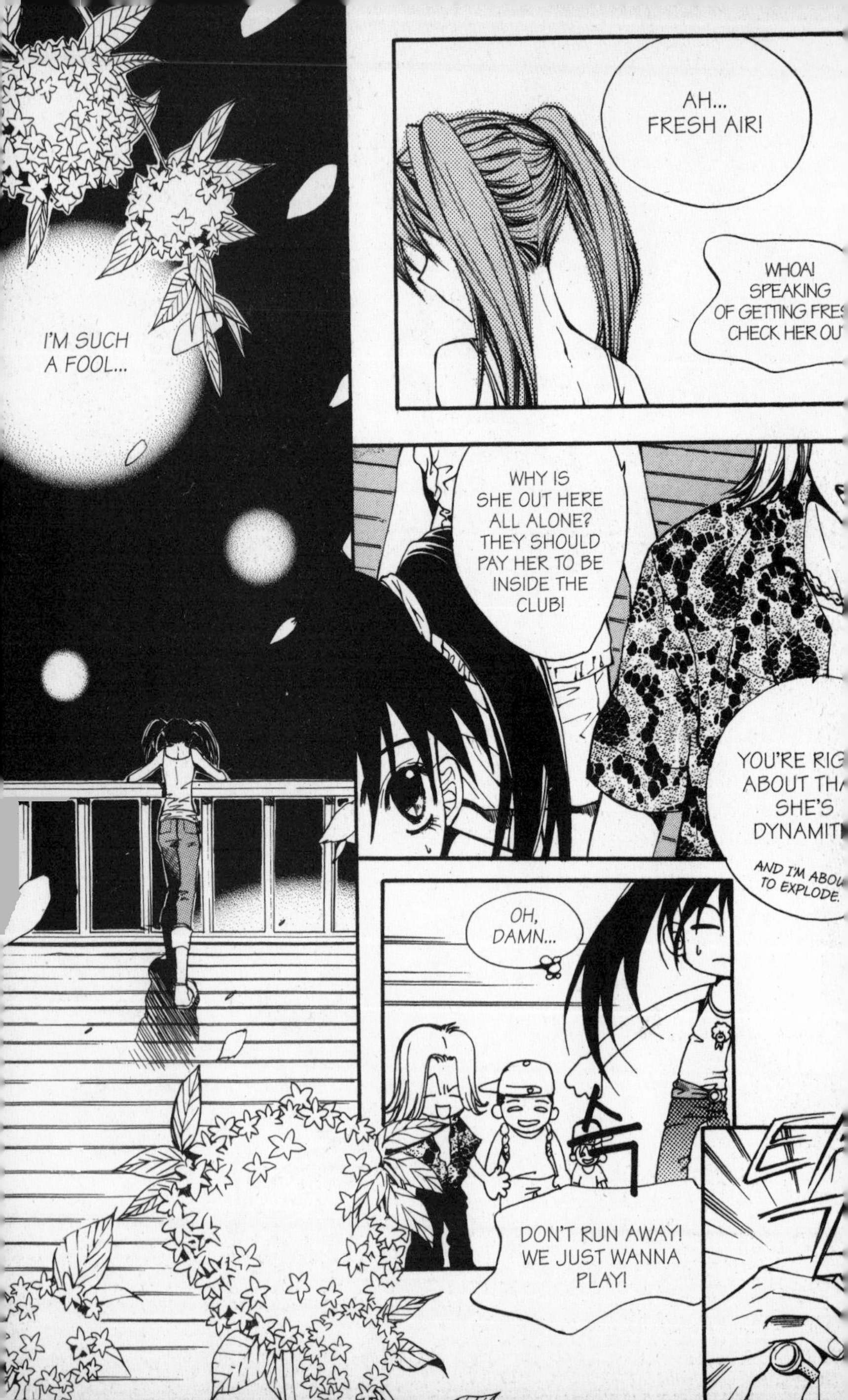
I'M SUCH A FOOL...
AH... FRESH AIR!
WHOA! SPEAKING OF GETTING FRES CHECK HER OU
WHY IS SHE OUT HERE ALL ALONE? THEY SHOULD PAY HER TO BE INSIDE THE CLUB!
YOU'RE RIG ABOUT TH SHE'S DYNAMIT
AND I'M ABOU TO EXPLODE.
OH, DAMN...
DON'T RUN AWAY! WE JUST WANNA PLAY!

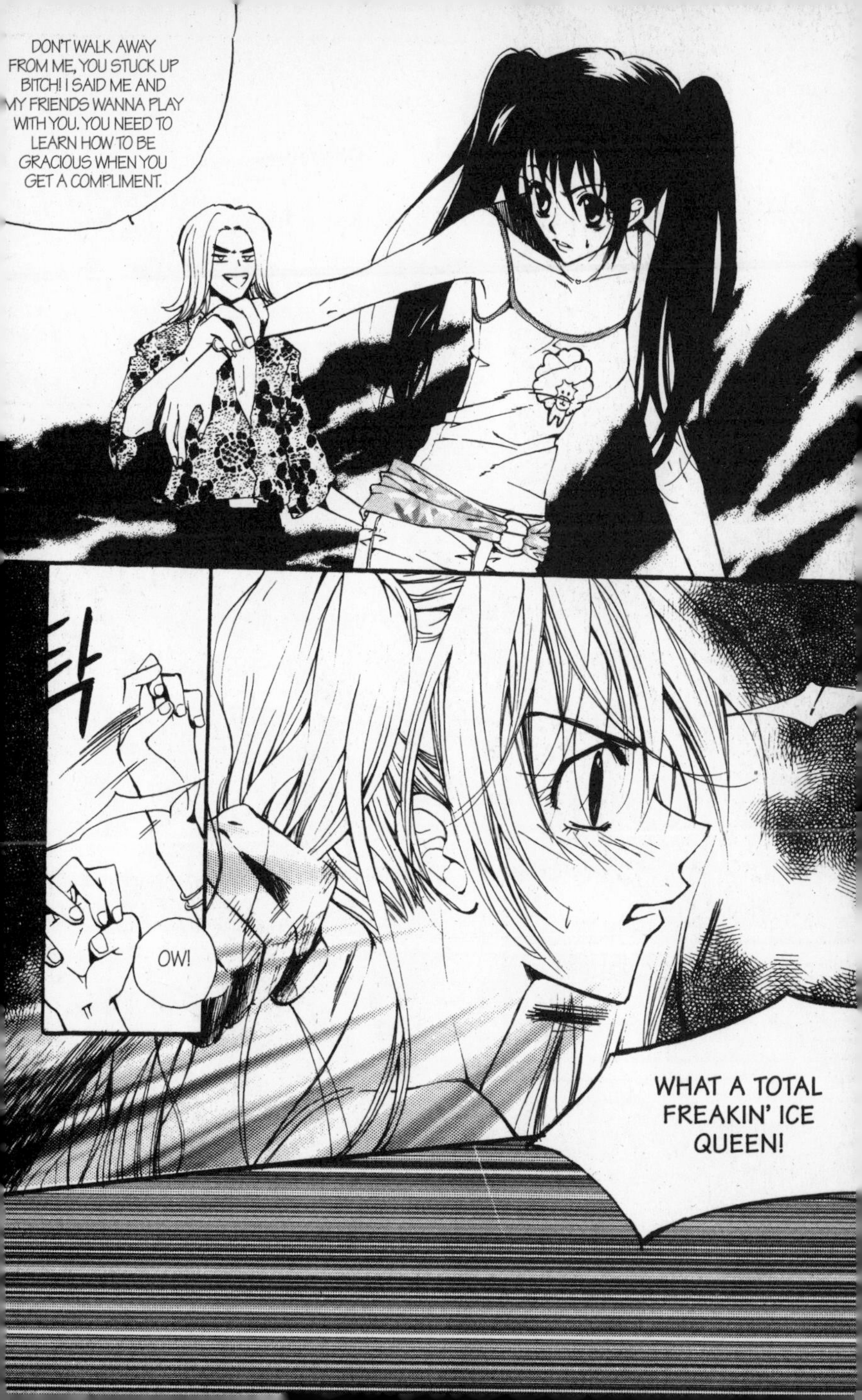
DON'T WALK AWAY FROM ME, YOU STUCK UP BITCH! I SAID ME AND MY FRIENDS WANNA PLAY WITH YOU. YOU NEED TO LEARN HOW TO BE GRACIOUS WHEN YOU GET A COMPLIMENT.
OW!
WHAT A TOTAL FREAKIN' ICE QUEEN!

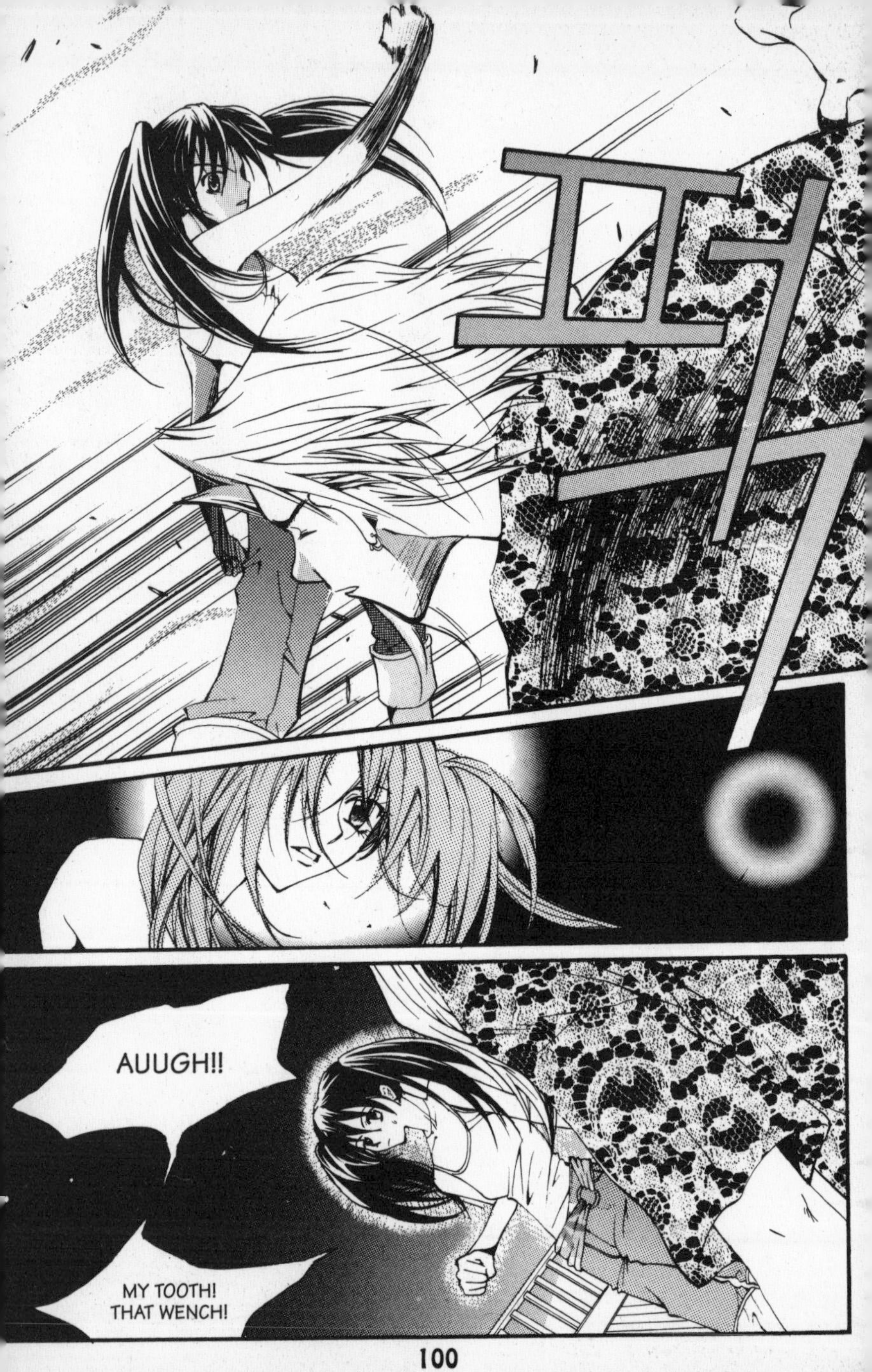

AUUGH!!
MY TOOTH! THAT WENCH!

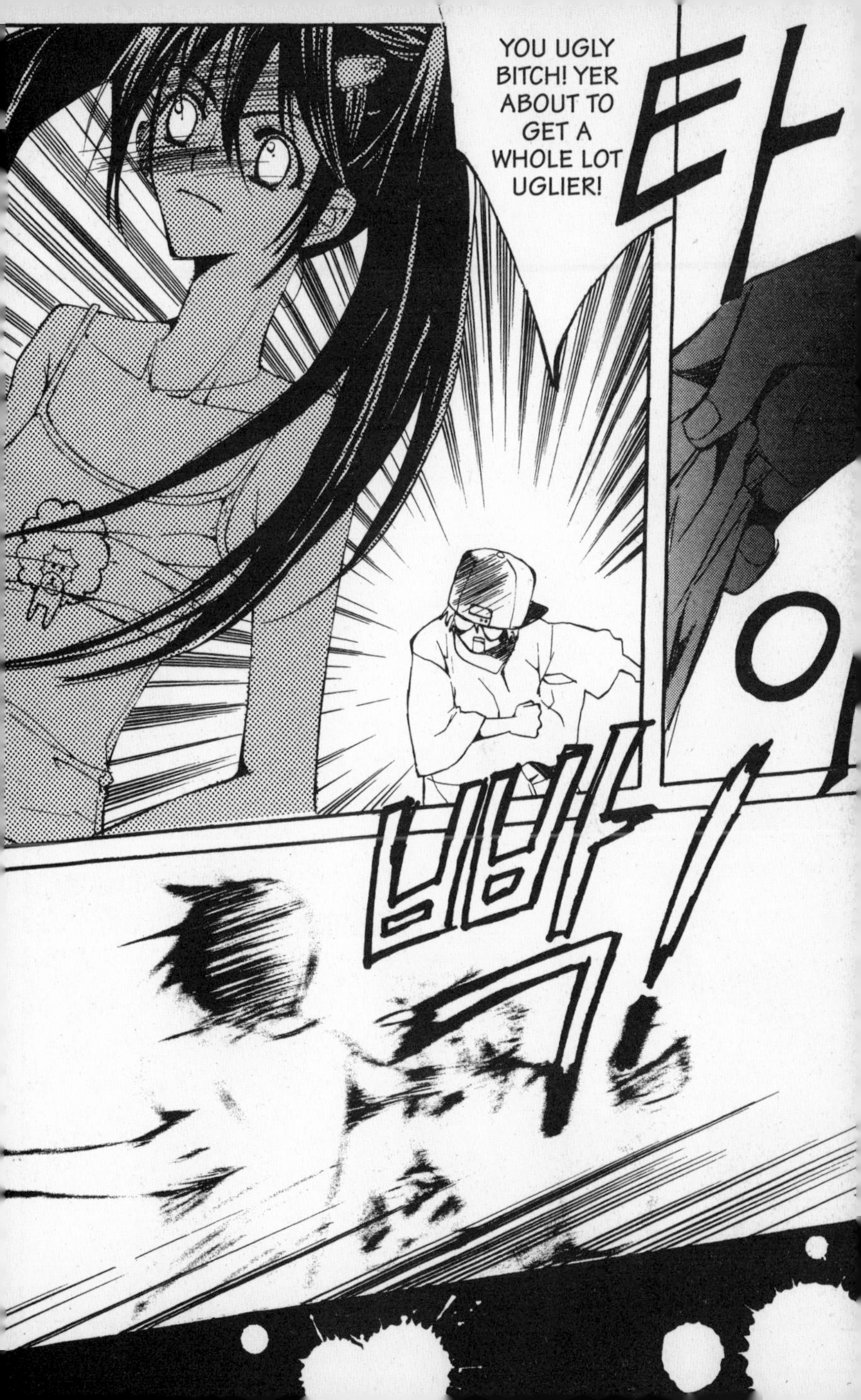
YOU UGLY BITCH! YER ABOUT TO GET A WHOLE LOT UGLIER!

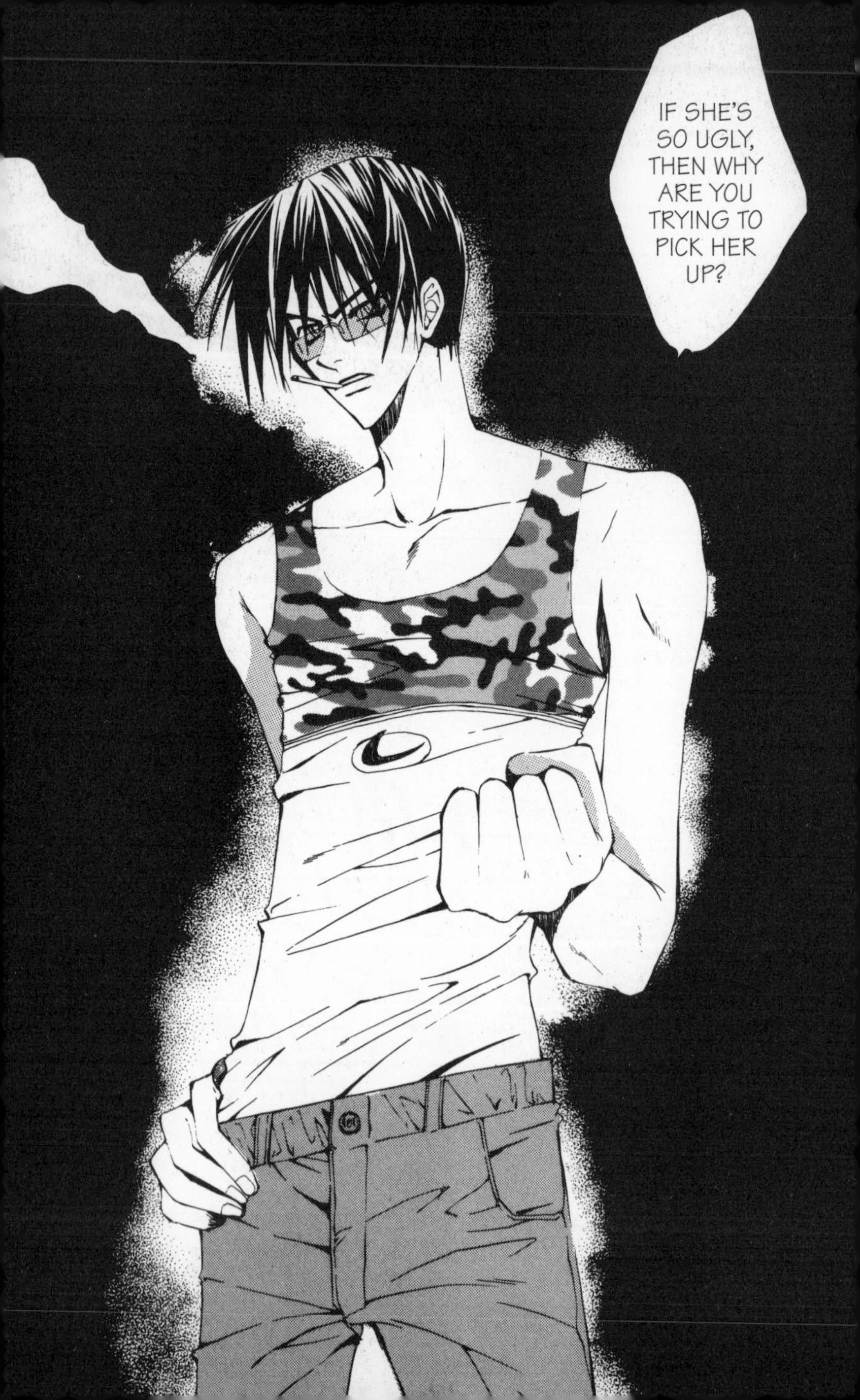
IF SHE'S SO UGLY, THEN WHY ARE YOU TRYING TO PICK HER UP?

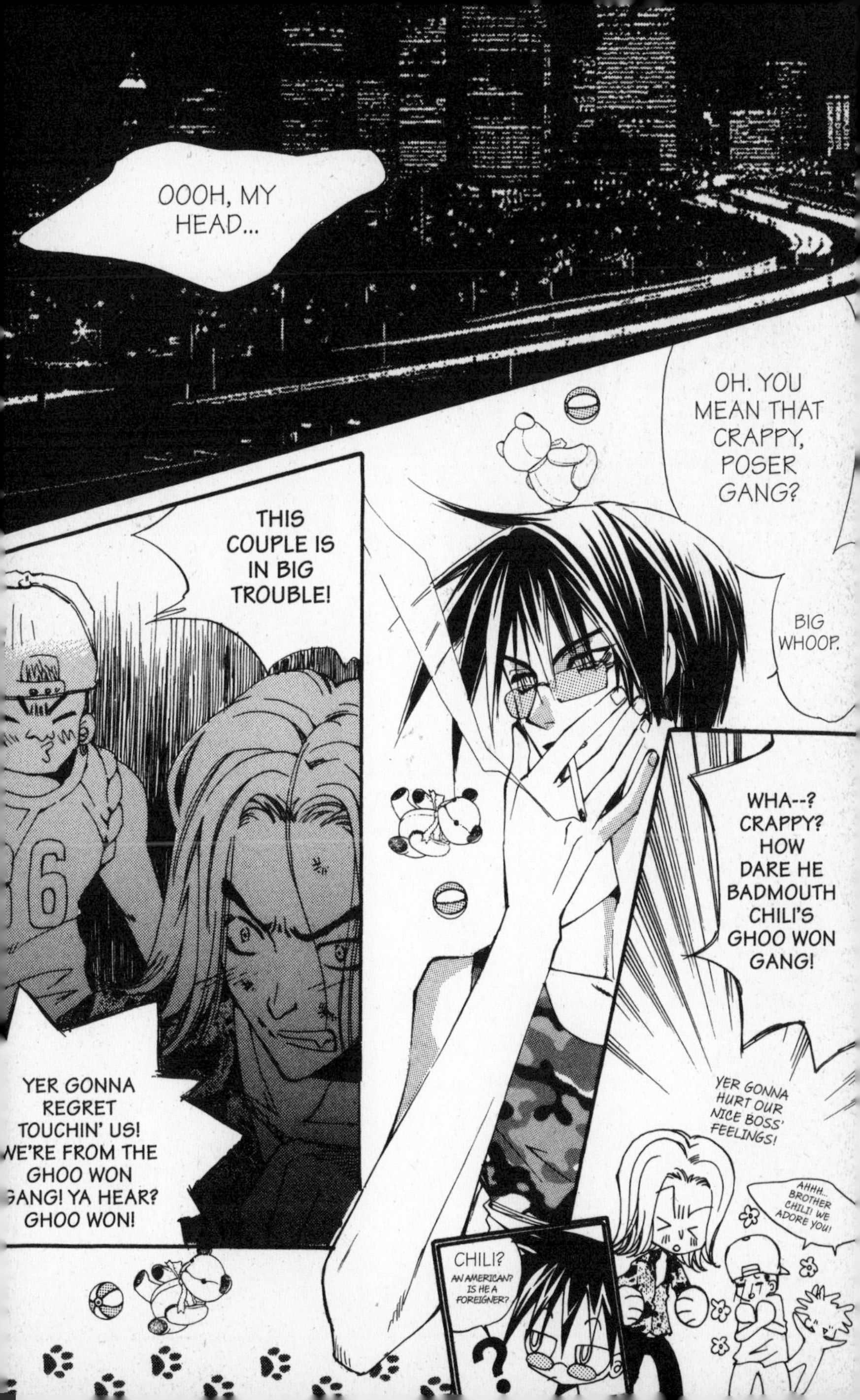
OOOH, MY HEAD...
THIS COUPLE IS IN BIG TROUBLE!
YER GONNA REGRET TOUCHIN' US! WE'RE FROM THE GHOO WON GANG! YA HEAR? GHOO WON!
OH. YOU MEAN THAT CRAPPY, POSER GANG?
BIG WHOOP.
WHA--? CRAPPY? HOW DARE HE BADMOUTH CHILI'S GHOO WON GANG!
YER GONNA HURT OUR NICE BOSS' FEELINGS!
AHHH... BROTHER CHILI! WE ADORE YOU!
CHILI?
AN AMERICAN? IS HE A FOREIGNER?

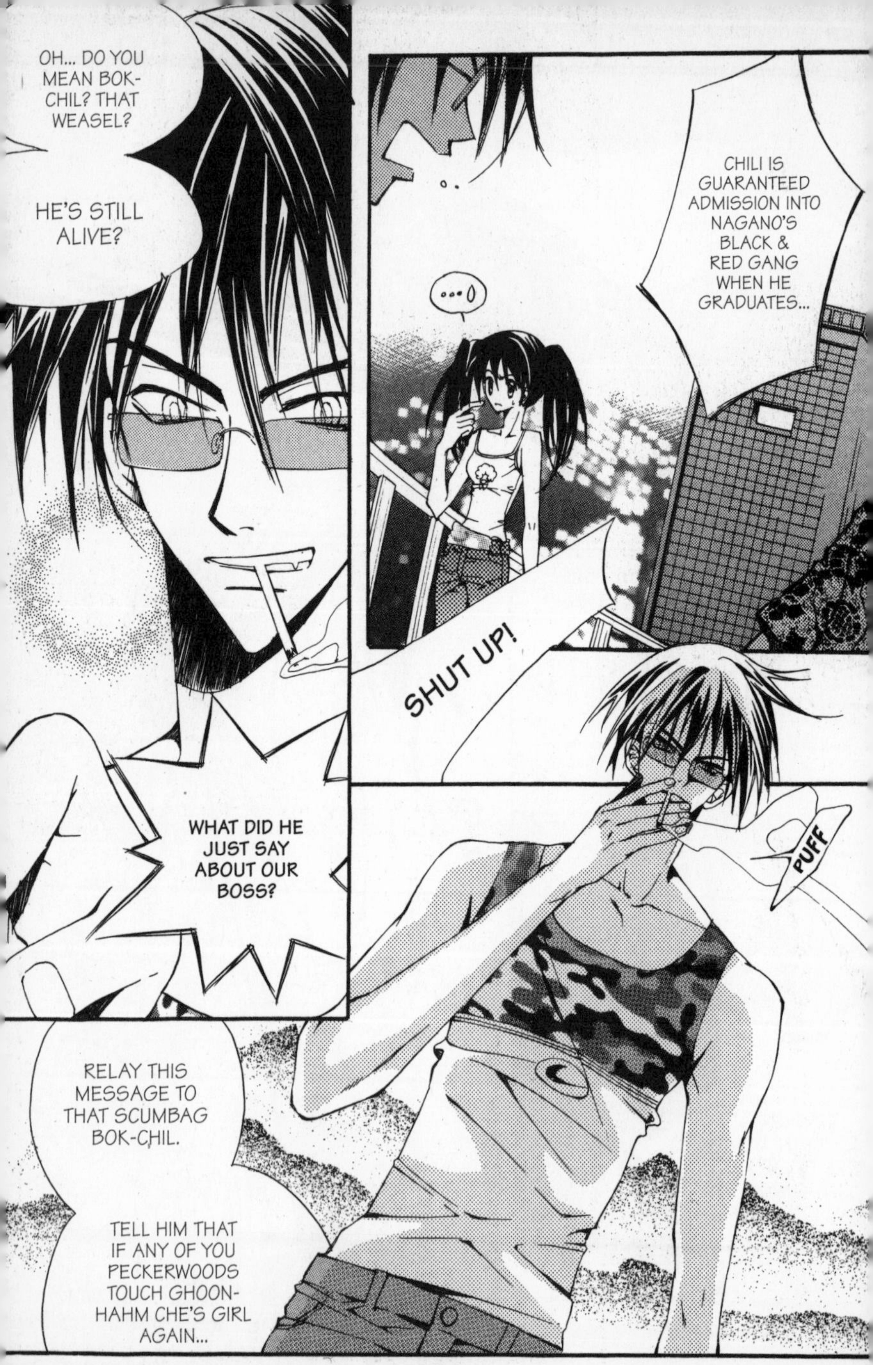

OH... DO YOU MEAN BOK-CHIL? THAT WEASEL?
HE'S STILL ALIVE?
WHAT DID HE JUST SAY ABOUT OUR BOSS?
CHILI IS GUARANTEED ADMISSION INTO NAGANO'S BLACK & RED GANG WHEN HE GRADUATES...
...
SHUT UP!
PUFF
RELAY THIS MESSAGE TO THAT SCUMBAG BOK-CHIL.
TELL HIM THAT IF ANY OF YOU PECKERWOODS TOUCH GHOON-HAHM CHE'S GIRL AGAIN...

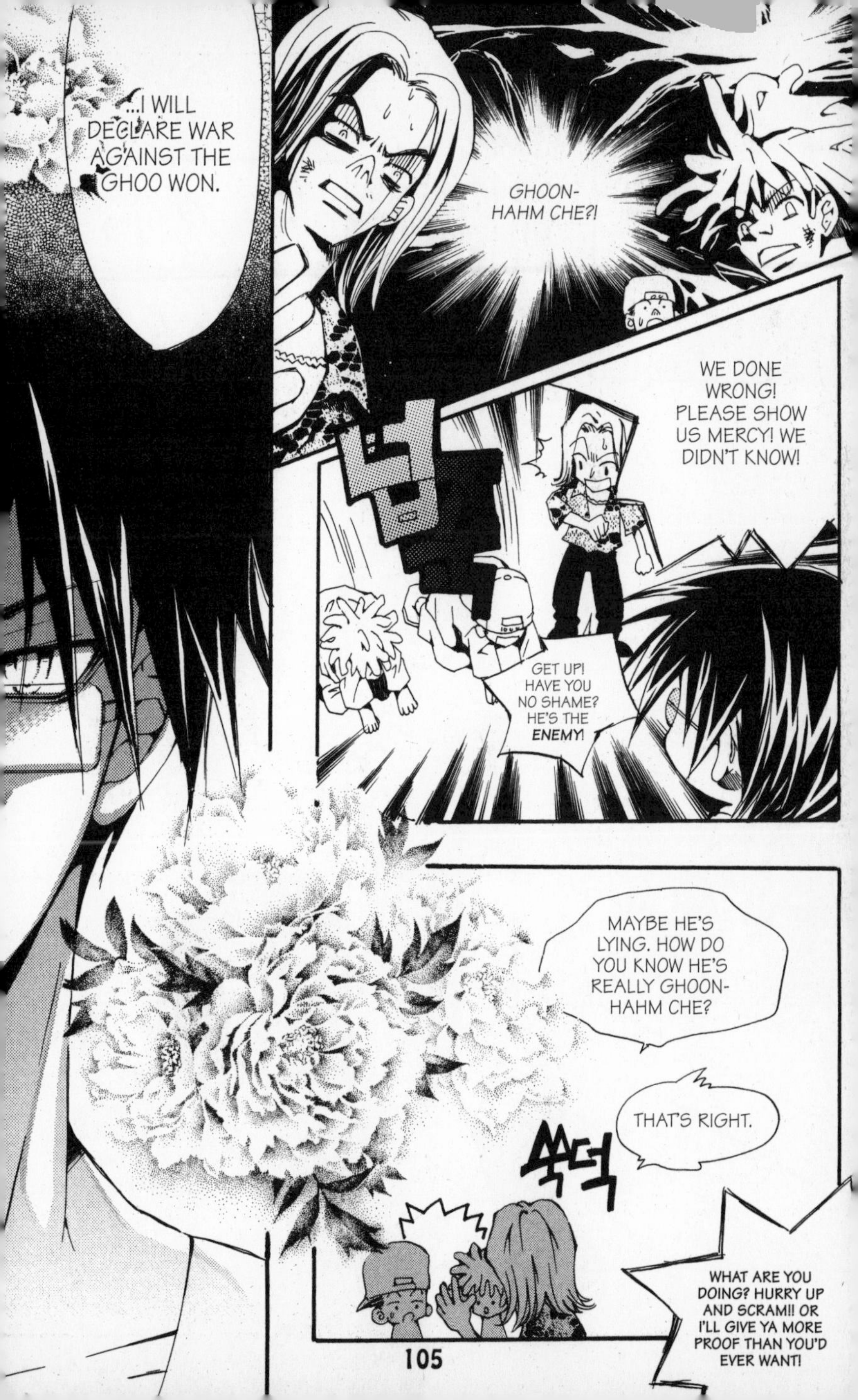
...I WILL DECLARE WAR AGAINST THE GHOO WON.
GHOON-HAHM CHE?!
WE DONE WRONG! PLEASE SHOW US MERCY! WE DIDN'T KNOW!
GET UP! HAVE YOU NO SHAME? HE'S THE ENEMY!
MAYBE HE'S LYING. HOW DO YOU KNOW HE'S REALLY GHOON-HAHM CHE?
THAT'S RIGHT.
WHAT ARE YOU DOING? HURRY UP AND SCRAM!! OR I'LL GIVE YA MORE PROOF THAN YOU'D EVER WANT!

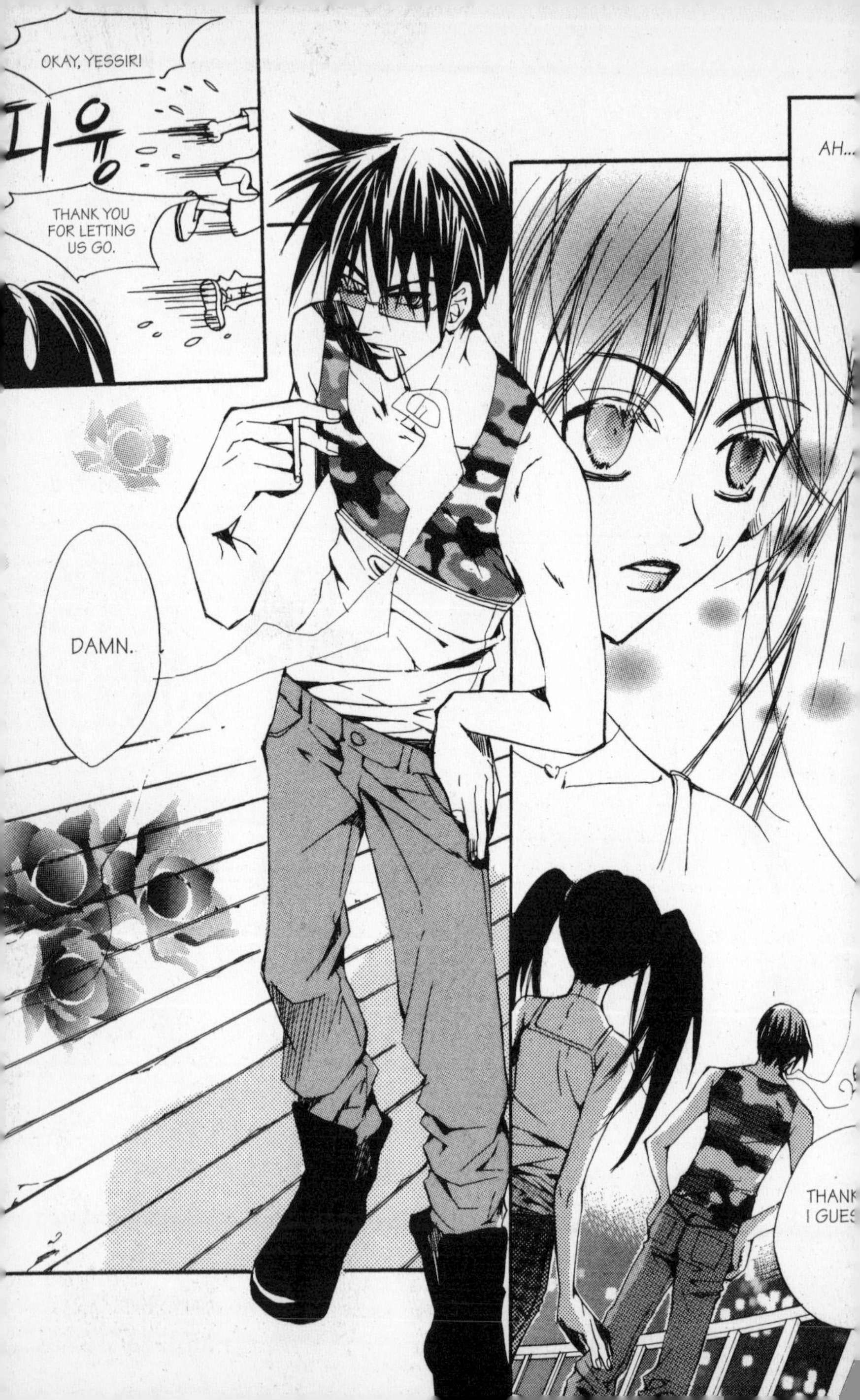

OKAY, YESSIR!
피웅
THANK YOU FOR LETTING US GO.
DAMN.
AH...
THANK
I GUES

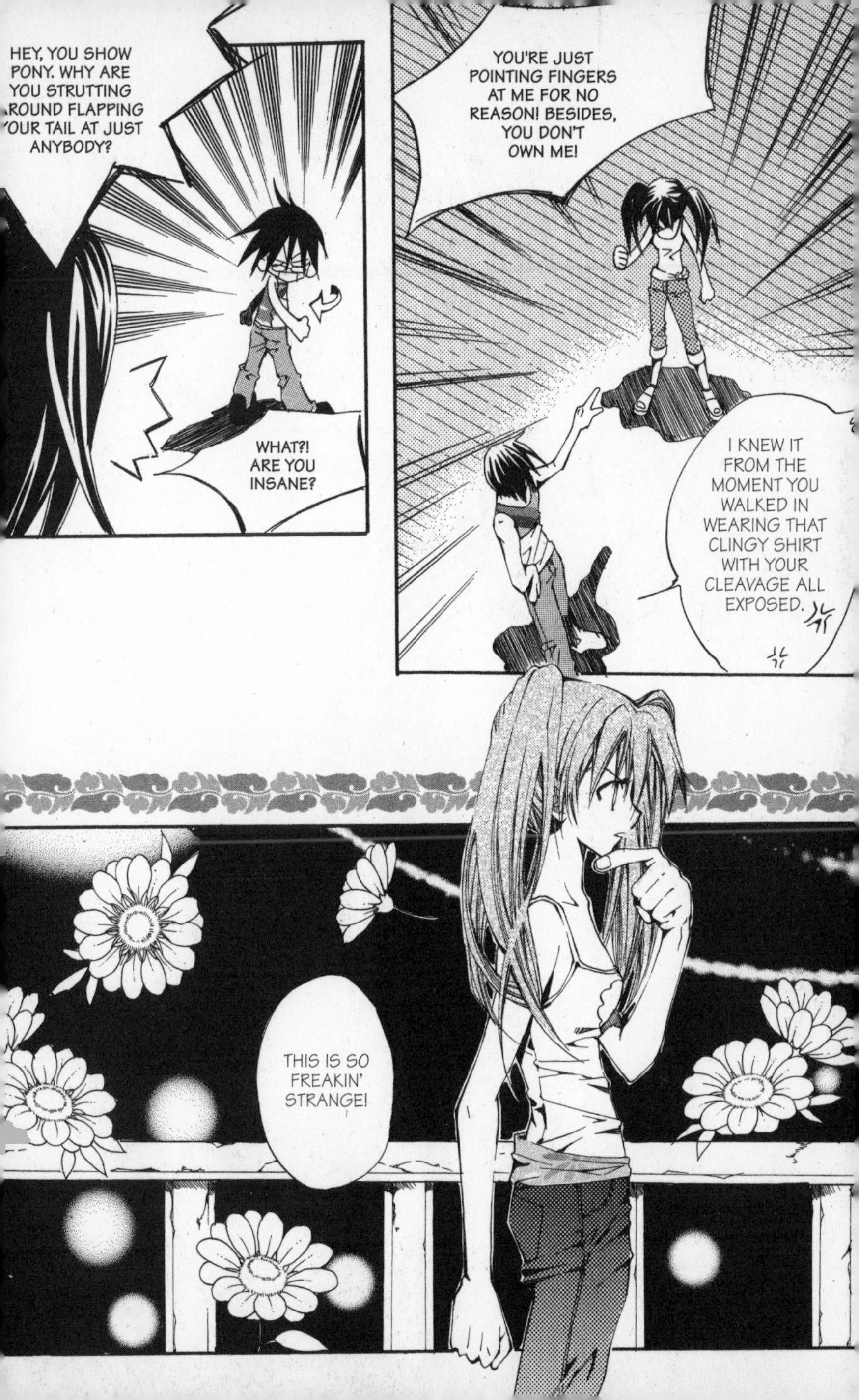
HEY, YOU SHOW PONY. WHY ARE YOU STRUTTING AROUND FLAPPING YOUR TAIL AT JUST ANYBODY?
WHAT?! ARE YOU INSANE?
YOU'RE JUST POINTING FINGERS AT ME FOR NO REASON! BESIDES, YOU DON'T OWN ME!
I KNEW IT FROM THE MOMENT YOU WALKED IN WEARING THAT CLINGY SHIRT WITH YOUR CLEAVAGE ALL EXPOSED.
THIS IS SO FREAKIN' STRANGE!

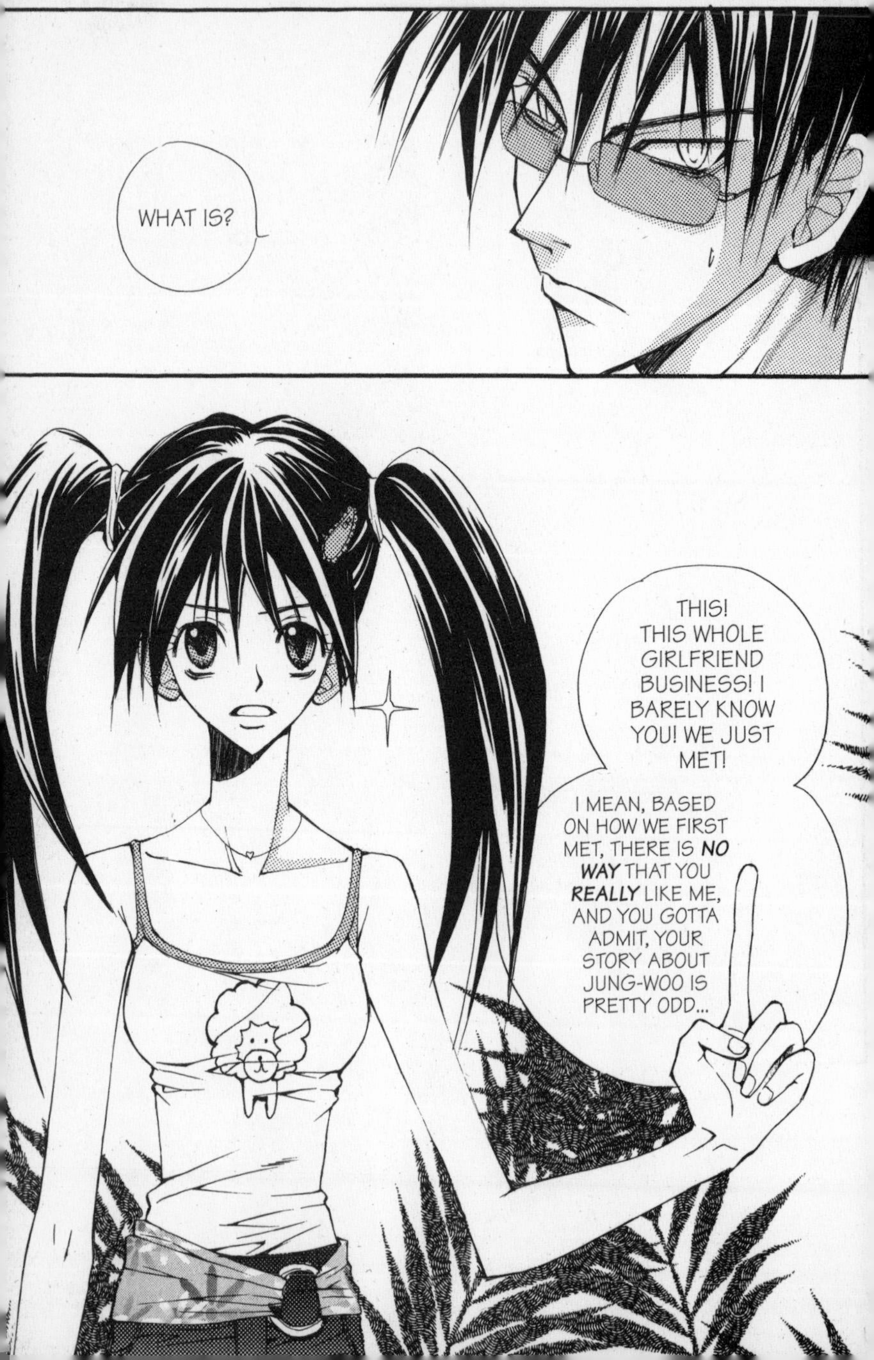
WHAT IS?
THIS! THIS WHOLE GIRLFRIEND BUSINESS! I BARELY KNOW YOU! WE JUST MET!
I MEAN, BASED ON HOW WE FIRST MET, THERE IS **NO WAY** THAT YOU **REALLY** LIKE ME, AND YOU GOTTA ADMIT, YOUR STORY ABOUT JUNG-WOO IS PRETTY ODD...

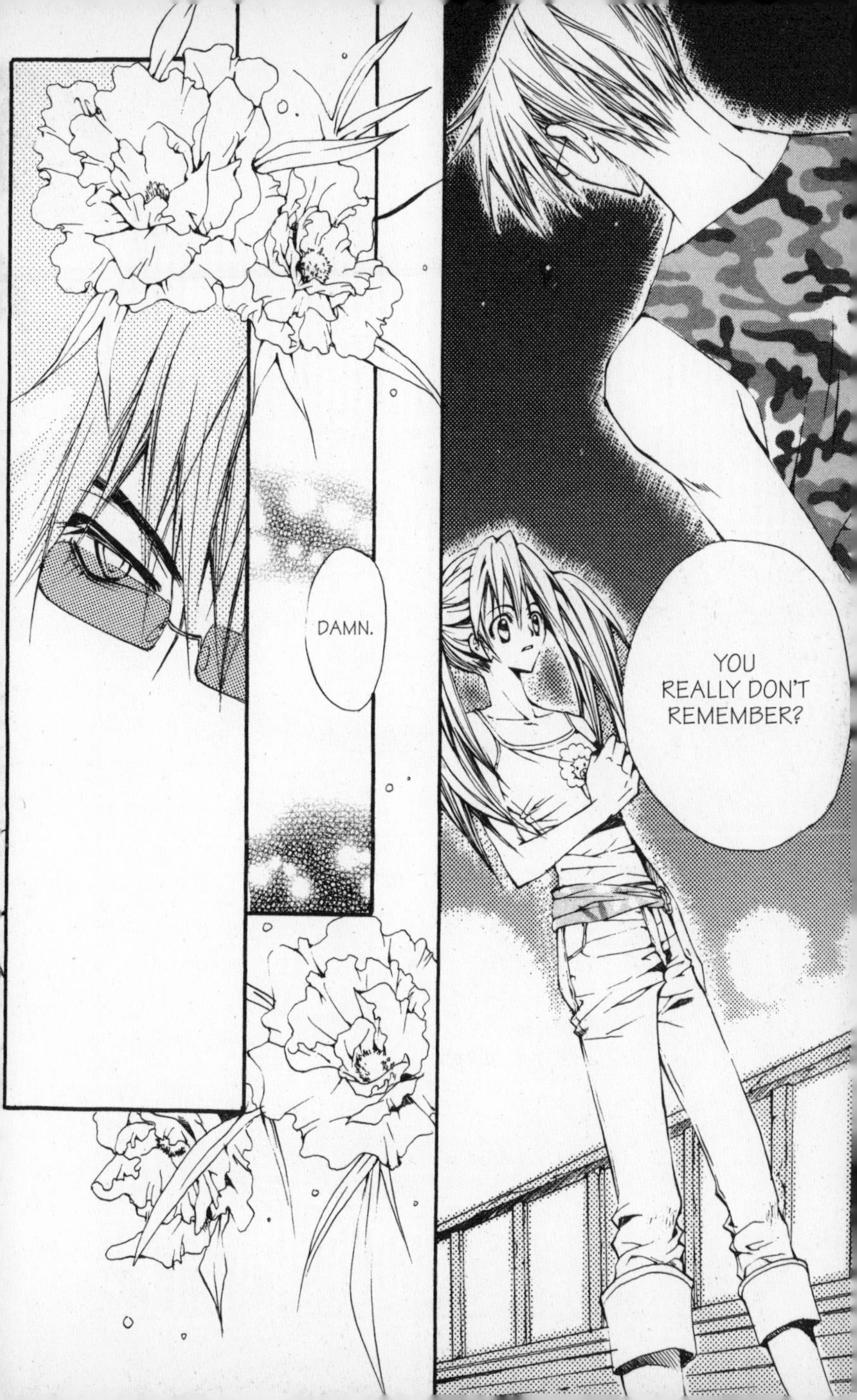
DAMN.
YOU REALLY DON'T REMEMBER?

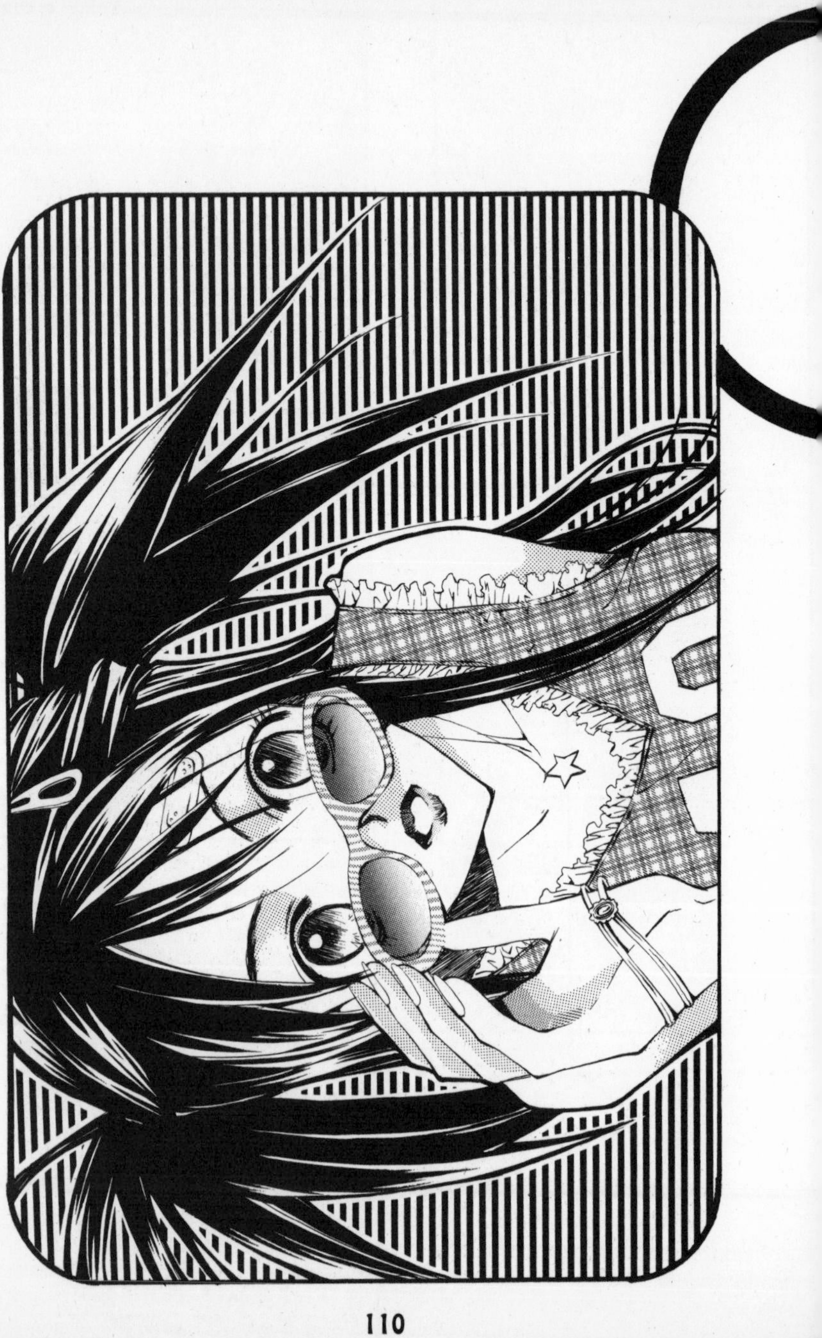

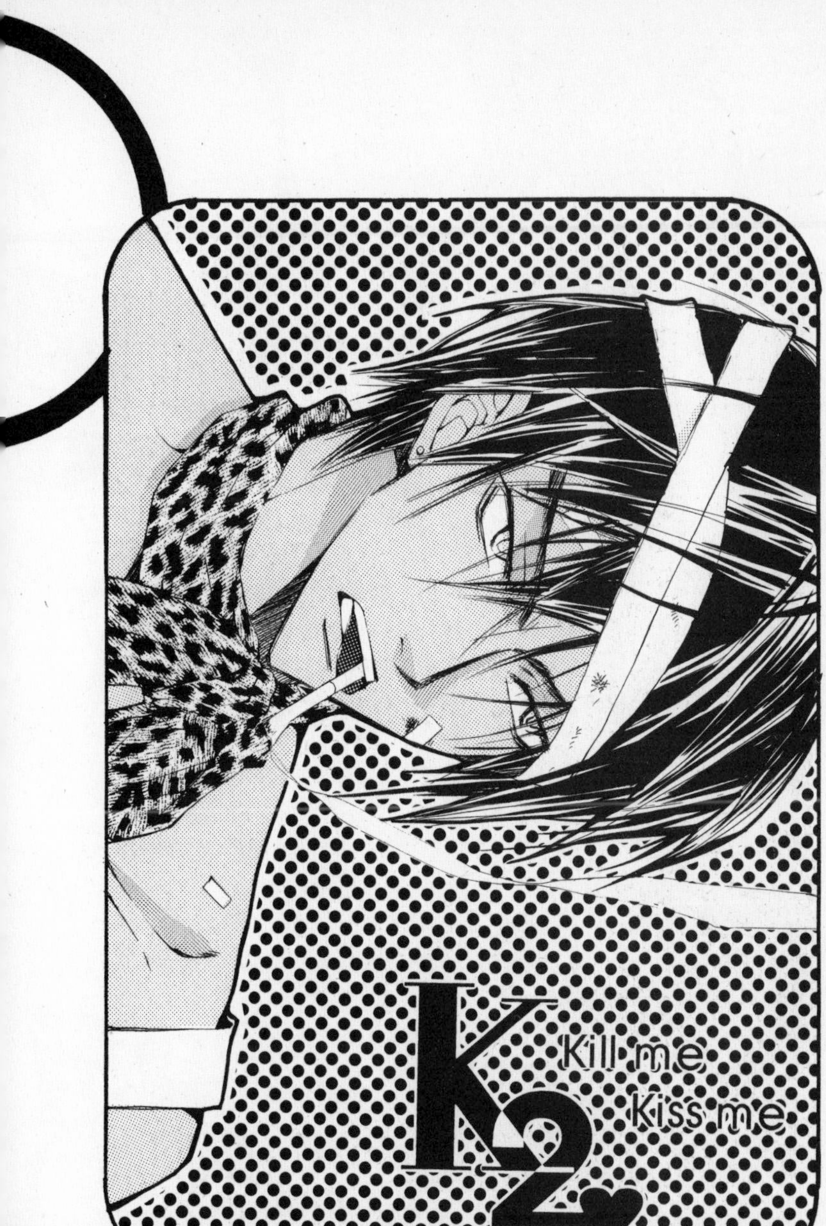
K2
Kill me
Kiss me

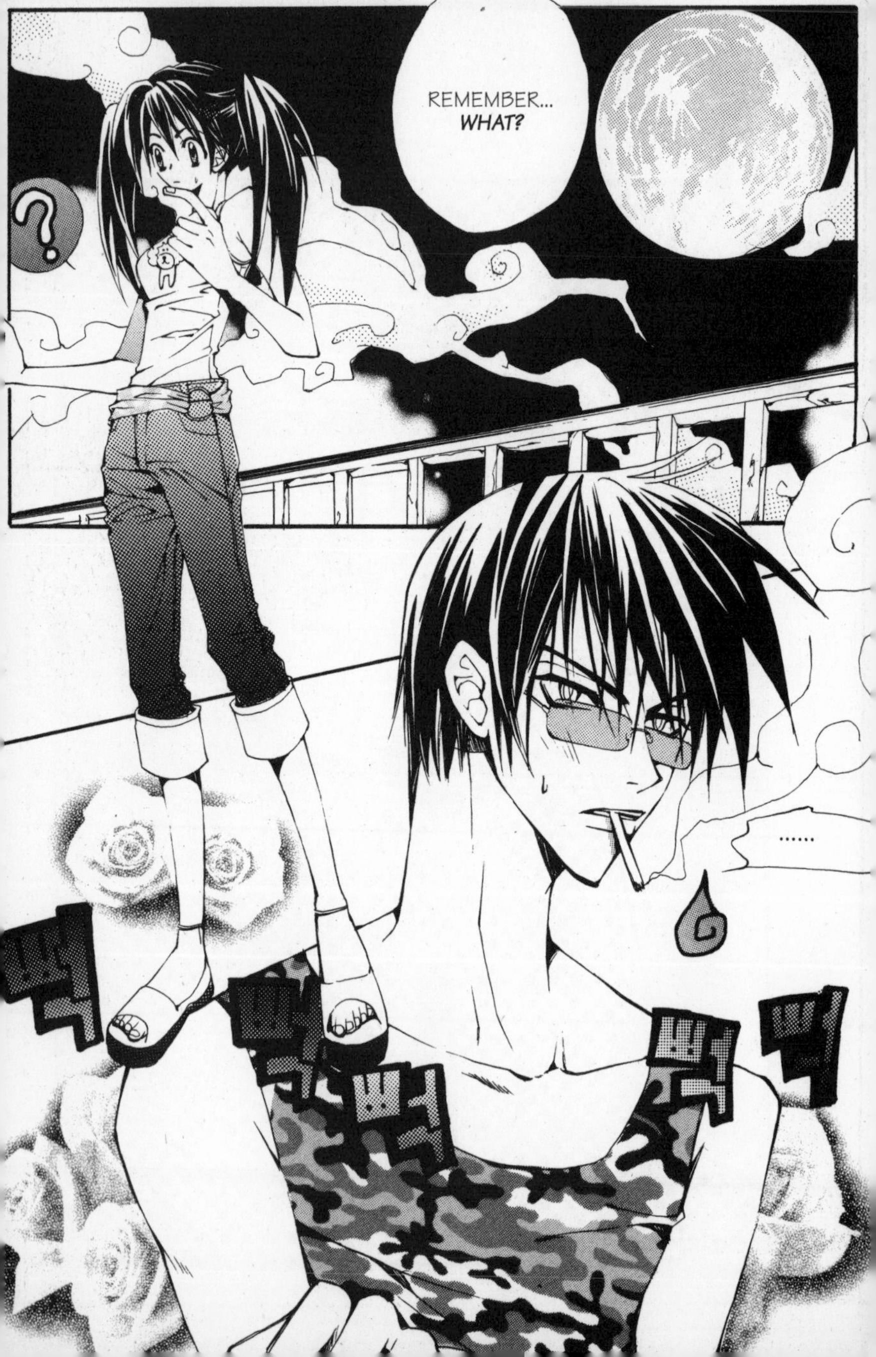
REMEMBER...
WHAT?
......

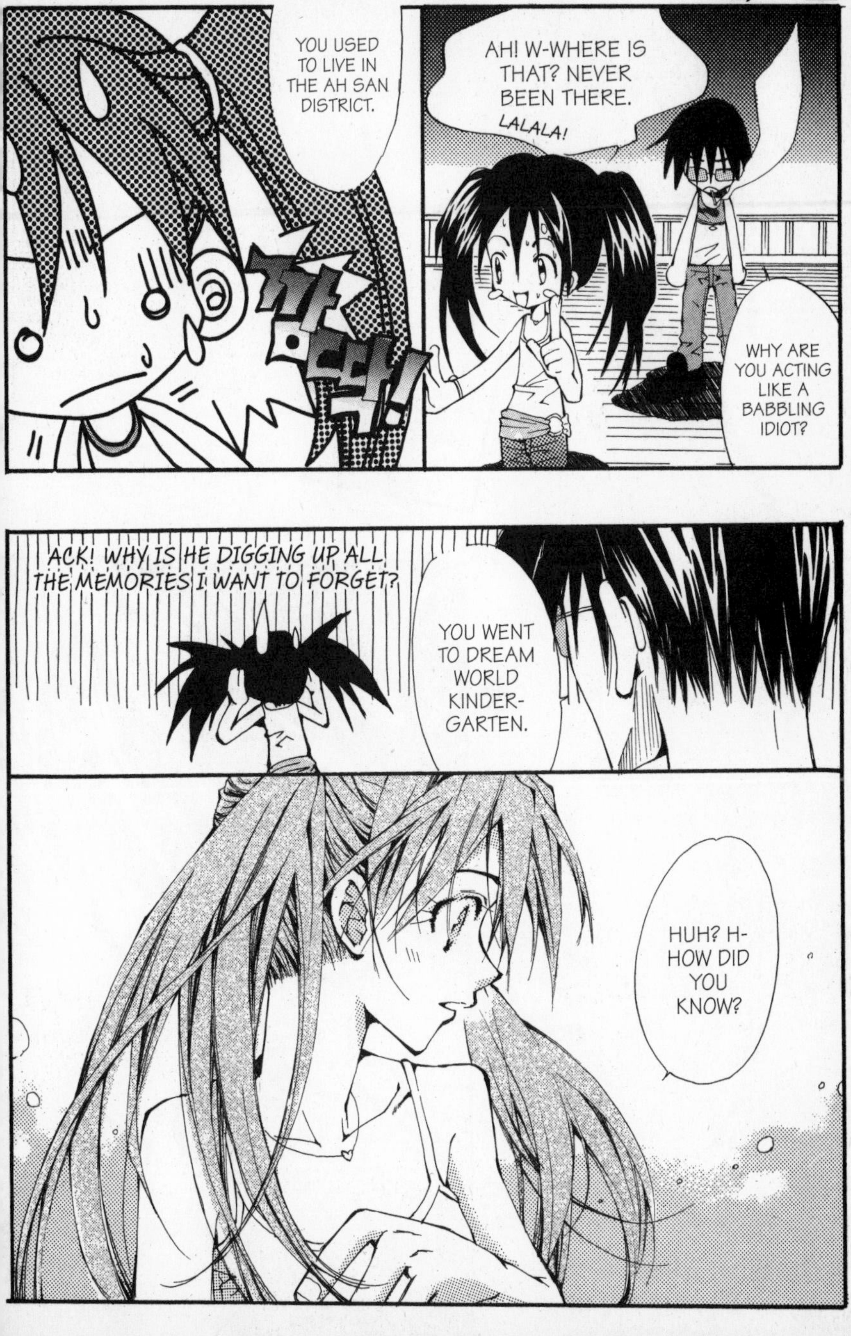
YOU USED TO LIVE IN THE AH SAN DISTRICT.
AH! W-WHERE IS THAT? NEVER BEEN THERE.
LALALA!
WHY ARE YOU ACTING LIKE A BABBLING IDIOT?
ACK! WHY IS HE DIGGING UP ALL THE MEMORIES I WANT TO FORGET?
YOU WENT TO DREAM WORLD KINDER-GARTEN.
HUH? H-HOW DID YOU KNOW?

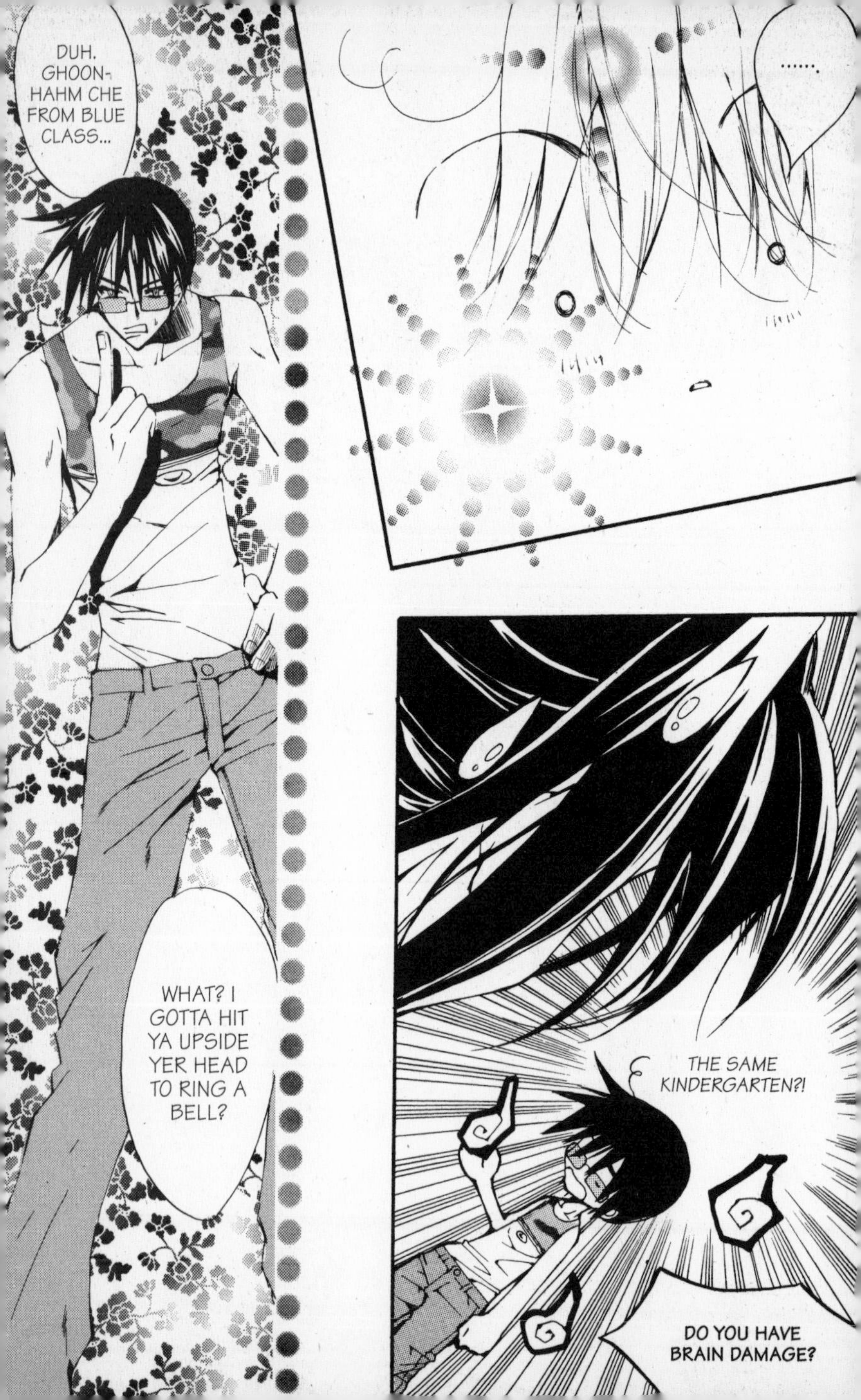
DUH. GHOON-HAHM CHE FROM BLUE CLASS...
WHAT? I GOTTA HIT YA UPSIDE YER HEAD TO RING A BELL?
......
THE SAME KINDERGARTEN?!
DO YOU HAVE BRAIN DAMAGE?

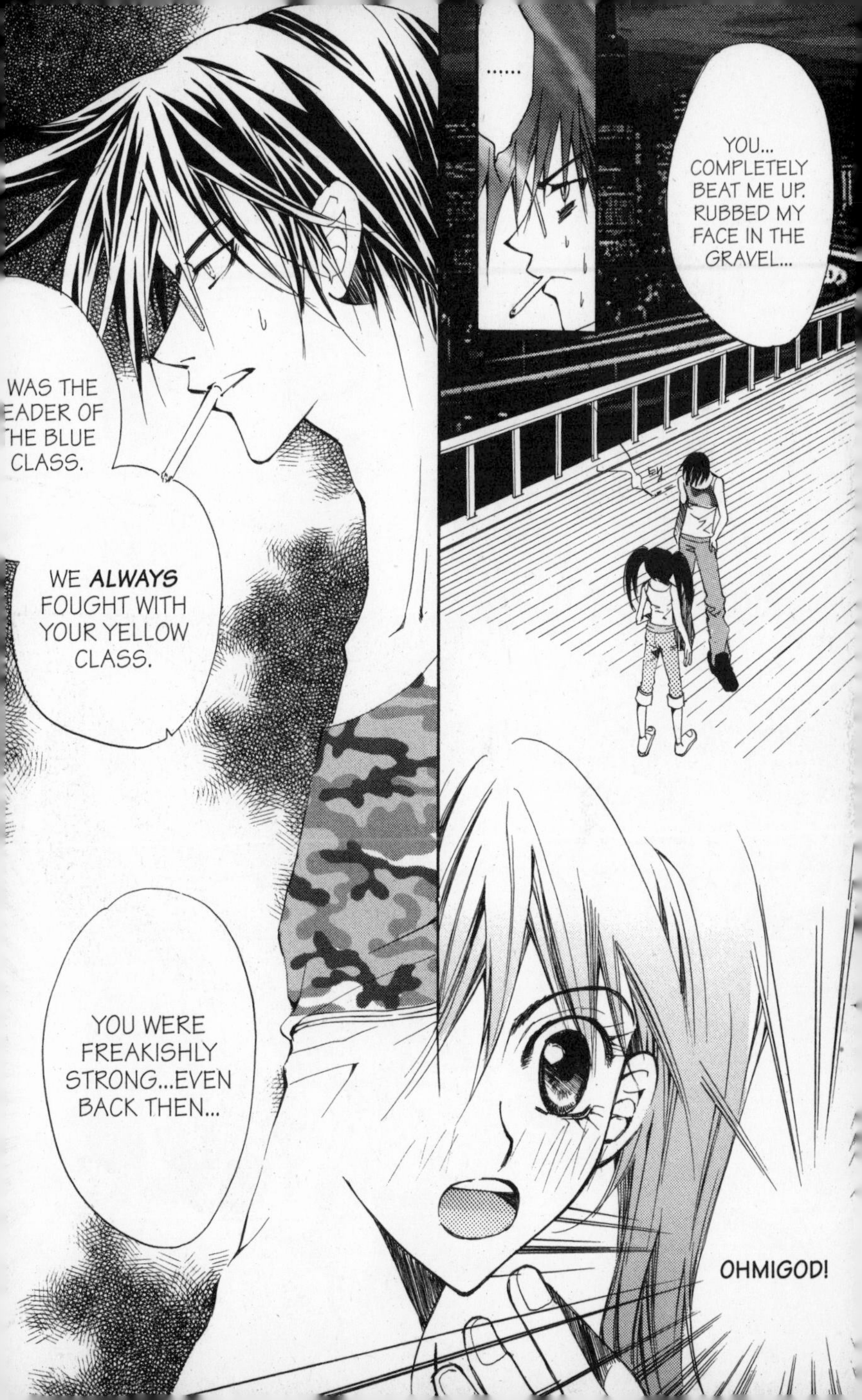
WAS THE EADER OF HE BLUE CLASS.
WE **ALWAYS** FOUGHT WITH YOUR YELLOW CLASS.
YOU WERE FREAKISHLY STRONG...EVEN BACK THEN...
......
YOU... COMPLETELY BEAT ME UP. RUBBED MY FACE IN THE GRAVEL...
OHMIGOD!

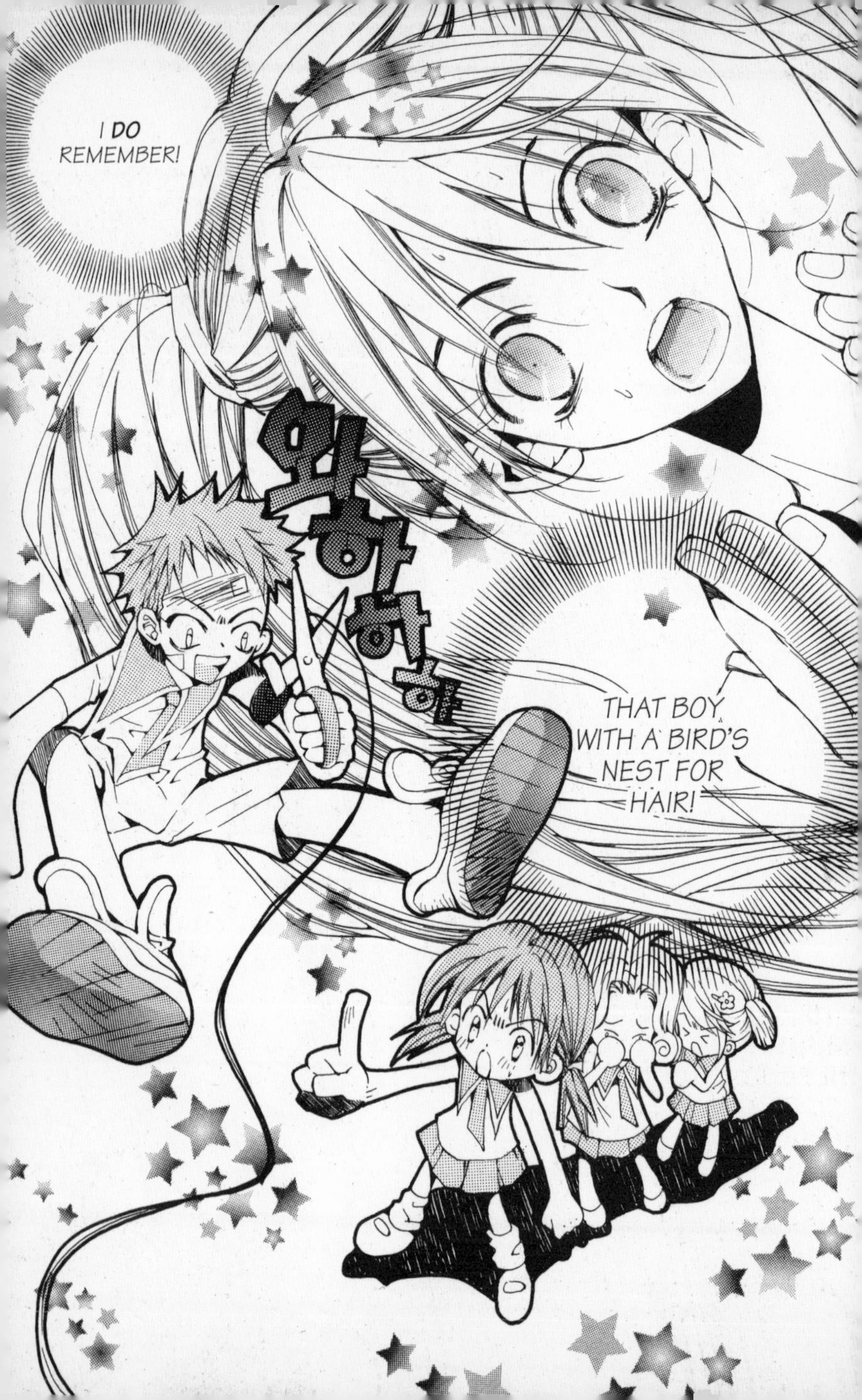
I DO REMEMBER!
와하하하
THAT BOY WITH A BIRD'S NEST FOR HAIR!

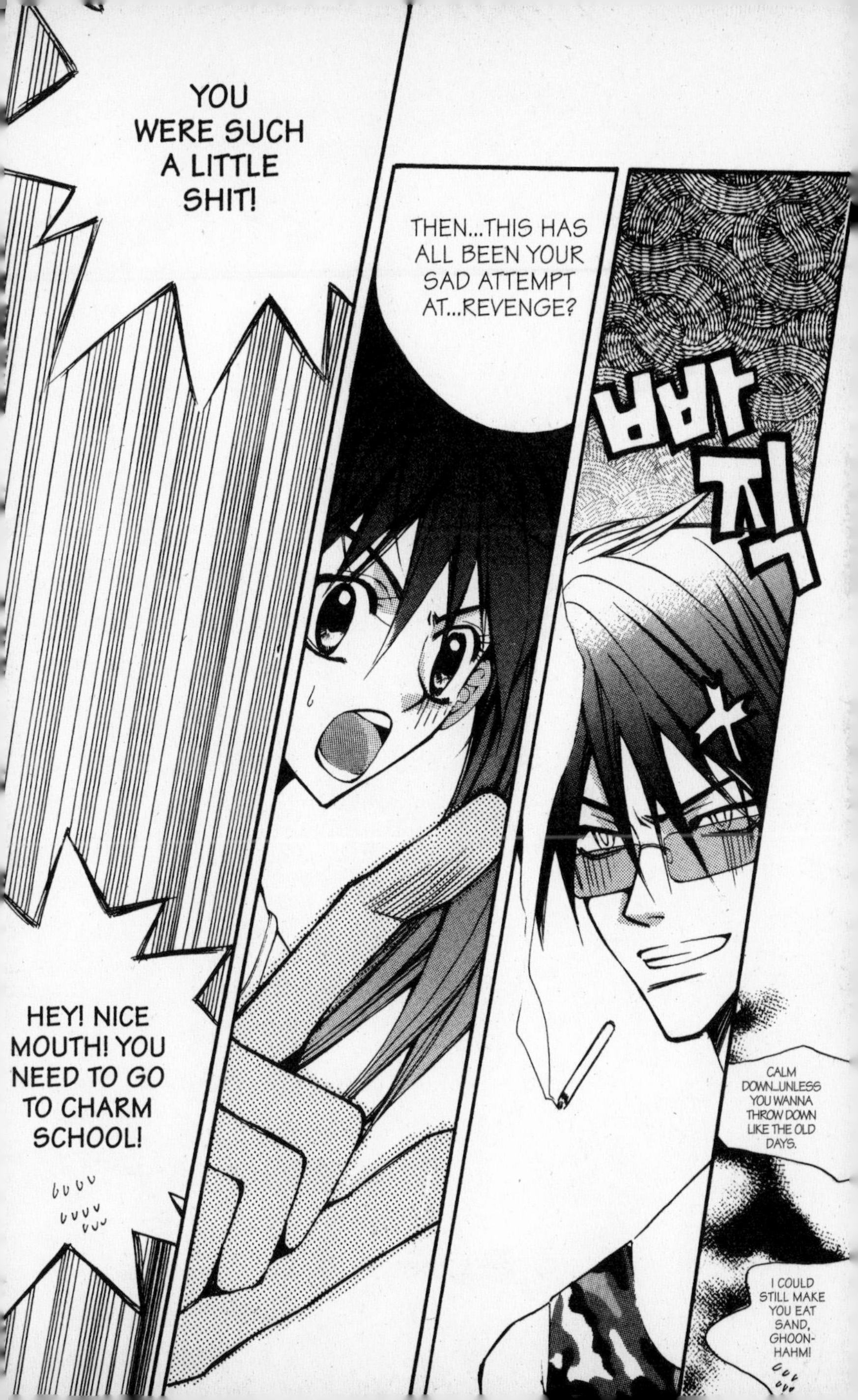
YOU WERE SUCH A LITTLE SHIT!
HEY! NICE MOUTH! YOU NEED TO GO TO CHARM SCHOOL!
THEN...THIS HAS ALL BEEN YOUR SAD ATTEMPT AT...REVENGE?
빠직
CALM DOWN...UNLESS YOU WANNA THROW DOWN LIKE THE OLD DAYS.
I COULD STILL MAKE YOU EAT SAND, GHOON-HAHM!

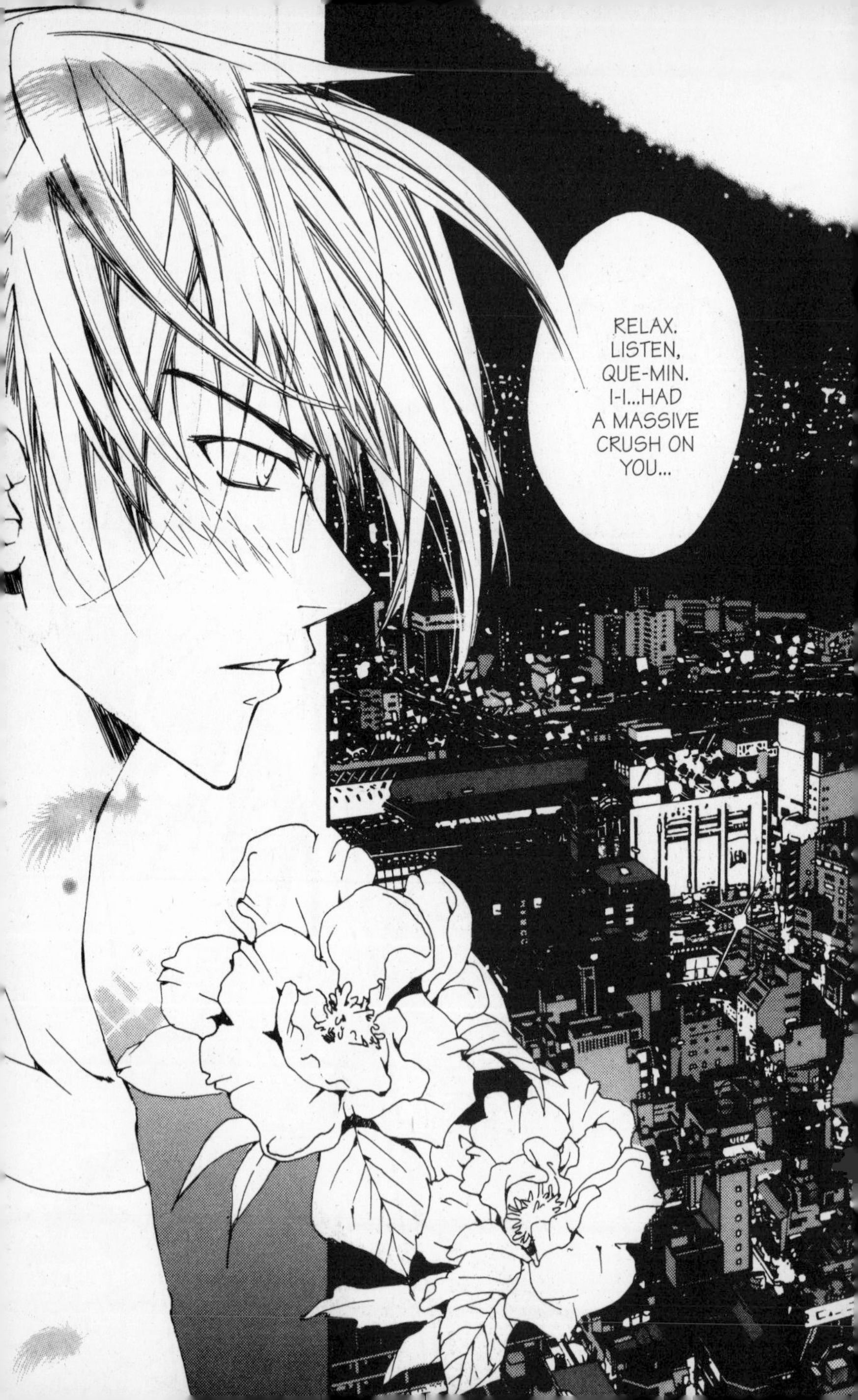
RELAX. LISTEN, QUE-MIN. I-I...HAD A MASSIVE CRUSH ON YOU...

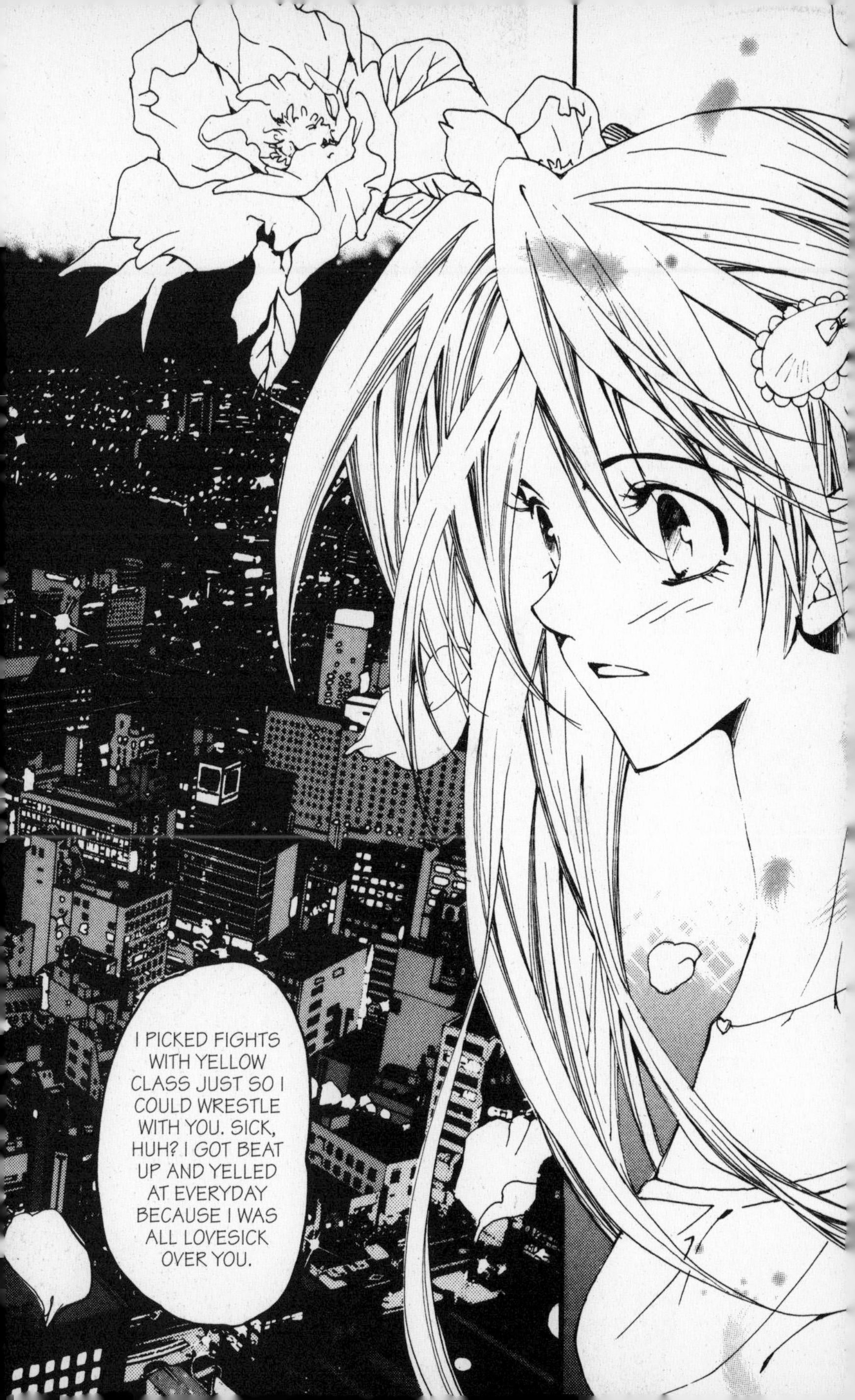
I PICKED FIGHTS WITH YELLOW CLASS JUST SO I COULD WRESTLE WITH YOU. SICK, HUH? I GOT BEAT UP AND YELLED AT EVERYDAY BECAUSE I WAS ALL LOVESICK OVER YOU.

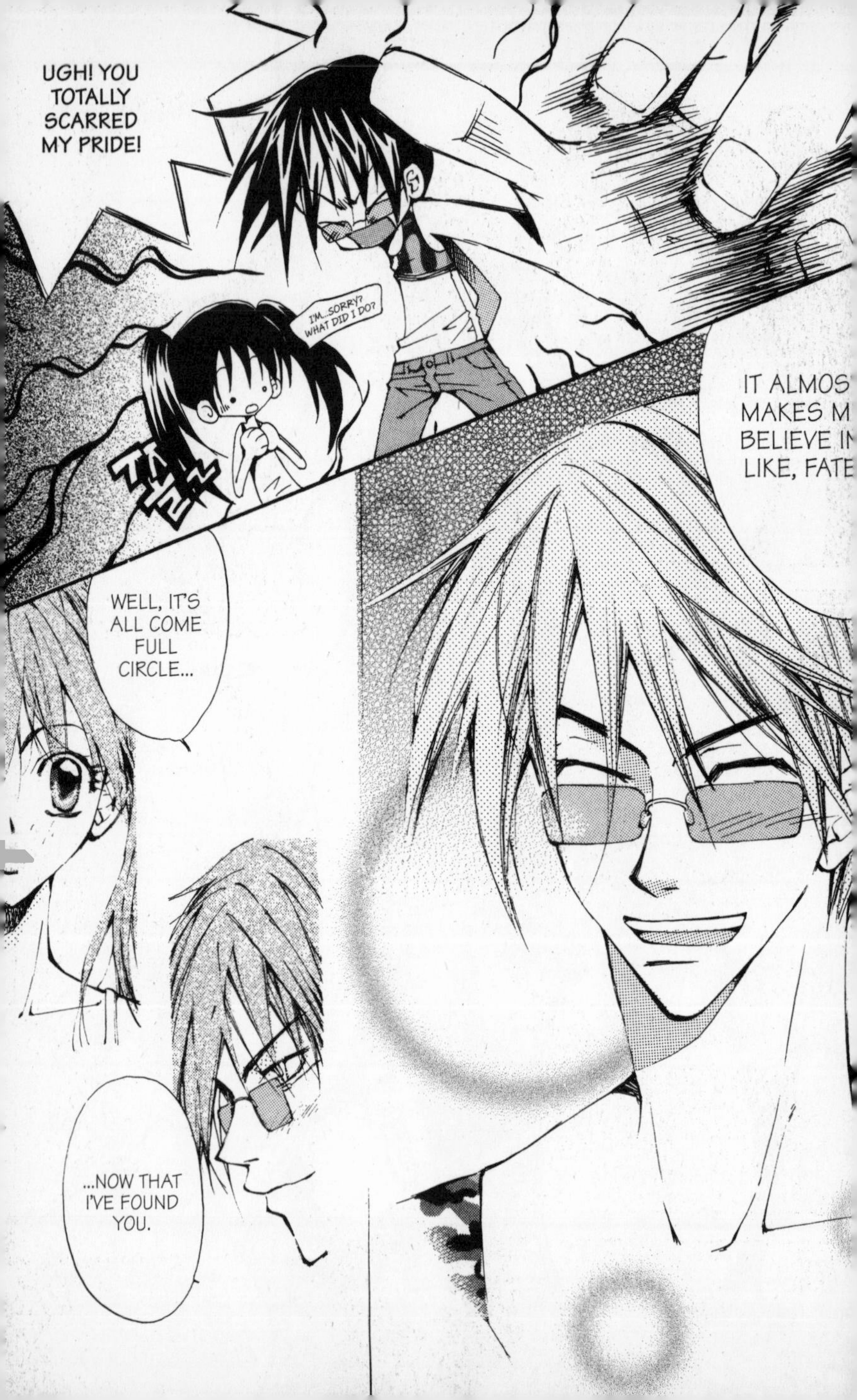
UGH! YOU TOTALLY SCARRED MY PRIDE!
I'M...SORRY? WHAT DID I DO?
WELL, IT'S ALL COME FULL CIRCLE...
...NOW THAT I'VE FOUND YOU.
IT ALMOS
MAKES M
BELIEVE IN
LIKE, FATE

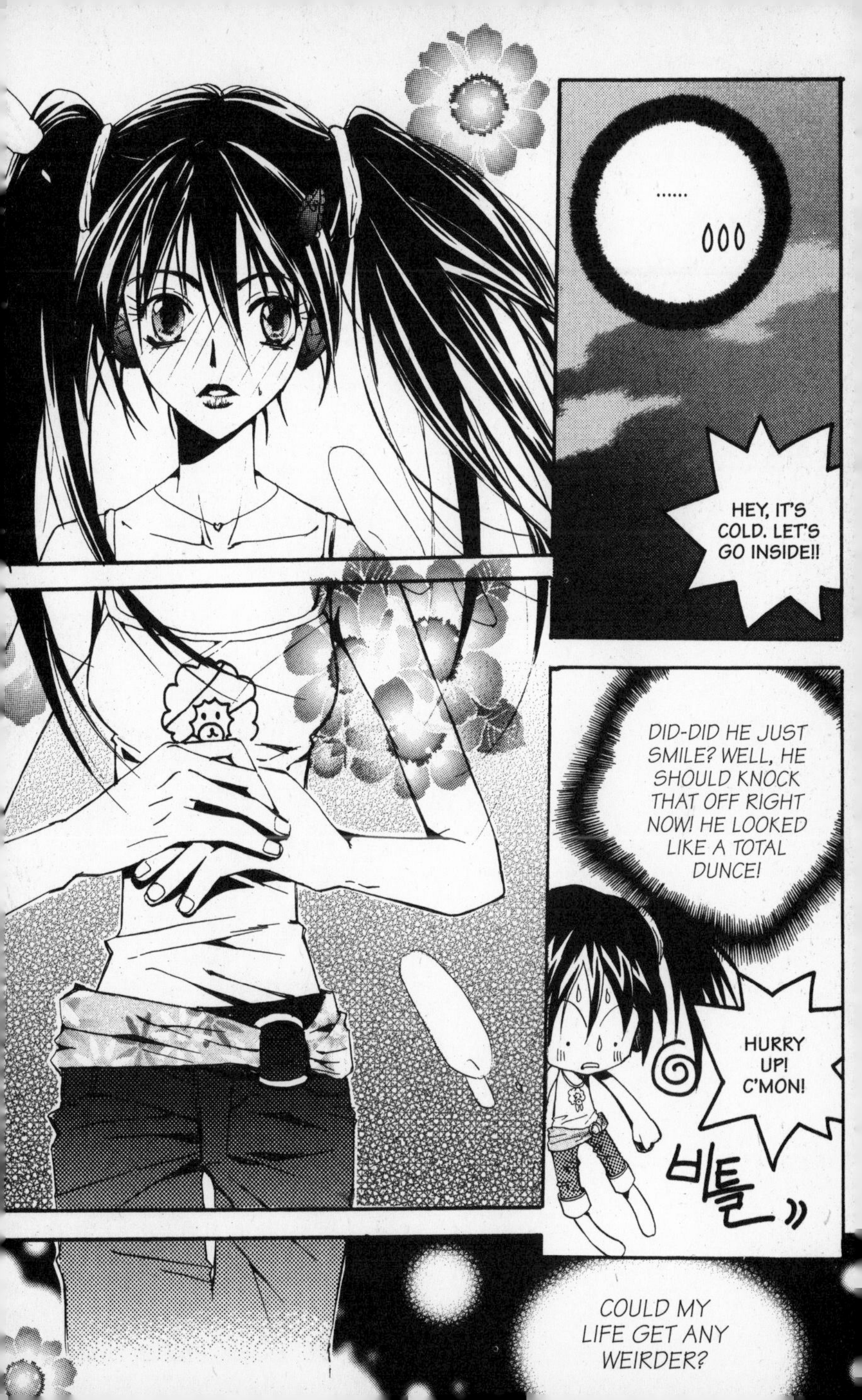
......
000
HEY, IT'S COLD. LET'S GO INSIDE!!
DID-DID HE JUST SMILE? WELL, HE SHOULD KNOCK THAT OFF RIGHT NOW! HE LOOKED LIKE A TOTAL DUNCE!
HURRY UP! C'MON!
비틀
COULD MY LIFE GET ANY WEIRDER?

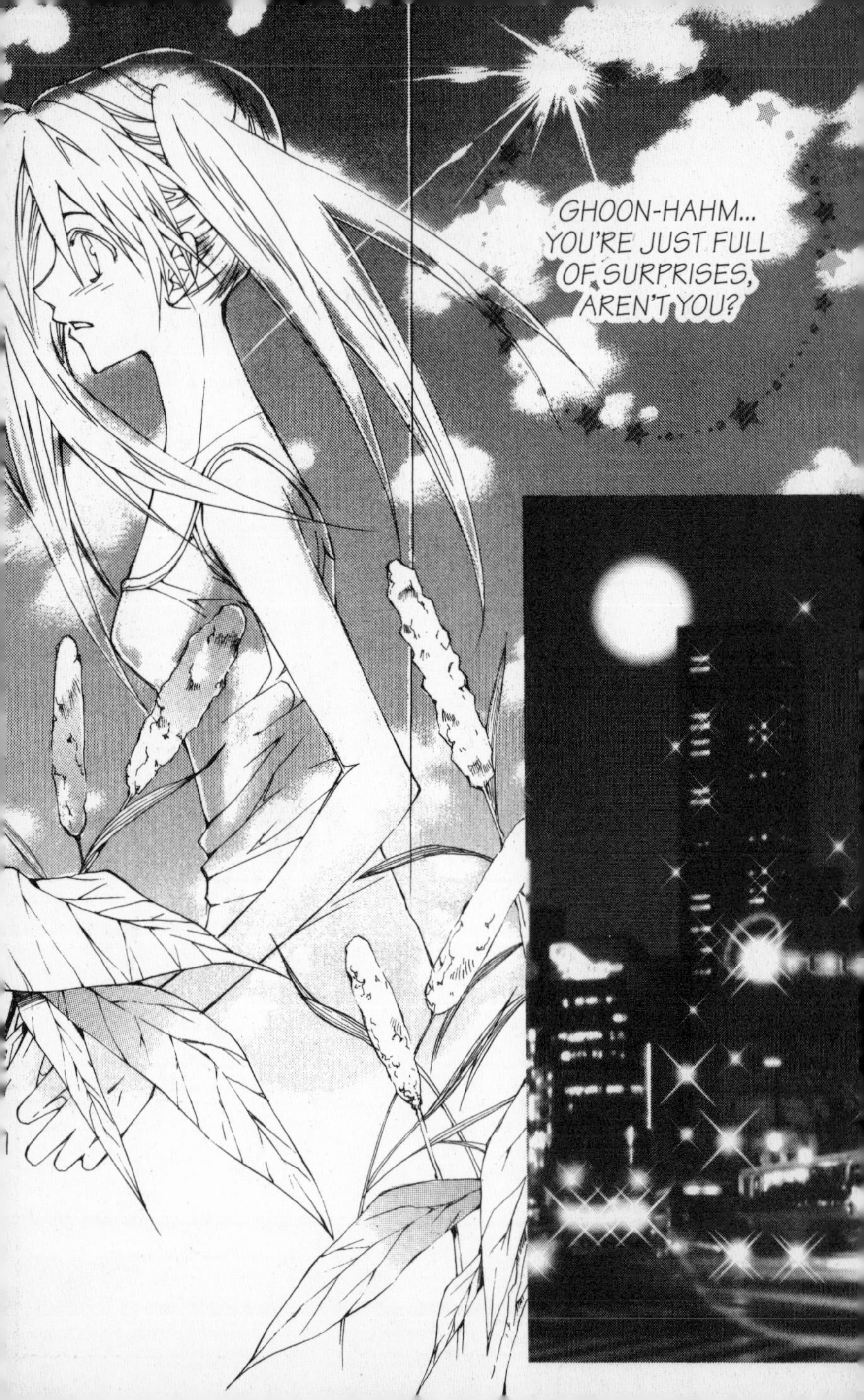
GHOON-HAHM... YOU'RE JUST FULL OF SURPRISES, AREN'T YOU?

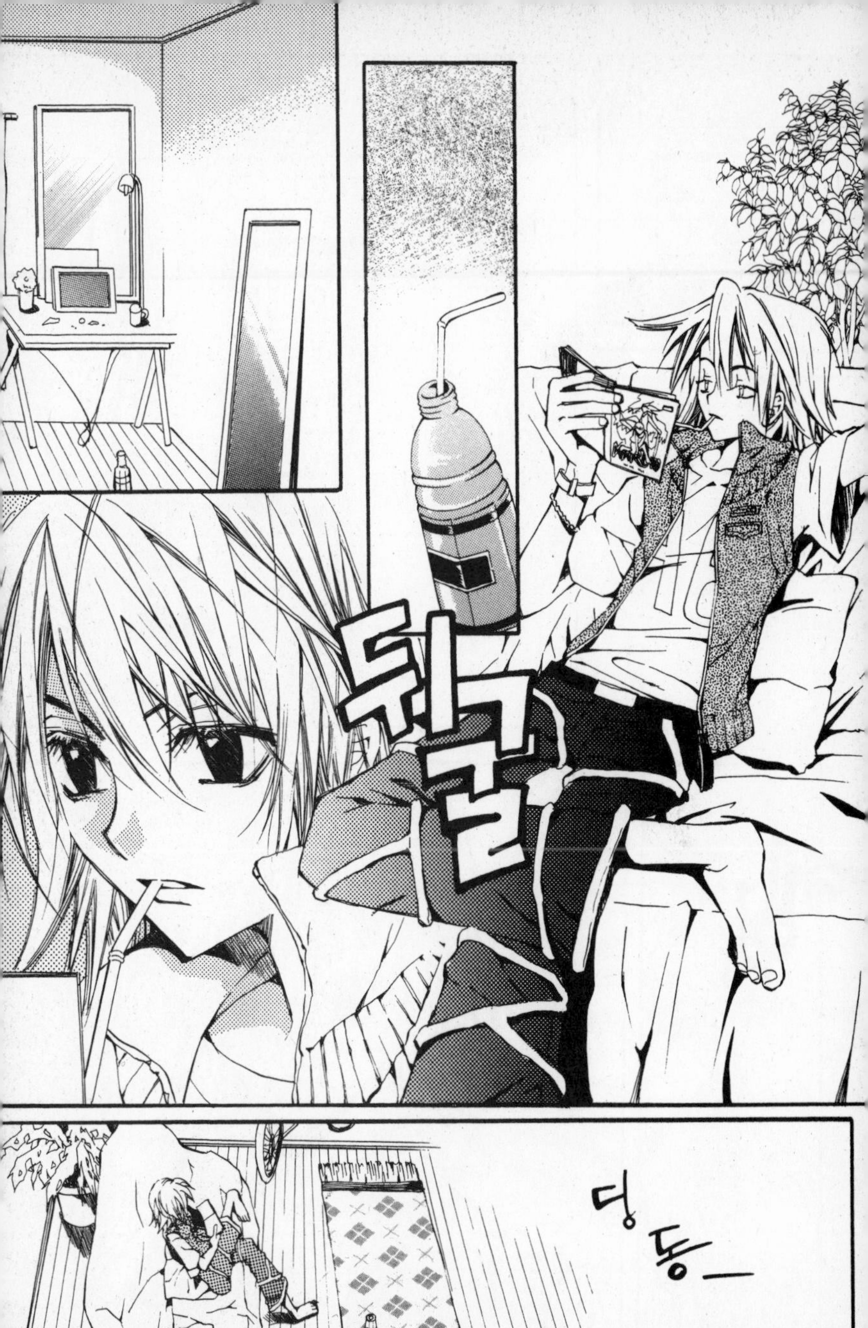
뒤굴
딩 동—

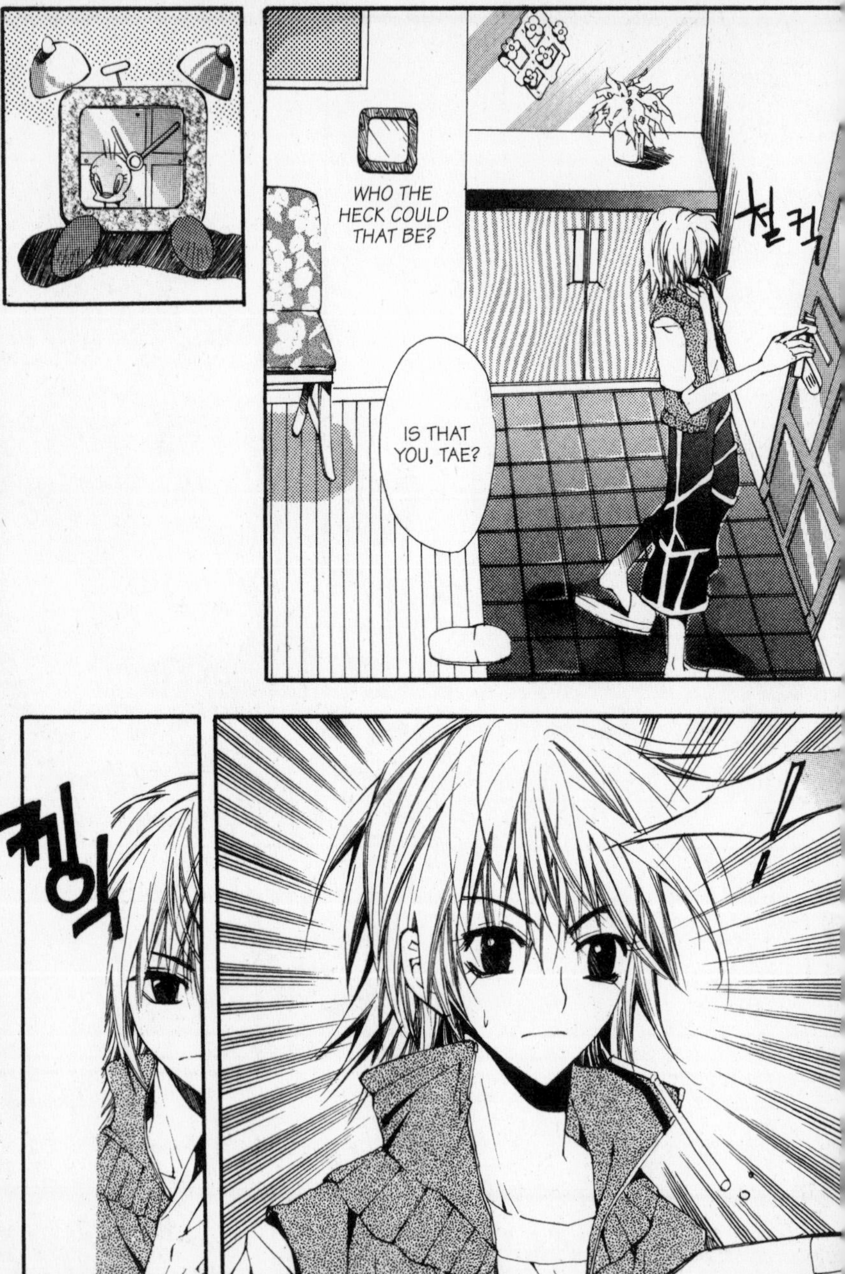
WHO THE HECK COULD THAT BE?
IS THAT YOU, TAE?
철컥

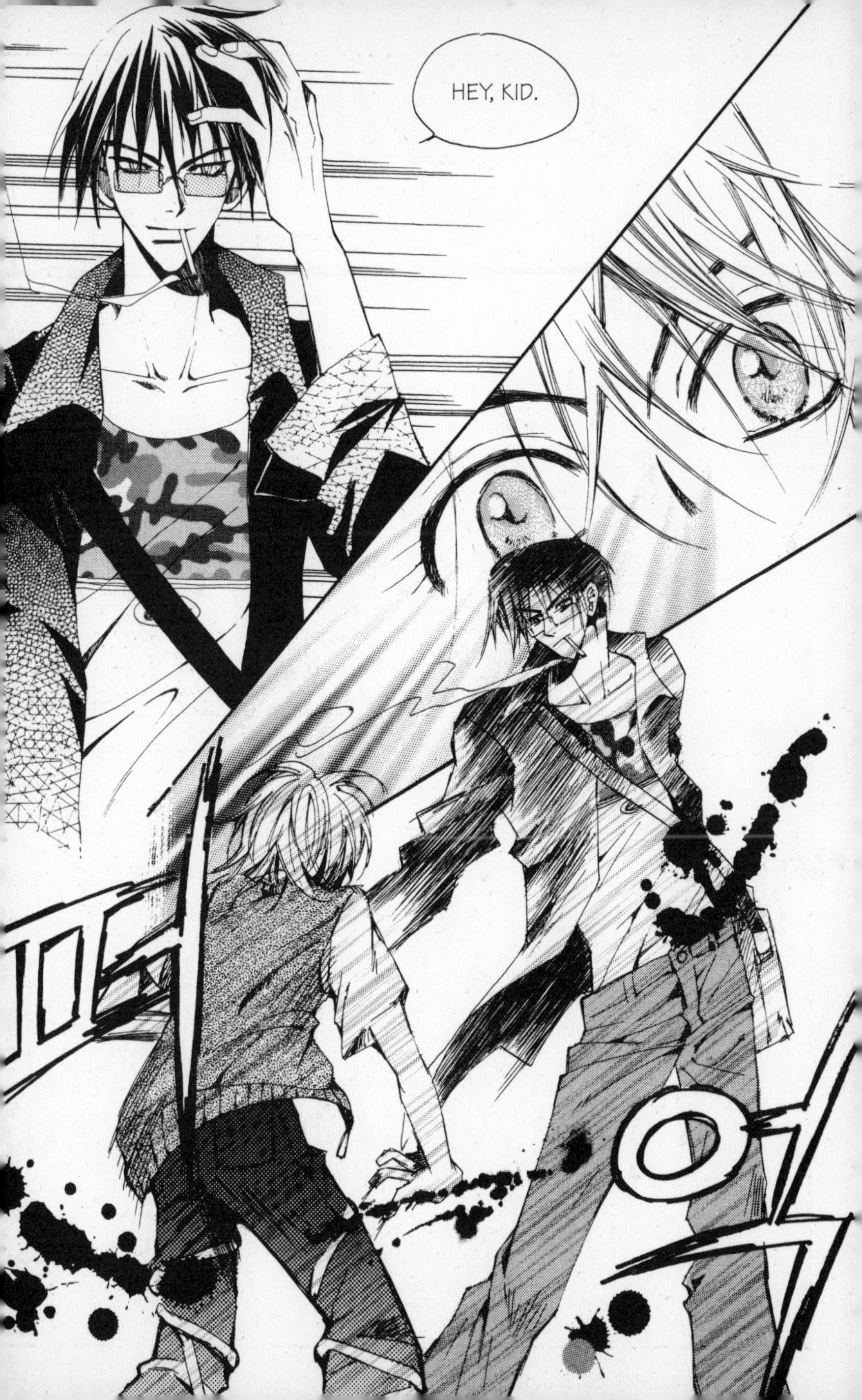
HEY, KID.

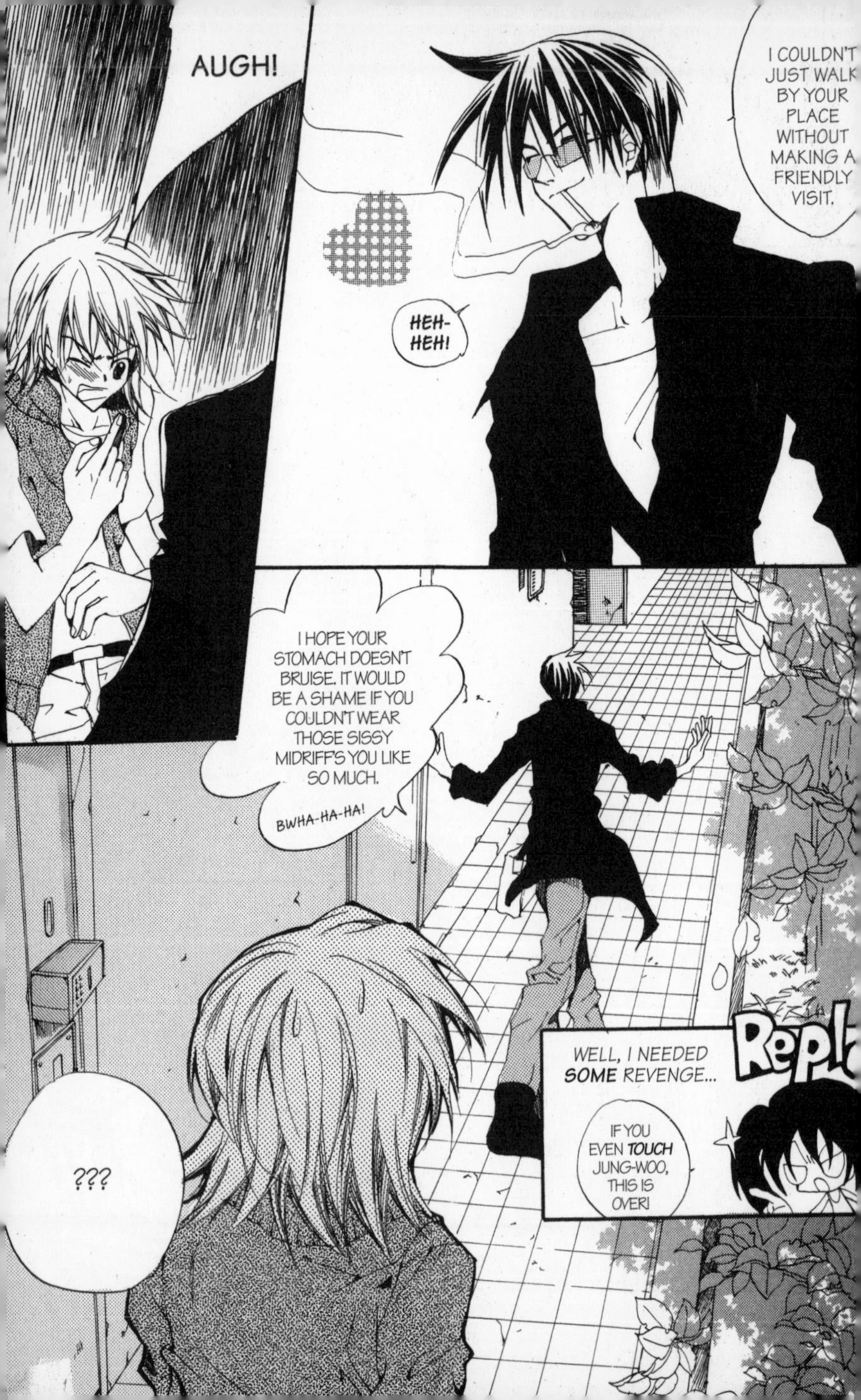
AUGH!
I COULDN'T JUST WALK BY YOUR PLACE WITHOUT MAKING A FRIENDLY VISIT.
HEH-HEH!
I HOPE YOUR STOMACH DOESN'T BRUISE. IT WOULD BE A SHAME IF YOU COULDN'T WEAR THOSE SISSY MIDRIFF'S YOU LIKE SO MUCH.
BWHA-HA-HA!
???
WELL, I NEEDED SOME REVENGE...
IF YOU EVEN TOUCH JUNG-WOO, THIS IS OVER!

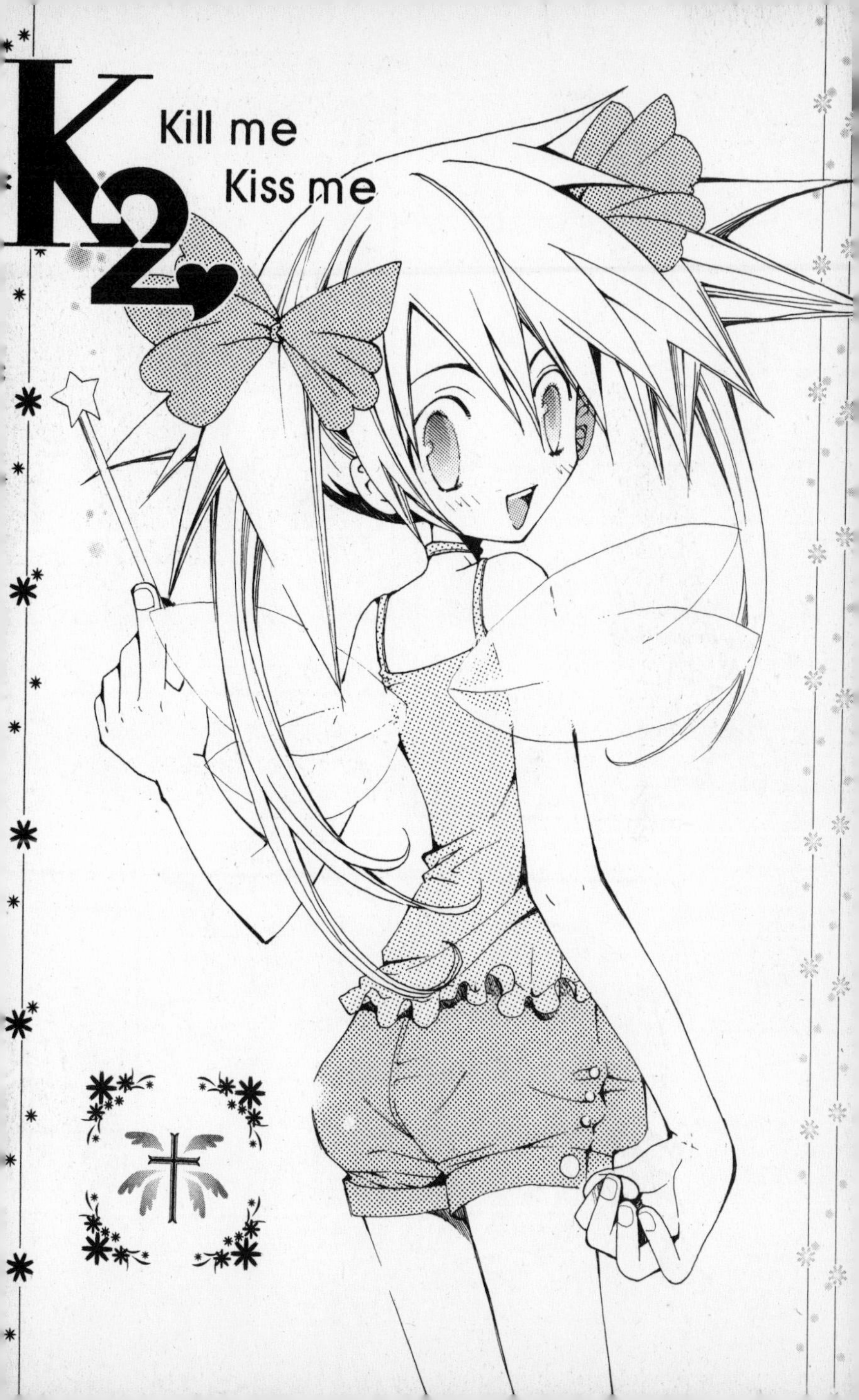
K2
Kill me
Kiss me

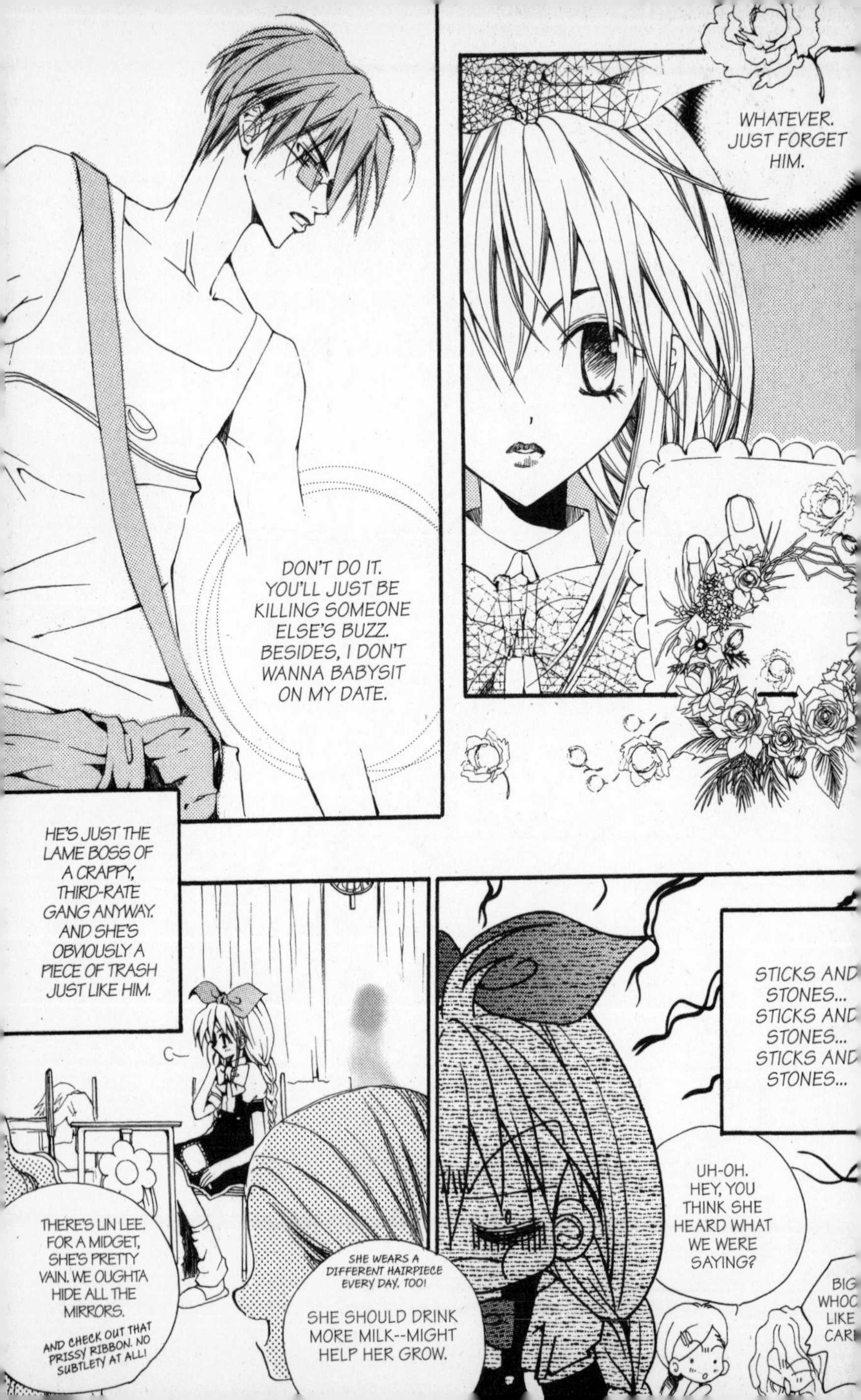

DON'T DO IT. YOU'LL JUST BE KILLING SOMEONE ELSE'S BUZZ. BESIDES, I DON'T WANNA BABYSIT ON MY DATE.
WHATEVER. JUST FORGET HIM.
HE'S JUST THE LAME BOSS OF A CRAPPY, THIRD-RATE GANG ANYWAY. AND SHE'S OBVIOUSLY A PIECE OF TRASH JUST LIKE HIM.
THERE'S LIN LEE. FOR A MIDGET, SHE'S PRETTY VAIN. WE OUGHTA HIDE ALL THE MIRRORS.
AND CHECK OUT THAT PRISSY RIBBON. NO SUBTLETY AT ALL!
SHE WEARS A DIFFERENT HAIRPIECE EVERY DAY, TOO!
SHE SHOULD DRINK MORE MILK--MIGHT HELP HER GROW.
STICKS AND STONES... STICKS AND STONES... STICKS AND STONES...
UH-OH. HEY, YOU THINK SHE HEARD WHAT WE WERE SAYING?
BIG WHOO LIKE CAR

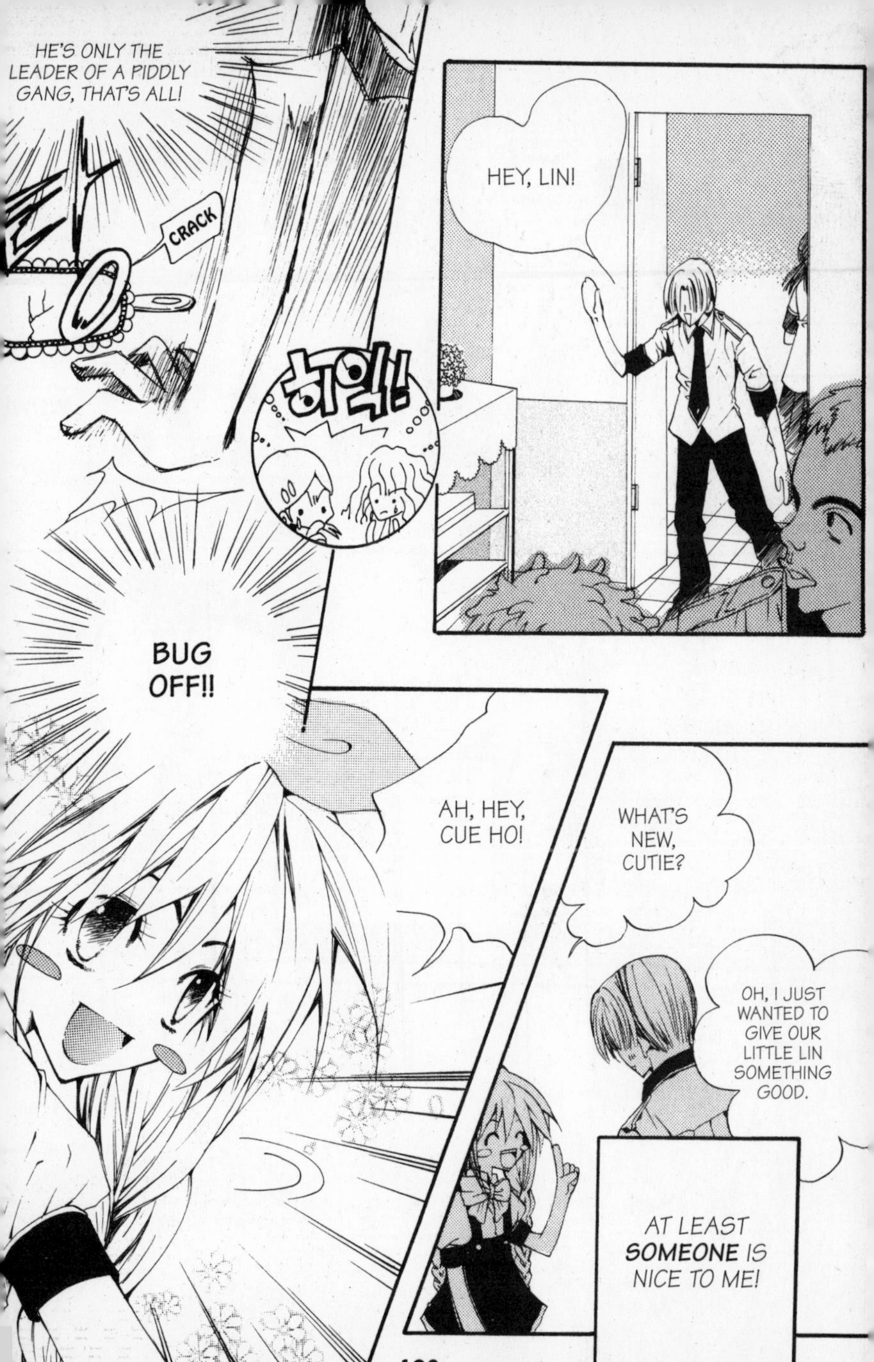
HE'S ONLY THE LEADER OF A PIDDLY GANG, THAT'S ALL!
CRACK
히익!!
BUG OFF!!
HEY, LIN!
AH, HEY, CUE HO!
WHAT'S NEW, CUTIE?
OH, I JUST WANTED TO GIVE OUR LITTLE LIN SOMETHING GOOD.
AT LEAST **SOMEONE** IS NICE TO ME!

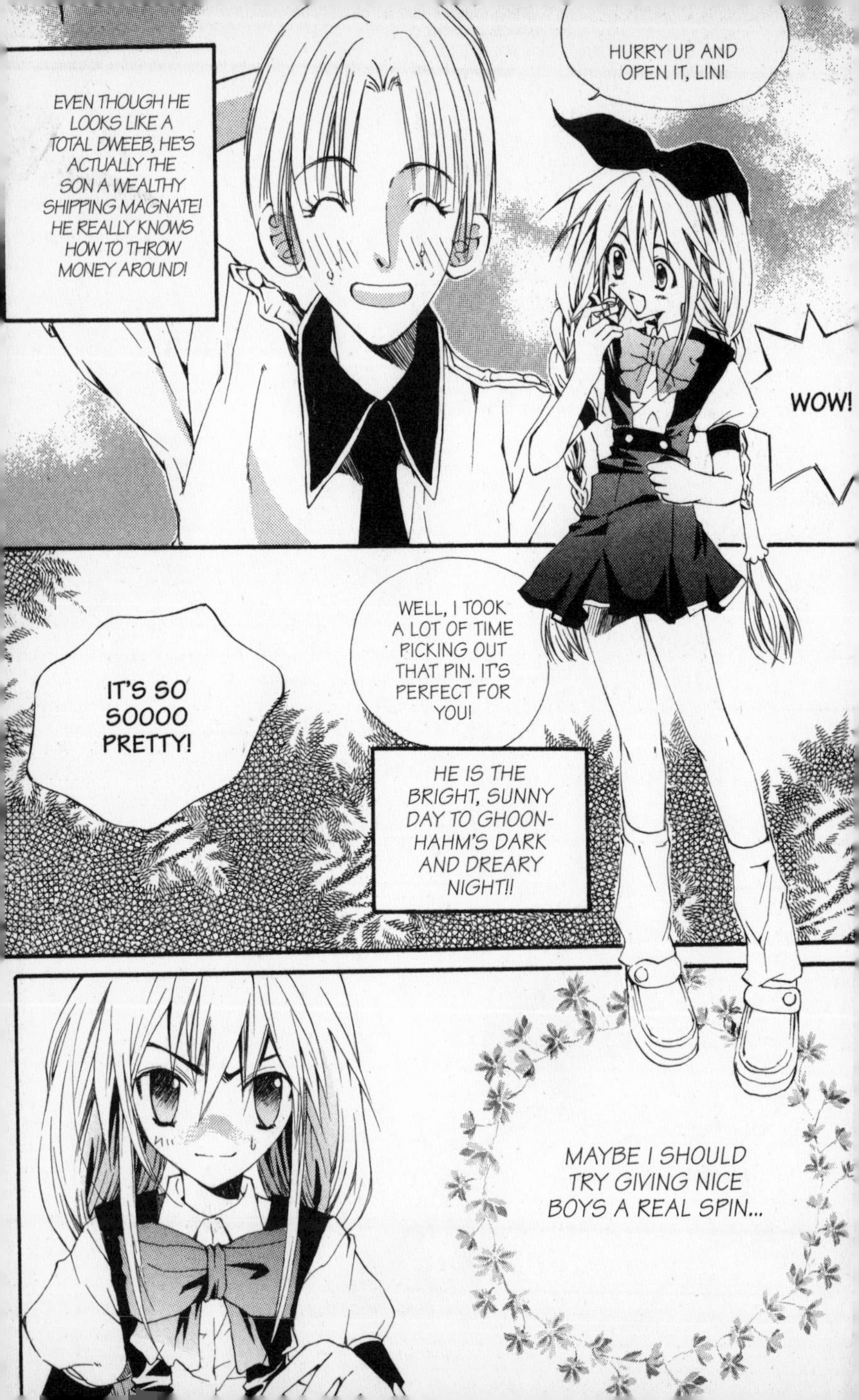
HURRY UP AND OPEN IT, LIN!
WOW!
EVEN THOUGH HE LOOKS LIKE A TOTAL DWEEB, HE'S ACTUALLY THE SON A WEALTHY SHIPPING MAGNATE! HE REALLY KNOWS HOW TO THROW MONEY AROUND!
WELL, I TOOK A LOT OF TIME PICKING OUT THAT PIN. IT'S PERFECT FOR YOU!
IT'S SO SOOOO PRETTY!
HE IS THE BRIGHT, SUNNY DAY TO GHOON-HAHM'S DARK AND DREARY NIGHT!!
MAYBE I SHOULD TRY GIVING NICE BOYS A REAL SPIN...

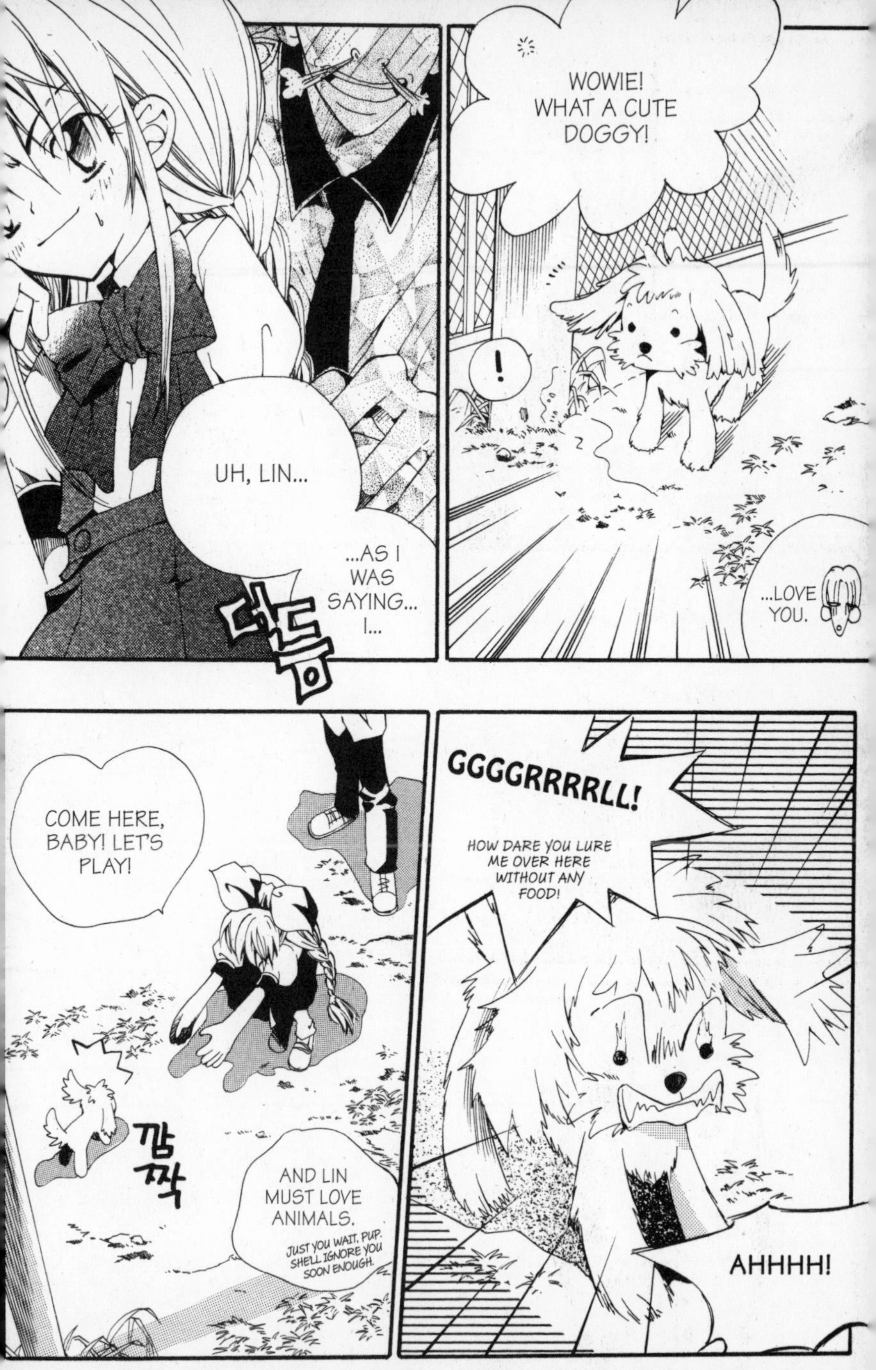
UH, LIN...
...AS I WAS SAYING... I...
더등
WOWIE! WHAT A CUTE DOGGY!
!
...LOVE YOU.
COME HERE, BABY! LET'S PLAY!
깜짝
AND LIN MUST LOVE ANIMALS.
JUST YOU WAIT, PUP. SHE'LL IGNORE YOU SOON ENOUGH.
GGGGRRRRLL!
HOW DARE YOU LURE ME OVER HERE WITHOUT ANY FOOD!
AHHHH!

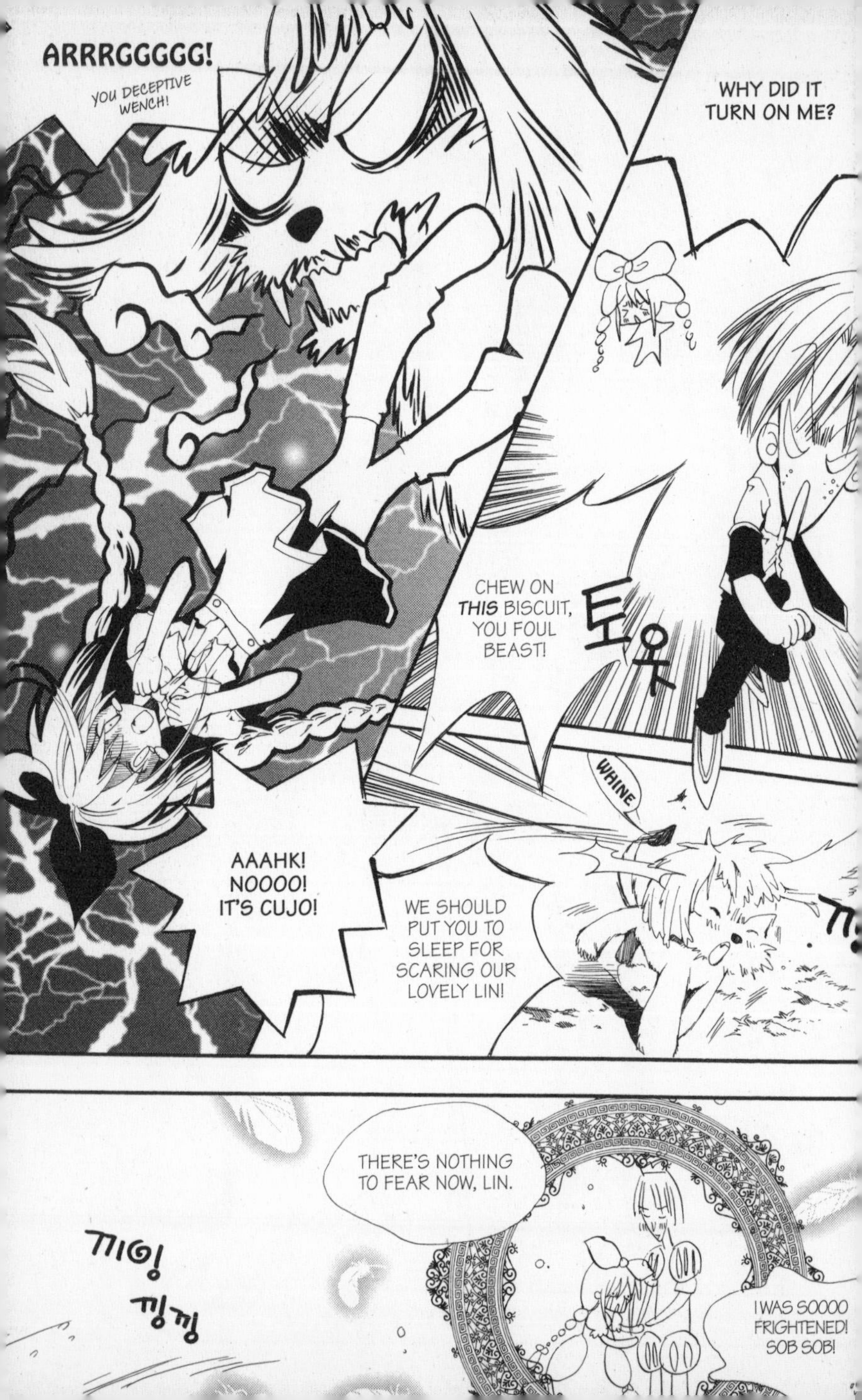
ARRRGGGGG!
YOU DECEPTIVE WENCH!
AAAHK! NOOOO! IT'S CUJO!
WHY DID IT TURN ON ME?
CHEW ON THIS BISCUIT, YOU FOUL BEAST!
토우
WHINE
WE SHOULD PUT YOU TO SLEEP FOR SCARING OUR LOVELY LIN!
끼잉!
낑낑
THERE'S NOTHING TO FEAR NOW, LIN.
I WAS SOOOO FRIGHTENED! SOB SOB!

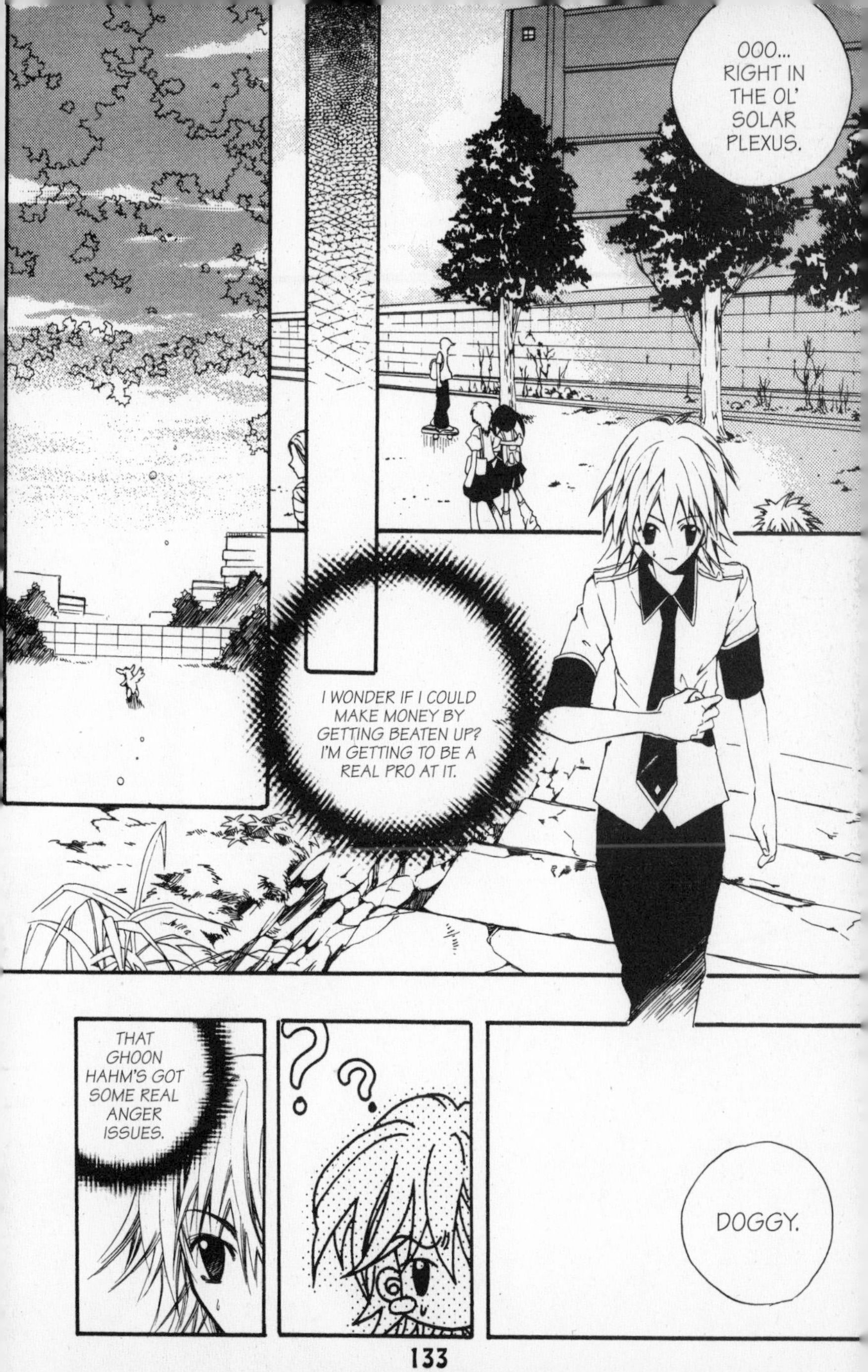
OOO... RIGHT IN THE OL' SOLAR PLEXUS.
I WONDER IF I COULD MAKE MONEY BY GETTING BEATEN UP? I'M GETTING TO BE A REAL PRO AT IT.
THAT GHOON HAHM'S GOT SOME REAL ANGER ISSUES.
? ?
DOGGY.

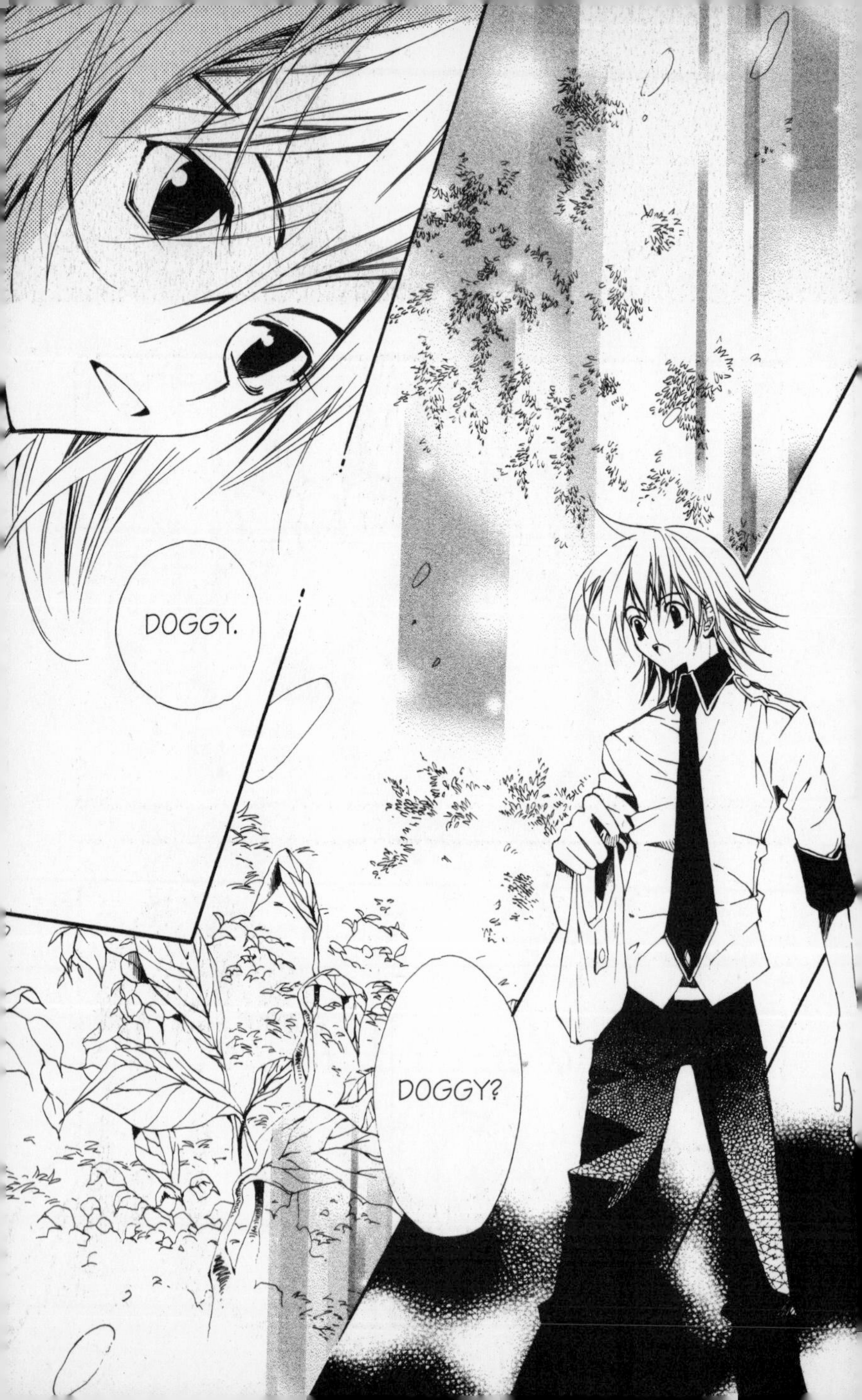
DOGGY.
DOGGY?

AH...MY MIND IS A TOTAL SHAMBLES.

I-I...HAD A MASSIVE CRUSH ON YOU...

I PICKED FIGHTS WITH YELLOW CLASS JUST SO I COULD WRESTLE WITH YOU.

NO MATTER HOW HARD I TRY, I CAN'T ESCAPE THE PAST...OR GHOON-HAHM.

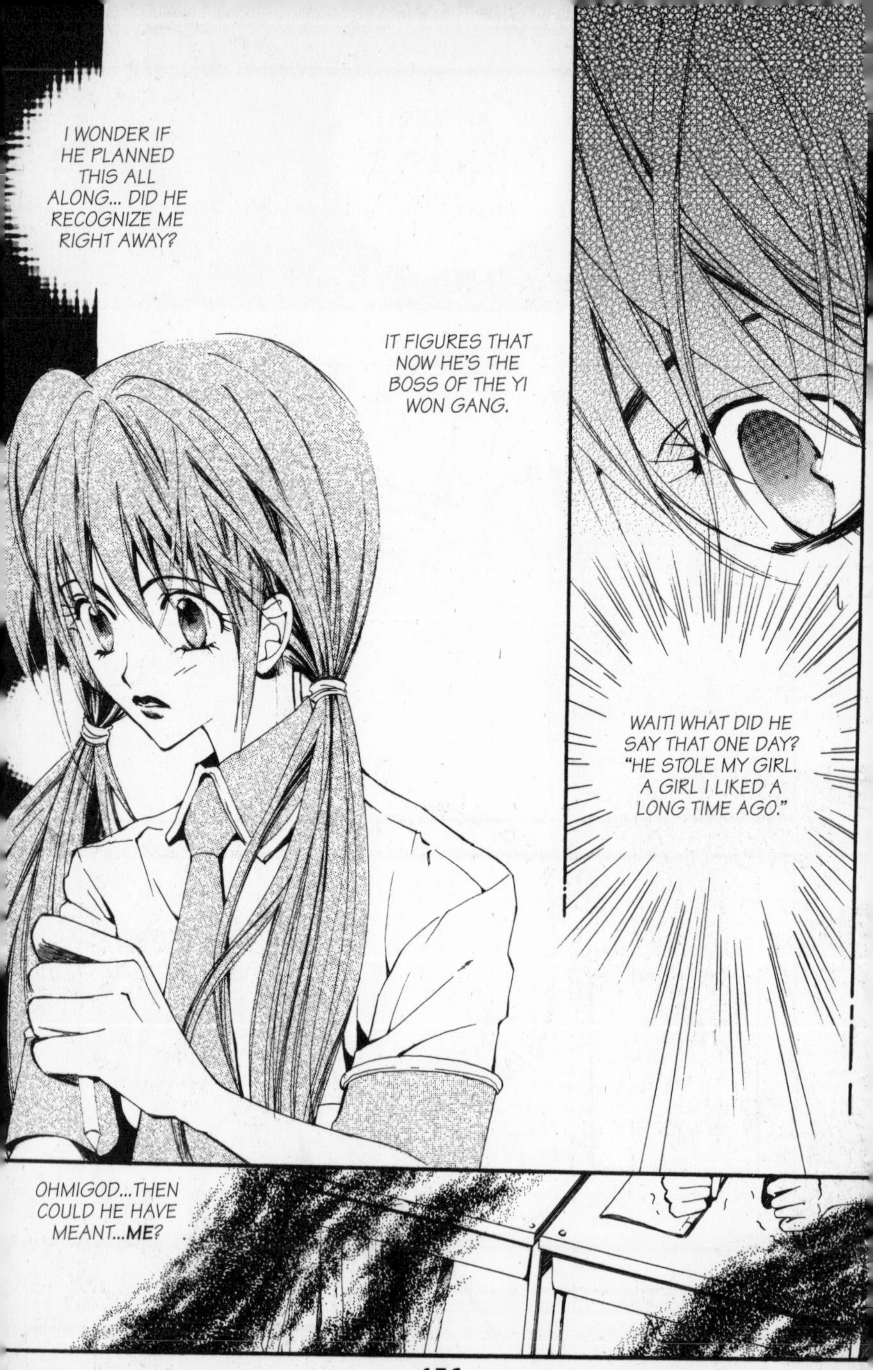
I WONDER IF HE PLANNED THIS ALL ALONG... DID HE RECOGNIZE ME RIGHT AWAY?
IT FIGURES THAT NOW HE'S THE BOSS OF THE YI WON GANG.
WAIT! WHAT DID HE SAY THAT ONE DAY? "HE STOLE MY GIRL. A GIRL I LIKED A LONG TIME AGO."
OHMIGOD...THEN COULD HE HAVE MEANT...ME?

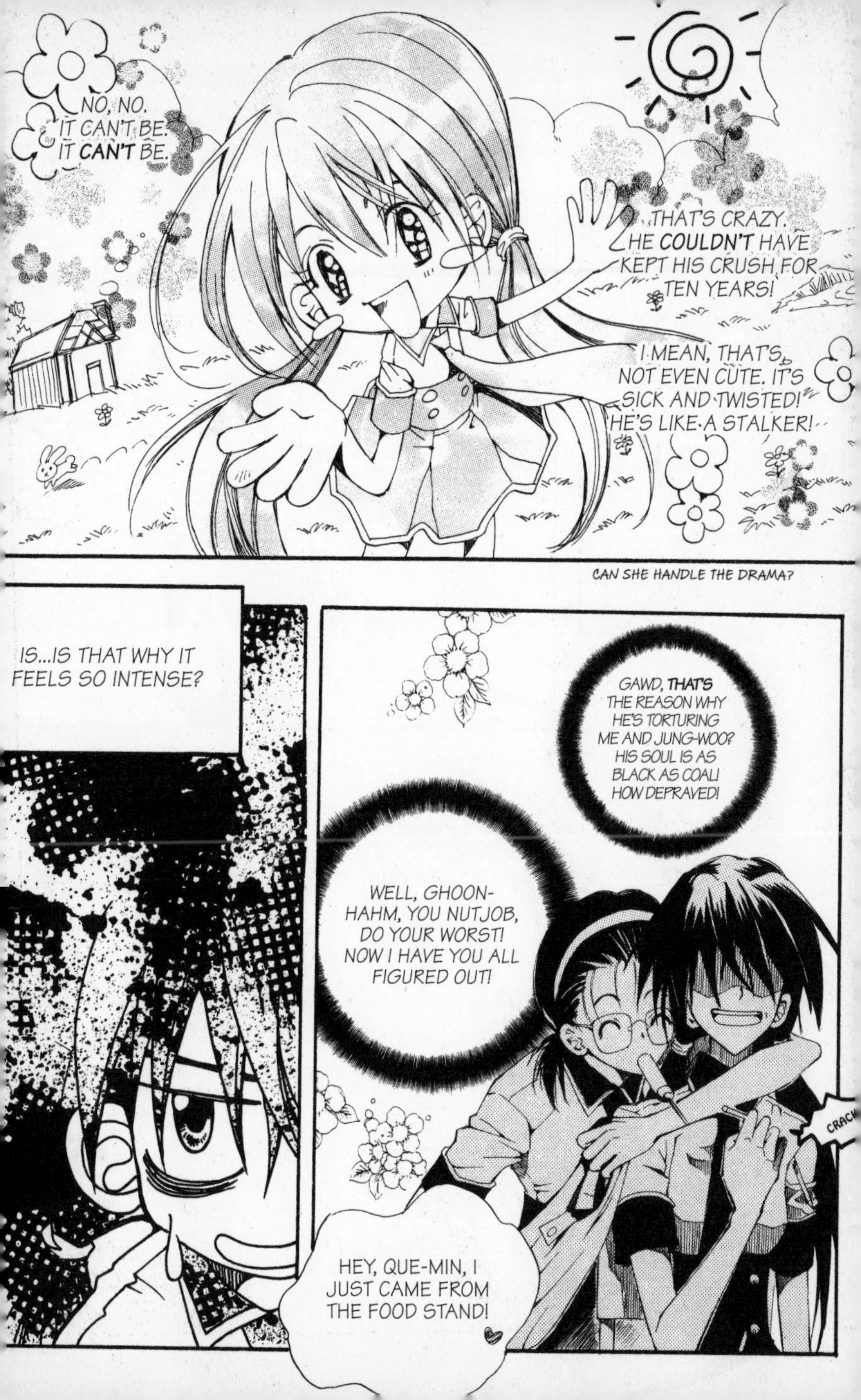
NO, NO. IT CAN'T BE. IT **CAN'T** BE.
THAT'S CRAZY. HE **COULDN'T** HAVE KEPT HIS CRUSH FOR TEN YEARS!
I MEAN, THAT'S NOT EVEN CUTE. IT'S SICK AND TWISTED! HE'S LIKE A STALKER!
CAN SHE HANDLE THE DRAMA?
IS...IS THAT WHY IT FEELS SO INTENSE?
GAWD, **THAT'S** THE REASON WHY HE'S TORTURING ME AND JUNG-WOO? HIS SOUL IS AS BLACK AS COAL! HOW DEPRAVED!
WELL, GHOON-HAHM, YOU NUTJOB, DO YOUR WORST! NOW I HAVE YOU ALL FIGURED OUT!
HEY, QUE-MIN, I JUST CAME FROM THE FOOD STAND!

HEY, SILLY GIRL! YOU STARTLED ME.

OWWWW!

TAKE IT EASY WITH THOSE MAN-HANDS!

THAT REALLY HURT!

SORRY. REFLEX.

LISTEN, ON THE WAY BACK, I RAN INTO YANG ME, AND SHE SAID JUNG-WOO IS, LIKE, M.I.A.

HE VANISHED AT LUNCH WITHOUT SAYING A WORD AND LEFT HIS BACKPACK BEHIND.

HE *CAN'T* HAVE BEEN KIDNAPPED, *RIGHT*? I BET A PRETTY BOY LIKE HIM WOULD FETCH A HIGH PRICE ON THE BLACK MARKET, THOUGH! I HOPE HE HASN'T BEEN SOLD INTO SEXUAL SLAVERY!

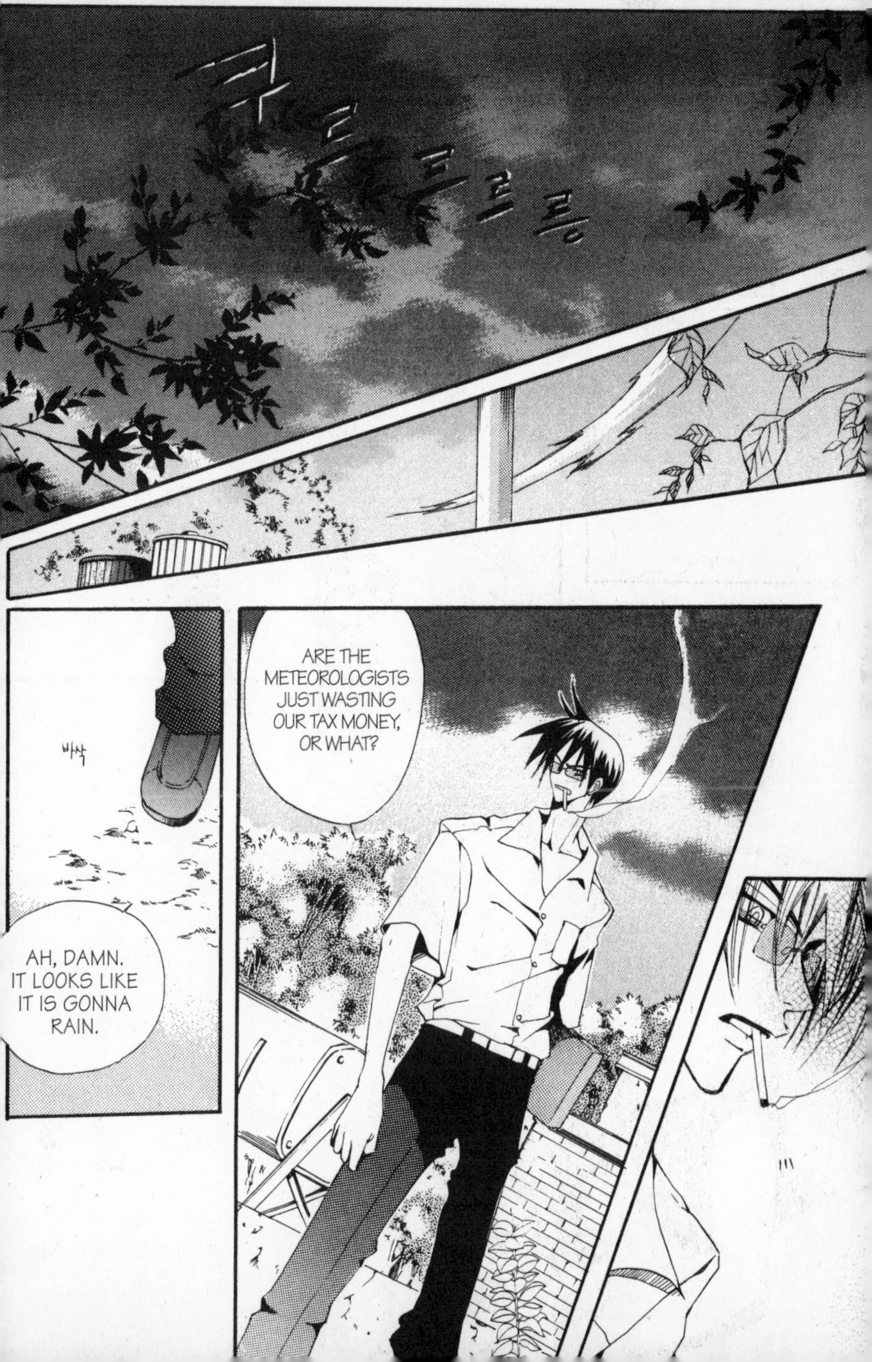
바삭
AH, DAMN. IT LOOKS LIKE IT IS GONNA RAIN.
ARE THE METEOROLOGISTS JUST WASTING OUR TAX MONEY, OR WHAT?

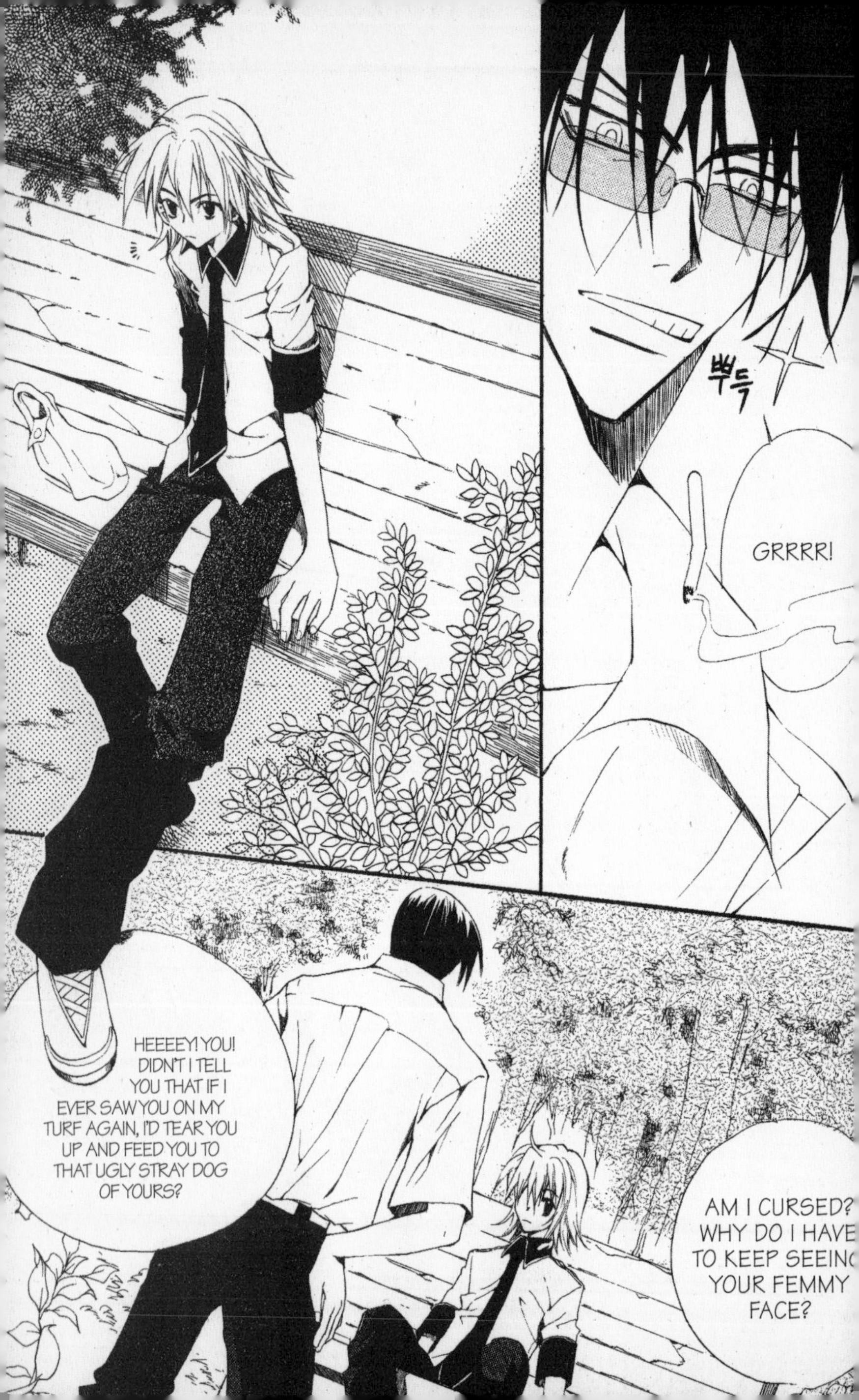
뿌득
GRRRR!
HEEEEY! YOU! DIDN'T I TELL YOU THAT IF I EVER SAW YOU ON MY TURF AGAIN, I'D TEAR YOU UP AND FEED YOU TO THAT UGLY STRAY DOG OF YOURS?
AM I CURSED? WHY DO I HAVE TO KEEP SEEIN YOUR FEMMY FACE?

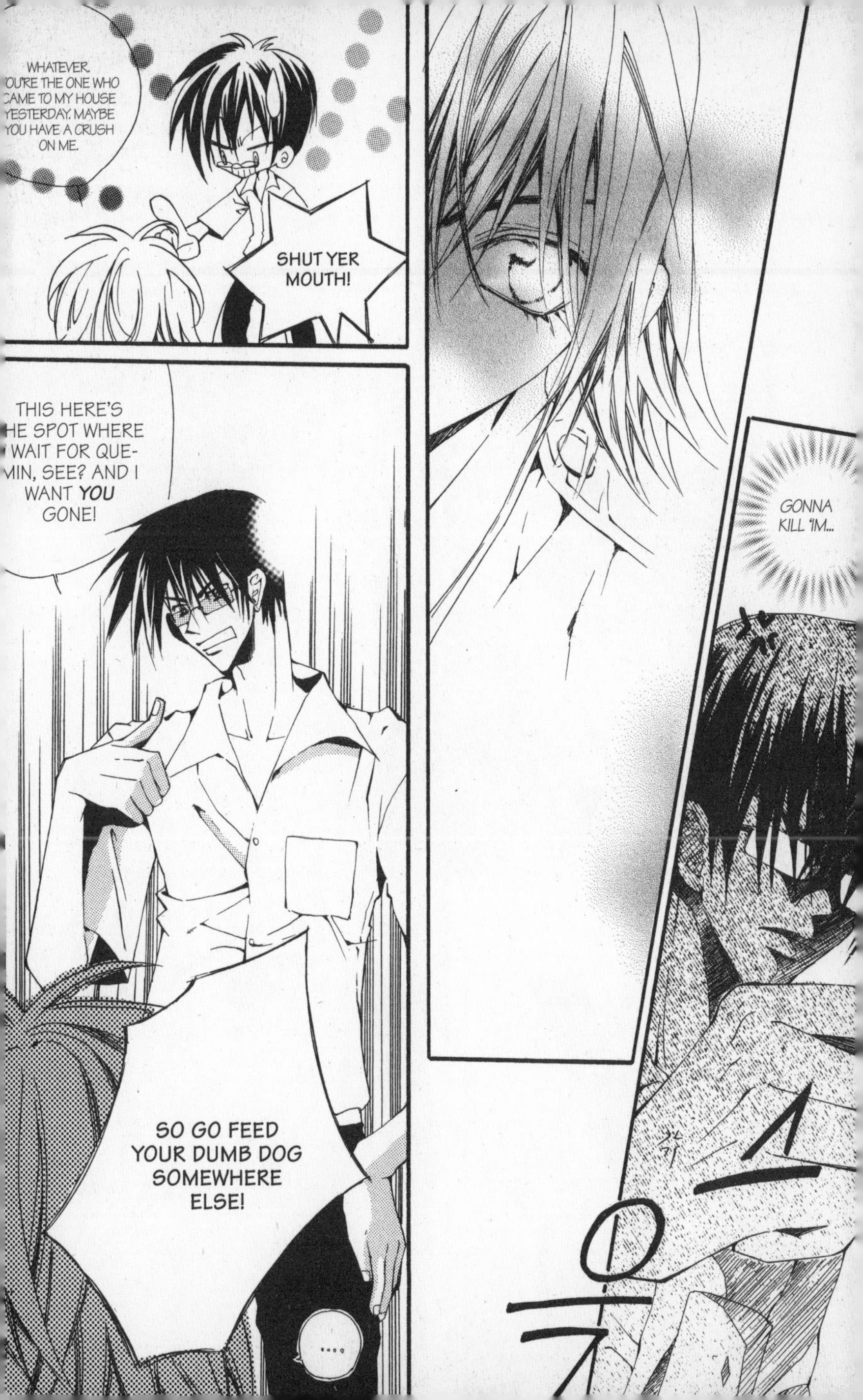
WHATEVER. OU'RE THE ONE WHO AME TO MY HOUSE ESTERDAY. MAYBE YOU HAVE A CRUSH ON ME.
SHUT YER MOUTH!
THIS HERE'S HE SPOT WHERE WAIT FOR QUE-MIN, SEE? AND I WANT *YOU* GONE!
SO GO FEED YOUR DUMB DOG SOMEWHERE ELSE!
....
GONNA KILL 'IM...

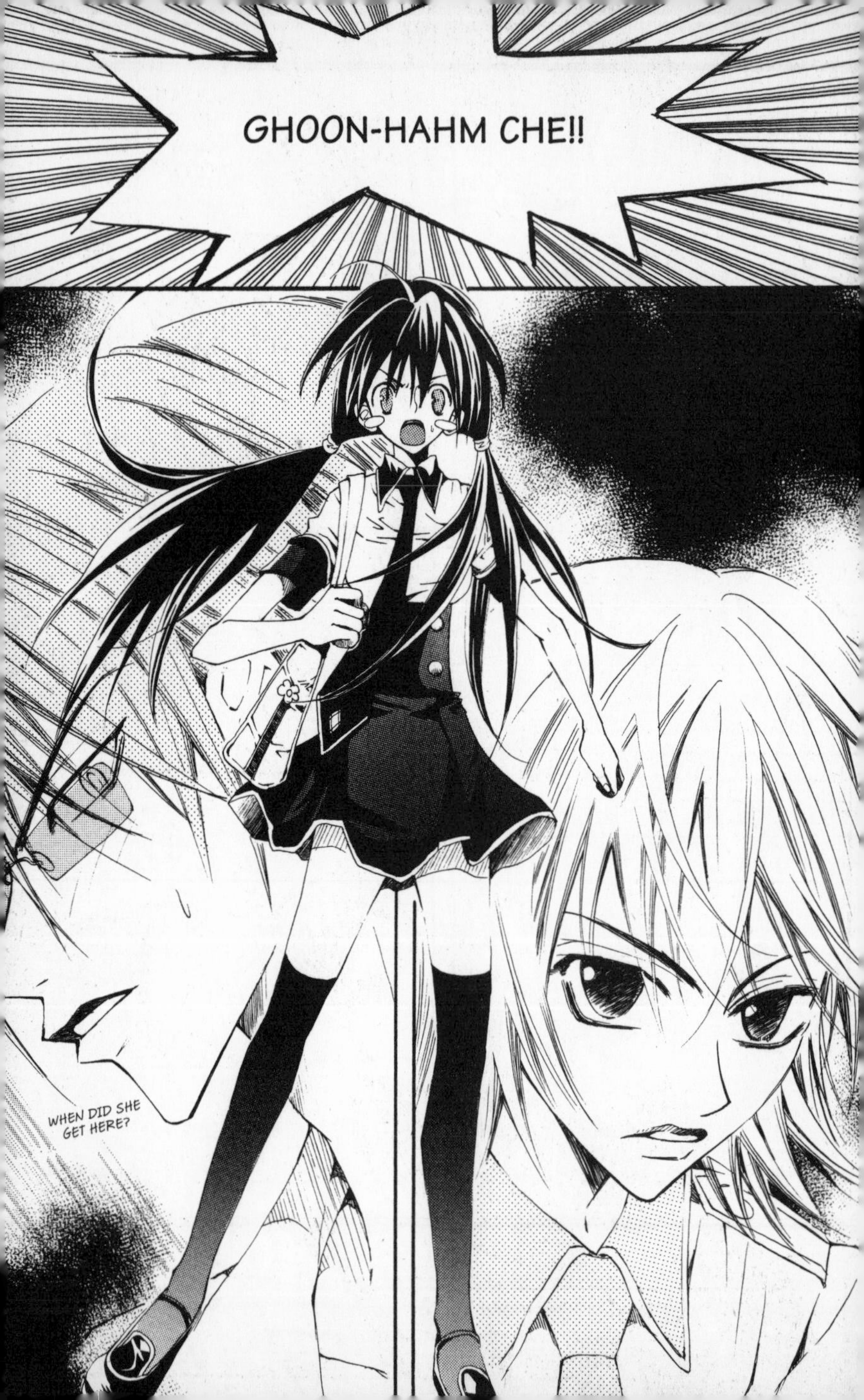
GHOON-HAHM CHE!!
WHEN DID SHE GET HERE?

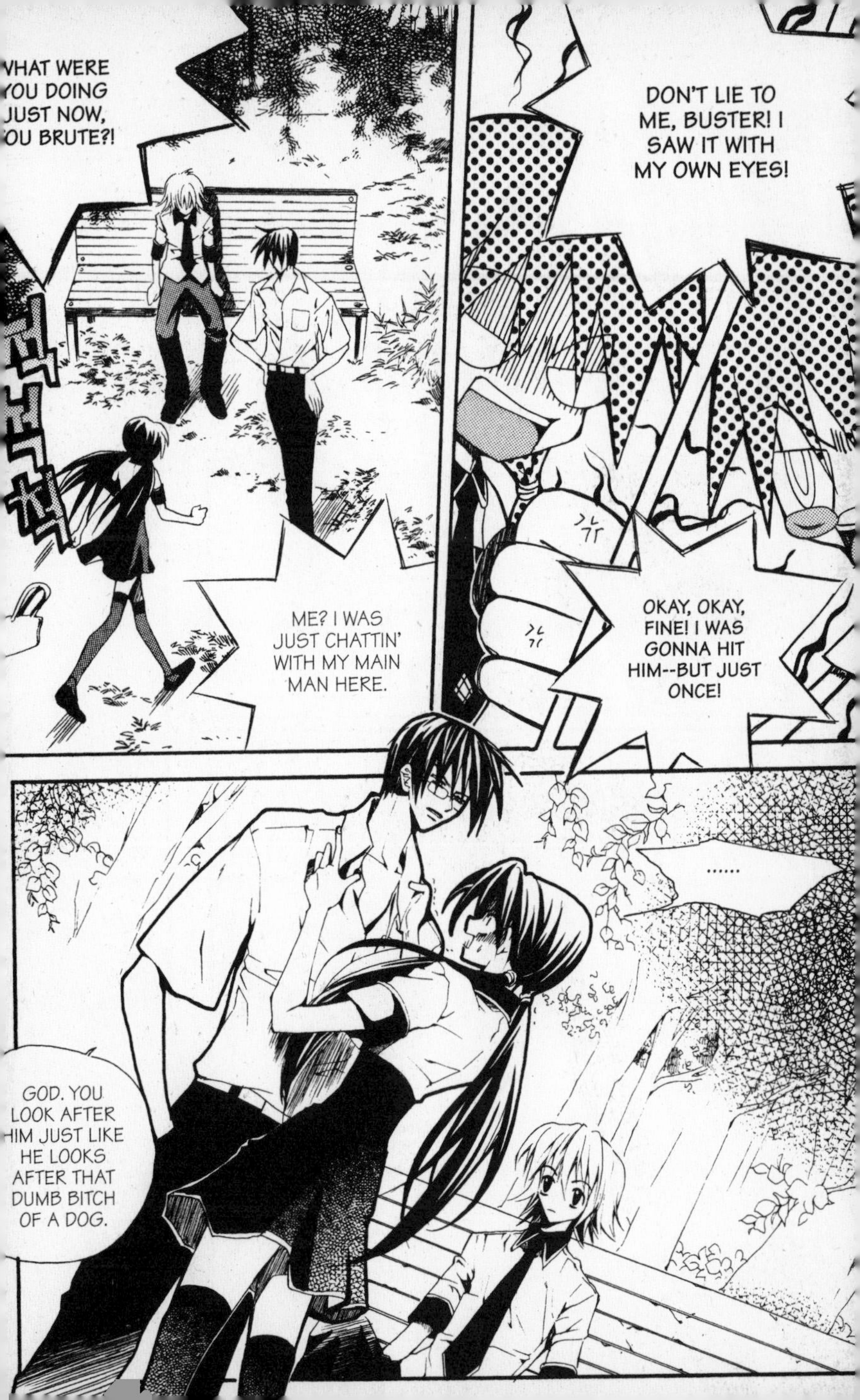
WHAT WERE YOU DOING JUST NOW, YOU BRUTE?!
ME? I WAS JUST CHATTIN' WITH MY MAIN MAN HERE.
DON'T LIE TO ME, BUSTER! I SAW IT WITH MY OWN EYES!
OKAY, OKAY, FINE! I WAS GONNA HIT HIM--BUT JUST ONCE!
......
GOD. YOU LOOK AFTER HIM JUST LIKE HE LOOKS AFTER THAT DUMB BITCH OF A DOG.

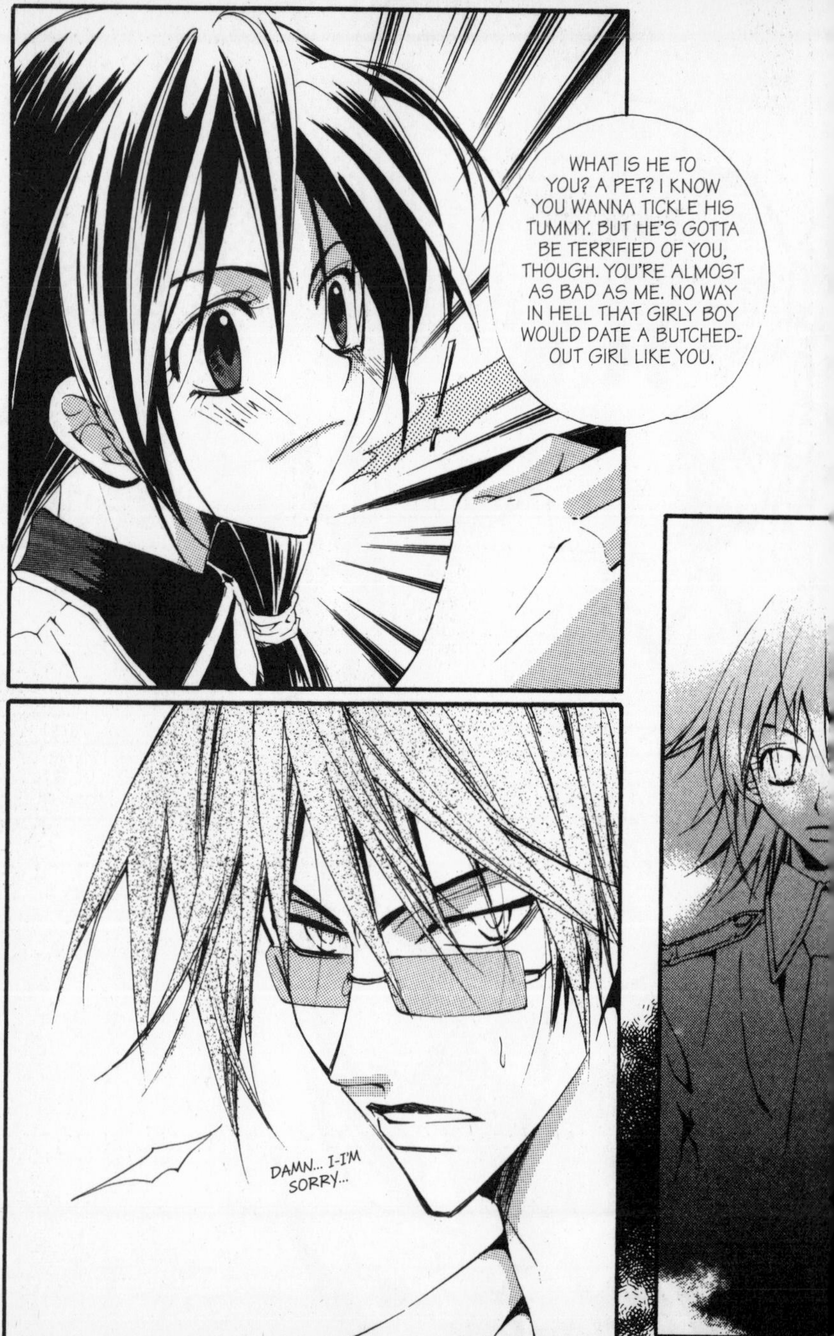
WHAT IS HE TO YOU? A PET? I KNOW YOU WANNA TICKLE HIS TUMMY. BUT HE'S GOTTA BE TERRIFIED OF YOU, THOUGH. YOU'RE ALMOST AS BAD AS ME. NO WAY IN HELL THAT GIRLY BOY WOULD DATE A BUTCHED-OUT GIRL LIKE YOU.
DAMN... I-I'M SORRY...

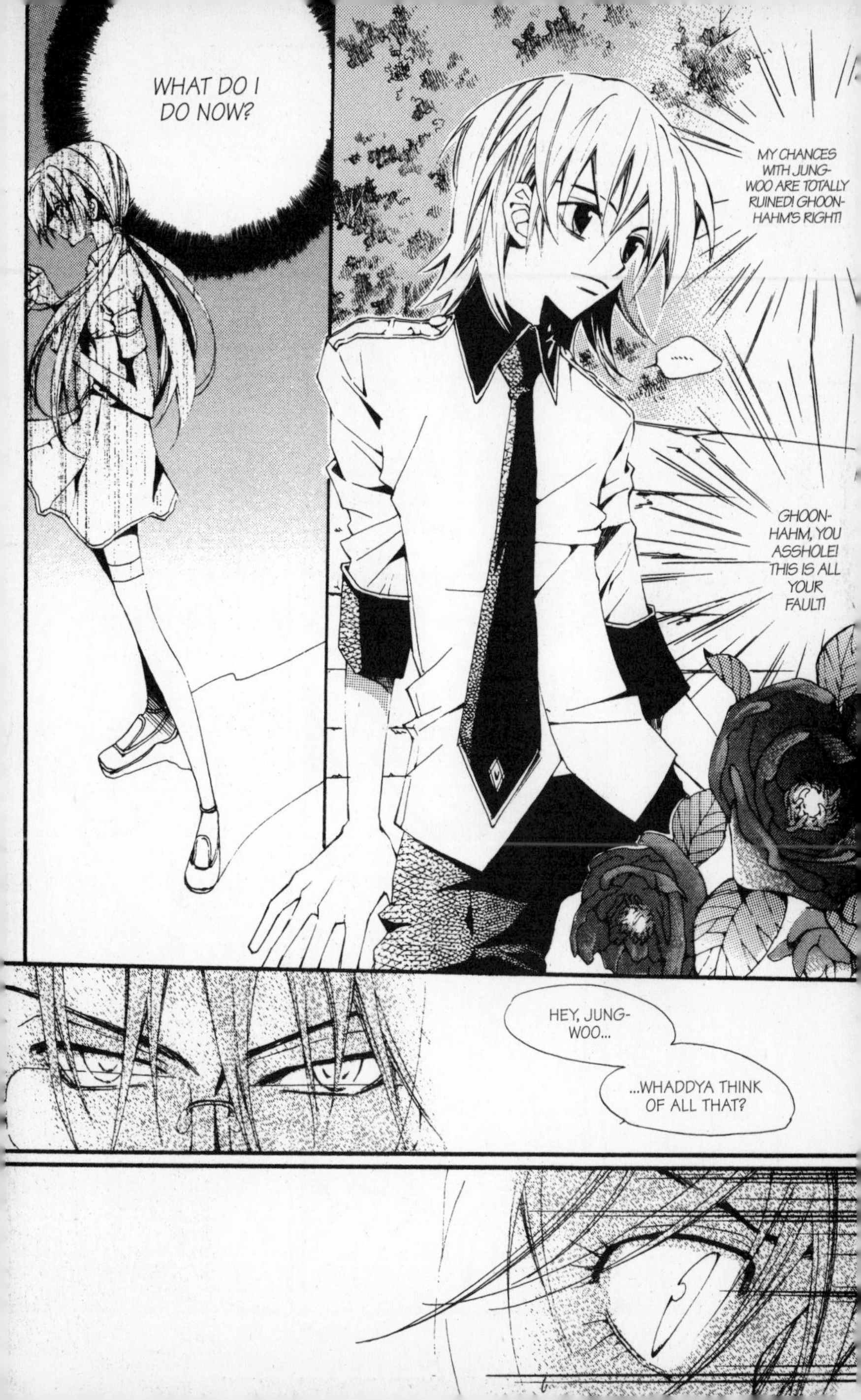
WHAT DO I DO NOW?
MY CHANCES WITH JUNG-WOO ARE TOTALLY RUINED! GHOON-HAHM'S RIGHT!
......
GHOON-HAHM, YOU ASSHOLE! THIS IS ALL YOUR FAULT!
HEY, JUNG-WOO...
...WHADDYA THINK OF ALL THAT?

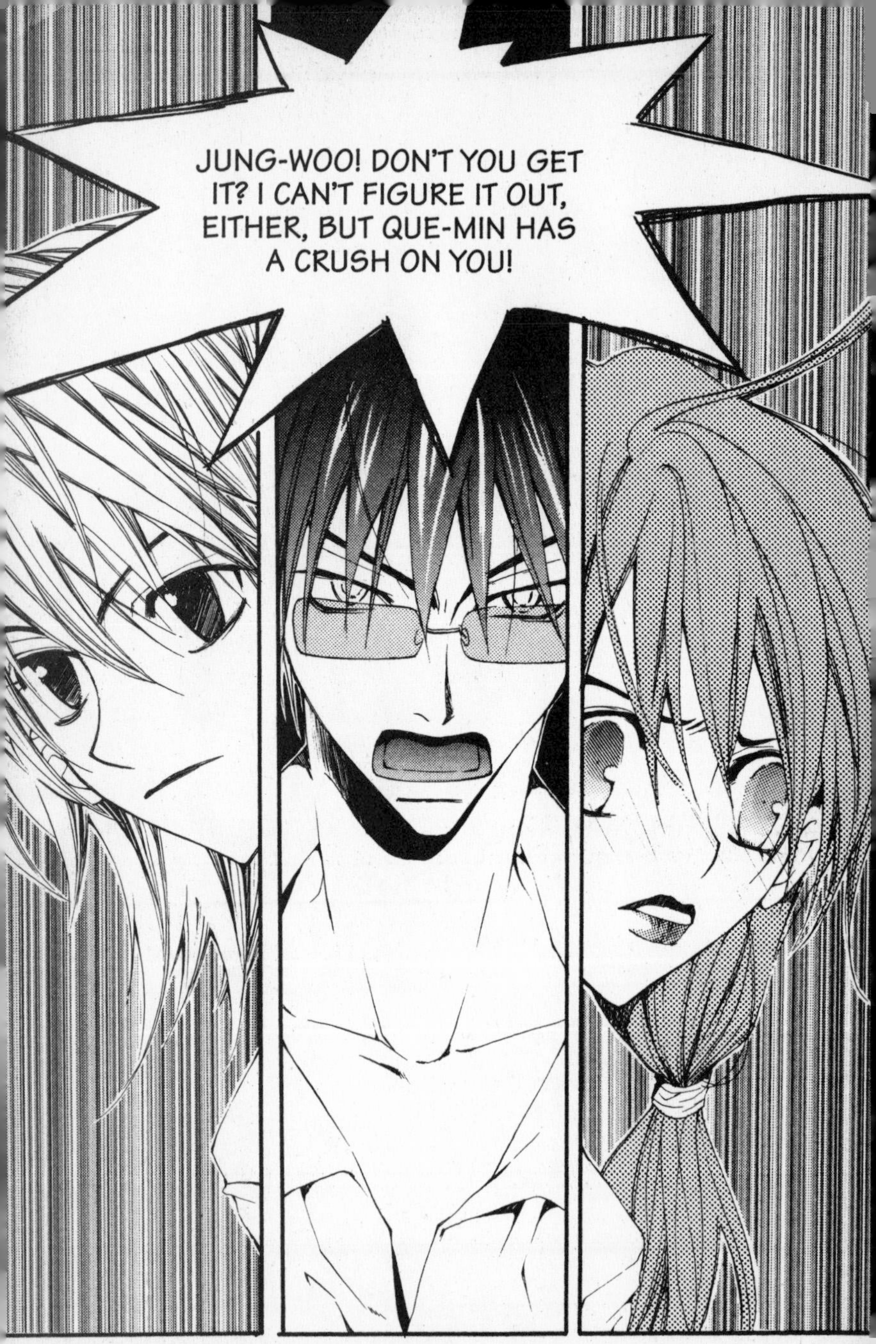
JUNG-WOO! DON'T YOU GET IT? I CAN'T FIGURE IT OUT, EITHER, BUT QUE-MIN HAS A CRUSH ON YOU!

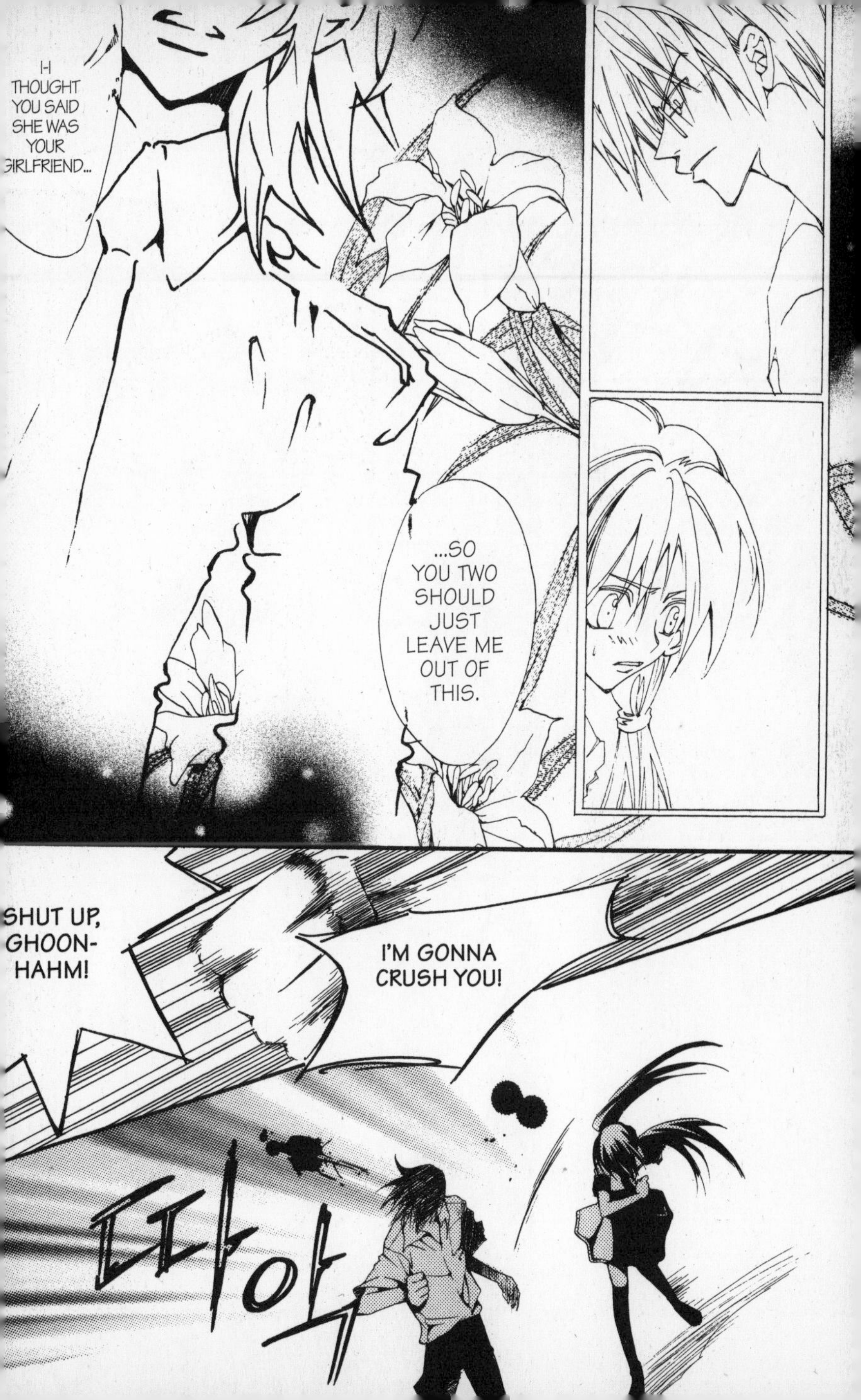
I-I THOUGHT YOU SAID SHE WAS YOUR GIRLFRIEND...
...SO YOU TWO SHOULD JUST LEAVE ME OUT OF THIS.
SHUT UP, GHOON-HAHM!
I'M GONNA CRUSH YOU!
ㄷㄷ아악

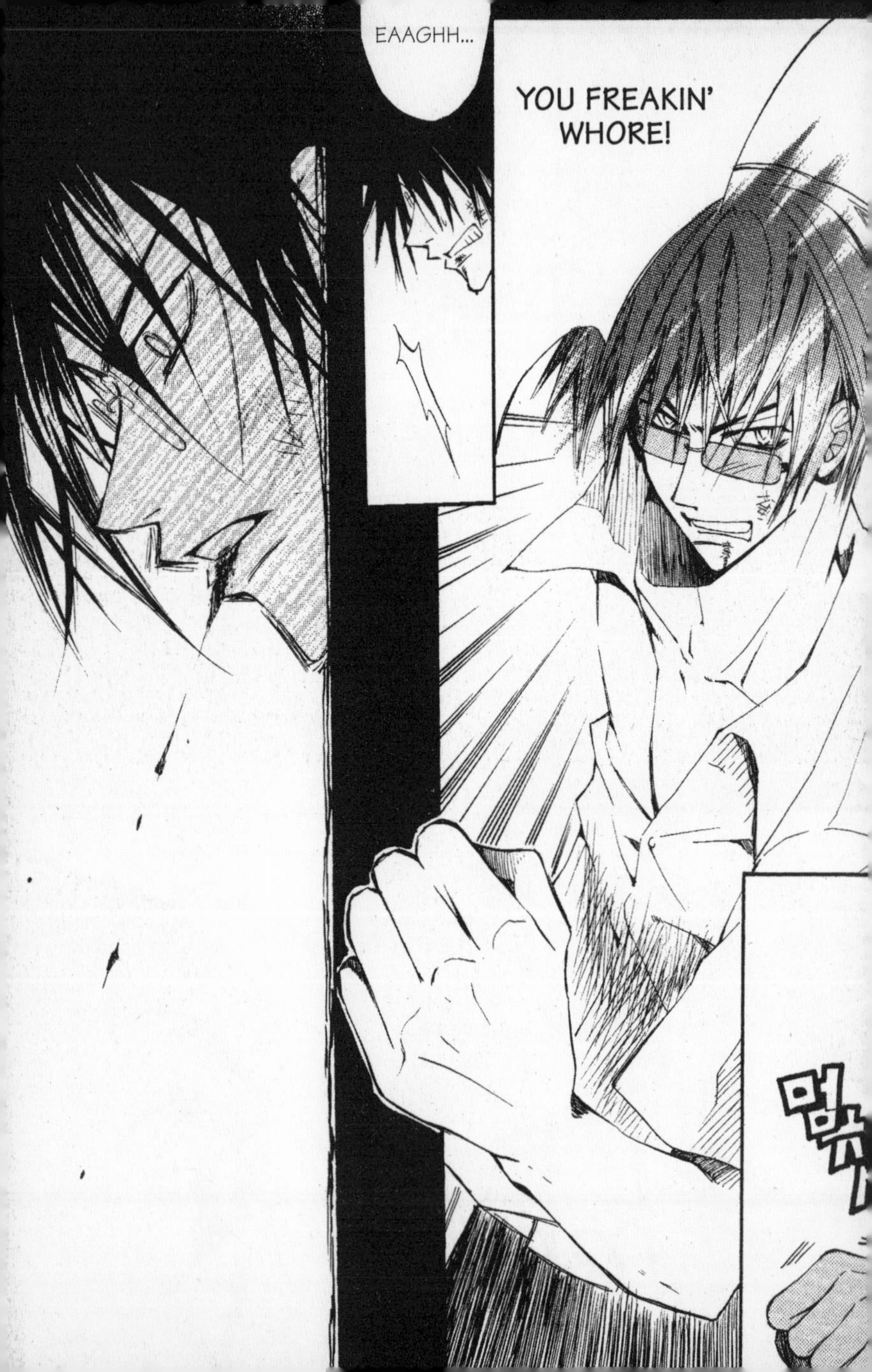
EAAGHH...
YOU FREAKIN' WHORE!

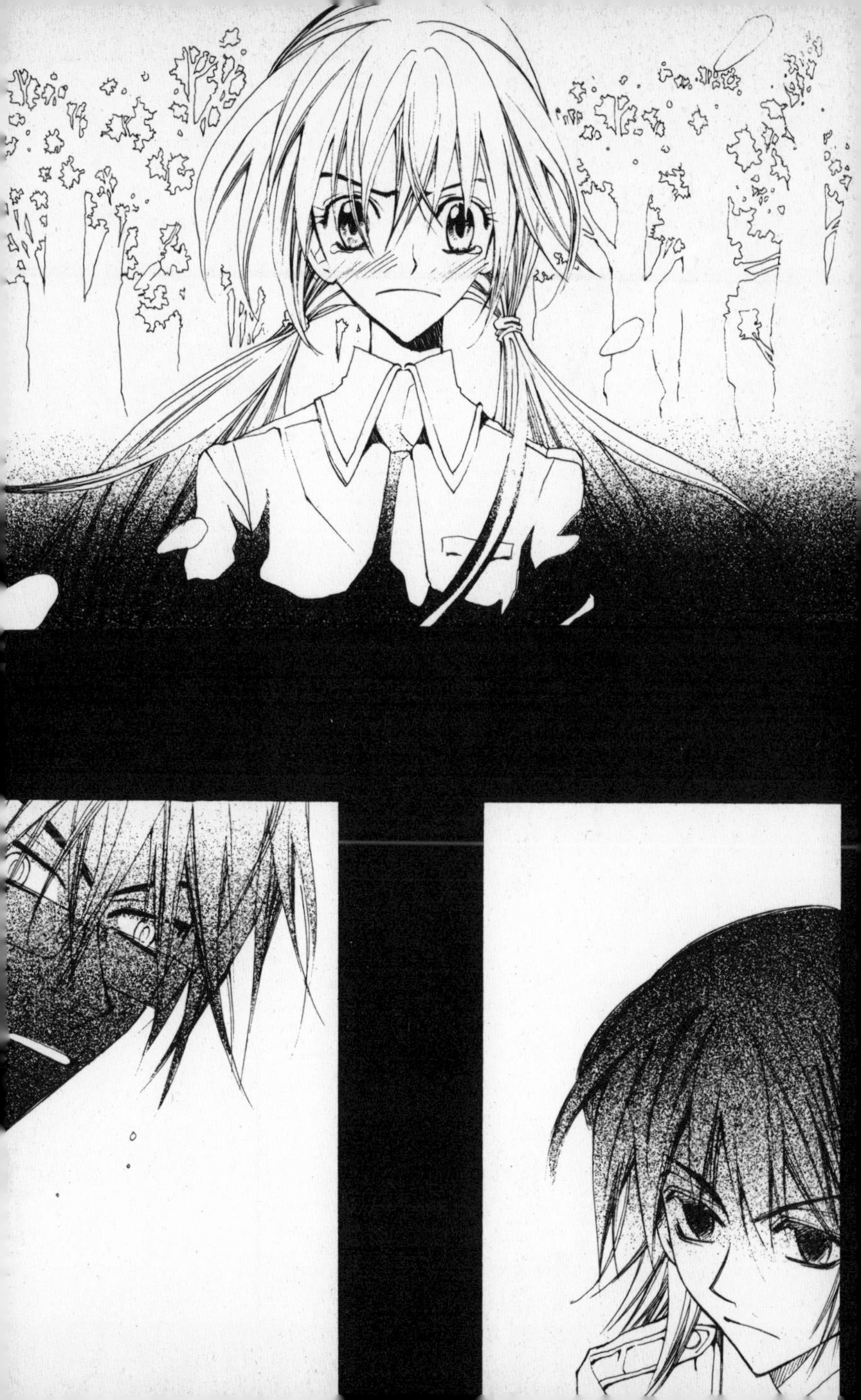

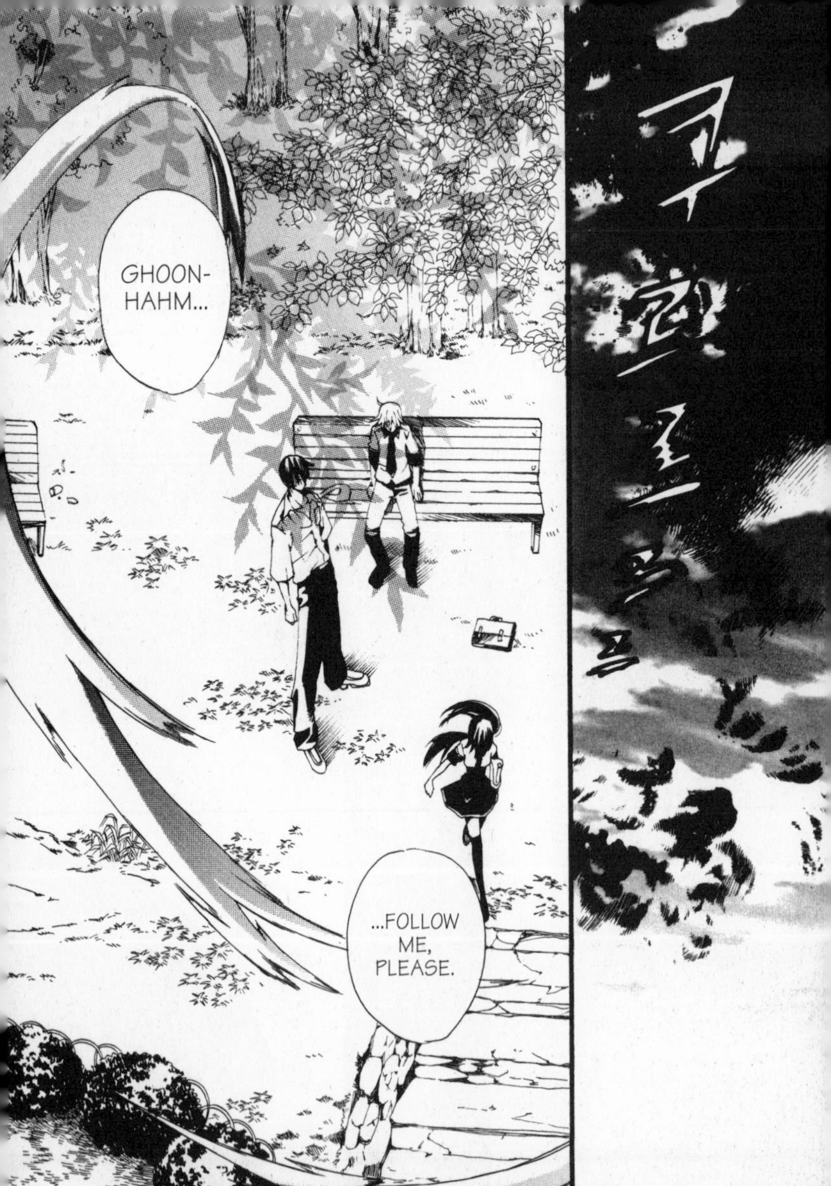
GHOON-HAHM...
...FOLLOW ME, PLEASE.

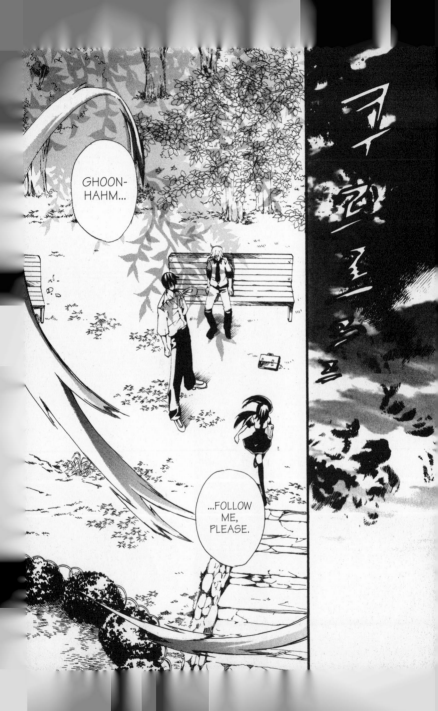

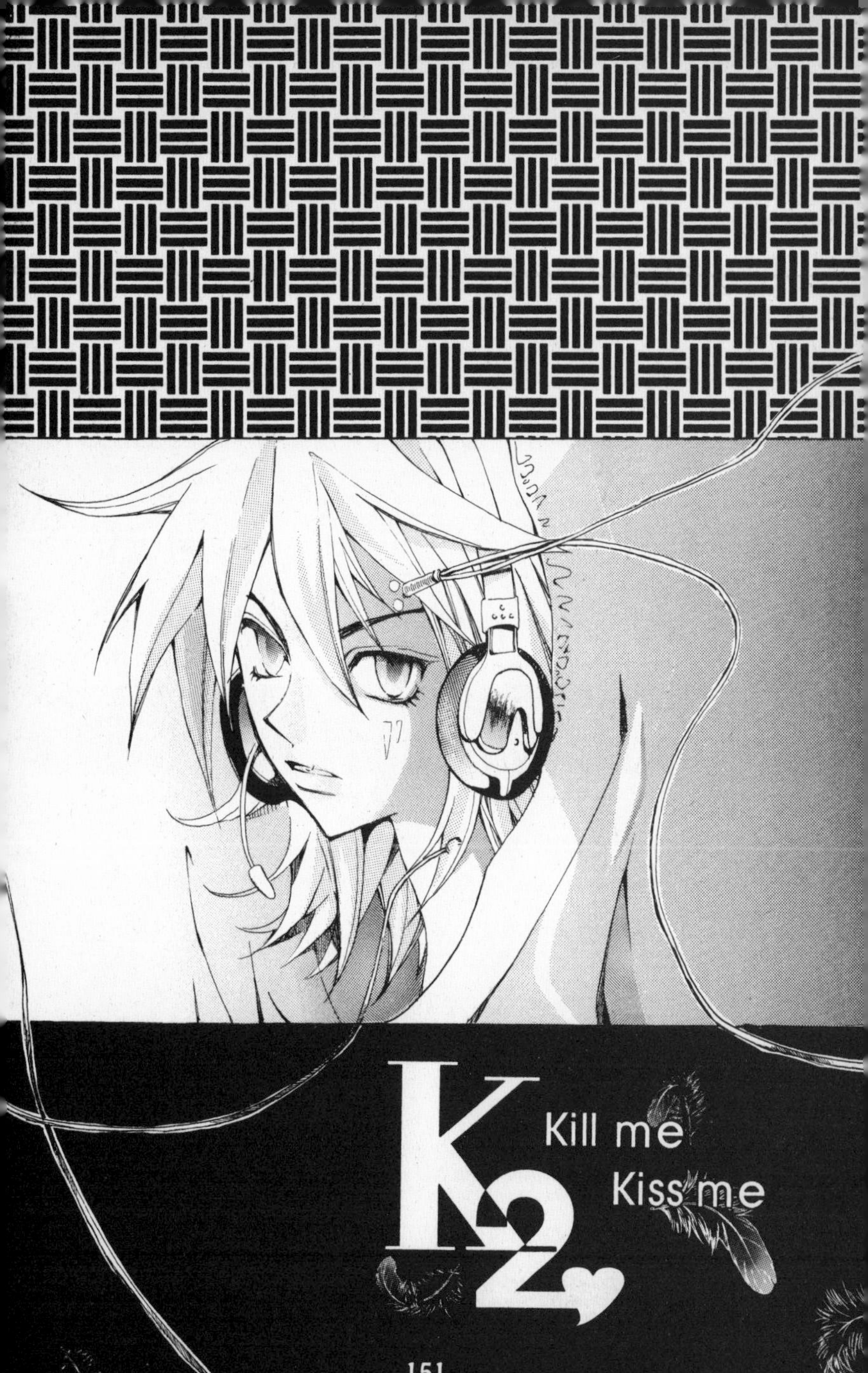
K2
Kill me
Kiss me

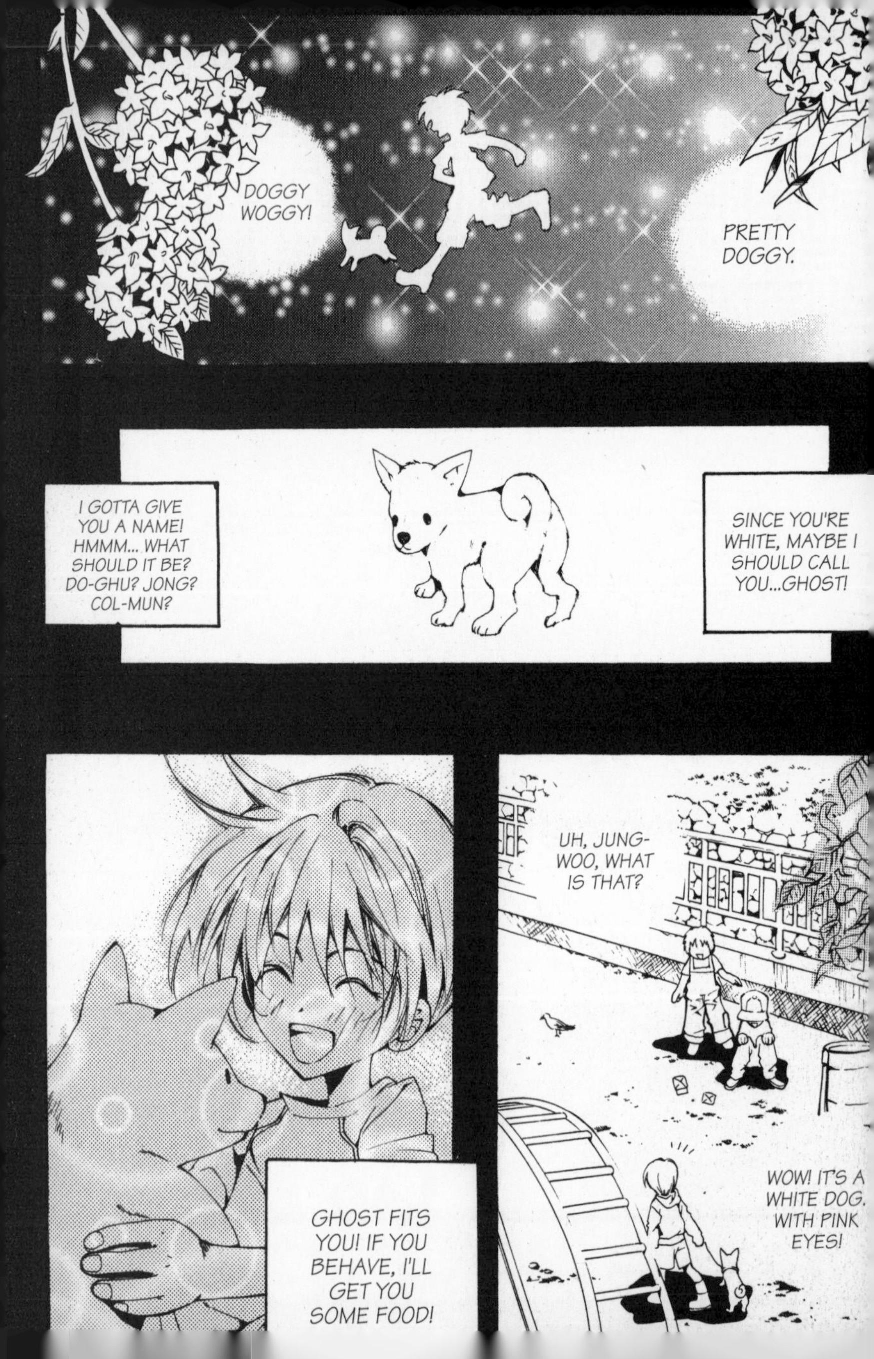
DOGGY WOGGY!
PRETTY DOGGY.
I GOTTA GIVE YOU A NAME! HMMM... WHAT SHOULD IT BE? DO-GHU? JONG? COL-MUN?
SINCE YOU'RE WHITE, MAYBE I SHOULD CALL YOU...GHOST!
GHOST FITS YOU! IF YOU BEHAVE, I'LL GET YOU SOME FOOD!
UH, JUNG-WOO, WHAT IS THAT?
WOW! IT'S A WHITE DOG. WITH PINK EYES!

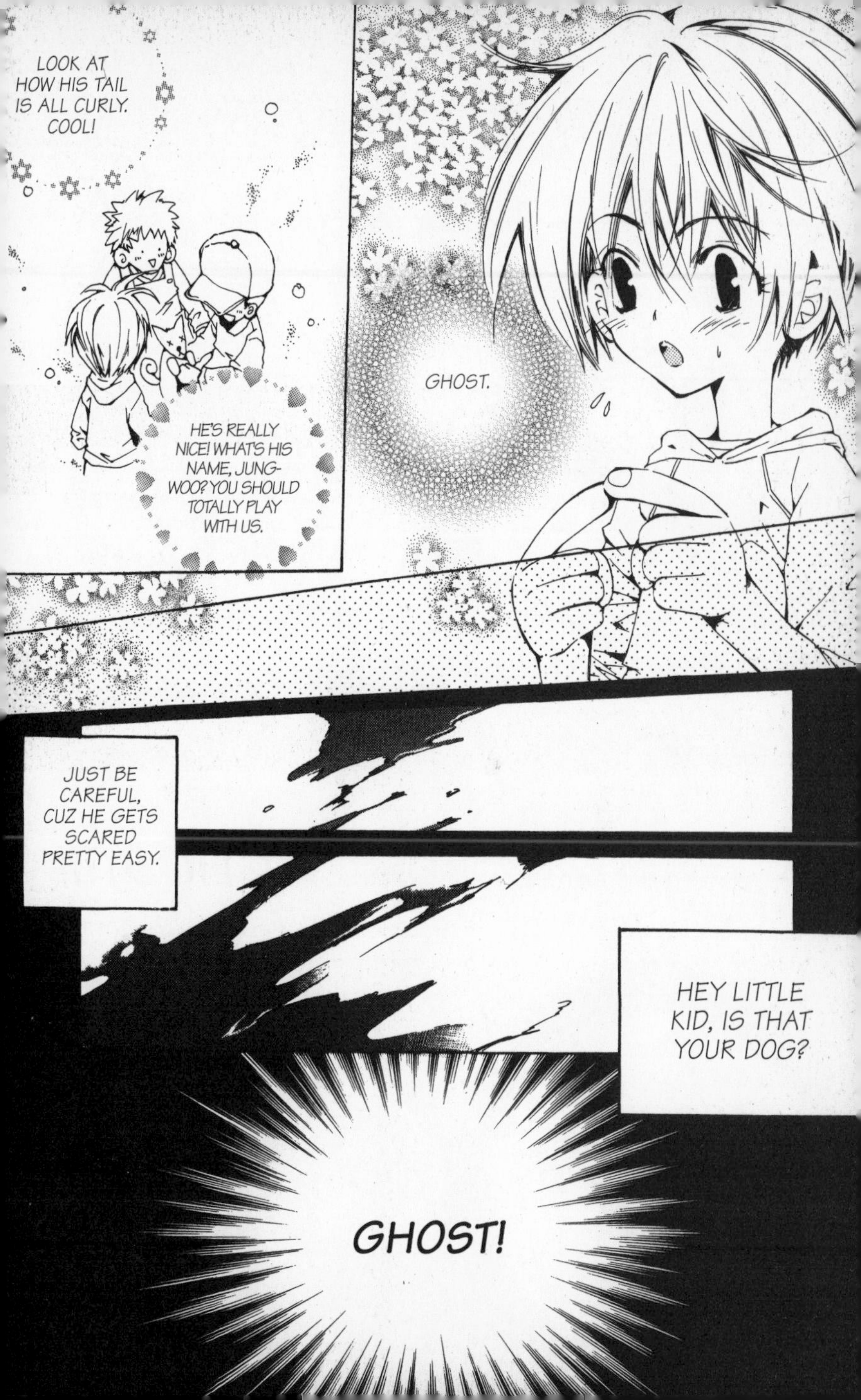
LOOK AT HOW HIS TAIL IS ALL CURLY. COOL!
HE'S REALLY NICE! WHAT'S HIS NAME, JUNG-WOO? YOU SHOULD TOTALLY PLAY WITH US.
GHOST.
JUST BE CAREFUL, CUZ HE GETS SCARED PRETTY EASY.
HEY LITTLE KID, IS THAT YOUR DOG?
GHOST!

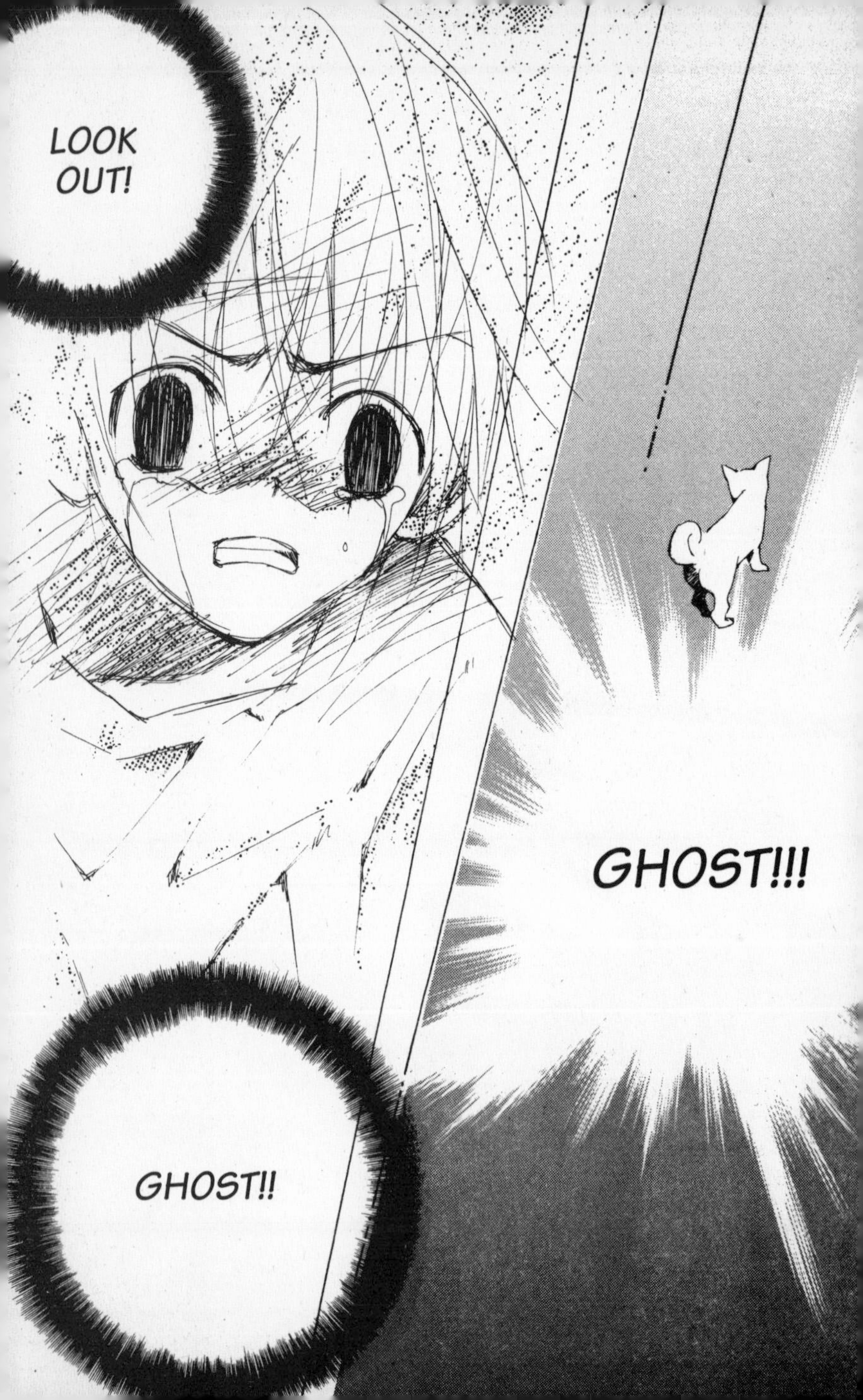
LOOK OUT!
GHOST!!!
GHOST!!

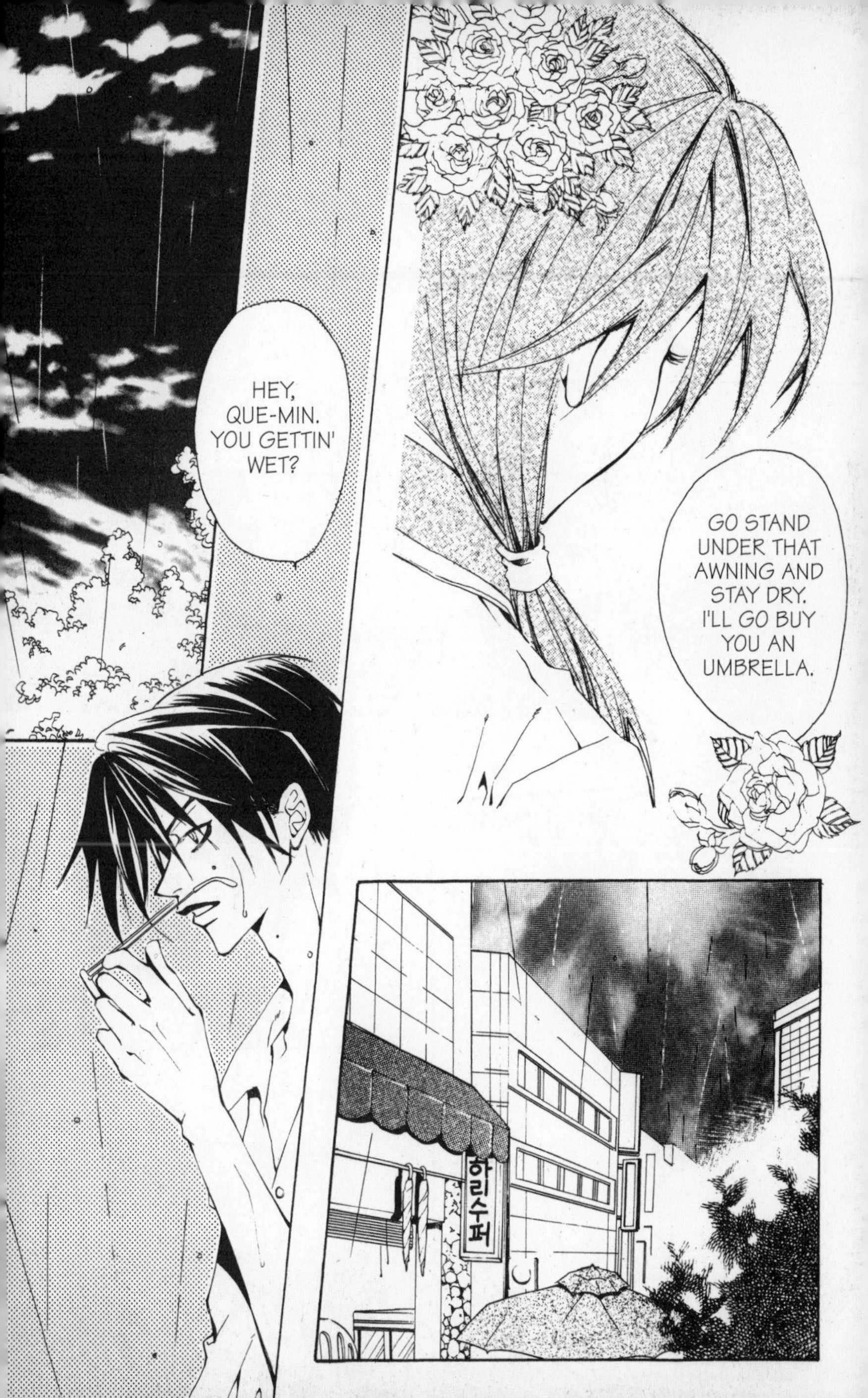
HEY, QUE-MIN. YOU GETTIN' WET?
GO STAND UNDER THAT AWNING AND STAY DRY. I'LL GO BUY YOU AN UMBRELLA.
하리수퍼

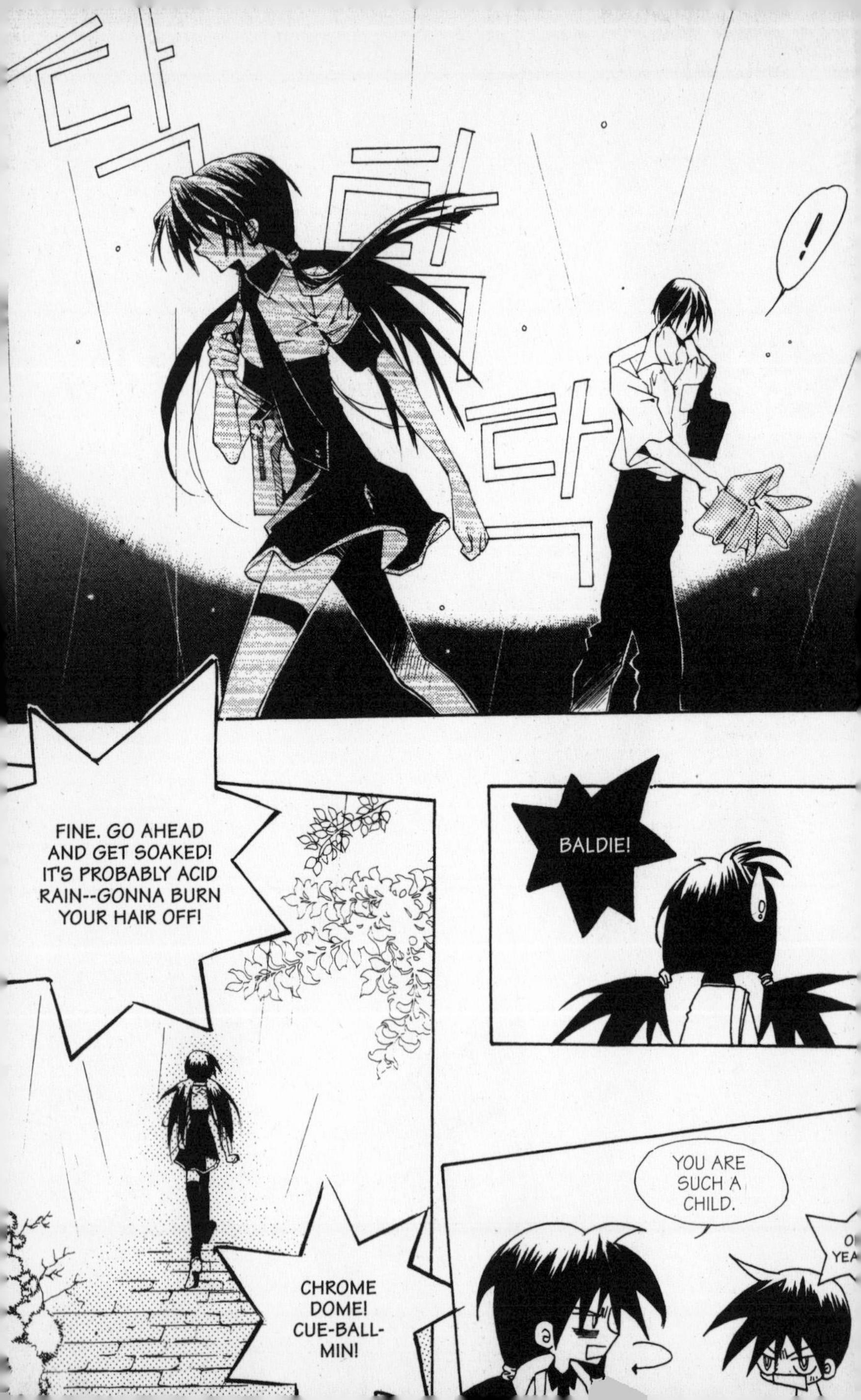
!
FINE. GO AHEAD AND GET SOAKED! IT'S PROBABLY ACID RAIN--GONNA BURN YOUR HAIR OFF!
BALDIE!
CHROME DOME! CUE-BALL-MIN!
YOU ARE SUCH A CHILD.

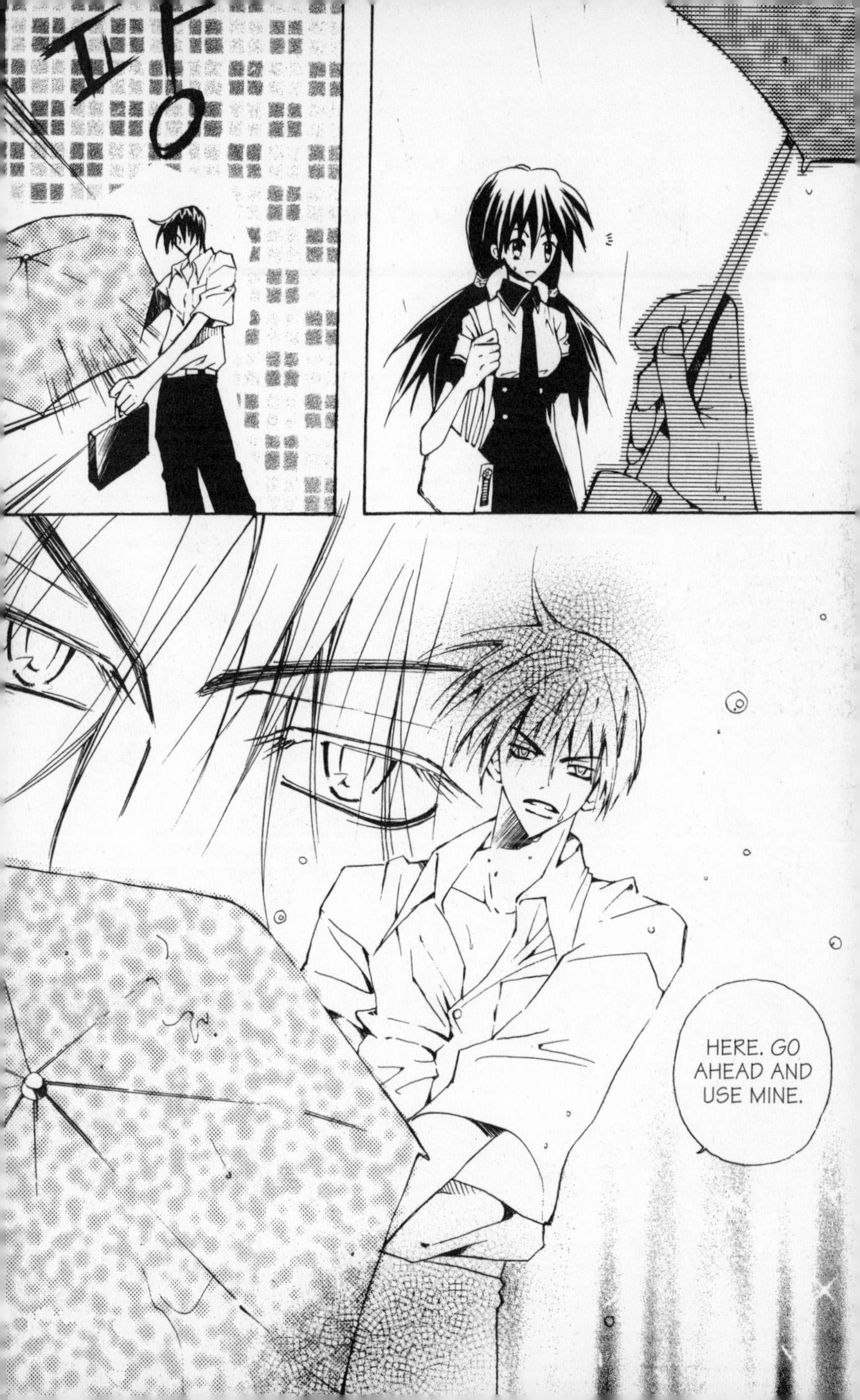
팡
HERE. GO AHEAD AND USE MINE.

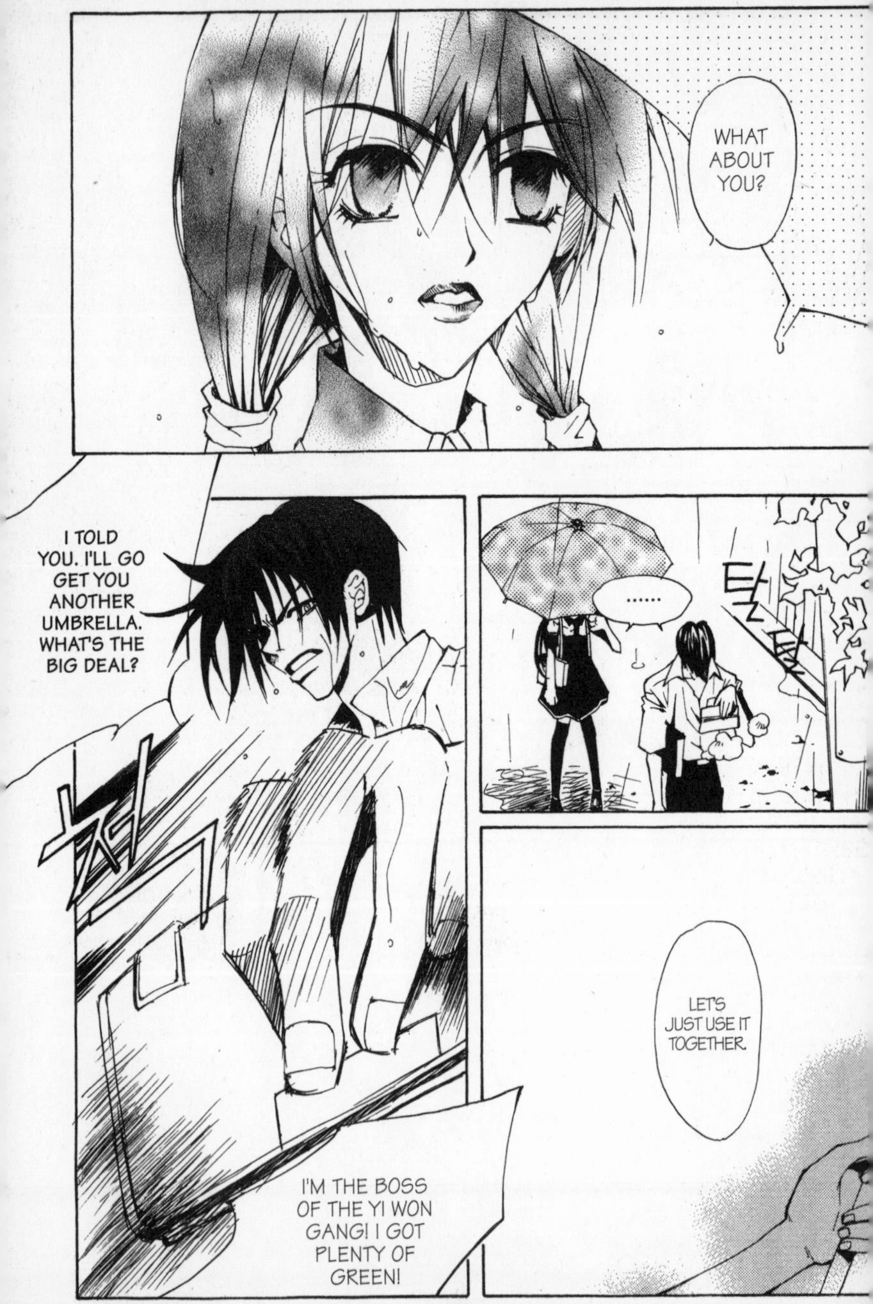
WHAT ABOUT YOU?
I TOLD YOU. I'LL GO GET YOU ANOTHER UMBRELLA. WHAT'S THE BIG DEAL?
I'M THE BOSS OF THE YI WON GANG! I GOT PLENTY OF GREEN!
......
LET'S JUST USE IT TOGETHER.

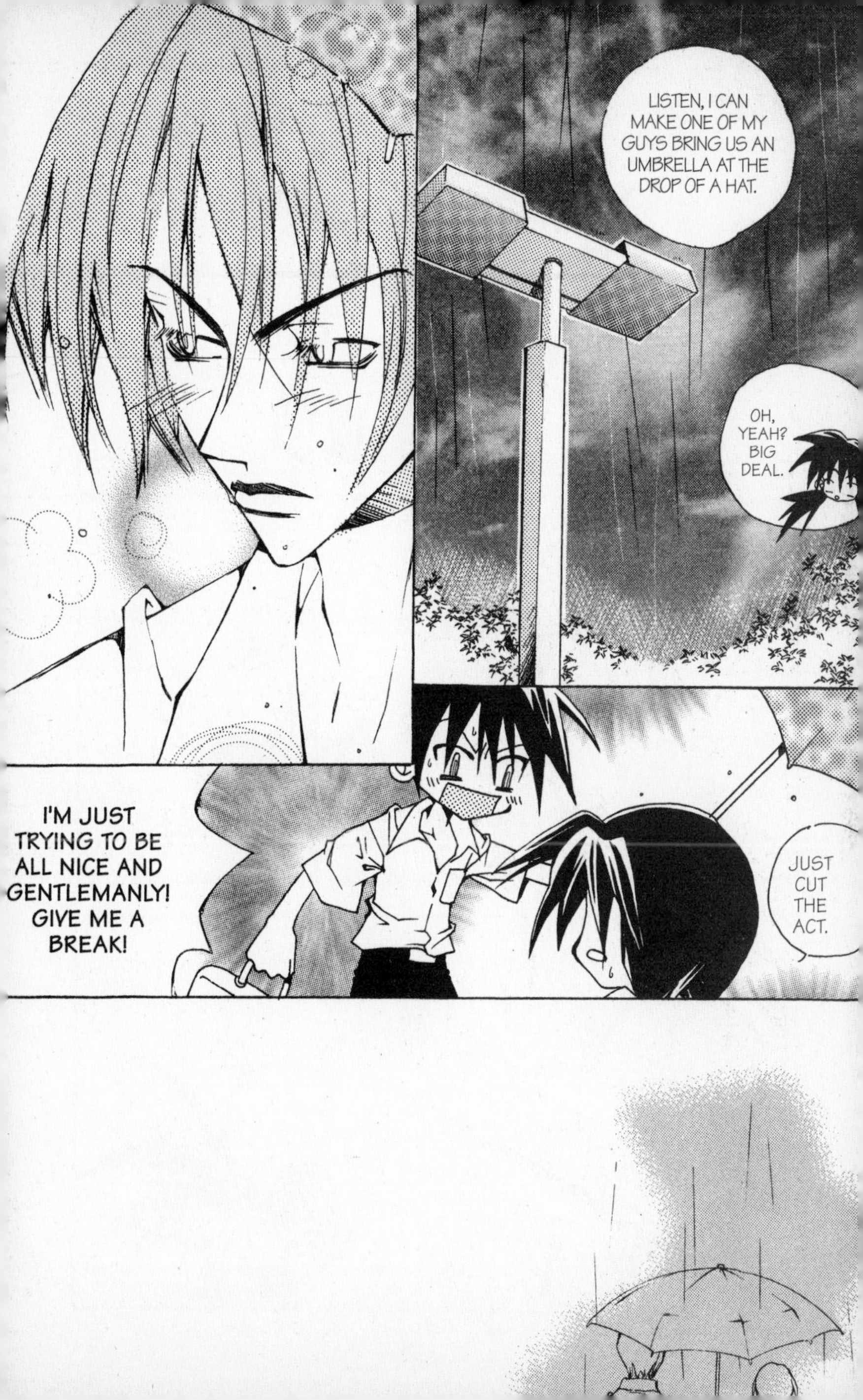
LISTEN, I CAN MAKE ONE OF MY GUYS BRING US AN UMBRELLA AT THE DROP OF A HAT.
OH, YEAH? BIG DEAL.
I'M JUST TRYING TO BE ALL NICE AND GENTLEMANLY! GIVE ME A BREAK!
JUST CUT THE ACT.

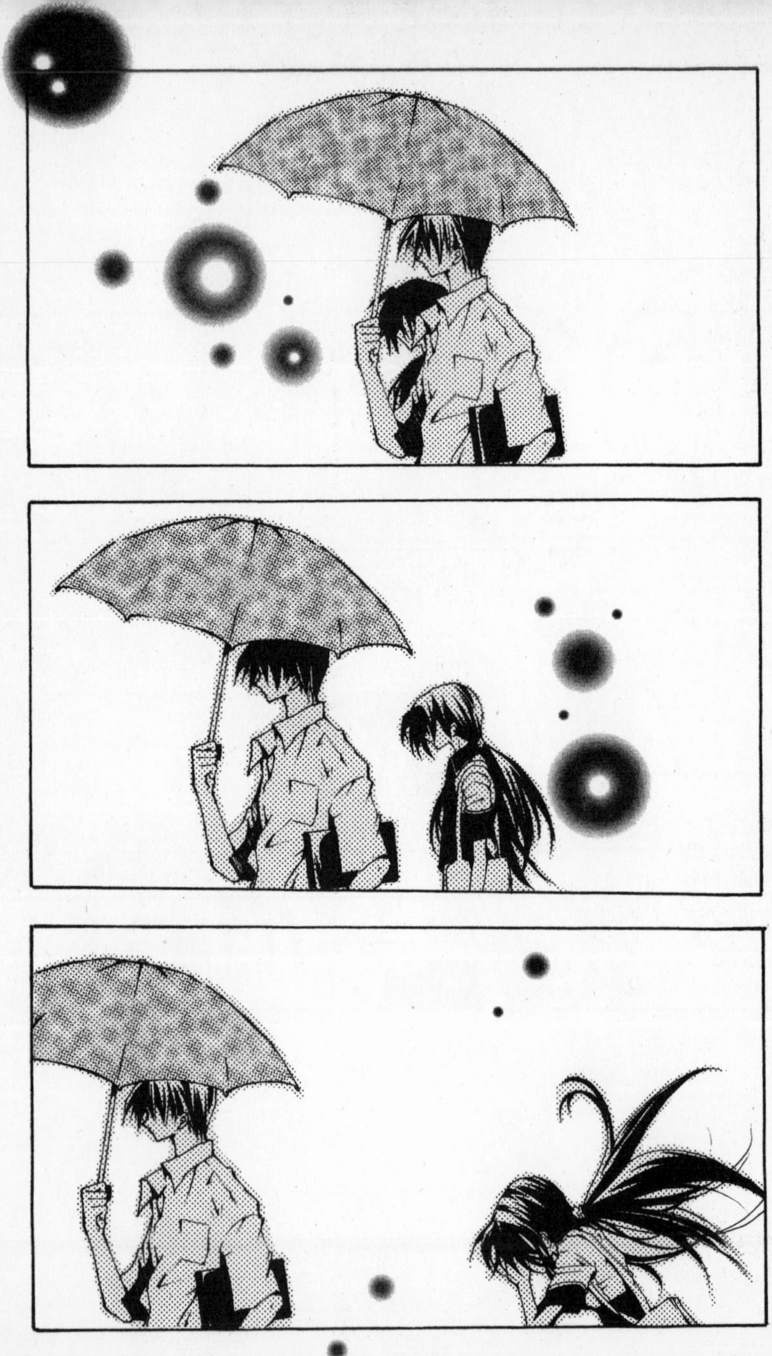

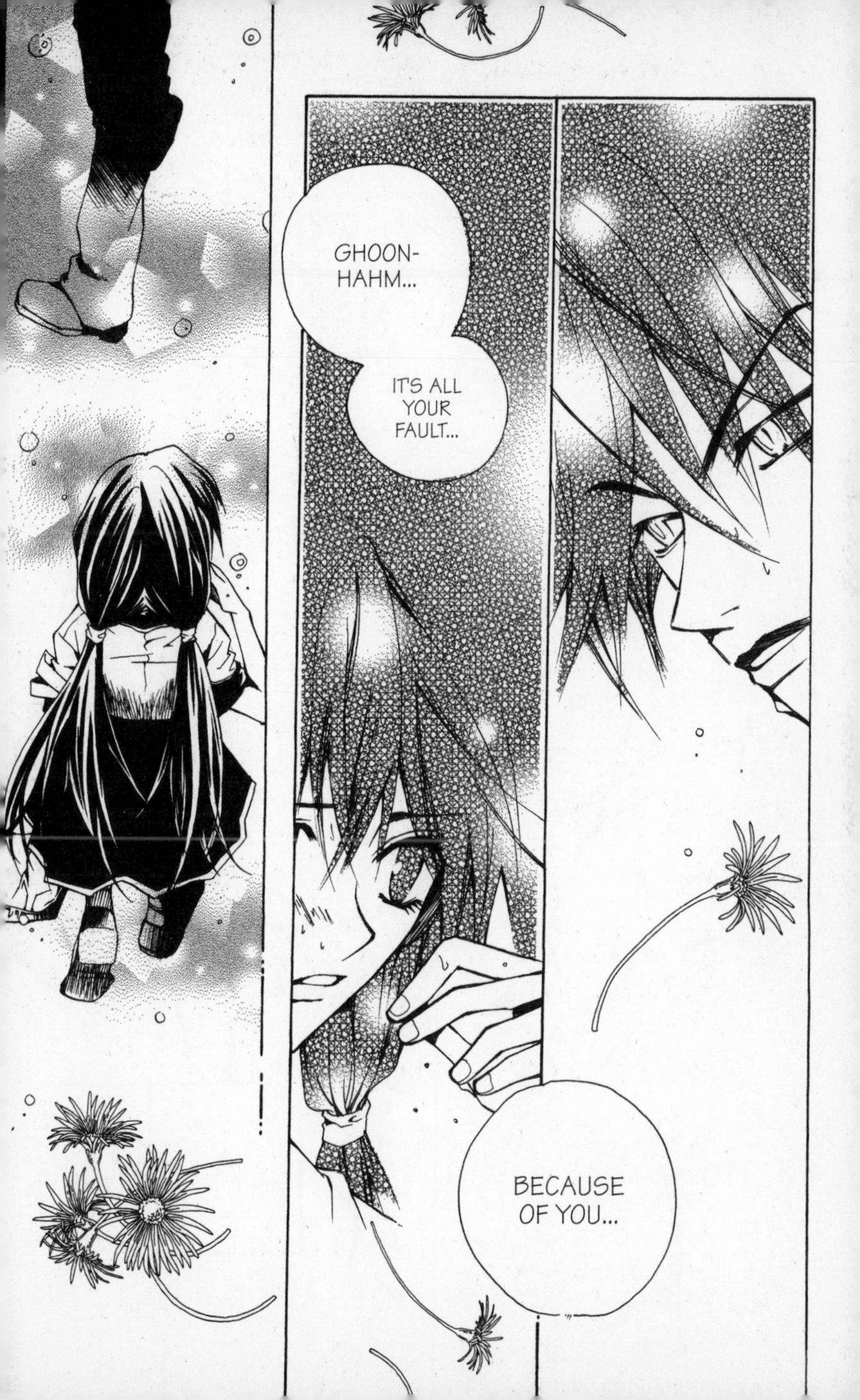
GHOON-HAHM...
IT'S ALL YOUR FAULT...
BECAUSE OF YOU...

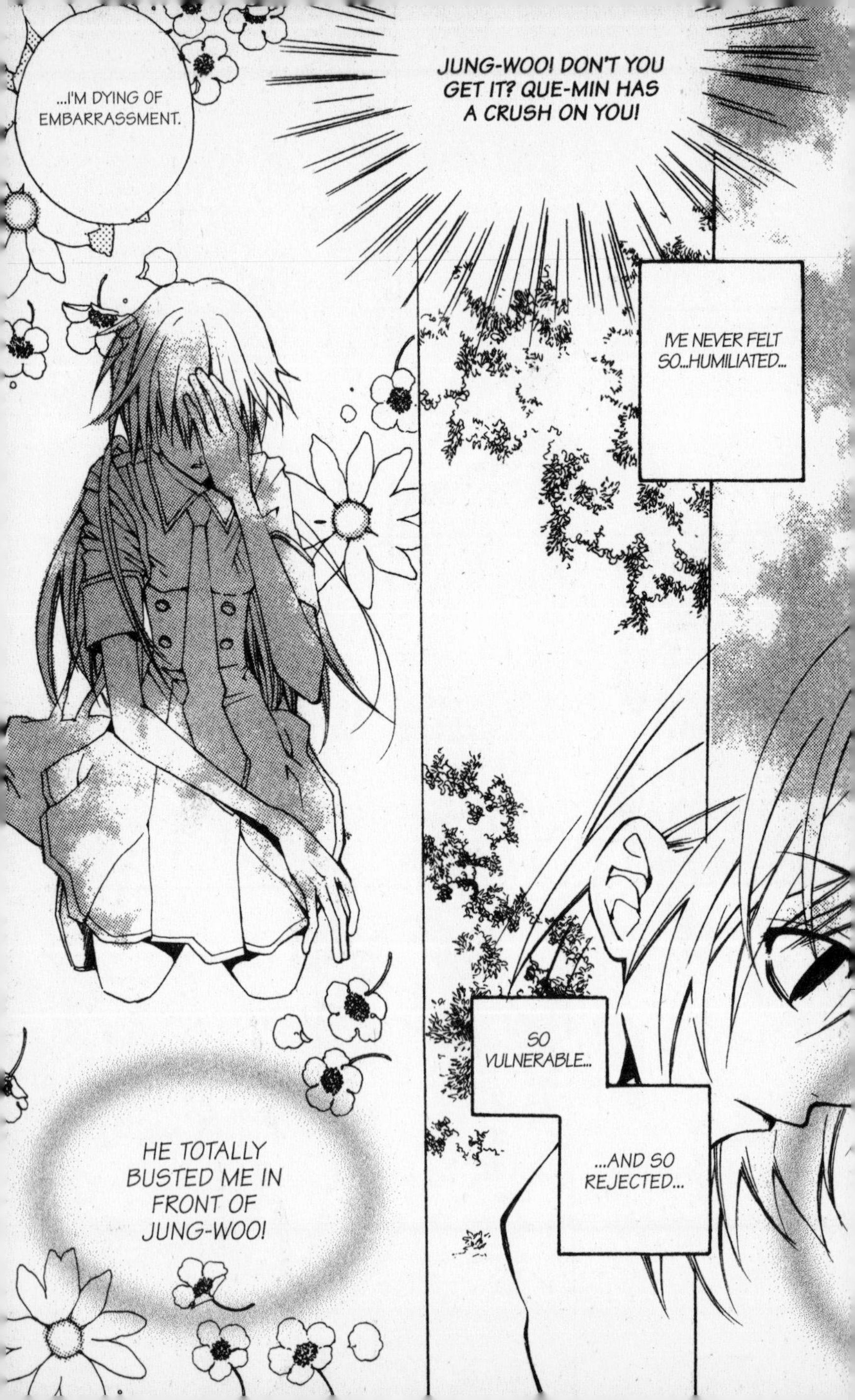
...I'M DYING OF EMBARRASSMENT.
JUNG-WOO! DON'T YOU GET IT? QUE-MIN HAS A CRUSH ON YOU!
HE TOTALLY BUSTED ME IN FRONT OF JUNG-WOO!
I'VE NEVER FELT SO...HUMILIATED...
SO VULNERABLE...
...AND SO REJECTED...

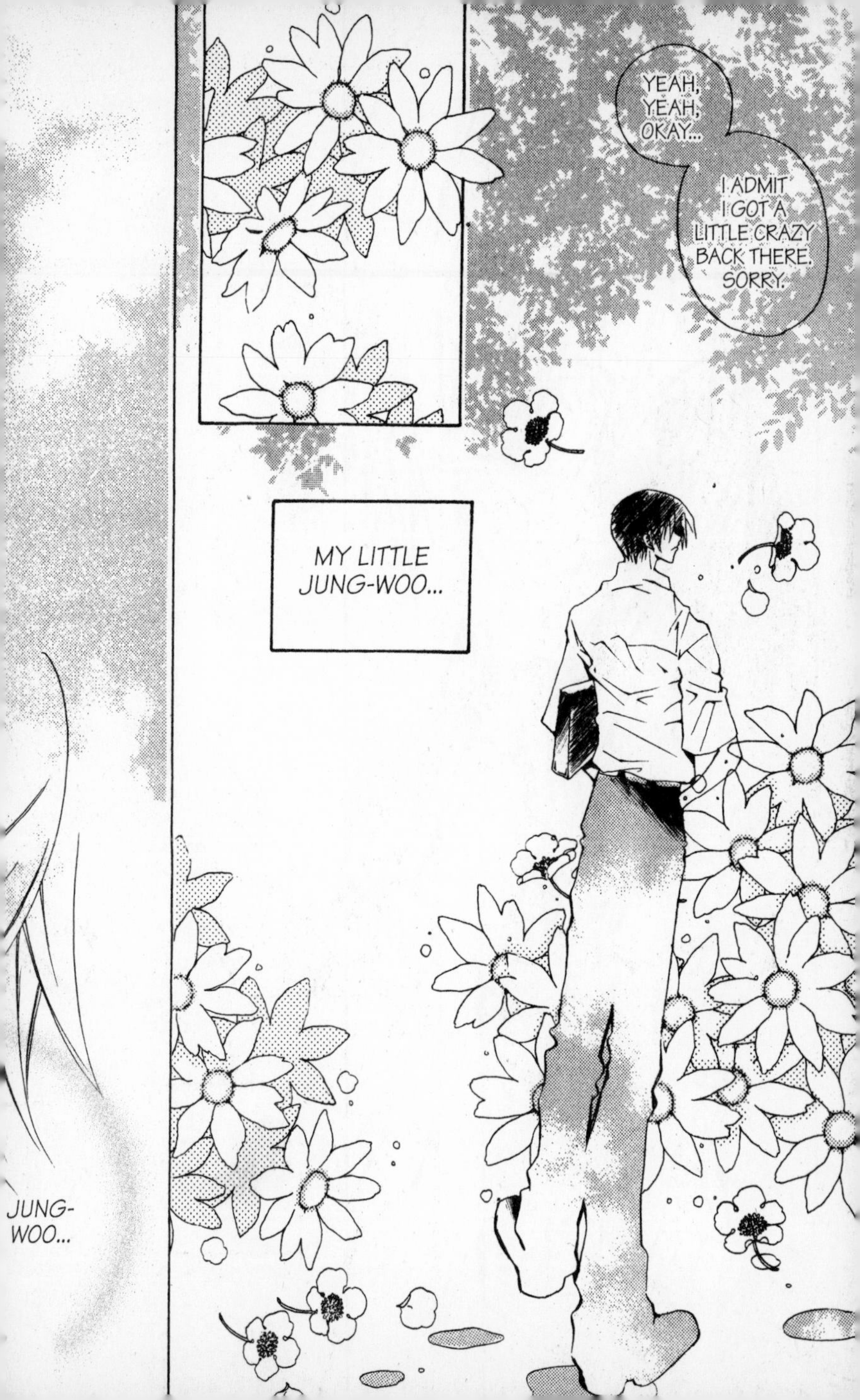
JUNG-WOO...
YEAH, YEAH, OKAY...
I ADMIT I GOT A LITTLE CRAZY BACK THERE. SORRY.
MY LITTLE JUNG-WOO...

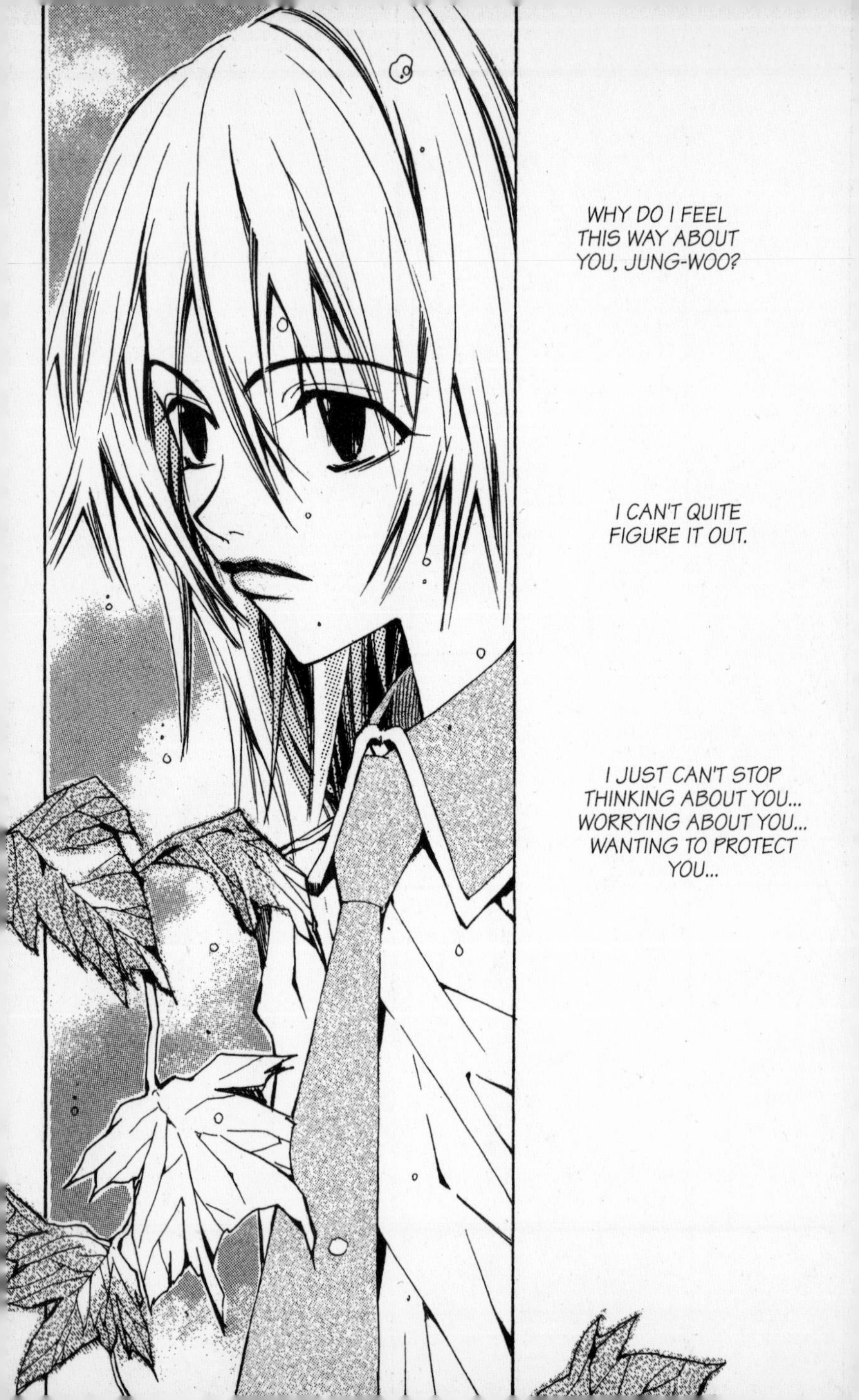
WHY DO I FEEL THIS WAY ABOUT YOU, JUNG-WOO?
I CAN'T QUITE FIGURE IT OUT.
I JUST CAN'T STOP THINKING ABOUT YOU... WORRYING ABOUT YOU... WANTING TO PROTECT YOU...

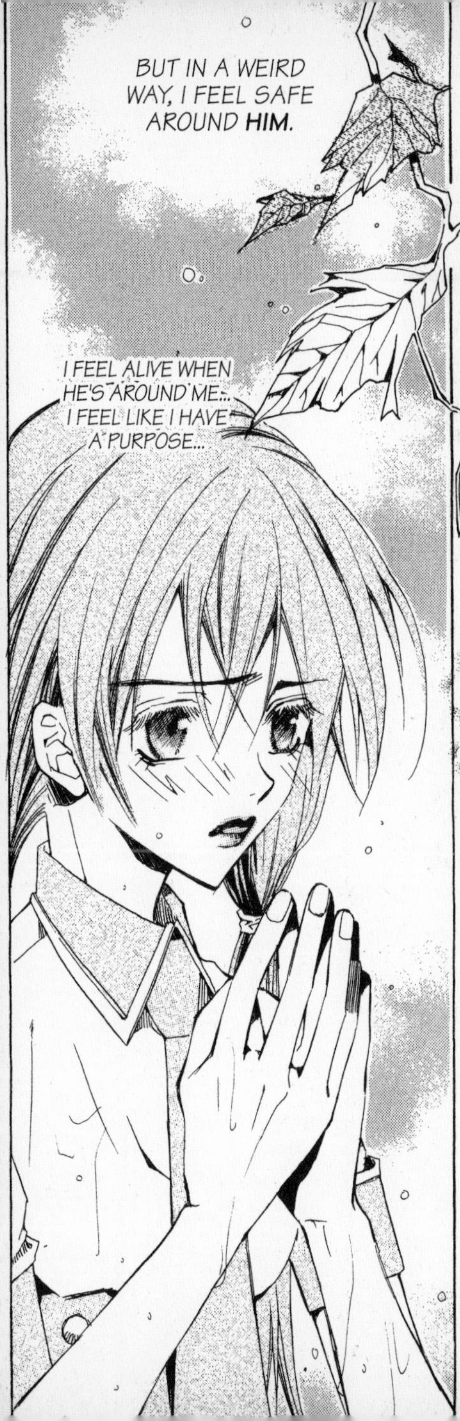
BUT IN A WEIRD WAY, I FEEL SAFE AROUND **HIM**.
I FEEL ALIVE WHEN HE'S AROUND ME... I FEEL LIKE I HAVE A PURPOSE...

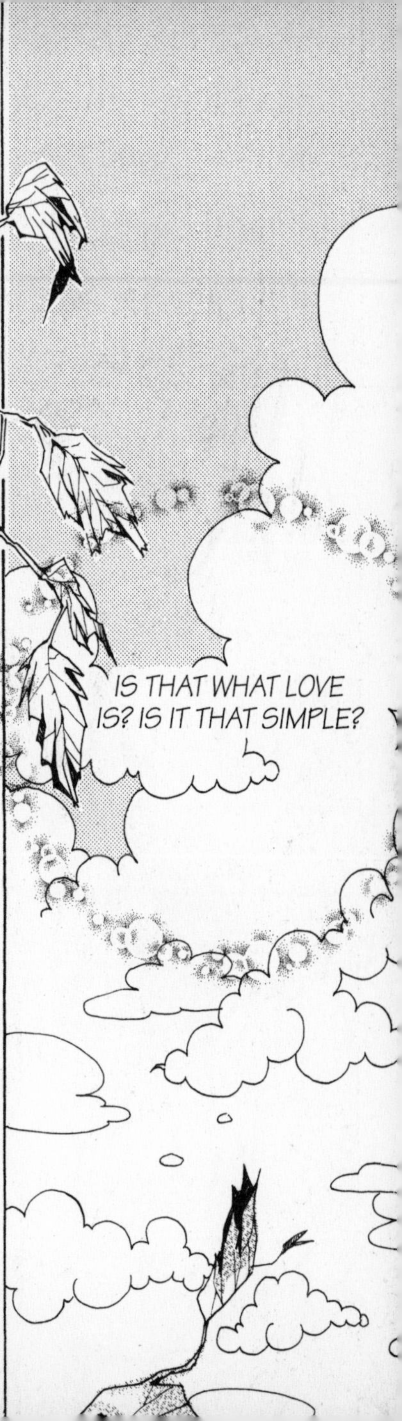
IS THAT WHAT LOVE IS? IS IT THAT SIMPLE?

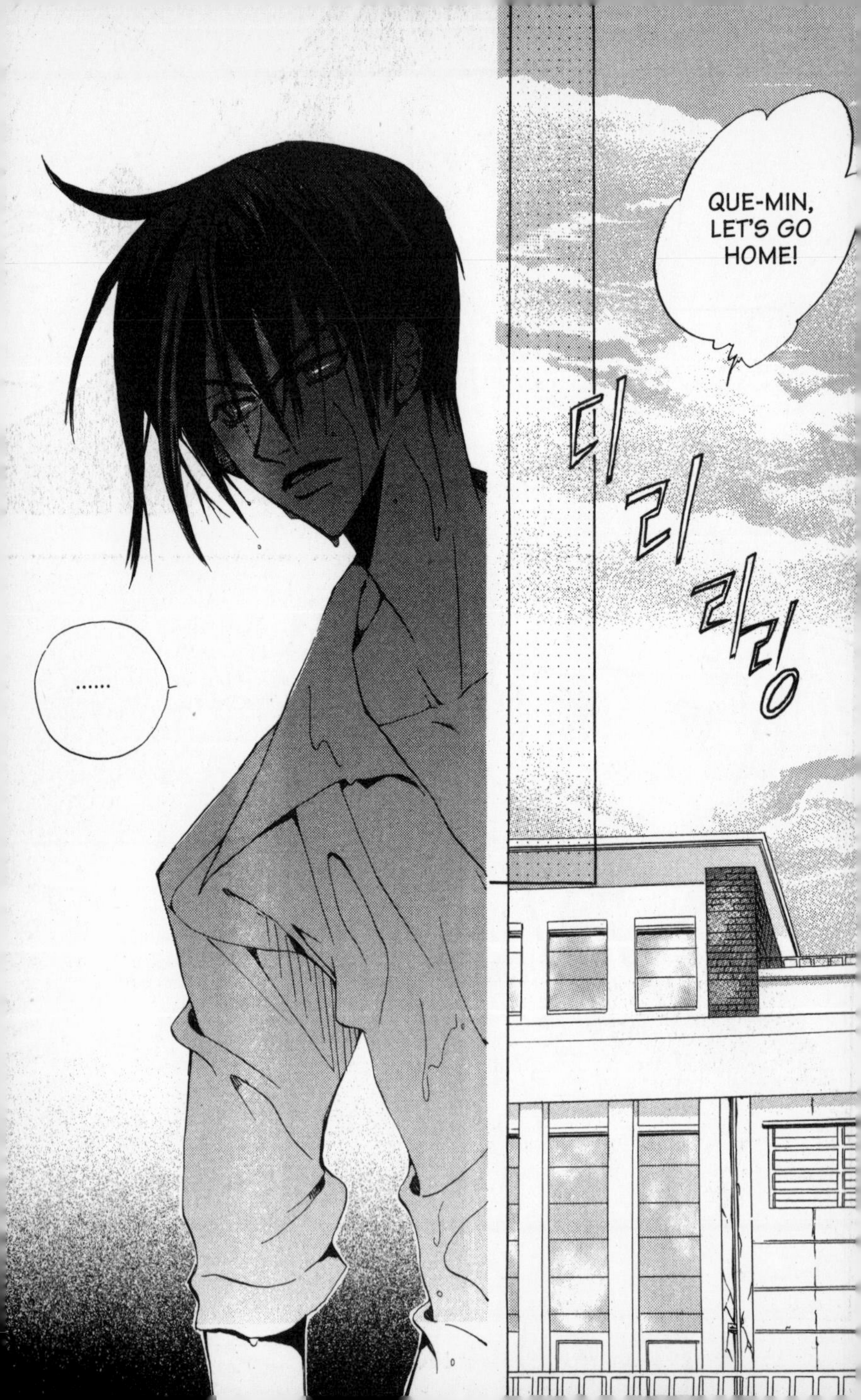
......
QUE-MIN, LET'S GO HOME!
디리라링

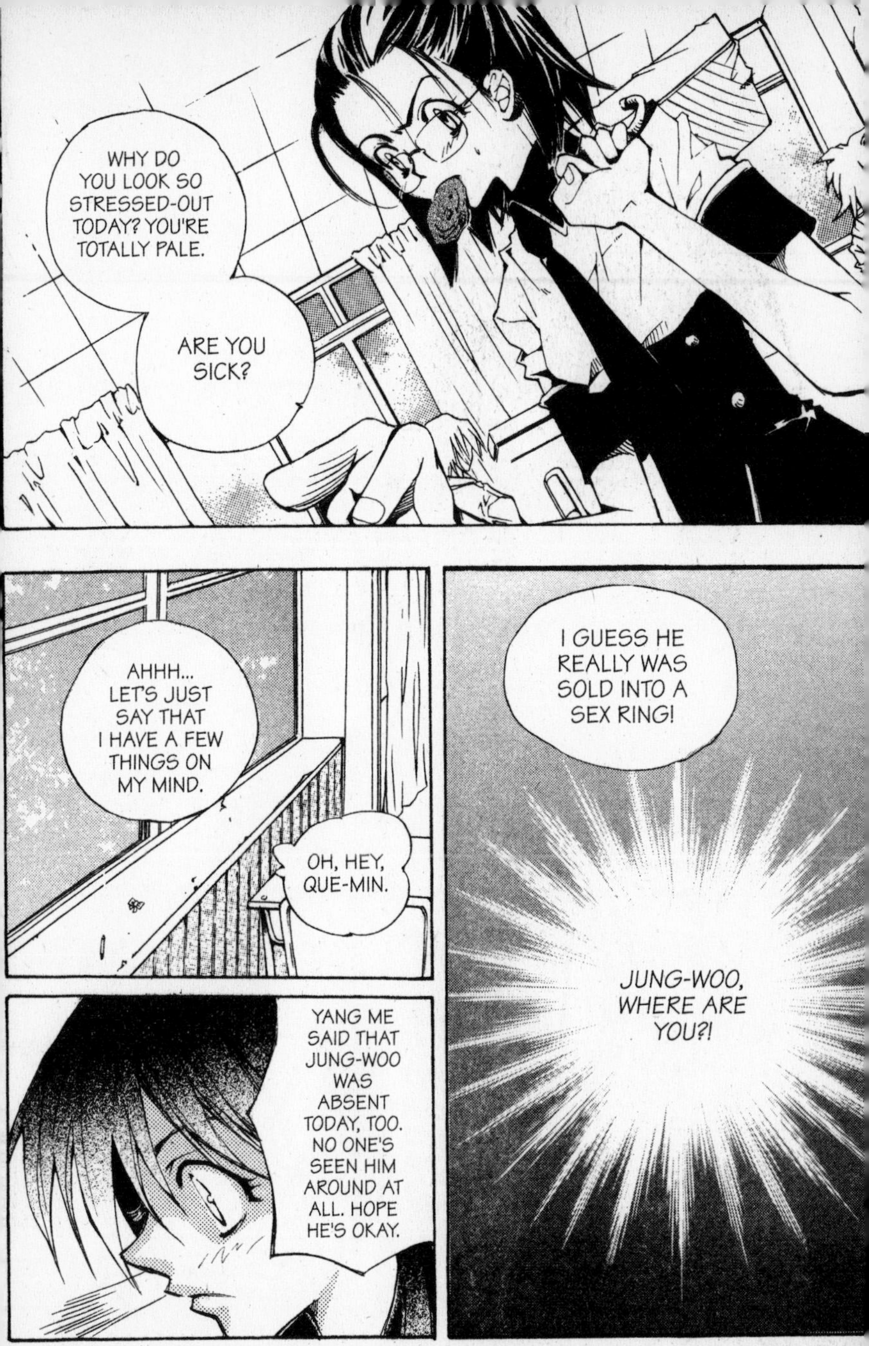
WHY DO YOU LOOK SO STRESSED-OUT TODAY? YOU'RE TOTALLY PALE.
ARE YOU SICK?
AHHH... LET'S JUST SAY THAT I HAVE A FEW THINGS ON MY MIND.
OH, HEY, QUE-MIN.
YANG ME SAID THAT JUNG-WOO WAS ABSENT TODAY, TOO. NO ONE'S SEEN HIM AROUND AT ALL. HOPE HE'S OKAY.
I GUESS HE REALLY WAS SOLD INTO A SEX RING!
JUNG-WOO, WHERE ARE YOU?!

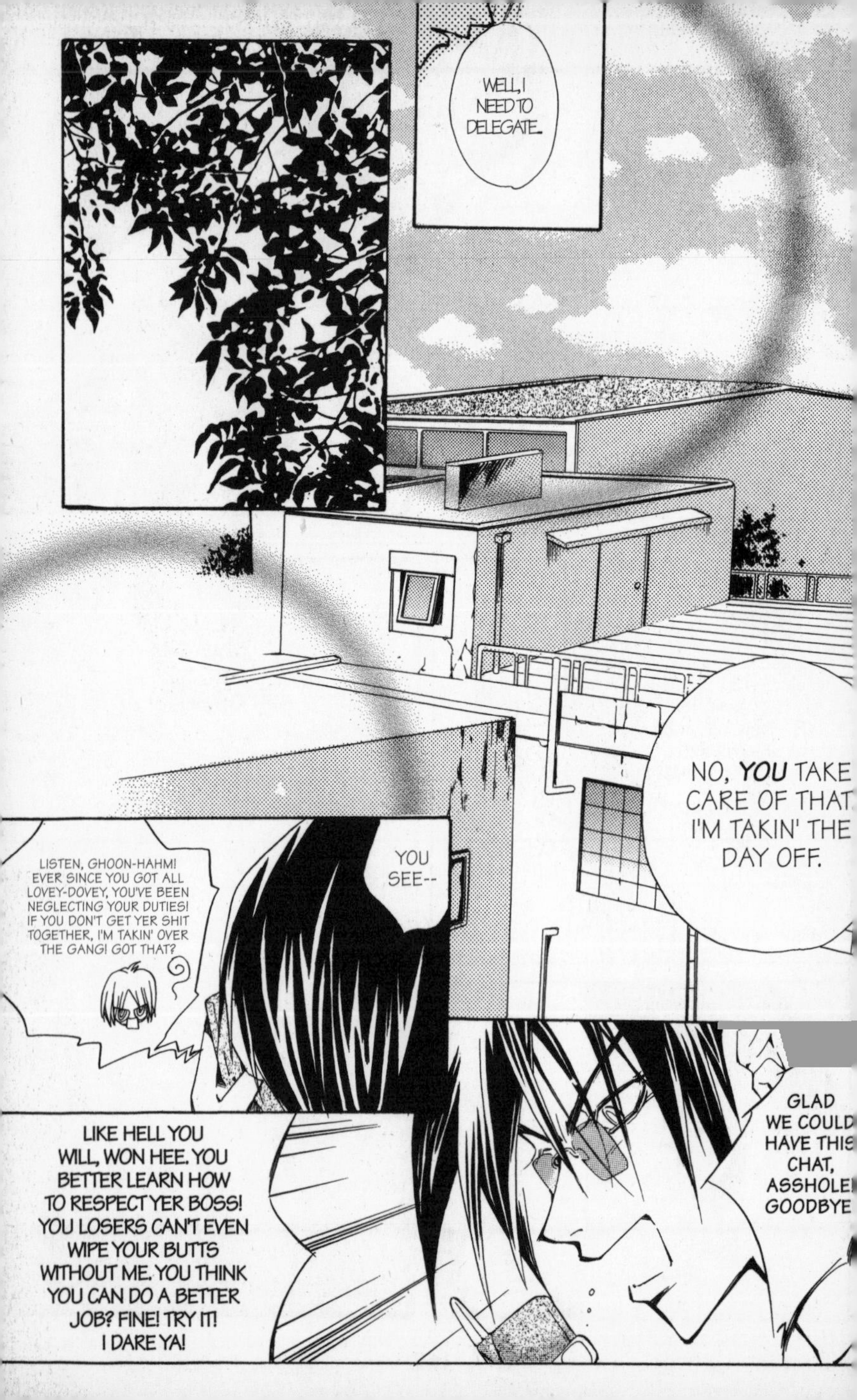
WELL, I NEED TO DELEGATE...
NO, YOU TAKE CARE OF THAT. I'M TAKIN' THE DAY OFF.
LISTEN, GHOON-HAHM! EVER SINCE YOU GOT ALL LOVEY-DOVEY, YOU'VE BEEN NEGLECTING YOUR DUTIES! IF YOU DON'T GET YER SHIT TOGETHER, I'M TAKIN' OVER THE GANG! GOT THAT?
YOU SEE--
LIKE HELL YOU WILL, WON HEE. YOU BETTER LEARN HOW TO RESPECT YER BOSS! YOU LOSERS CAN'T EVEN WIPE YOUR BUTTS WITHOUT ME. YOU THINK YOU CAN DO A BETTER JOB? FINE! TRY IT! I DARE YA!
GLAD WE COULD HAVE THIS CHAT, ASSHOLE! GOODBYE

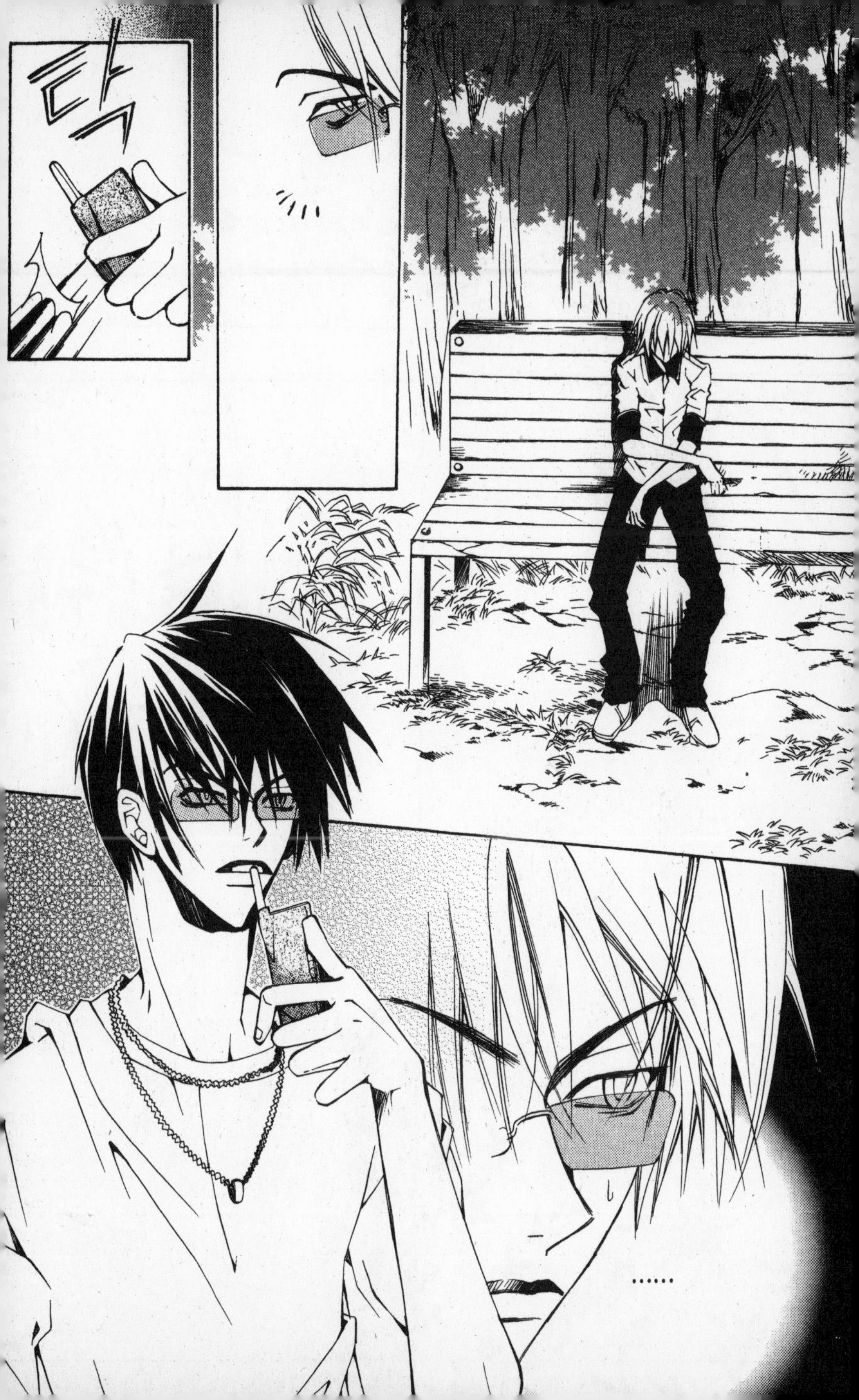
......

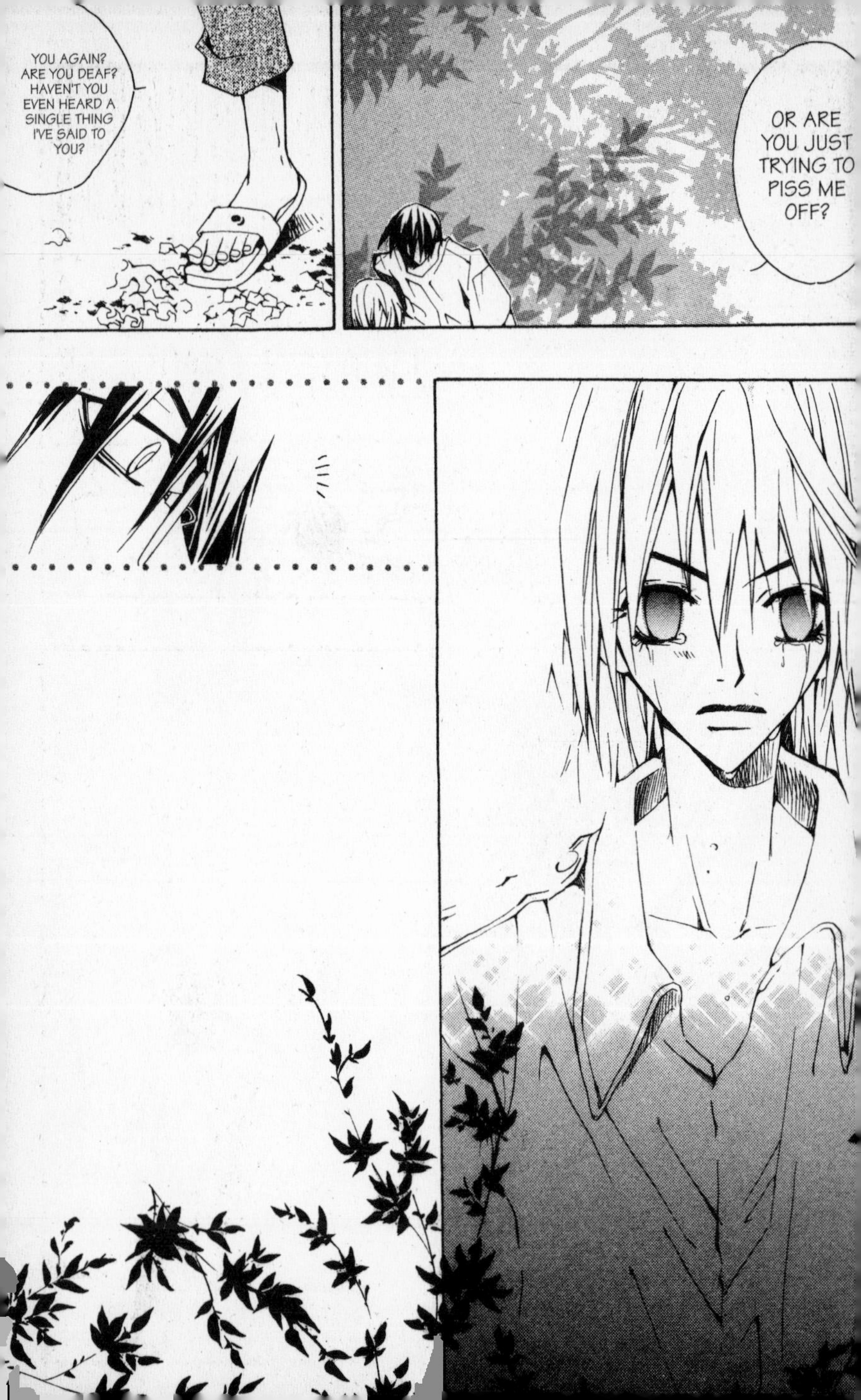
YOU AGAIN? ARE YOU DEAF? HAVEN'T YOU EVEN HEARD A SINGLE THING I'VE SAID TO YOU?
OR ARE YOU JUST TRYING TO PISS ME OFF?

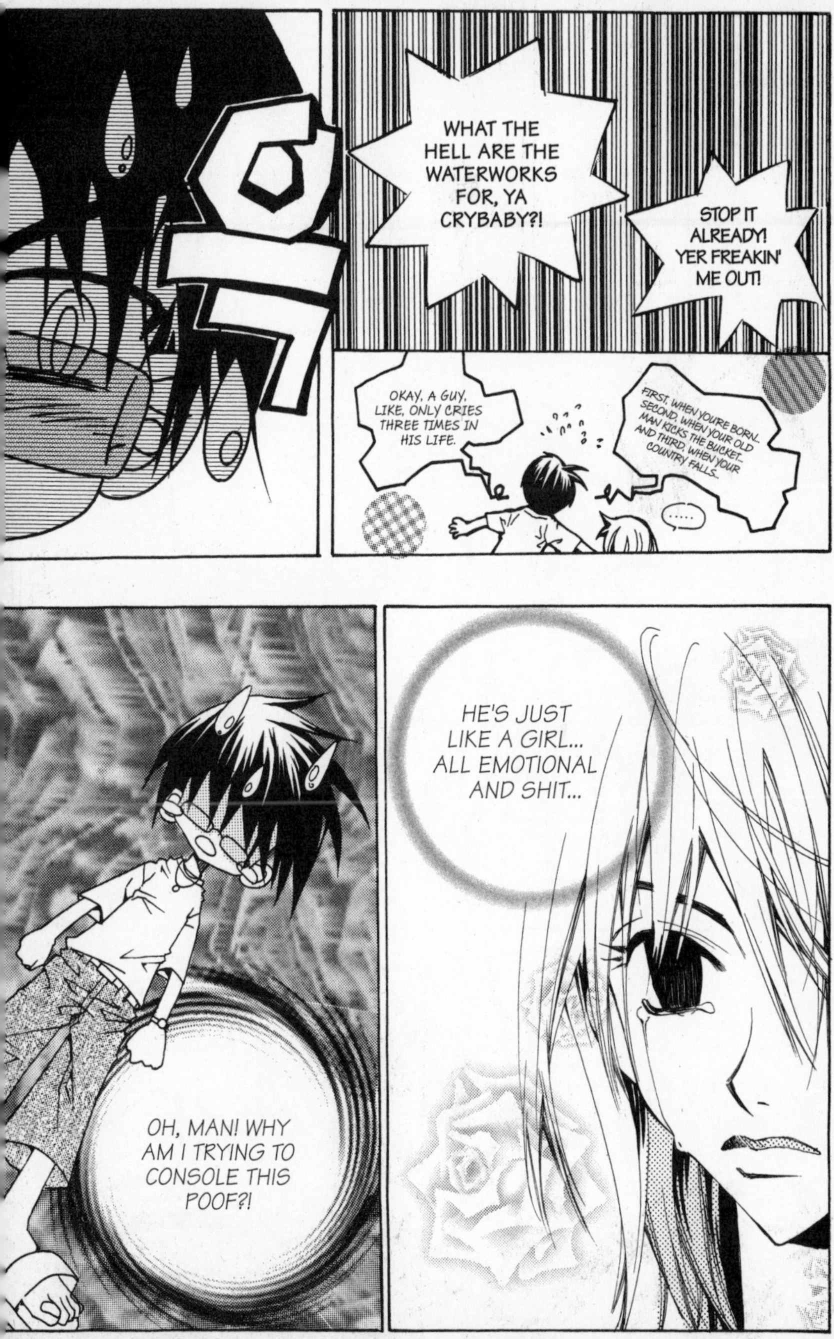
WHAT THE HELL ARE THE WATERWORKS FOR, YA CRYBABY?!
STOP IT ALREADY! YER FREAKIN' ME OUT!
OKAY, A GUY, LIKE, ONLY CRIES THREE TIMES IN HIS LIFE.
FIRST, WHEN YOU'RE BORN... SECOND, WHEN YOUR OLD MAN KICKS THE BUCKET... AND THIRD, WHEN YOUR COUNTRY FALLS...
.....
OH, MAN! WHY AM I TRYING TO CONSOLE THIS POOF?!
HE'S JUST LIKE A GIRL... ALL EMOTIONAL AND SHIT...

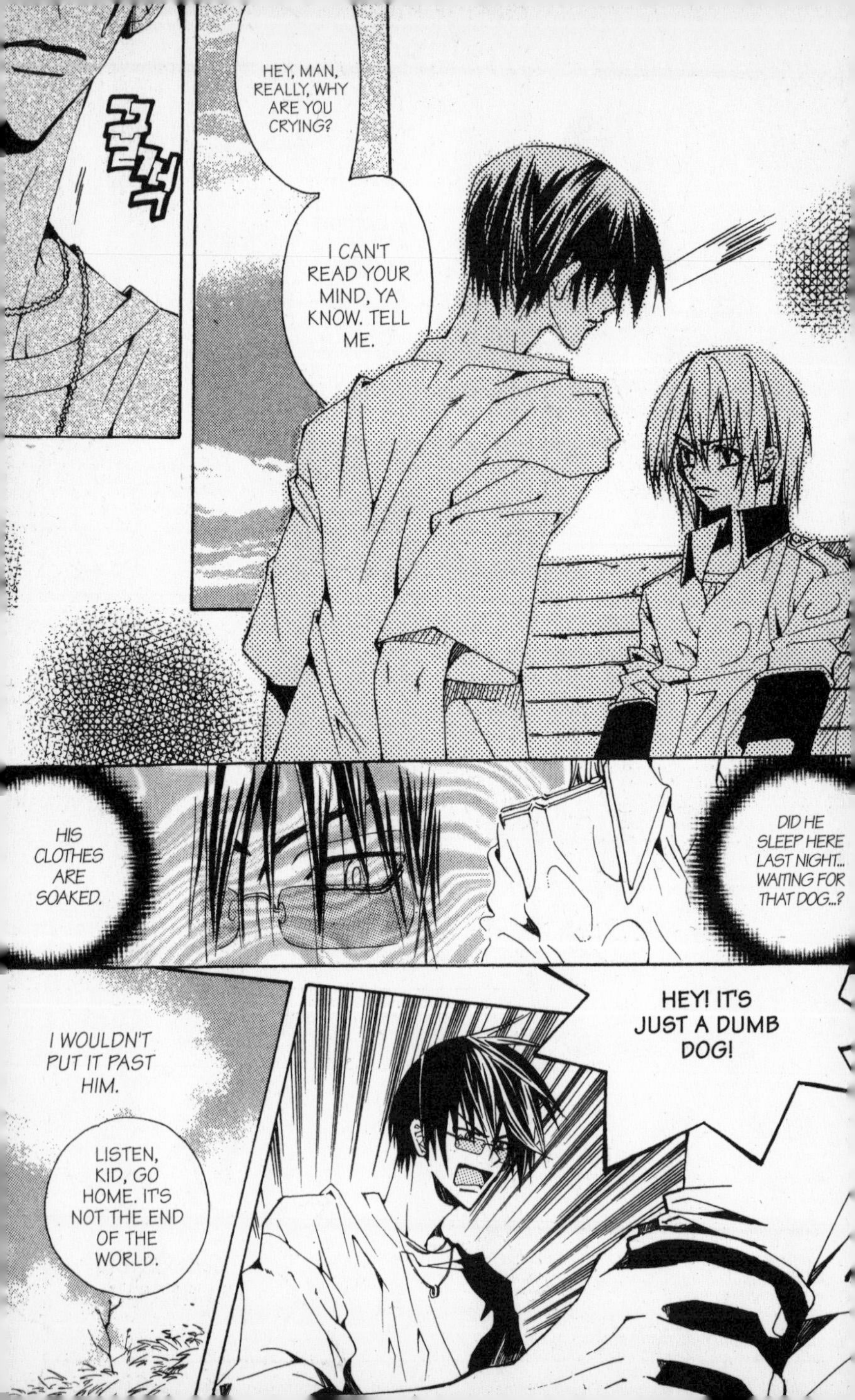

HEY, MAN, REALLY, WHY ARE YOU CRYING?
I CAN'T READ YOUR MIND, YA KNOW. TELL ME.
HIS CLOTHES ARE SOAKED.
DID HE SLEEP HERE LAST NIGHT... WAITING FOR THAT DOG...?
I WOULDN'T PUT IT PAST HIM.
LISTEN, KID, GO HOME. IT'S NOT THE END OF THE WORLD.
HEY! IT'S JUST A DUMB DOG!

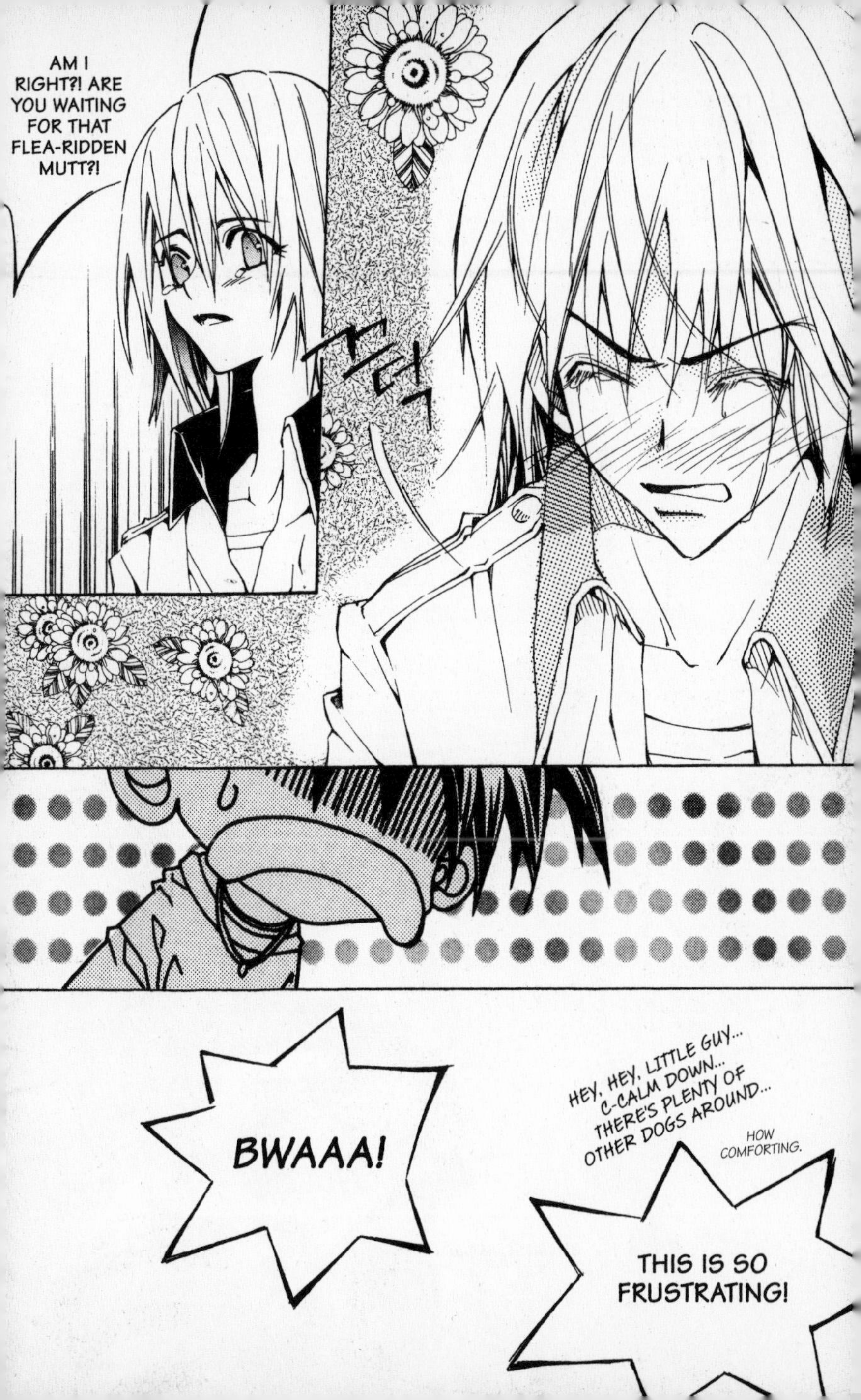
AM I RIGHT?! ARE YOU WAITING FOR THAT FLEA-RIDDEN MUTT?!
BWAAA!
HEY, HEY, LITTLE GUY... C-CALM DOWN... THERE'S PLENTY OF OTHER DOGS AROUND...
HOW COMFORTING.
THIS IS SO FRUSTRATING!

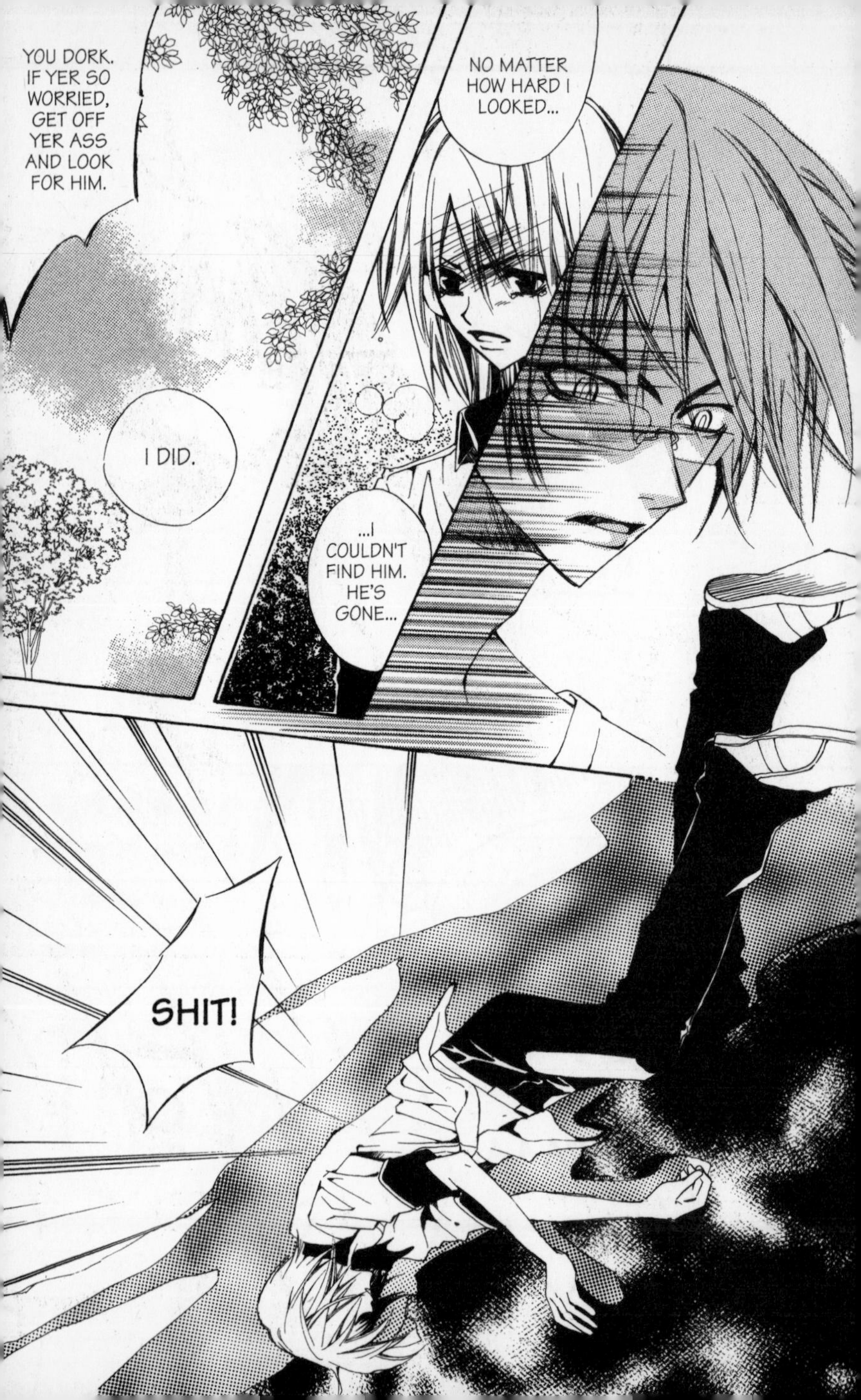
YOU DORK. IF YER SO WORRIED, GET OFF YER ASS AND LOOK FOR HIM.
I DID.
NO MATTER HOW HARD I LOOKED...
...I COULDN'T FIND HIM. HE'S GONE...
SHIT!

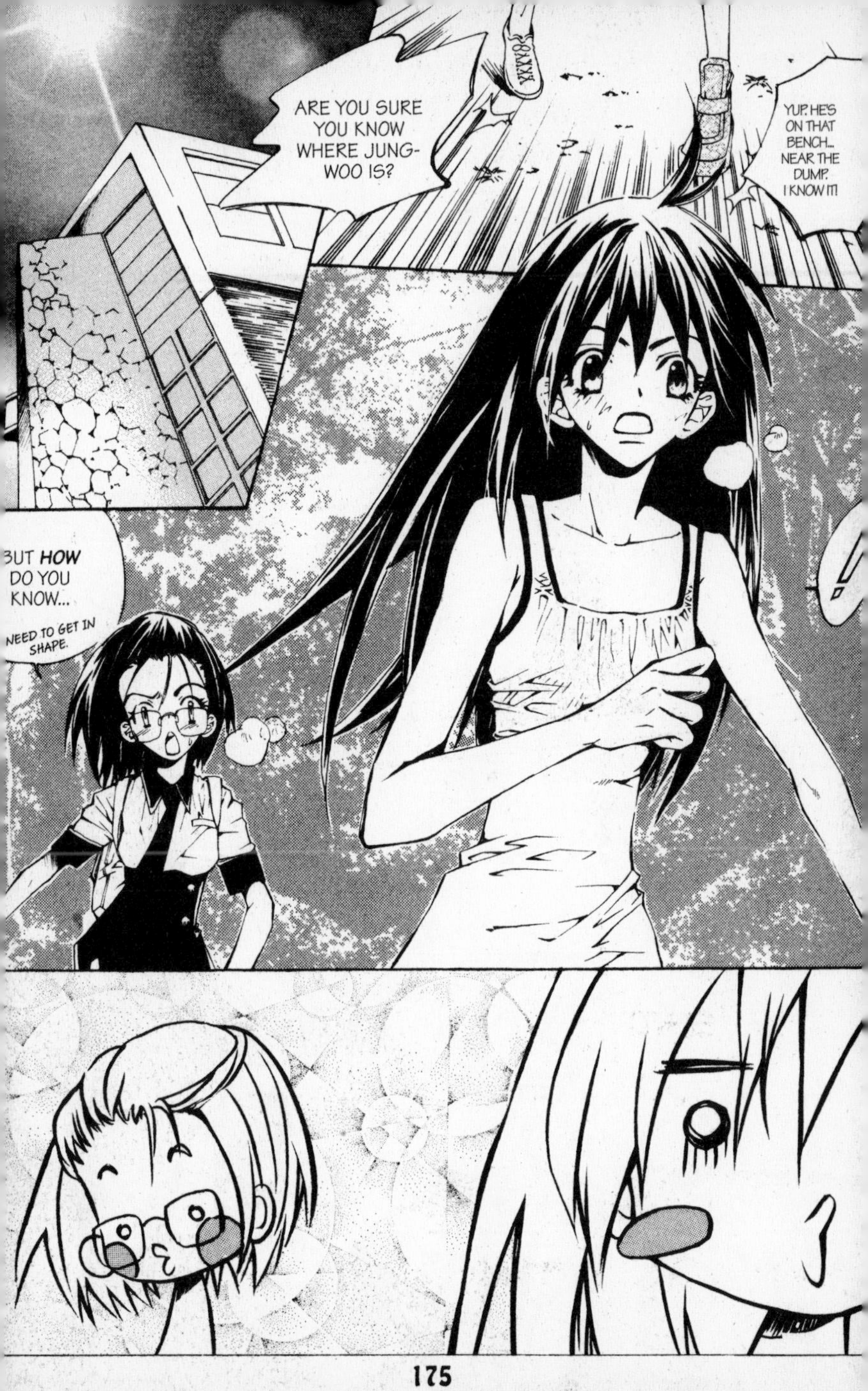
ARE YOU SURE YOU KNOW WHERE JUNG-WOO IS?
YUP. HE'S ON THAT BENCH... NEAR THE DUMP. I KNOW IT!
BUT **HOW** DO YOU KNOW...
NEED TO GET IN SHAPE.

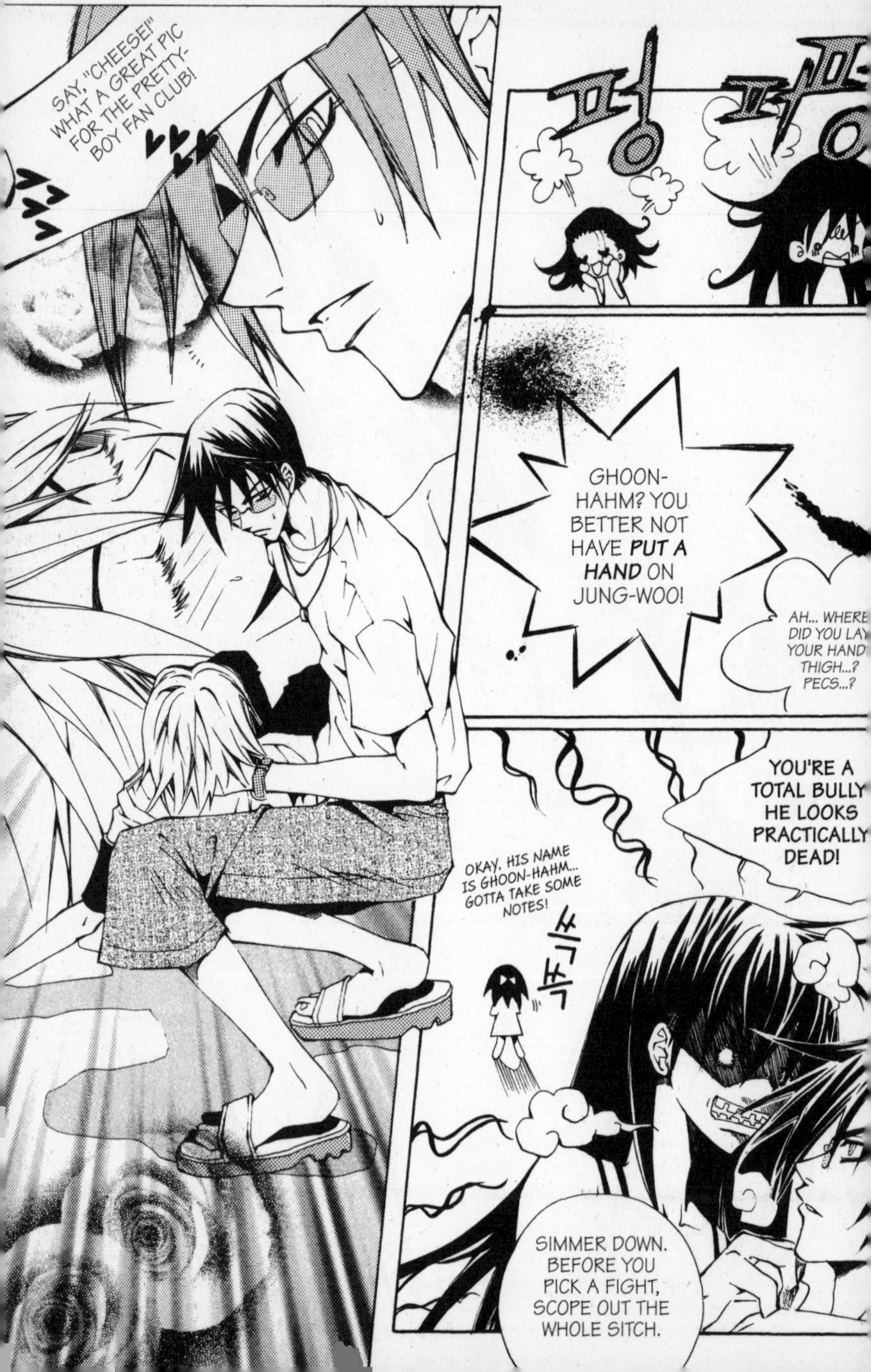

SAY, "CHEESE!" WHAT A GREAT PIC FOR THE PRETTY-BOY FAN CLUB!
펑
GHOON-HAHM? YOU BETTER NOT HAVE **PUT A HAND** ON JUNG-WOO!
AH... WHERE DID YOU LAY YOUR HAND THIGH...? PECS...?
YOU'RE A TOTAL BULLY HE LOOKS PRACTICALLY DEAD!
OKAY, HIS NAME IS GHOON-HAHM... GOTTA TAKE SOME NOTES!
쓱 쓱
SIMMER DOWN. BEFORE YOU PICK A FIGHT, SCOPE OUT THE WHOLE SITCH.

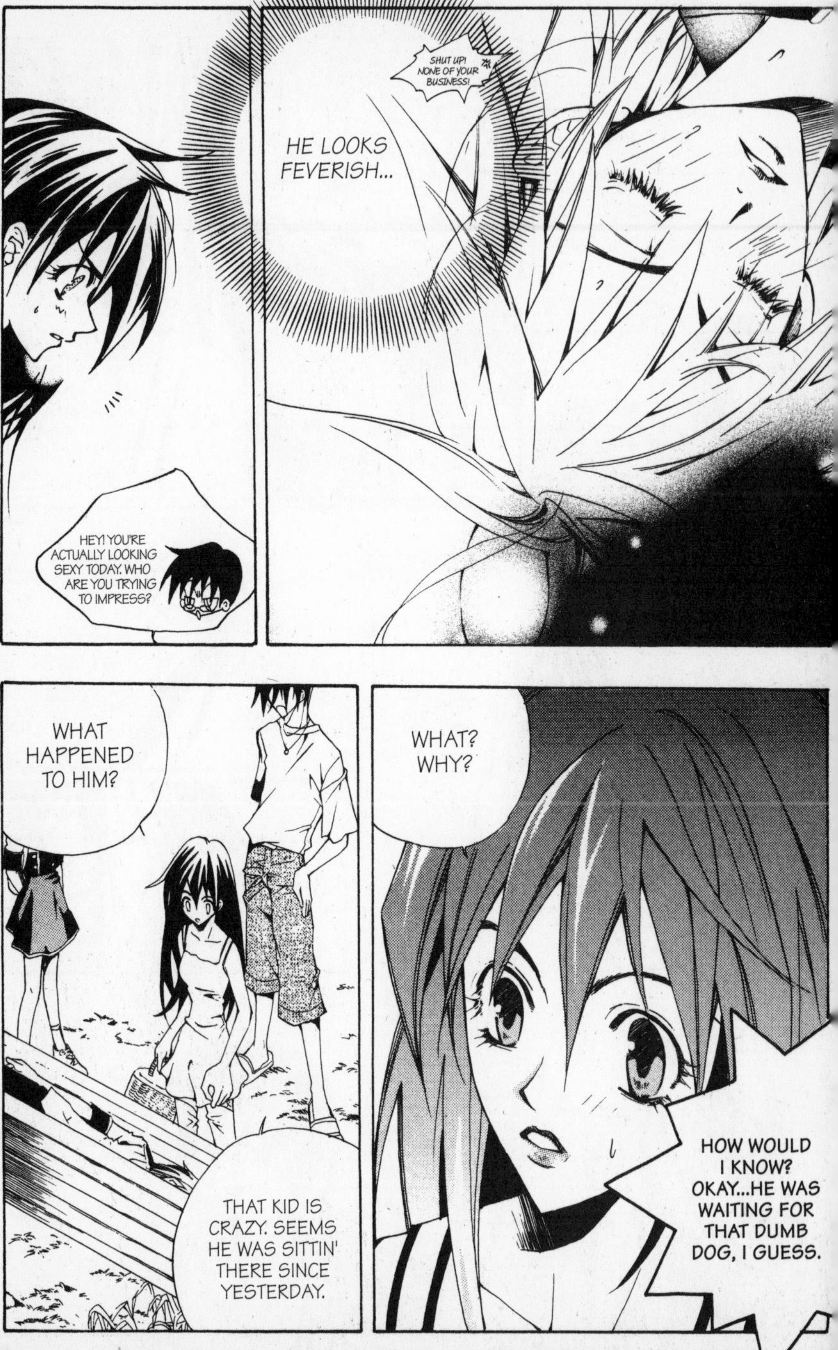
HEY! YOU'RE ACTUALLY LOOKING SEXY TODAY. WHO ARE YOU TRYING TO IMPRESS?
SHUT UP! NONE OF YOUR BUSINESS!
HE LOOKS FEVERISH...
WHAT HAPPENED TO HIM?
THAT KID IS CRAZY. SEEMS HE WAS SITTIN' THERE SINCE YESTERDAY.
WHAT? WHY?
HOW WOULD I KNOW? OKAY...HE WAS WAITING FOR THAT DUMB DOG, I GUESS.

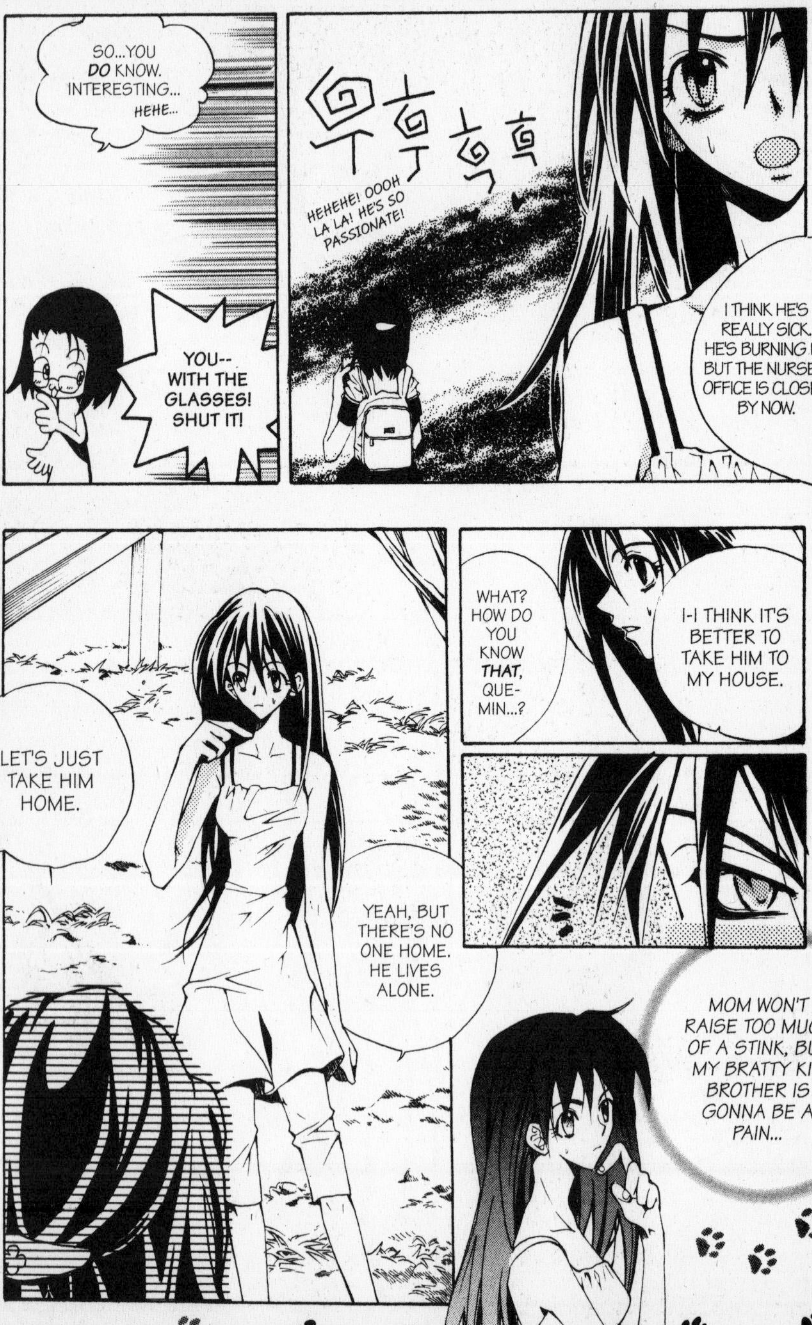
SO...YOU DO KNOW. INTERESTING... HEHE...
YOU-- WITH THE GLASSES! SHUT IT!
HEHEHE! OOOH LA LA! HE'S SO PASSIONATE!
I THINK HE'S REALLY SICK. HE'S BURNING UP. BUT THE NURSE'S OFFICE IS CLOSED BY NOW.
LET'S JUST TAKE HIM HOME.
YEAH, BUT THERE'S NO ONE HOME. HE LIVES ALONE.
WHAT? HOW DO YOU KNOW THAT, QUE-MIN...?
I-I THINK IT'S BETTER TO TAKE HIM TO MY HOUSE.
MOM WON'T RAISE TOO MUCH OF A STINK, BUT MY BRATTY KID BROTHER IS GONNA BE A PAIN...

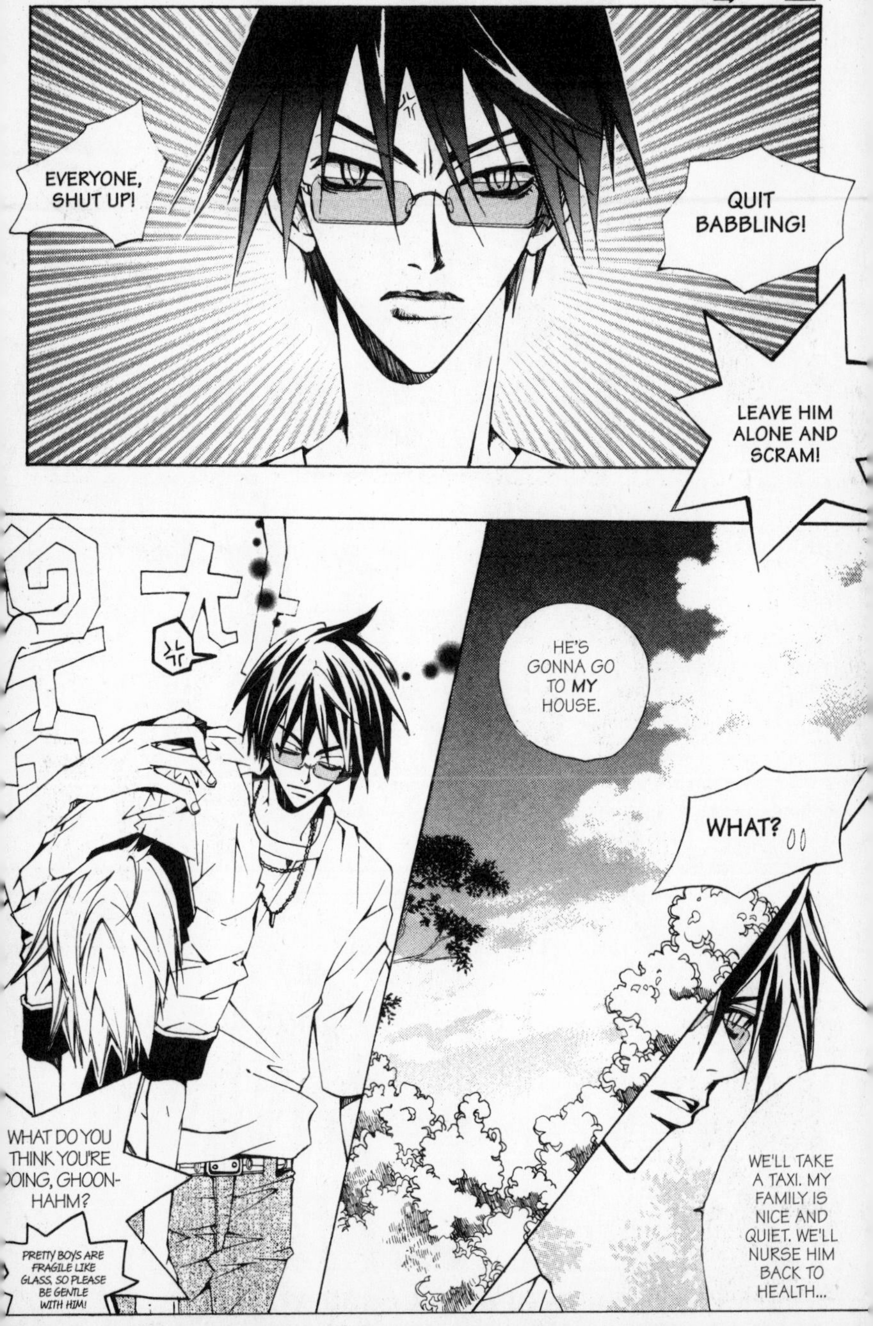
EVERYONE, SHUT UP!
QUIT BABBLING!
LEAVE HIM ALONE AND SCRAM!
WHAT DO YOU THINK YOU'RE DOING, GHOON-HAHM?
PRETTY BOYS ARE FRAGILE LIKE GLASS, SO PLEASE BE GENTLE WITH HIM!
HE'S GONNA GO TO MY HOUSE.
WHAT?
WE'LL TAKE A TAXI. MY FAMILY IS NICE AND QUIET. WE'LL NURSE HIM BACK TO HEALTH...

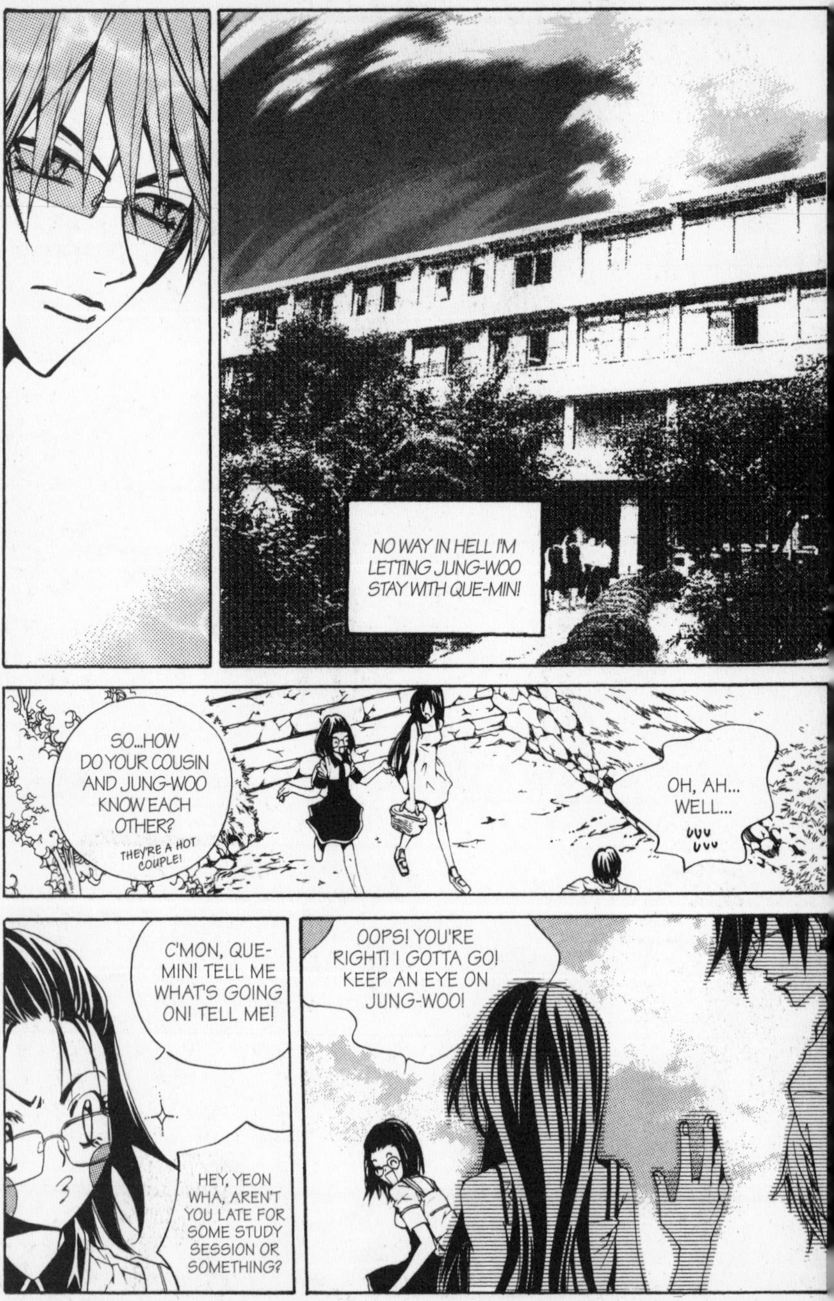
NO WAY IN HELL I'M LETTING JUNG-WOO STAY WITH QUE-MIN!
SO...HOW DO YOUR COUSIN AND JUNG-WOO KNOW EACH OTHER?
THEY'RE A HOT COUPLE!
OH, AH... WELL...
C'MON, QUE-MIN! TELL ME WHAT'S GOING ON! TELL ME!
HEY, YEON WHA, AREN'T YOU LATE FOR SOME STUDY SESSION OR SOMETHING?
OOPS! YOU'RE RIGHT! I GOTTA GO! KEEP AN EYE ON JUNG-WOO!

TO BE CONTINUED IN KILL ME, KISS ME VOL.4

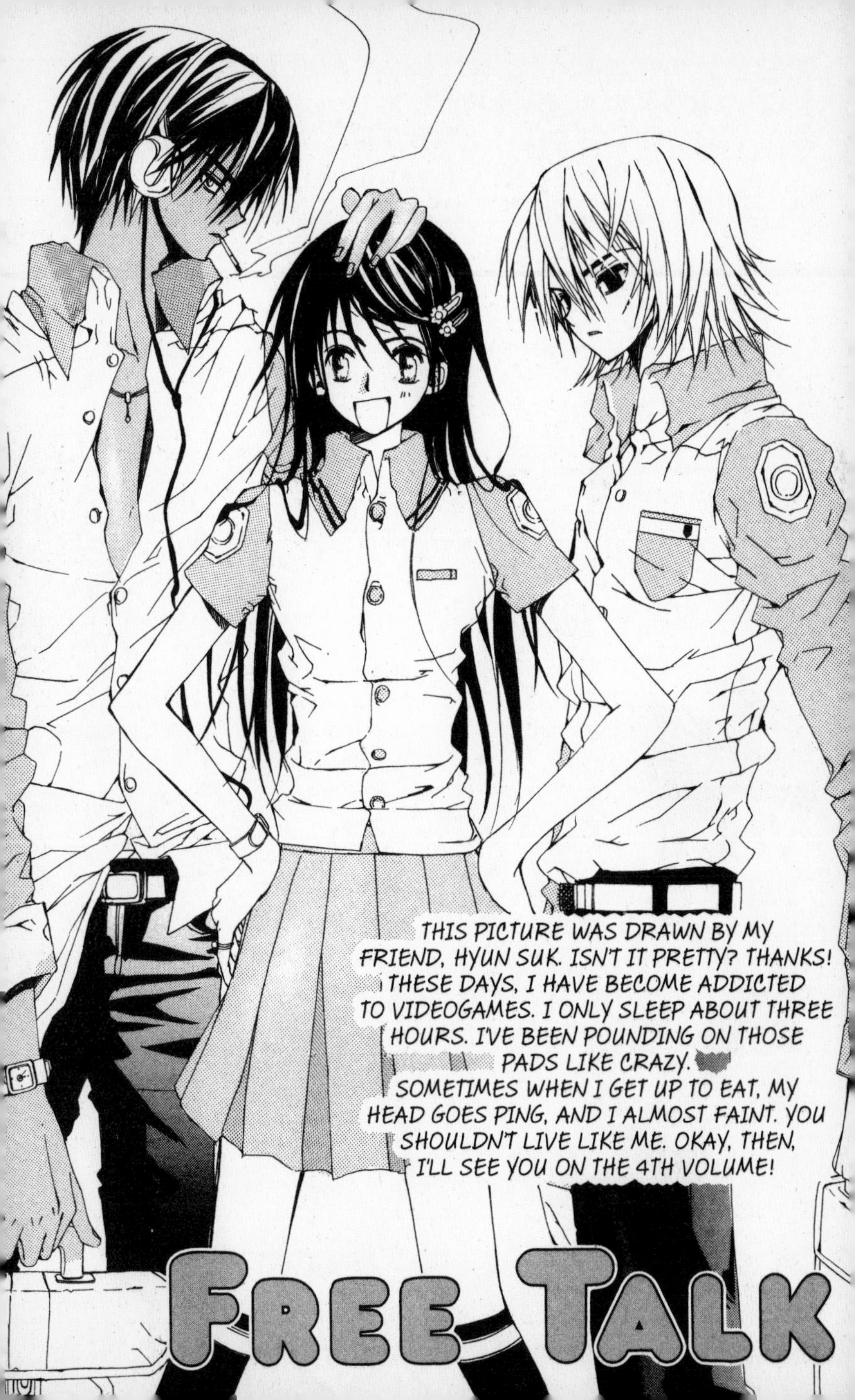

FREE TALK

THIS PICTURE WAS DRAWN BY MY FRIEND, HYUN SUK. ISN'T IT PRETTY? THANKS! THESE DAYS, I HAVE BECOME ADDICTED TO VIDEOGAMES. I ONLY SLEEP ABOUT THREE HOURS. I'VE BEEN POUNDING ON THOSE PADS LIKE CRAZY.
SOMETIMES WHEN I GET UP TO EAT, MY HEAD GOES PING, AND I ALMOST FAINT. YOU SHOULDN'T LIVE LIKE ME. OKAY, THEN, I'LL SEE YOU ON THE 4TH VOLUME!

WILL THERE BE A BATTLE ROYALE BETWEEN TOUGH GUY GHOON-HAHM AND THE MONSTER-POWERFUL QUE- MIN? WILL LIN LEE EVER USE PUBLIC TRANSPORTATION AGAIN?

WILL THERE BE A BATTLE ROYALE BETWEEN TOUGH GUY HOON-HAHM AND THE MONSTER-POWERFUL QUE- MIN? WILL LIN LEE EVER USE PUBLIC TRANSPORTATION AGAIN?

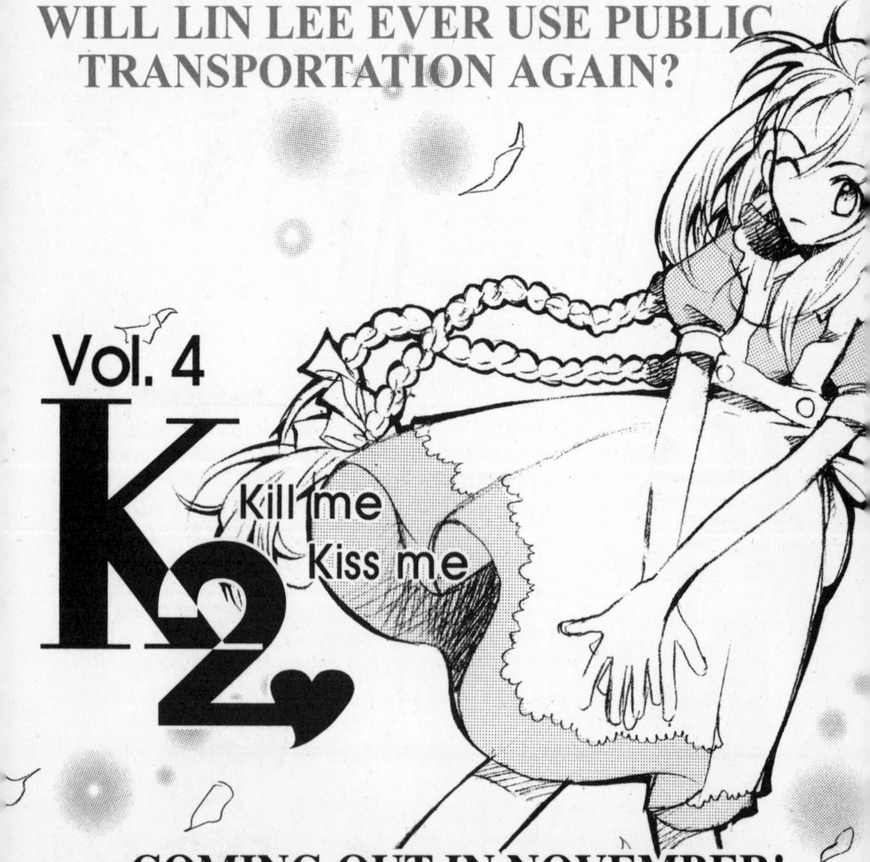
Vol. 4
K2
Kill me
Kiss me

COMING OUT IN NOVEMBER!

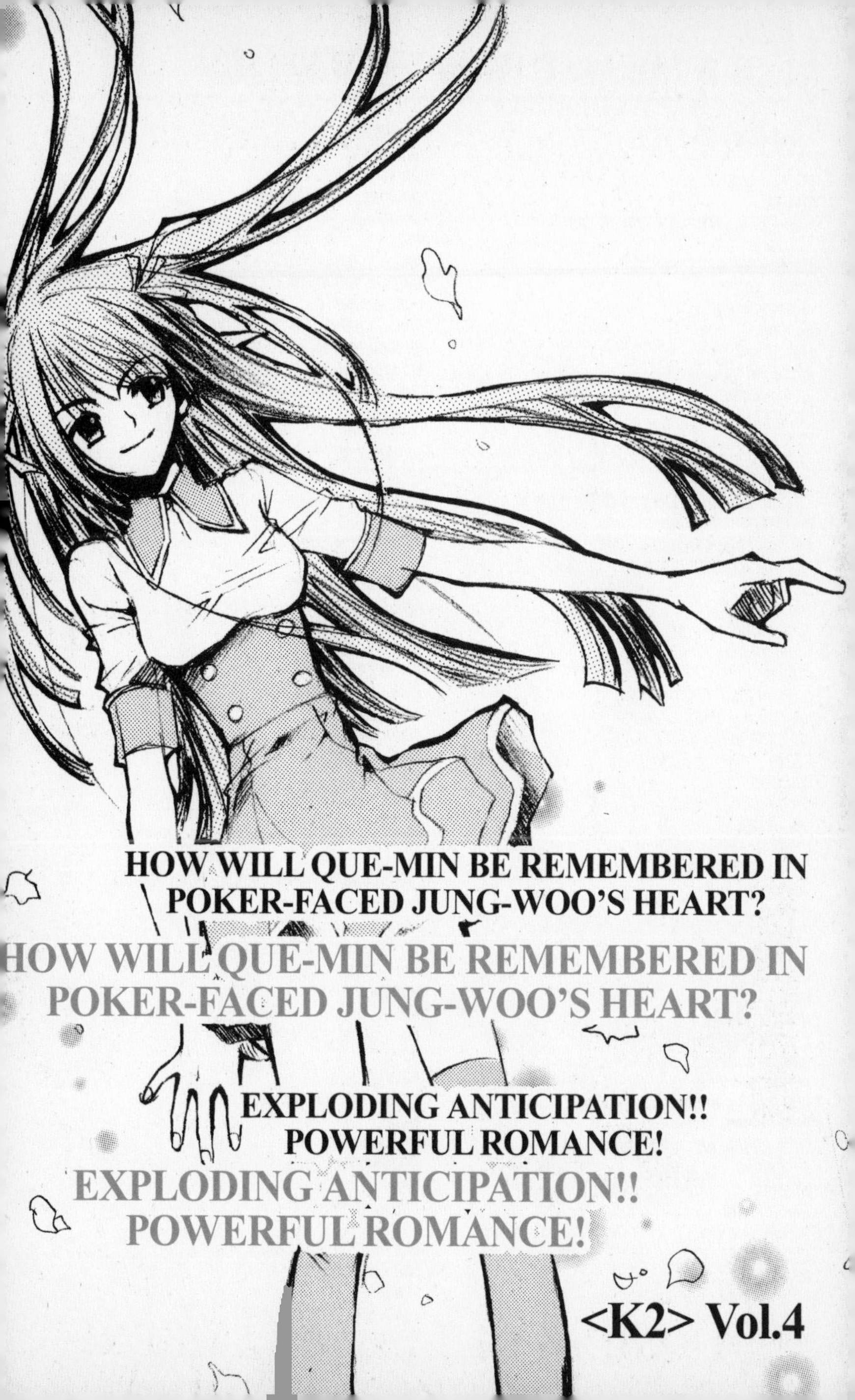
HOW WILL QUE-MIN BE REMEMBERED IN POKER-FACED JUNG-WOO'S HEART?
HOW WILL QUE-MIN BE REMEMBERED IN POKER-FACED JUNG-WOO'S HEART?
EXPLODING ANTICIPATION!! POWERFUL ROMANCE!
EXPLODING ANTICIPATION!! POWERFUL ROMANCE!
<K2> Vol.4

ALSO AVAILABLE FROM

MANGA

.HACK//LEGEND OF THE TWILIGHT
@LARGE
ABENOBASHI: MAGICAL SHOPPING ARCADE
A.I. LOVE YOU
AI YORI AOSHI
ANGELIC LAYER
ARM OF KANNON
BABY BIRTH
BATTLE ROYALE
BATTLE VIXENS
BRAIN POWERED
BRIGADOON
B'TX
CANDIDATE FOR GODDESS, THE
CARDCAPTOR SAKURA
CARDCAPTOR SAKURA - MASTER OF THE CLOW
CHOBITS
CHRONICLES OF THE CURSED SWORD
CLAMP SCHOOL DETECTIVES
CLOVER
COMIC PARTY
CONFIDENTIAL CONFESSIONS
CORRECTOR YUI
COWBOY BEBOP
COWBOY BEBOP: SHOOTING STAR
CRAZY LOVE STORY
CRESCENT MOON
CROSS
CULDCEPT
CYBORG 009
D•N•ANGEL
DEMON DIARY
DEMON ORORON, THE
DEUS VITAE
DIABOLO
DIGIMON
DIGIMON TAMERS
DIGIMON ZERO TWO
DOLL
DRAGON HUNTER
DRAGON KNIGHTS
DRAGON VOICE
DREAM SAGA
DUKLYON: CLAMP SCHOOL DEFENDERS
EERIE QUEERIE!
ERICA SAKURAZAWA: COLLECTED WORKS
ET CETERA
ETERNITY
EVIL'S RETURN
FAERIES' LANDING
FAKE
FLCL
FLOWER OF THE DEEP SLEEP
FORBIDDEN DANCE
FRUITS BASKET
G GUNDAM

GATEKEEPERS
GETBACKERS
GIRL GOT GAME
GIRLS' EDUCATIONAL CHARTER
GRAVITATION
GTO
GUNDAM BLUE DESTINY
GUNDAM SEED ASTRAY
GUNDAM WING
GUNDAM WING: BATTLEFIELD OF PACIFISTS
GUNDAM WING: ENDLESS WALTZ
GUNDAM WING: THE LAST OUTPOST (G-UNIT)
GUYS' GUIDE TO GIRLS
HANDS OFF!
HAPPY MANIA
HARLEM BEAT
I.N.V.U.
IMMORTAL RAIN
INITIAL D
INSTANT TEEN: JUST ADD NUTS
ISLAND
JING: KING OF BANDITS
JING: KING OF BANDITS - TWILIGHT TALES
JULINE
KARE KANO
KILL ME, KISS ME
KINDAICHI CASE FILES, THE
KING OF HELL
KODOCHA: SANA'S STAGE
LAMENT OF THE LAMB
LEGAL DRUG
LEGEND OF CHUN HYANG, THE
LES BIJOUX
LOVE HINA
LUPIN III
LUPIN III: WORLD'S MOST WANTED
MAGIC KNIGHT RAYEARTH I
MAGIC KNIGHT RAYEARTH II
MAHOROMATIC: AUTOMATIC MAIDEN
MAN OF MANY FACES
MARMALADE BOY
MARS
MARS: HORSE WITH NO NAME
MINK
MIRACLE GIRLS
MIYUKI-CHAN IN WONDERLAND
MODEL
MY LOVE
NECK AND NECK
ONE
ONE I LOVE, THE
PARADISE KISS
PARASYTE
PASSION FRUIT
PEACH GIRL
PEACH GIRL: CHANGE OF HEART
PET SHOP OF HORRORS
PITA-TEN

ALSO AVAILABLE FROM TOKYOPOP®

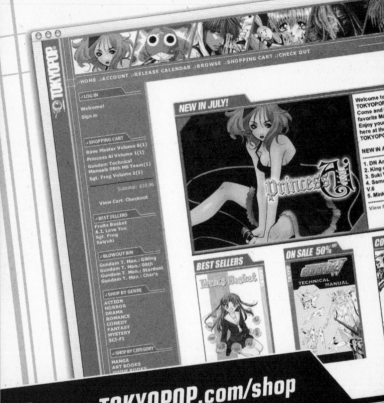

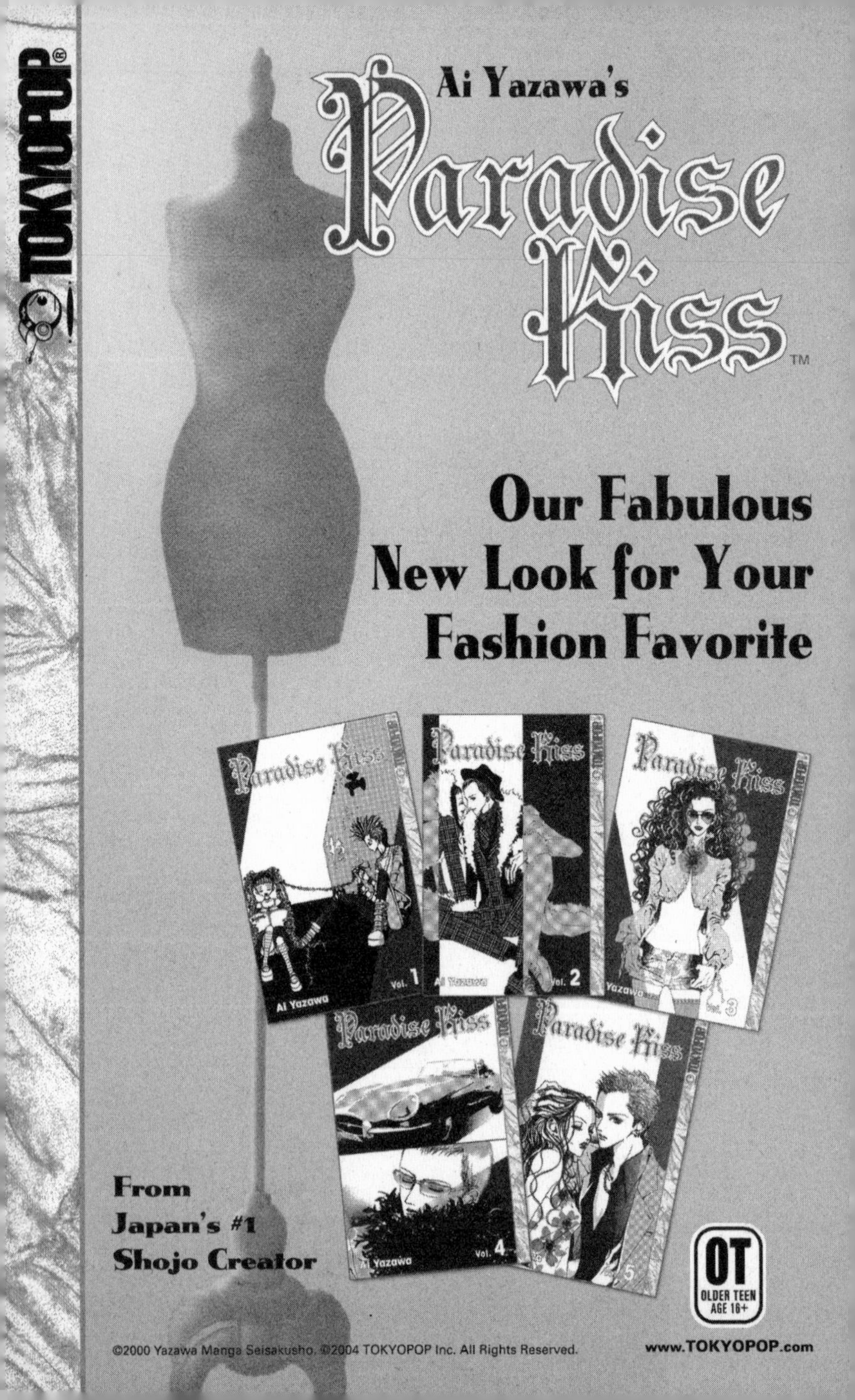
TOKYOPOP®
Ai Yazawa's
Paradise Kiss™
Our Fabulous
New Look for Your
Fashion Favorite
From
Japan's #1
Shojo Creator
OT
OLDER TEEN
AGE 16+
©2000 Yazawa Manga Seisakusho. ©2004 TOKYOPOP Inc. All Rights Reserved.
www.TOKYOPOP.com

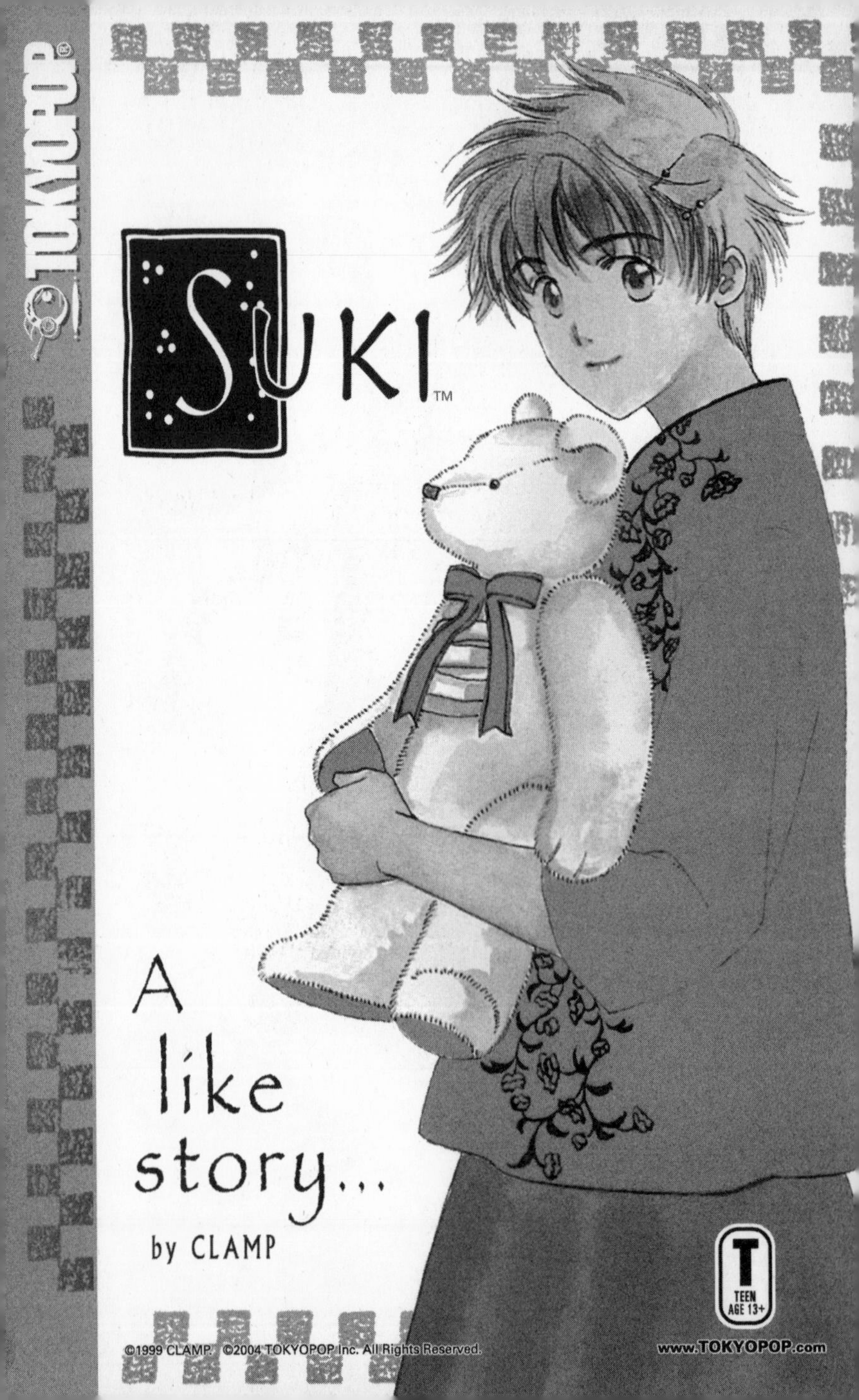
TOKYOPOP
SUKI™
A like story...
by CLAMP
T
TEEN
AGE 13+
©1999 CLAMP. ©2004 TOKYOPOP Inc. All Rights Reserved.
www.TOKYOPOP.com

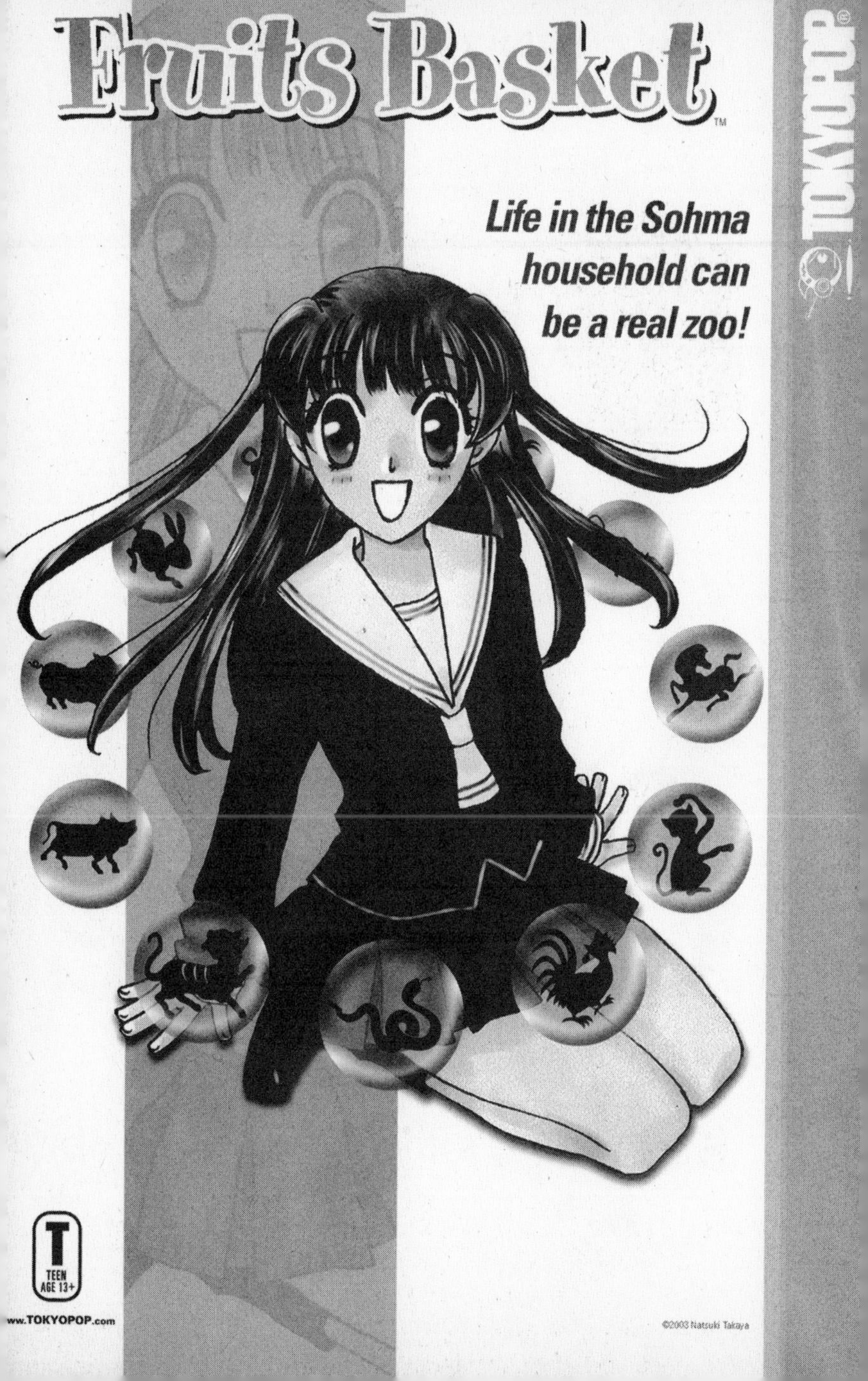
Fruits Basket™
TOKYOPOP®
Life in the Sohma household can be a real zoo!
T TEEN AGE 13+
www.TOKYOPOP.com
©2003 Natsuki Takaya